CONSTITUTIONAL COMPETENCE FOR PUBLIC MANAGERS

Cases and Commentary

David H. Rosenbloom
James D. Carroll
Jonathan D. Carroll

CENGAGE
Learning™

Australia • Brazil • Japan • Korea • Mexico • Singapore • Spain • United Kingdom • United States

CENGAGE
Learning™

Constitutional Competence for Public Managers: Cases and Commentary
David H. Rosenbloom, James D. Carroll, and Jonathan D. Carroll

Executive Editors: Michele Baird, Maureen Staudt, Michael Stranz

Project Development Manager: Linda deStefano

Senior Marketing Coordinators: Sara Mercurio, Lindsay Shapiro

Sr. Production/Manufacturing Manager: Donna M. Brown

PreMedia Services Supervisor: Joel Brennecke

Rights & Permissions Specialist: Kalina Hintz

Cover Image: Getty Image

For product information and technology assistance, contact us at
Cengage Learning Customer & Sales Support, 1-800-354-9706
For permission to use material from this text or product, submit all requests online at **www.cengage.com/permissions**
Further permissions questions can be emailed to
permissionrequest@cengage.com

ISBN-13: 978-0-534-27078-0

ISBN-10: 0-534-27078-6

Cengage Learning
5191 Natorp Blvd.
Mason, OH 45040
USA

Cengage Learning is a leading provider of customized learning solutions with office locations around the globe, including Singapore, the United Kingdom, Australia, Mexico, Brazil, and Japan. Locate your local office at **international.cengage.com/region**

Cengage Learning products are represented in Canada by Nelson Education, Ltd.

To learn more about Cengage Learning, visit **www.cengage.com**

Purchase any of our products at your local college store or at our preferred online store **www.ichapters.com**

Printed in the United States of America
7 8 9 10 11   19 18 17 16 15

CONSTITUTIONAL COMPETENCE
for PUBLIC MANAGERS

Cases and Commentary

It may seem contrary to common sense to assert that a municipality will actually have a policy of not taking reasonable steps to train its employees. But it may happen that in light of the duties assigned to specific officers and employees the need for more or different training is so obvious, and the inadequacy so likely to result in the violation of constitutional rights, that the policymakers of the city can reasonably be said to have been deliberately indifferent to the need. In that event, the failure to provide proper training may fairly be said to represent a policy for which the city is responsible, and for which the city may be held liable if it actually causes injury.

The U.S. Supreme Court in City of
Canton v. Harris, *489 U.S. 378, 390 (1989)*

[A] reasonably competent public official should know the law governing his conduct.

The U.S. Supreme Court in Harlow v. *Fitzgerald,*
457 U.S. 800, 819 (1982)

For Megan, Christopher, Rachael, Catherine, Joseph Patrick, and Melvin D.

CONTENTS

Chapter 5
Administrative Effectiveness   105

Chapter 6
Efficiency   125

Chapter 7
Administrative Standardization   149

Chapter 8
Economy 173

Chapter 9
The Promise of Constitutional Competence 196

FOREWORD

In the foreword to an earlier version of this book, I wrote: "During the past few years, the public administration community has contributed substantially to the impressive literature that has marked the observance of the bicentennial of the Constitution of the United States. A generous array of books, articles, monographs, and symposia has enriched the field and made us all aware of the constitutional foundations of our work. As a result of this scholarship, we are witnessing the gradual reintegration of constitutionalism and public administration. I say *re*integration because of the obvious connection between public administration and constitutionalism in *The Federalist Papers*. So integral was administration to the intent of the framers that the authors of *The Federalist Papers* made more frequent use of the word *administration* and its cognates than they did of the words *Congress, President,* or *Supreme Court.*

"Scholars and practitioners concerned with constitutionalism and public administration can only applaud this reintegration. And yet there is an undercurrent of concern about its permanence. Is it merely a flower of a day? Will public administrators forget about constitutionalism after the nation concludes its bicentennial remembrances by commemorating the two-hundredth anniversary of the Bill of Rights in 1991? I do not believe this will be the case.

"The reason for my optimism is threefold. First, for all federal employees and for the vast majority of state employees, the oath of office is an oath to uphold the Constitution of the United States. If this oath is administered in a meaningful way, it will serve as a powerful symbol of the moral foundation of public service in the United States. We can hope that alert personnel officers will see to it that the oath is not squeezed into a brief lull between the lecture on retirement benefits and the instruction on how to fill out a W-2 form.

"Secondly, there is the leadership that is currently being exercised by the United States Office of Personnel Management (OPM) in proclaiming constitutional literacy in the federal work force as one of the goals of its training program. This effort follows up on Constance Horner's thoughtful remarks in an address at the Federal Executive Institute shortly before she concluded her service as director of OPM. Horner's remarks and the subsequent OPM follow-through augur well for institutionalizing the current interest in the Constitution.

"The third reason for my optimism is this superb book, which I have the honor of introducing in this foreword. David Rosenbloom and James Carroll have rendered signal service to the public administration community by providing us with an eminently readable book that integrates public administration into the American constitutional tradition. In their preface, they promise to 'address . . . constitutional concerns squarely from a public administrative perspective,' and throughout the book they redeem this pledge. The constitutional themes are organized around such garden-variety administrative matters as efficiency, effectiveness, economy, and decision-making. One need not be a specialist in constitutional law to learn the lessons this book teaches so well.

"It is my earnest hope that this fine book will be used in introductory public administration courses throughout the United States. It will provide a new generation of public administration students with a thoughtful and reflective appreciation of the fundamental political order they are sworn to uphold."

Regarding the question of whether the newly found interest in constitutional questions in public administration circles would prove to be merely "a flower of a day," clearly, the answer is a resounding and unequivocal "no." I raised the question because the sudden salience of constitutionalism in public administration literature a decade or so ago was grounded in the celebration of the bicentennial of the great constitutional events from the Philadelphia Convention of 1787 to the approval of the Bill of Rights in 1791. Today, constitutionalism has been so well integrated into administrative practice and literature that its permanent place is assured. The appearance of this fine book witnesses to this important and most welcome change in the field of public administration, just as its illustrious predecessor helped to bring it about.

The present volume gives considerable attention to the New Public Management movement, thereby revealing the dynamic character of the administrative-constitutional relationship. In years gone by, constitutionalists worried about delegation of legislative authority and the quasi-adjudicative powers of agencies. Today they worry about empowering street-level bureaucrats and celebrating results over process. Of particular significance is the addition of an entirely new chapter tellingly entitled "Privatization and Outsourcing." These practices were well underway at the time of the earlier version, but there was little constitutional law to guide them. All this has changed. The new chapter reveals the Constitution's inevitable way of catching up with administrative innovations, purging them of their excesses, and providing a solid normative base for their advancement.

The public administration community remains deeply in debt to David Rosenbloom, James Carroll, and Jonathan Carroll for continuing to provide their wise constitutional guidance.

John A. Rohr

PREFACE

Constitutional Competence for Public Managers: Cases and Commentary is an indispensable tool for helping students of public management and practitioners to understand the constitutional principles, concepts, and values that apply directly to American public administration. The book is intended for use in courses in public management, public administration and law, and public administrative ethics. It grows out of the recognition that, although law is central to public management, it has not been well integrated into public administrative education in the United States. Too often, law is treated as a "stand alone" subject, due partly to the traditional materials available for teaching it. *Constitutional Competence for Public Managers: Cases and Commentary* explains key constitutional concerns wholly within the context of public administrative practice. Its message applies to public management at all levels of government in the United States.

American public administration is based on the proposition that government decisions and activities should follow the rule of law. As the authors of the Declaration of Independence, the Constitution, and the *Federalist Papers* repeatedly emphasized, government under law is the basis of liberty. For the framers, the absence of the rule of law was tyranny. The Declaration of Independence provides an enduring statement of the purpose of government: "We hold these Truths to be self-evident, that all Men are created equal, that they are endowed by their Creator with certain unalienable Rights, that among these are Life, Liberty, and the Pursuit of Happiness—That to secure these Rights, Governments are instituted among Men, deriving their just Powers from the Consent of the Governed...."

To govern according to law, public managers must understand the law that applies to their conduct. They need two kinds of legal knowledge: First, they need an understanding of the basic constitutional principles, concepts, and values upon which all governmental action in the United States rests. This is constitutional knowledge not just for lawyers and judges; it is a job requirement for all public managers as well. Article VI of the Constitution underscores the point: "The Senators and Representatives, ... the Members of the several State Legislatures, and all executive and judicial Officers, both of the United States and of the several States, shall be bound by Oath or Affirmation, to support this Constitution...."[1]

Article VI presupposes knowledge of constitutional law as it applies to public managers. We call this knowledge "constitutional competence," and the purpose of this book is to provide a firm grounding in it.

The second kind of legal knowledge that public managers need is the substantive and administrative law that is specific to different units of government, individual agencies, policies, programs, and so forth. *Constitutional Competence for Public Managers* does not cover these legal requirements, which vary greatly among state and local governments, agencies, functions, and administrative arrangements.

Public Values

The book makes a basic point about government in the United States that can be easily overlooked. Public values—defined as the core beliefs Americans hold about what is worth striving for through governmental action—are central to the daily decisions and operations of public managers. Different kinds of public values may apply to particular issues or situations; they may conflict. For example, constitutional procedural due process may clash with administrative efficiency or cost-effectiveness. When a conflict occurs, the task of the responsible public manager is to reconcile it—with full recognition that constitutional requirements will trump administrative values.

Constitutional Competence for Public Managers contrasts two kinds of public values that are central to American government: (1) constitutional values, and (2) managerial values—those of both traditional public administration and the current movement toward "reinventing" government. It explains these values, comprehensively illustrates through court cases how they often conflict, and discusses the analytical and intellectual processes through which tensions may be resolved or mitigated. The goal is to provide public managers with a framework for ensuring that public administrative activity is consistent with constitutional requirements.

As noted, public managers should have constitutional competence because they pledge to uphold the Constitution. However, there is a second, very practical reason for such competence—avoiding *personal* liability for violating individuals' constitutional rights. The old adage that the best offense is a good defense is nowhere truer. Constitutional competence can go a very long way toward reducing the likelihood that public managers will be sued for "constitutional torts"—that is, breaches of individuals' constitutional rights.

In *Harlow v. Fitzgerald* (1982), the Supreme Court concluded that "... a reasonably competent official should know the law governing his conduct," and that most public personnel can be held personally liable for violating "clearly established statutory or constitutional rights of which a reasonable person would have known."[2] With these words, the Court clearly *established constitutional competence as a job requirement for public managers at all levels of government.* Moreover, a municipality's failure to train its employees in constitutional competence can trigger liability.[3] Even a private party to which a governmental function has been outsourced is potentially liable for violating individuals' constitutional rights (see Chapter 3).[4]

The Book's Plan and Method

Constitutional Competence for Public Managers is unique among books for teaching law in public administration courses and programs. The first and last chapters broadly frame the key concerns—constitutional concepts, structure, and the limits of judicial involvement in public administration. Chapter 2 explains public administrators' liability for constitutional torts. Chapters 3 through 8 turn academic tradition on its head by beginning with an essay analyzing a central *managerial* process or value, and then introducing cases—primarily at the Supreme Court level—that explain competing constitutional values in plain, nontechnical language. The focus is on the relationship between managerial values and constitutional values, and how these can be reconciled to a greater extent.

The cases were selected because they clearly discuss the logical structure and application of specific constitutional rights in actual public managerial situations. All the cases are valid as constitutional law, of course, but beyond that they explain how to think about constitutional rights. For instance, what factors must be balanced when considering the applicability of procedural due process? What is the threshold requirement for asserting a Fourth Amendment privacy right? How are various classifications treated under equal protection analysis? Constitutional competence requires knowing what questions to ask, which factors to balance, and the tests that must be met. Even though judges often disagree over the outcome in a specific case, they overwhelmingly use the same reasoning when analyzing rights. Their differences are over the weight of subjective factors within the framework of those rights, such as the relative importance of the individual's or the government's interests.

The cases have been edited for efficiency and clarity, and footnotes have been omitted. Citations are provided at the beginning of each case and in the Table of Cases so that the reader who is interested in the complete text can readily find it in a law library, through a computerized legal service, or on the Internet.[5]

Our ideas have been shaped through discussions with hundred of students and public managers in many settings during the past two decades. Two of the authors, Rosenbloom and James Carroll, developed the book's central concept and method in the early 1980s while team-teaching a course on Public Administration and Democracy at the Maxwell School of Citizenship and Public Affairs of Syracuse University. The initial results were published in 1990 under the title *Toward Constitutional Competence: A Casebook for Public Administrators* (Prentice-Hall). The present volume has been updated and expanded, with additional contributions by Jonathan D. Carroll, who recently earned his M.P.A. and J.D. degrees. It squarely addresses traditional public administration, as well as the reinventing government movement (which is also called the "New Public Management").

We continued to develop the book's method and content throughout the 1990s in work done at the Brookings Institution, the U.S. Office of Personnel Management, American University (Washington, D.C.), Georgetown University, Florida International University, and other settings, including consultations in Chile, China, Hong Kong, Israel, and Singapore.

The book is organized as a teaching tool with an underlying intellectual message of fundamental importance to public management in the American constitutional system. Constitutional government cannot function effectively without public management that embraces constitutional values. Public management should not expect to be supported by the American people unless it internalizes these values and respects constitutional rights. Constitutional competence should be central to public management education in the United States. The book is designed both to demonstrate this proposition and to help put it into practice.[6]

Acknowledgments

We thank the hundreds of public managers and students who contributed to the book's approach and brought materials to our attention. Space prevents us from naming everyone who advanced our thinking and thereby improved the book's substance. However, we can personally thank a few individuals who made particularly strong contributions. John A. Rohr provided very useful ideas for the first and current versions of the book. His work on the role of public administration in the constitutional system remains classic.[7] Patricia Ingraham, Melvin Dubnick, Norma Riccucci, and Philip Joyce are among several faculty who have been very helpful in testing the materials. Robert Roberts, David Sadofsky, and Rosemary O'Leary, all of whom hold law and Ph.D. degrees in public administration, provided invaluable assistance in developing the book's approach and substantive core. Henry Hogue's editorial work greatly improved the text. We also thank Bernard H. Ross for his editorial comments and strong support of the project. Of course, we take full responsibility for the book's contents.

Notes

1. The oath encompasses local government officials as well because constitutional law regards local governments as creations and parts of the state governments. See Joan Williams, "The Constitutional Vulnerability of American Local Government: The Politics of City Status in American Law," *Wisconsin Law Review*, vol. 1986 (1986): 83.

2. *Harlow v. Fitzgerald*, 457 U.S. 800, 818–819 (1982).

3. *City of Canton v. Harris*, 489 U.S. 378 (1989).

4. *West v. Atkins*, 487 U.S. 42 (1988); *Richardson v. McKnight*, 117 S.Ct. 2100 (1997).

5. See the Virtual law Library, http://www.law.indiana.edu/law/v-lib/lawindex.html; The Legal Information Institute, http://www.fatty.law.Cornell.edu/; and the Law and Politics Internet Guide, http://www.geocities.com/Capitol Hill/Lobby/5011. For current-term Supreme Court decisions see http://www.usscplus.com.

6. The following works advance some version of this basic idea: John A. Rohr, *To Run a Constitution: The Legitimacy of the Administrative State* (Lawrence, KS: University Press of Kansas, 1986); Michael W. Spicer, *The Founders, the Constitution, and Public Administration: A Conflict in World Views* (Washington, DC: Georgetown University Press, 1995); David H. Rosenbloom and Rosemary O'Leary, *Public Administration and Law*, 2nd ed. (New York: Marcel Dekker, 1997); Ronald Moe and Robert Gilmour, "Rediscovering Principles of Public Administration: The Neglected Foundation of Public Law," *Public Administration Review*, vol. 55 (March/April 1995): 135–146; G. Wamsley, R. Bacher, C. Goodsell, P. Kronenberg, J. Rohr, C. Stivers, O. White, and J. Wolf, *Refounding Public Administration* (Newbury Park, CA: Sage, 1990).

7. John A. Rohr, *To Run a Constitution: The Legitimacy of the Administrative State* (Lawrence, KS: University Press of Kansas, 1986).

ONE

Constitutional Competence, Interpretation, and Structure

The Need for Constitutional Competence

In Texas, a constable fires a deputized employee who, after hearing of an assassination attempt on President Ronald Reagan, remarks, "Shoot, if they go for him again, I hope they get him." In Cleveland, a public school guard is dismissed for lying on his job application by failing to note having been convicted of a felony. Over the years, a small Mississippi town concentrates its economic development and new infrastructure in the business district and adjacent neighborhoods. Following a California law, police arrest an apparent vagrant who cannot produce credible and reliable identification or account for his presence. In Delaware, for no particular reason, a police officer makes a routine stop of a car to check the driver's license and registration. In Cook County, Illinois, a newly elected sheriff dismisses some of the previous administration's political appointees. Clarkstown, New York, requires trash within its borders to be deposited at a specific solid waste transfer station with which it has a public-private partnership. In order to promote equal economic opportunity, the federal Department of Transportation gives preference to disadvantaged business enterprises in contracting highway work. In Tigard, Oregon, a businesswoman is told that she will not be given a permit to expand her plumbing and electric supply store unless she agrees to dedicate a 15-foot strip of her land to a pedestrian/bicycle pathway. Alaska rewards its residents for their tangible and intangible contributions to the state by giving them a financial dividend for each year they have lived there since statehood. What do all these cases have in common? In each, the action taken was unconstitutional.[1]

Today, as these examples suggest, whole areas of public management are permeated by constitutional law. This is true of human resources management, social services and "street-level" administration, public education and mental health, some aspects of decisionmaking, zoning, environmental regulation, and corrections. Public administrative relationships with clients, customers, contractors, property owners, public employees, prisoners, and public mental health patients, as well as with individuals engaged in street-level encounters with law enforcement agents, are currently regulated to one degree or another by the Constitution. More than ever before, to do their jobs properly public managers must understand the nation's constitutional framework, as well as the substance and structure of individuals' constitutional rights. The body of knowledge they need can be thought of as *constitutional competence.* Public administrators who lack it may not only fail to perform appropriately, but may also become the targets of successful lawsuits seeking financial compensation. The costs of inadequate constitutional competence can be substantial to both public administrators and the members of the public whose rights they harm.

The purpose of this book is to aid students of public administration and public managers in gaining constitutional competence. It focuses on conflicts between public managerial and constitutional values. It discusses the content of constitutional rights within the framework of public management. The book is especially accessible to students and practitioners of public management because it is arranged according to standard administrative values and processes. It uses actual legal cases that challenge apparently reasonable administrative action as a springboard for consideration of countervailing or otherwise pertinent constitutional concerns. In addition, discussion questions following each case are an integral part of the book's method. They are intended to provoke deeper thinking about how to integrate public managerial and constitutional values in a practical way. These questions should be wrestled with at some length.

Constitutional competence does not require that public managers become constitutional lawyers any more than statistical or economic competence requires them to be statisticians or economists. Just as public managers need to know how to interpret statistical findings and cost-effectiveness analyses, they must often have knowledge of the constitutional rights of their subordinates and other individuals directly affected by their official actions.

Our objective is to provide students and practitioners of public management with the knowledge that will make them constitutionally competent. The remainder of this chapter takes some basic first steps. It discusses constitutional interpretation, the standards courts use when assessing the constitutionality of public administrative and other governmental action, the structure of individual constitutional rights, the importance of maintaining the Constitution's integrity, the separation of powers, and the key constitutional parameters of today's federalism.

This chapter serves as a platform for understanding the cases in Chapters 3 through 8 and for considering how the constitutional values they discuss may be effectively integrated into administrative practice. To address any doubts about the relevance of constitutional competence to contemporary public management, Chapter 2 explains the scope of public administrative liability for violating individuals' constitutional rights. Chapter 9 concludes the book with a reminder that the courts are only part of the equation in improving the fit between public management and the Constitution. Constitutionally competent public managers can do much on their own.

The Constitution as the Supreme Law of the Land

Article VI of the Constitution provides that in cases of conflict between a state or federal law and the Constitution, the latter will *always* prevail. The question that often arises is: What does the Constitution say, and who determines what it means? The answer has been well settled since the Supreme Court's decision in

Marbury v. Madison in 1803.[2] The Court held that the federal judiciary has the power and duty to declare federal statutes unconstitutional and to refuse to enforce them if they conflict with the Constitution. In perhaps its most famous and often quoted language, the Court held "It is emphatically the province and duty of the Judicial Department to say what the law is."[3] Accordingly it is the courts, and not the legislature, that must determine whether a law is in conflict with the Constitution.

Following *Marbury*, the federal judiciary's power to determine the constitutionality of state laws and actions was firmly established in *Martin v. Hunter's Lessee* (1816).[4] This power was vastly expanded by the ratification of the Fourteenth Amendment in 1868. The amendment prohibits the state and local governments from depriving individuals of life, liberty, or property without due process of law. It also forbids them from denying equal protection of the laws to anyone within their jurisdictions.

The word "liberty" in the Fourteenth Amendment is now read to incorporate many of the rights in the Bill of Rights (that is, the first ten amendments), which became part of the Constitution in 1791. Originally the Bill of Rights provided protection only against federal encroachment. For instance, the First Amendment prohibits the federal government from abridging free speech and free exercise of religion. But until the Fourteenth Amendment was read to apply these restrictions to the states, there was nothing enforceable in the U.S. Constitution to prevent them from treading on such fundamental freedoms. Although the various state constitutions may have included similar protections, they could not be enforced in federal court.

The Fourteenth Amendment fundamentally changes the nature of American federalism. It enables the federal courts to apply parts of the Bill of Rights to the state governments and to strike down state and local regulations, policies, or court decisions that violate them. The power of the federal courts to check state and local governmental actions is enhanced further by the fact that liberty protected by the Fourteenth Amendment is not confined to the specific provisions of the Bill of Rights. Under a concept called "Substantive Due Process," which is discussed later on in this chapter, liberty includes fundamental personal rights, such as the right to terminate a pregnancy during the first trimester. Using the Fourteenth Amendment to place constraints on the states and their subdivisions extends the Constitution's reach and enhances its position as the supreme law of the land.[5]

Approaches to Constitutional Interpretation

At one time or another, many Americans have declared that something would be "unconstitutional."[6] The Constitution occupies a very important place in the American political culture. We tend to view it in broad general and abstract terms as a guide to public policy and fair treatment, as well as a guarantor of individual rights. But constitutional interpretation has some very concrete features and constitutional rights have clear, logical structures. Grasping these is an absolute prerequisite to gaining the constitutional competence required of today's public managers.

The federal courts use five main approaches when deciding cases under the Constitution. In general order of preference they are:

1. The text of the Constitution
2. Constitutional history
3. Precedents found in case law
4. The Constitution's structure
5. Values embodied in the Constitution and in the political culture generally

A court usually will look first at whether the Constitution specifically addresses the issues the case raises. If it does, then often the court goes no further. However, even if the text appears to provide an answer, the court may still use one or more of the other approaches. For example, the Second Amendment states that "…the right to bear arms shall not be infringed." Although the text is plain, the Supreme Court has refused to hold statutes restricting the right to own guns unconstitutional because, in its view, the Constitution envisioned neither the firepower nor lethality of today's weapons.[7]

There is great debate about the weight to give to these approaches. Supreme Court Justice Antonin Scalia strongly prefers the textual approach.[8] However, even he relies on historical and other approaches to decide cases when the Constitution's text does not provide a clear answer. In order to understand judicial decisions fully, it is often helpful to focus on which approach the court is using, and more importantly, why.

Textual Approach

When the Constitution provides a clear answer to a question, it generally resolves the issue. For example, *Immigration and Naturalization Service v. Chadha* (1983), Case 1.1, concerns the constitutionality of the "legislative veto." This type of veto was found in a wide variety of statutes. It enabled Congress to nullify specific executive actions taken under grants of delegated legislative authority. The specific question pertains to the constitutional procedures prescribed for congressional enactment of federal law. Article I, section 7, requires that Congress present the president with bills, orders, and resolutions for his approval or veto. The Supreme Court admitted that the legislative veto was a convenient shortcut, but held that it violates the Constitution's text because it is not submitted to the president for approval or rejection. Moreover, the legislative veto at issue was exercised by one House of Congress, which violates the constitutional requirements for bicameralism.

The textual approach is very strong because the Constitution is binding. But sometimes the plain text cannot resolve an issue.

Historical Approach

A second approach, which is related to textualism, is the historical approach. Here the jurist looks to history to determine the meaning or intent of constitutional provisions. For example, in *Church of Lukumi Babalu Aye, Inc. v. City of Hialeah* (1993), Case 7.2, the Supreme Court relied on history to reaffirm the principle that the government may not enact laws that intentionally suppress religious beliefs or practices. The Court explained the historical reasons why freedom of religion is afforded specific constitutional protection.

Precedent

Almost all Supreme Court decisions discuss precedent. Under a principle of law called *stare decisis* (Latin for "let the decision stand"), the Court will follow previous holdings. For example, in Case 6.1, *Cleveland Board of Education v. Loudermill (1985)*, Justice Byron White's opinion cited precedent in holding that procedural due process generally requires some kind of hearing before a public employee with civil service job protection can be dismissed.

Precedent does not prevent the courts from adapting to changing conditions. However, when they do not follow it, judges often explain in detail why earlier cases should no longer be considered binding. Perhaps time has shown that the precedent was a mistake—adhering to values, perspectives, or reasoning that has proven untenable or undesirable. Legal history reveals both rapid flip-flops as well as stubborn adherence to unrealistic precedent.[9] Note how the Supreme Court moves away from precedent in Case 1.2, *Morrison v. Olson* (1988).

The Structural Approach

The structural approach to constitutional interpretation requires analysis of the text's major provisions in conjunction with one another. For example, constitutional federalism requires an assessment of the national government's power under the Commerce Clause (Article 1, section 8) in tandem with the Tenth Amendment's reservation of some unspecified powers to the states. See Cases 1.4, 1.5 and 1.6: *United States v. Lopez* (1995), *Printz v. United States* (1997), and *C & A Carbone, Inc. v. Town of Clarkstown* (1994). In *Morrison*, the Court also assessed the interaction of different constitutional clauses and provisions.

Values

There are at least three versions of the values approach. One looks to the fundamental values embodied in the Constitution. For example, in Case 8.3, *Shapiro v. Thompson* (1969), the Supreme Court invalidated state regulations that interfered with the constitutional right to travel interstate. Although that right is not specifically mentioned in the text of the Constitution, it can be inferred from several values, including general liberty interests and the federal union's creation of national citizenship.

The second version of the values approach emphasizes that, as a living document, the Constitution should be responsive to the changing needs of the times. Case 6.4, *Vernonia School District 47J v. Acton* (1995), is an example. The Supreme Court accommodated the needs of public school authorities to control student drug use. It upheld a policy authorizing random urinalysis of students who participate in school athletic programs. The Court found that the value of controlling the illegal drug epidemic in the schools justified a major exception to the normal Fourth Amendment requirement that to be reasonable a search must be based on a well-founded suspicion that an individual has violated a law or regulation.

A third form of the values approach centers on the advantages and burdens of the action in question for the government, other organizations, and/or the individual. Here, the judges or justices ask, What would be the result of a particular decision for the specific parties involved in the case? Such "results–oriented jurisprudence" is nuanced and tied closely to the facts of a case. On the one hand, it is the product of the hard task of judging, as Justice Sandra Day O'Connor notes in Case 3.3, *Board of County Commissioners, Wabaunsee County v. Umbehr* (1996). On the other, it can be criticized as unprincipled, ad hoc balancing, as Justice Scalia frequently complains.[10]

Standards of Review

When the federal courts decide a case they normally will use one of three standards of review. The first is *mere rationality,* sometimes called the "any rational basis test." The second is *middle-level review,* and the third is *strict scrutiny.* The court's choice of which standard to use is extremely important to the analysis and outcome of cases. Nevertheless, judges are not always explicit about which one they are employing. Gaining constitutional competence enables the public manager to understand the standard invoked, why the court adopted it, and what its implications for similar cases may be.

When mere rationality review is used, the burden of persuasion is on the party challenging the governmental action. The court presumes that the government is acting properly within its powers. Under strict scrutiny, the opposite is true. The government has to demonstrate why its action is constitutionally justified, and the court will extend very little deference to its claims. Middle-level review is mixed—either party may bear the burden of persuasion for some or all facets of the case.

Mere Rationality

When a court uses the mere rationality test, the government will win insofar as two requirements are met. First, the government must be acting pursuant to a *legitimate state (i.e., governmental) objective,* such as promoting public safety, health, or the general welfare. Under this requirement both the objective and the power of the government involved to pursue it must be legitimate. Second, the means the government uses must be rationally related to the objective. Only if the government acts irrationally or totally arbitrarily will it fail to meet this requirement. Case 7.4, *Zobel v. Williams* (1982), is an unusual example of a state's failure to prevail under both prongs of the mere rationality test.

Middle-Level Review

When a court uses middle-level review, it requires the governmental objective to be *important.* It will also consider whether the means employed by the government are *substantially related* to attaining the objective. This level is often used when the government's legitimate interests seriously compete with an individual's enjoyment of his or her constitutional rights. In Case 6.3, *Rankin v. McPherson* (1987), the Supreme Court tacitly uses middle-level review in analyzing the scope of public employees' free speech rights.

Middle-level review is used in equal protection cases involving alleged discrimination based on gender. According to Case 7.3, *United States v. Virginia* (1996), the government will have to provide an "exceedingly persuasive justification" for policies that interfere with gender equality. However, in other types of middle-level review cases the burden of persuasion varies and is somewhat unpredictable.

Strict Scrutiny

When a court uses this standard to assess the constitutionality of a public policy or action, the government will typically lose, because it has to meet two difficult tests. First, the governmental objective must be *compelling* or *paramount*. Second, the means selected to achieve that objective must be either the least restrictive of constitutional rights or "narrowly tailored" to minimize infringement on them. The *least restrictive alternative* and *narrow tailoring* tests are intended to protect against unnecessary abridgment of protected freedoms. It is important for students and practitioners of public management to note that these tests look toward the extent to which constitutional rights are constricted, not the cost-effectiveness of various means. Under strict scrutiny, a more expensive—but affordable—means that is less invasive of protected constitutional rights will be preferred to a cheaper one that encroaches on such rights to a greater degree.

Strict scrutiny is used when the government is infringing on a fundamental right that is implicitly protected by the Constitution, such as the right to travel from state to state or explicitly guaranteed, as in the case of freedom of speech. For instance, in *Lukumi,* the Supreme Court applied strict scrutiny because a right that enjoys clear constitutional protection, free exercise of religion, was being abridged by the city council. The Court noted that government action targeting religious beliefs or practices will be subject to the "most rigorous of scrutiny" because freedom of religion is specifically protected by the first Amendment. In the course of its analysis, the Court cogently discusses the requirements of narrow tailoring in the context of religious freedom. Strict scrutiny is also applied in equal protection cases involving claims of racial or ethnic discrimination, as discussed below.

The Structure of Individual Constitutional Rights

Understanding the levels of review makes it easier to appreciate the logical structure of basic constitutional rights. For the most part, First Amendment, Fourth Amendment, procedural due process, and equal protection rights can be understood as a series of "if, then" statements. Judges will overwhelmingly follow the same line of reasoning when construing rights. Their disagreements with one another frequently concern the scope of rights in specific circumstances, not how the rights are constructed in the abstract. Therefore, constitutional competence demands a thorough understanding of how constitutional rights are logically structured and analyzed by the courts.

Substantive Rights

Substantive rights include the First Amendment freedoms of speech, assembly or association, press, and exercise of religion. None of these rights is absolute, but their structure places a heavy burden on the government when it seeks to abridge them. Alleged violations are subject to strict judicial scrutiny.

The threshold question in the structure of substantive rights is whether a governmental practice infringes on a protected right, even indirectly. If not, there is no violation of the Constitution. If so, the next question is whether the policy or practice is tightly connected to a governmental interest. If not, the infringement is gratuitous and consequently unconstitutional.

If the action at issue does serve a governmental interest, then it will be constitutional only if it satisfies strict scrutiny review. The interest must be compelling or paramount, and the means of achieving it must be the least restrictive alternative in terms of its infringement on constitutional rights.

Case 5.2, *Elrod v. Burns* (1976), clearly illustrates the structure of substantive rights. In assessing the constitutionality of patronage dismissals from the public service, the Supreme Court elaborates on both the requirement that governmental interests be paramount and that the means meet the least restrictive alternative test. Case 7.1, *Goldman v. Weinberger* (1986), analyzes a governmental policy that abridges the substantive right of free exercise of religion, but meets the requirements for constitutionality.

When dealing with freedom of speech or press, a few additional dimensions should be considered. The structure of substantive rights applies to governmental policies or actions that regulate the *content* of speech or publications. But not all content is fully protected. Pure political speech, such as partisan campaigning or policy advocacy, enjoys the greatest protection. It is easier to regulate commercial speech to prevent false advertising or other unfair trade practices. "Fighting words," such as incitement to riot or violence, can be suppressed when the speaker is intentionally trying to provoke disorder *and* such a reaction is imminent. Pornography enjoys no protection at all. Slander and libel can be grounds for civil suits for damages. Truth is an absolute defense in such suits. When a public figure, such as a celebrity or politician, is the object of slander or libel, he or she must show that the remarks were made with the knowledge that they were false or with reckless disregard of their truth or falsity.

The nature of the forum in which the speech takes place or the publication appears is also important. An *open public forum* is a place that has been used for the free and open exchange of ideas from time immemorial. A public park where people have discussed politics and policy for as long as anyone can remember is an example. A *designated public forum* is a place that the government has chosen to make available for indiscriminate speech, such as a community meeting room in a public library. In both cases, regulations affecting the content of speech are analyzed according to the structure of substantive rights.

A *closed or limited public forum,* such as a military base or the interior of a government office building, is treated differently. In a closed forum, all public speech can be prohibited. In a limited public forum, speech on some subjects is allowed, but not on others. For example, an agency may make a bulletin board available for work-related notices only. Political statements not related to the workplace can then be banned. However, the First Amendment bars the government from regulating viewpoints within the area of speech allowed. If such a bulletin board is open to antiunion speech, the expression of prounion points of view must also be allowed.

Content-neutral regulations face a lower level of review. These are restrictions on the time, place, and manner of speech, but not on its substance. For instance, a government can prohibit the use of loudspeakers in residential neighborhoods at night or require permits for parades and rallies in order to promote public order and prevent crowding or congestion. In assessing the constitutionality of time, place, and manner restrictions, the courts balance the importance of the governmental objective against the burden on expressive activity. The level of review varies from case to case, depending on the purpose and severity of the restriction.

In addition to *Elrod* and *Rankin, Umbehr* squarely addresses First Amendment rights in a common public administrative context—the free speech rights of contractors performing work for a government.

Fourth Amendment Privacy Rights

The Fourth Amendment protects individuals against "unreasonable searches and seizures" by the government. It is intended to give private individuals security against official intrusions into their personal spheres, including their "persons, houses, papers, and effects." But the protection is only against "unreasonable" searches and seizures—and what is reasonable is inherently given to subjective interpretations that vary with the situation. Nevertheless, the amendment has a tight logical structure.

Once it is determined that a governmental action involves an individual's protected Fourth Amendment privacy rights, the key question is whether the individual has a reasonable expectation of privacy under the circumstances. Such an expectation is one that society is prepared to support, as assessed by judges. In the absence of a reasonable expectation of privacy there can be no violation of the Fourth Amendment. For instance, there is no reasonable expectation of privacy in carry-on luggage when it is undergoing screening at an airport or in something one does openly, in plain view of the public or police.

Assuming that the individual has a reasonable expectation of privacy, then ideally the government should have a warrant to carry out the search. The appropriate judicial authority will issue a search warrant if the government can show probable cause that the individual has committed an act that may be the subject of proper criminal, civil, or administrative proceeding. Probable cause essentially means reasonable belief that the individual is involved in whatever wrongdoing is being investigated. Today, it is sometimes possible for police to obtain warrants electronically via laptop computers.

It is frequently impractical for government officers to seek warrants. A suspect may flee or dispose of contraband. In law enforcement cases, the government may conduct a warrantless search as long as there is the same probable cause upon which a warrant would be issued if the circumstances permitted. A non–law enforcement search, such as looking in a civil servant's desk at work for evidence of misconduct, faces a weaker standard. It must only be reasonable in its inception and scope.

Although the structure of Fourth Amendment privacy rights involves considerable subjective judgment with regard to reasonableness, it is hardly amorphous. Government employees who violate clearly established Fourth Amendment rights of which a reasonable person would have known are subject to civil suits for compensatory and punitive money damages (see Chapter 2). Furthermore, unconstitutionally obtained evidence is excluded from criminal trials. Case 4.1, *Deleware v. Prouse* (1979), and *Vernonia* show how the Fourth Amendment applies in different contexts.

Procedural Due Process

Procedural due process is guaranteed by the Fifth and Fourteenth Amendments. It seeks to assure fundamental fairness when the government takes action that injures the life, liberty, or property interests of a specific individual or a few people. It relies on procedural checks to prevent arbitrary, capricious, biased, or otherwise unfair governmental decisions that substantially compromise protected constitutional interests. Procedural due process generally cannot be used to challenge legislative or administrative regulations or policies that apply broadly to the society or economy. For instance, dismissals from the civil service based on a government-wide reduction in force typically do not trigger procedural due process concerns, whereas individual dismissals for misconduct do.

The Supreme Court notes that procedural due process is "an elusive concept. Its exact boundaries are indefinable, and its content varies according to specific factual contexts."[11] But, like substantive and Fourth Amendment rights, procedural due process has a clear logical structure. It requires balancing three factors:

1. The importance of the individual's protected interests;
2. The likelihood that the governmental decisionmaking procedure used will yield errors, and the probable value of other procedures in reducing that error rate; and
3. The government's financial, administrative, or other interests in using the procedure in place.

This structure implicitly assumes that the government's error rate can often be reduced by relying on substitute or additional procedures that may be more costly and/or time-consuming. As the importance of the individual's interest increases, procedural due process becomes less tolerant of errors and more willing to impose higher costs on the government to avoid them. When life is at stake, as in the case of capital punishment, there is essentially zero tolerance for errors; when liberty or property interests are implicated, more leeway is often available. Of course, when the facts upon which an administrative decision is based are neither in dispute nor subject to varying interpretations, there may be no possibility of error. In that case, only very minimal procedures will be necessary. Nothing more than informing the individual of the government's reasons for taking the action may be required.

When procedural due process applies in public administration it usually requires at least an explanation of the reasons for the government's action and an opportunity for the individual concerned to respond orally or in writing. If the individual's interest is substantial and the error rate potentially significant, a hearing may be required either before the action is taken or within a reasonable time thereafter.

How elaborate such a hearing must be is also determined by the structure of procedural due process balancing. It may include the right to confrontation and cross-examination of adverse witnesses, the opportunity to present witnesses on one's behalf, limits on the kind of information that can be presented as evidence, the right to be represented by an attorney (generally at one's own expense), a decision on the record by an impartial decisionmaker, and the opportunity to appeal an adverse decision. The *Loudermill* case explains the structure of procedural due process rights and applies it to the dismissal of a public employee.

Equal Protection

The Fourteenth Amendment provides that no state shall "deny to any person within its jurisdiction the equal protection of the laws." Equal protection applies to the federal government through "reverse" incorporation of this provision into the word "liberty" in the Fifth Amendment. Adopted after the Civil War, the Equal Protection Clause had as its original purpose at least the protection of the newly freed slaves from discriminatory treatment by the states in which they resided. Today, equal protection has an elaborate structure.

The threshold question for contemporary equal protection analysis is whether a governmental policy classifies individuals according to some criterion such as race, gender, citizenship, residency, wealth, or age. If there is no classification, there is no equal protection issue. This is not to say that the classification has to be explicit. It can sometimes be inferred from the government's policies or actions. A law or administrative practice that appears to be neutral but has a discriminatory purpose can be challenged under equal protection because it implicitly classifies people in distributing burdens or benefits. However, a regulation that has no discriminatory purpose, but simply a disparate impact on different social or demographic groups, will not violate equal protection. Similarly, a public administrator who treats two identically situated individuals, one black and one white, differently without classifying them by race does not abridge equal protection (though arbitrary or capricious action may raise procedural due process concerns).

If the policy, program, pattern of enforcement, or other governmental action does manifest a classification, a three-tier test is used to analyze its constitutionality.

1. *Suspect classifications.* Classifications based on race or ethnicity[12] are considered "suspect." On the one hand, in view of the nation's history there is reason to suspect that they may be used to discriminate invidiously against minorities. On the other, even if such classifications are intended to be "benign," as in the case of public sector affirmative action, they contravene the contemporary ideal of a color-blind society.

Suspect classifications face strict scrutiny review and are currently very difficult to sustain. The government has a heavy burden of persuasion to show that they serve a compelling governmental interest in a narrowly tailored way.

One *possible* constitutional use of suspect classifications is to remedy past, proven violations of equal protection in public personnel systems. In *United States v. Paradise* (1987),[13] a divided Supreme Court upheld the use of quota-based racial hiring and promotion to correct years of discrimination in the Alabama Department of Public Safety. The plurality opinion agreed that the remedial scheme served a compelling governmental interest.[14] The requisites of narrow tailoring were also satisfied because: (a) the remedy was efficacious vis-à-vis alternative approaches; (b) it had a fixed stopping point; (c) the percentage of minority workers to be employed and promoted was reasonable in view of the relevant population and workforce; (d) waiver provisions were available if the government needed to add staff but could not meet the hiring and promotion requirements; and (e) the remedy did not substantially compromise the employment interests of nonminority employees. See Case 5.3, *Adarand Constuctors, Inc. v. Pena* (1995) for the Supreme Court's current analysis of suspect classifications.

2. *Nonsuspect classifications.*Classifications based on age, residency, or wealth are common in public policy. For example, all the states regulate the age at which one can obtain a driver's license, marry, enter into valid contracts, and buy alcoholic beverages. Residency is frequently the basis for eligibility to attend a specific public school, work for a local government, or qualify for lower tuition at public universities. Income tax codes and social welfare policies that are means-tested make distinctions based on wealth. Such classifications are subject to mere rationality review and, therefore, will be constitutional unless the challenger can show that they do not serve a legitimate governmental interest in a rational fashion. As noted earlier, *Zobel* is an unusual example of a nonsuspect classification that fails to satisfy the mere rationality test.

3. *Quasi-suspect classifications.* Classifications based on gender fall in between the suspect and nonsuspect categories. They are subject to middle-level review: they must be substantially related to the achievement of important governmental objectives. The government's justification of gender classifications must be exceedingly persuasive.

Prior to the 1970s, gender classifications were treated as nonsuspect. They could be sustained under mere rationality as using sensible means to promote a legitimate governmental interest in protecting women. For instance, the exclusion of women from juries "protected" them from the depravity revealed in criminal trials; restrictions on the number of hours they could work "shielded" them from some of the harshness of factory and other work; exclusion from some jobs, including positions in the public service, "saved" them from "moral dangers."[15] As the society became more cognizant of gender inequality, such regulations were increasingly considered discriminatory rather than protective. The application of middle-level review to all gender classifications is an illustration of how the federal courts can adapt constitutional law to changes in the nation's social and political views. Eventually, gender classifications may be treated as suspect. Case 4.3, *Craig v. Boren* (1976), explains the Supreme Court's rationale for treating gender classifications as quasi-suspect.

Substantive Due Process

The Due Process Clauses of the Fifth and Fourteenth Amendments have a substantive as well as a procedural aspect. They protect substantive rights that are considered to be of fundamental importance to democratic constitutionalism in the United States, but which are not specifically mentioned in the Constitution. These "substantive due process" rights are declared by the judiciary in the course of deciding cases. For example, in Case 6.2, *Cleveland Board of Education v. LaFleur* (1974), the Supreme Court noted that "…it has long recognized that freedom of personal choice in matters of marriage and family life is one of the liberties protected by the Due Process Clause of the Fourteenth Amendment…."Case 8.1, *Wyatt v. Stick-*

ney (1971), finds a substantive due process right to treatment for those involuntarily confined to public mental health facilities.

By its very nature, substantive due process is open-ended and controversial. It enables federal judges, who serve indefinite terms and are removable only through impeachment, to insert their personal policy preferences into constitutional law. From the 1890s to the mid-1930s, laissez-faire-oriented judges relied on "economic" substantive due process to frustrate many governmental attempts to regulate markets. For instance, the Supreme Court struck down laws for regulating the number of hours an employee could work, child labor, and the rates common carriers could charge.[16] Today, substantive due process centers on the scope of such personal liberties as the right to terminate a pregnancy and the right to die.[17]

Although the reasonableness of particular substantive due process decisions is often hotly contested, it is well accepted that the Constitution's protection of fundamental liberty reaches beyond the rights that are specifically mentioned in its text. Little used in litigation, the Ninth Amendment stands for the grand principle that fundamental rights are antecedent to the Constitution rather than created by it: "The enumeration in the Constitution of certain rights shall not be construed to deny or disparage others retained by the people." The amendment embraces the concept that the United States is a "natural rights" society. In the enduring words of the Declaration of Independence, individuals are "endowed by their Creator with certain unalienable Rights." Substantive due process is a constitutional vehicle for defining and protecting those rights.

As a field of law, substantive due process is not as clearly structured as the other rights reviewed here. The key issue may be whether a right, such as the right to die, exists at all rather than what the government must show to abridge it. If the court rules that the right does exist, its scope may still have to be defined. In practice, judges tend to use either middle-level or strict scrutiny review, depending on the precise issues involved.

Property Rights

The protection of private property was one of the framers' primary interests. Property enjoys a variety of constitutional protections. The Fifth Amendment prohibits the federal government from taking private property except for public use and with just compensation. The same restrictions apply to the state and local governments through the Fourteenth Amendment. Both amendments prohibit governments from depriving individuals of property without due process.

In general, the courts view property rights as "a bundle of sticks," or separate components, such as the right to exclude others from one's land and to build on it. However, property is necessarily subject to extensive governmental regulation through zoning, environmental, and nuisance abatement measures. Sometimes these regulations go so far as to constitute a "taking" under the Fifth and Fourteenth Amendments because the owner is deprived of the use of the property even though he or she retains ownership of it.

Toward the end of the 1980s, the Supreme Court strengthened land owners' protection against regulatory takings. Case 8.4, *Dolan v. City of Tigard* (1994), examines an issue that often confronts local governments. When do conditions attached to a building permit constitute a taking that must be compensated? The

Supreme Court's answer strengthened property rights and complicated regulatory efforts. First, the government bears the burden of showing an "essential nexus" (connection) between the conditions it seeks to impose and the promotion of a legitimate public purpose, such as reducing traffic congestion. Second, based on the individual circumstances involved, the government must show that the conditions at issue are roughly proportional to the impact that the proposed development of the property will have.

Indirect Interference with Protected Rights

Laws and administrative actions that directly seek to curtail the exercise of constitutional rights are subject to the levels of review and tests outlined above. However, sometimes governmental regulations will indirectly interfere with protected rights. This may be unintentional and primarily the result of poor drafting. The courts have identified four areas of particular concern:

1. Overbreadth. A regulation that prohibits more constitutionally protected activity than necessary to achieve its purpose is overbroad. The problem may be that it applies to too many categories of people and/or that it covers behavior unrelated to its objectives. For instance, in *Coates v. City of Cincinnati* (1971),[18] the Supreme Court struck down an ordinance that made it a crime for three or more persons to assemble on a sidewalk and "annoy" persons passing by. Part of the constitutional problem was that the regulation was overbroad because it could be construed to outlaw protected as well as unprotected behavior. Three people urging passersby to vote Republican may annoy Democrats and vice versa, but the content of their speech is protected by the First Amendment. If the three were panhandling, their behavior might constitutionally be prohibited. *Elrod* presents an example of a practice that is overbroad in relation to its putative objectives.

2. Chilling effect. A regulation may "chill" one's ardor for exercising a constitutional right even though it does not specifically penalize it. *Shelton v. Tucker* (1960)[19] is an example. An Arkansas statute required every teacher employed in a state-supported school or college to file "annually an affidavit listing without limitation every organization to which he has belonged or regularly contributed within the preceding five years."[20] The state's purpose was somewhat unclear, and there was no barrier to membership in any particular organization or in numerous organizations. The Supreme Court ruled that the law was constitutionally defective in part because it placed heavy "pressure upon a teacher to avoid any ties which might displease those who control his professional destiny."[21] In other words, it had a chilling effect on the teachers' freedom of association. The problem of chilling effect is central to the *Umbehr* case.

3. Vagueness. There are at least three constitutional problems with vague laws. First, they undercut the rule of law because they do not clearly indicate which behavior is illegal or what is demanded for compliance. If people do not understand a law's requirements, they cannot knowingly obey it. Second, vague laws can have a chilling effect on the exercise of protected rights. Efforts at state

universities to ban racist, sexist, homophobic, and other "hate speech" may suffer from this defect. Their imprecise definitions may make students reluctant to express opinions on matters related to the status of minorities, women, homosexuals, disabled persons, and others in the society. Third, vague regulations can encourage arbitrary enforcement. In Case 5.1, *Kolender v. Lawson* (1983), the Supreme Court explains the constitutional problem with criminal statutes that vest excessive discretion in the police.

4. Underinclusiveness. Sometimes a law impinging on constitutional rights will have a legitimate, important, or compelling governmental purpose, but will be unconstitutional because it is "underinclusive." Such laws fail to regulate sufficiently all the behavior necessary to achieve their purposes. Consequently, their interference with constitutional rights is not narrowly tailored. For example, in *Lukumi,* the city sought to prevent cruelty to animals and to protect public health by outlawing animal sacrifices. However, its ordinances were underinclusive. They did not prevent mistreatment of animals in all contexts or provide for the safe disposal of animal remains generally. The underinclusiveness was unconstitutional because it restricted religiously motivated, but not other, behavior.

Constitutional Integrity

A document written in 1787 that still governs a complex nation such as the United States must be both flexible and brilliant. Flexibility allows it to accommodate vast social, economic, intellectual, and technological change. Brilliance helps it endure. Adherence to the value of constitutional integrity ensures that adjustments and new interpretations do not diminish brilliance. Change, other than through the nearly consensual process of constitutional amendment, must be consonant with the framers' design. But the framers could not have envisioned the scale of the contemporary administrative state, and the Constitution's provisions for public administration are rudimentary. Unlike the federal government, many of the states have adopted new constitutions or extensive amendments partly to deal with administrative change. But at the national level, it has been necessary to "retrofit" the government's large and powerful administrative component into the constitutional scheme without damaging its integrity.

Chadha demonstrates the importance the Supreme Court attaches to constitutional integrity. The Court insists that the letter of the Constitution's procedure for legislating be followed. Then Chief Justice Warren Burger noted that the Constitution imposes some heavy procedural burdens on government, sometimes making it inefficient or unworkable. However, the procedures were carefully crafted by the framers in order to preserve freedom. Shortcuts that damage constitutional integrity are not permitted. The Court made the same point more recently in *Clinton v. City of New York* (1998).[22] No matter how attractive providing the president with a line item veto may be, legislation must comport strictly with constitutional procedure. The theme of constitutional integrity runs through many of the cases in subsequent chapters as well.

The Separation of Powers

Ever since 1887, when Woodrow Wilson called for "The Study of Administration"[23] in a systematic way, mainstream public administrative thought in the United States has identified public management primarily as an executive endeavor. Federal administration is typically viewed as taking place in the executive branch and subordinate to the president. But the constitutional reality is much closer to Lewis Meriam's 1939 observation that "…under our system of divided powers, the executive branch of the national government is not exclusively controlled by the President, by the Congress, or by the courts. All three have a hand in controlling it, each from a different angle and each in a different way."[24] The separation of powers has a tremendous impact on the operations of federal agencies.

The Constitution authorizes the president to "take Care that the Laws be faithfully executed" (Article II, section 3). However, almost all the powers necessary to do so are shared with Congress. The president's appointment of department heads requires the advice and consent of the Senate. Appointments to such positions when the Senate is in recess expire at the end of the next legislative session. The missions, powers, structure, procedures, size, budget, and personnel systems of all agencies are established by statute. Acting alone, presidents can ask the "principal officers" in the executive departments for their opinions in writing and can issue executive orders. However, neither formal opinions nor executive orders can supersede law. Congress can restrict the president's power to fire ordinary federal employees, and even to dismiss the heads of the independent regulatory commissions (which constitutionally are not considered part of the executive branch).[25]

The courts also play a major role in federal administration. They are often called upon to review agency actions for legality under both the Constitution and statutes that generically regulate the federal administration, such as the Administrative Procedure Act (1946), the National Environmental Policy Act (1969), and various sections of the Civil Service Reform Act (1978).[26] The courts also rule on challenges to the exercise of administrative powers pursuant to the broad variety of statutes that empower agencies and define their missions. As Chapter 2 explains, since the 1970s, the federal judiciary has also made many public administrators personally liable for violating individuals' constitutional rights.

Morrison broadly discusses contemporary separation of powers theory and shows how the Constitution subordinates federal administration to all three branches. Specifically, the Supreme Court's decision explains why it is constitutionally permissible for a *court* to appoint an Independent Counsel in the Department of Justice and for Congress to limit strictly the president's authority to dismiss him or her. *Morrison* erases any notion that the executive branch is compartmentalized under the president.

Case 1.3, *Local 2677, The American Federation of Government Employees v. Phillips* (1973), illustrates how the separation of powers can complicate the jobs of federal executives and managers. What if the president and Congress disagree? Who should be followed? The court's answer is in keeping with a tenet that reaches all the way back to an 1838 case in which the Supreme Court ruled that "It would be an alarming doctrine that [C]ongress cannot impose upon any executive officer any duty they may think proper, which is not repugnant to any rights secured and protected by the [C]onstitution; and in such cases, the duty and responsibility grow out of and are subject to the control of law, and not to the direction of the President."[27] Of course! But what happens after you say "no!" to the president?

Constitutional Federalism

Federalism has a major impact on public administration at all levels of government. The Constitution established a system of dual sovereignty that was unique at its inception in 1789 and has been intermittently perplexing ever since. The national government is sovereign in some areas and the states in others. Local governments are considered subunits of the states and, however central they have become to the implementation of federal and state programs, have no independent standing in constitutional federalism. The national and state governments also share sovereignty in many policy areas. Because there is so much overlap and partnering between the national and subnational governments, it has become customary for public managers to think in terms of "cooperative federalism."[28] However, three key Supreme Court decisions in the 1990s reestablish some constitutional parameters for dual sovereignty.

Constitutional federalism turns largely on the federal courts' reading of two provisions. The Commerce Clause provides that "The Congress shall have Power…To regulate Commerce with foreign Nations, and among the several States, and with the Indian Tribes…" (Article I, section 8). From the late 1930s until its 1995 decision in the *Lopez* case, no law was struck down by the Supreme Court for exceeding Congress's powers under the Commerce Clause. To the contrary, a great deal of environmental, economic, and civil rights legislation was upheld under the national government's power to regulate interstate commerce. In *Lopez,* a 5-4 majority of the Court held that Congress does not have the power to prohibit individuals from bringing guns into school zones. The Court reasoned that if Congress were allowed to regulate such an act, its powers would almost endlessly overlap those of the states, and the distinctions that constitutional federalism tries to protect would disappear. *Lopez* includes a concise and incisive history of Commerce Clause interpretation.

Endless overlap would damage a second provision in the structure of constitutional federalism. The Tenth Amendment provides that "The powers not delegated to the United States by the Constitution, nor prohibited by it to the States, are reserved to the States respectively, or to the people." In other words, the national government is one of enumerated powers. If the scope of congressional power to regulate local social behavior were no different than that of the states, then what powers would be reserved to the states? In short, the Tenth Amendment stands for the principle that some powers must be reserved exclusively to the states; that is, the states retain exclusive sovereign authority in some policy areas.

But which ones and which governmental institutions should decide? These questions have plagued Tenth Amendment jurisprudence. For a time during the latter half of the 1980s, it even looked as if the Tenth Amendment was not judicially enforceable. The Supreme Court reasoned that the states' main protection from national regulation lay in the structure of Congress, especially the Senate, which represents each state equally.[29] However, in its 1997 decision in *Printz,* the Court did much to rehabilitate the language and concept of dual sovereignty.

Determining the parameters of dual sovereignty in contemporary constitutional federalism is complicated by an additional consideration of importance to public management. As interpreted by the federal courts, the Commerce Clause has a "negative" or "dormant" aspect that prohibits state and local governments from regulating interstate commerce. As *Carbone* explains, state and local governments cannot discriminate against interstate commerce or excessively burden it. For instance, a state with a natural resource, such as timber or shellfish, cannot require that whatever is harvested in-state be processed there as well. *Carbone* is particularly interesting because it involved a fairly common type of local regulation aimed at assuring the mutual profitability of an innovative public–private partnership.

Conclusion

The material in this chapter lays the groundwork for gaining constitutional competence. Constitutional interpretation is not a science, but there are patterns of reasoning that act almost like formulas. Understanding the three levels of review and the structures of the rights reviewed here will go a long way toward helping one to analyze the cases in Chapters 3 through 8 and to appreciate their centrality to public management. The cases that follow in the next section explain why the Supreme Court values strict adherence to the letter of constitutional procedures— even when simpler ones might yield better accountability or cost-effectiveness— and how constitutional authority regarding public administration is organized. Although the constitutional integrity and separation of powers cases focus on the federal government, their overall reasoning has broad application in the states as well. Constitutional federalism, of course, directly affects the state and local governments.

Much of the discussion in this chapter may seem alien to traditional education for public management. In many respects it is. Nonetheless, it is central to doing American public administration well. After reading the cases that follow carefully, and working through the discussion questions, the foundation for constitutional competence will be well established.

Notes

1. In this book, see Cases 6.3, *Rankin, v. McPherson* (1987); 6.1, *Cleveland Board of Education v. Loudermill* (1985); 4.4, *Hawkins v. Town of Shaw* (1971); 5.1, *Kolender v. Lawson* (1983); 4.1, *Delaware v. Prouse* (1979); 5.2, *Elrod v. Burns* (1976); 1.6, *C & A Carbone, Inc. v. Town of Clarkstown* (1994); 5.3, *Adarand Constructors, Inc. v. Pena* (1995); 8.4, *Dolan v. City of Tigard* (1994); 7.4, *Zobel v. Williams* (1982).

2. 1 Cranch 137 (1803).

3. 1 Cranch 137, 177 (1803).

4. 14 U.S. 304 (1816).

5. When citizens of two or more states have a conflict involving $100,000 or more, the federal courts may interpret state law to decide the case. This is called diversity jurisdiction. The theory is that the state whose law controls (usually where the dispute occurred) would favor its citizens over those from other states. The federal courts' jurisdiction in such cases is established by law rather than by the Constitution.

6. This section relies on the methodology established in Steven L. Emanuel, *Constitutional Law* (Larchmont, NY: Emanuel Publishing, 1998). See also Lawrence Tribe, *American Constitutional Law* (Westbury, NY: Foundation Press, 1989); Gerald Gunther and Kathleen Sullivan, *Constitutional Law*, 8th ed. (Westbury, NY: Foundation Press, 1997); Walter Murphy, James Fleming, and Sotorious Barber, *American Constitutional Interpretation* (Westbury, NY: Foundation Press, 1995).

7. See *Quilici v. Village of Morton Grove,* 695 F.2d 261 (1982); *Humphrey v. United States,* 464 U.S. 863 (1983).

8. Antonin Scalia, *A Matter of Interpretation* (Princeton, NJ: Princeton University Press, 1997).

9. For example, compare *West Virginia State Board of Education v. Barnette,* 319 U.S. 624 (1943) and *Flood v. Kuhn,* 407 U.S. 258 (1972).

10. For example, see Scalia's dissent in *O'Hare Truck Service v. City of Northlake,* 518 U.S. 668 at 711 (1996).

11. *Hannah v. Larche,* 363 U.S. 420, 442 (1960).

12. As a general rule, classifications based on citizenship are suspect at the state and local levels, but nonsuspect at the federal level. The difference is that the federal government has substantial constitutional powers with regard to immigration and naturalization. State and local classifications based on citizenship may serve a compelling governmental interest when they promote political community, as in the case of restricting employment as public school teachers or police to citizens. See *Ambach v. Norwick,* 441 U.S. 68 (1979); *Foley v. Connelie,* 435 U.S. 291 (1978).

13. 480 U.S. 149 (1987).

14. A plurality opinion occurs when a majority of the justices deciding the case do not subscribe to a single opinion. In *Paradise* only Justices William Brennan, Thurgood Marshall, Harry Blackmun, and Lewis Powell specifically agreed on this point.

15. See *J.E.B. v. Alabama, ex rel. T.B.,* 511 U.S. 127 (1994); *Muller v. Oregon,* 208 U.S. 412 (1908); *Goesaert v. Cleary,* 335 U.S. 464 (1948). See also David H. Rosenbloom, *Federal Equal Employment Opportunity* (New York: Praeger, 1977), pp. 56–58, 70.

16. *Lochner v. New York,* 198 U.S. 45 (1905); *Hammer v. Dagenhart,* 247 U.S. 251 (1918); *Chicago, Milwaukee and St. Paul Railway Co. v. Minnesota,* 134 U.S. 418 (1890).

17. See *Vacco v. Quill,* 117 S.Ct. 2293 (1997); *Washington v. Glucksberg,* 117 S.Ct. 2258 (1997).

18. 402 U.S. 611 (1971).

19. 364 U.S. 479 (1960).

20. 364 U.S. 479 (1960).

21. 364 U.S. 479, 486 (1960).

22. *Clinton v. City of New York,* 118 S.Ct. 2091 (1998).

23. Woodrow Wilson, "The Study of Administration," in Jay Shafritz and A. Hyde, eds., *Classics of Public Administration,* 2nd ed. (Chicago: Dorsey Press, 1987), pp. 10–25. (Wilson's essay was originally published in 1887.)

24. Lewis Meriam, *Reorganization of the National Government: Part I: An Analysis of the Problem* (Washington, DC: Brookings Institution, 1939), p. 125.

25. *Humphrey's Executor v. United States,* 295 U.S. 602 (1935); Angel Moreno, "Presidential Coordination of the Independent Regulatory Process," *Administrative Law Journal,* 8 (1994): 461–516.

26. Administrative Procedure Act, 60 Stat. 237 (1946); National Environmental Policy Act, 83 Stat. 852 (1969); Civil Service Reform Act, 92 Stat. 1111 (1978).

27. *Kendall v. United States,* 37 U.S. 524, 610 (1838).

28. See Deil Wright, "The Origins, Emergence, and Maturity of Federalism and Intergovernmental Relations: Two Centuries of Territory and Power," in Jack Rabin, W. Bartley Hildreth, and Gerald Miller, eds., *Handbook of Public Administration* (New York: Marcel Dekker, 1989), pp. 331–386.

29. *Garcia v. San Antonio Metropolitan Transit Authority,* 469 U.S. 528 (1985).

Additional Reading

Carp, Robert, and Ronald Stidham. *Judicial Process in America.* 4th ed. Washington, DC: Congressional Quarterly, 1998.

Fisher, Louis, *The Politics of Shared Power: Congress and the Executive.* 4th ed. College Station, TX: Texas A & M University Press, 1998.

Rosenbloom, David, and Bernard Ross, "Toward A New Jurisprudence of Constitutional Federalism: The Supreme Court in the 1990s and Public Administration." *American Review of Public Administration* 28 (June 1998): 107–125.

Case 1.1
Constitutional Integrity

IMMIGRATION AND NATURALIZATION SERVICE v. CHADHA et al.
Argued February 22, 1982
Reargued December 7, 1982
Decided June 23, 1983
462 US 919

CHIEF JUSTICE BURGER delivered the opinion of the Court.

• • •

I

Chadha is an East Indian who was born in Kenya and holds a British passport. He was lawfully admitted to the United States in 1966 on a nonimmigrant student visa. His visa expired on June 30, 1972. On October 11, 1973, the District Director of the Immigration and Naturalization Service ordered Chadha to show cause why he should not be deported for having "remained in the United States for a longer time than permitted." ...Pursuant to § 242(b) of the Immigration and Nationality Act (Act), 8 USC § 1252(b), ...a deportation hearing was held before an Immigration Judge on January 11, 1974. Chadha conceded that he was deportable for overstaying his visa and the hearing was adjourned to enable him to file an application for suspension of deportation....

After Chadha submitted his application for suspension of deportation, the deportation hearing was resumed on February 7, 1974. On the basis of evidence adduced at the hearing, affidavits submitted with the application, and the results of a character investigation conducted by the INS, the Immigration Judge, on June 25, 1974, ordered that Chadha's deportation be suspended. The Immigration Judge found that Chadha met the requirements of § 244(a)(1): he had resided continuously in the United States for over seven years, was of good moral character, and would suffer "extreme hardship" if deported.

Pursuant to § 244(c)(1) of the Act, 8 USC § 1254(c)(1), ...the Immigration Judge suspended Chadha's deportation and a report of the suspension was transmitted to Congress...[in the form of a recommendation by the Attor-

ney General that Chadha's deportation be suspended].

Once the Attorney General's recommendation for suspension of Chadha's deportation was conveyed to Congress, Congress had the power under § 244(c)(2) of the Act, 8 USC § 1254(c)(2),...to veto the Attorney General's determination that Chadha should not be deported. Section 244(c)(2) provides:

"if during the session of the Congress at which a case is reported, or prior to the close of the session of the Congress next following the session at which a case is reported, either the Senate or the House of Representatives passes a resolution stating in substance that it does not favor the suspension of such deportation, the Attorney General shall thereupon deport such alien or authorize the alien's voluntary departure at his own expense under the order of deportation in the manner provided by law. If, within the time above specified, neither the Senate nor the House of Representatives shall pass such a resolution, the Attorney General shall cancel deportation proceedings."

The June 25, 1974, order of the Immigration Judge suspending Chadha's deportation remained outstanding as a valid order for a year and a half. For reasons not disclosed by the record, Congress did not exercise the veto authority reserved to it under § 244(c)(2) until the first session of the 94th Congress.

• • •

After the House veto of the Attorney General's decision to allow Chadha to remain in the United States, the Immigration Judge reopened the deportation proceedings to implement the House order deporting Chadha. Chadha moved to terminate the proceedings on the ground that § 244(c)(2) is unconstitutional. The Immigration Judge held that he had no authority to rule on the constitutional validity of § 244(c)(2). On November 8, 1976, Chadha was ordered deported pursuant to the House action.

Chadha appealed the deportation order to the Board of Immigration Appeals, again contending that § 244(c)(2) is unconstitutional. The Board held that it had "no power to declare unconstitutional an act of Congress" and Chadha's appeal was dismissed....

...Chadha filed a petition for review of the deportation order in the United States Court of Appeals for the Ninth Circuit. The Immigration and Naturalization Service agreed with Chadha's position before the Court of Appeals and joined him in arguing that § 244(c)(2) is unconstitutional. In light of the importance of the question, the Court of Appeals invited both the Senate and the House of Representatives to file briefs amici curiae.

After full briefing and oral argument, the Court of Appeals held that the House was without constitutional authority to order Chadha's deportation; accordingly it directed the Attorney General "to cease and desist from taking any steps to deport this alien based upon the resolution enacted by the House of Representatives." ...The essence of its holding was that § 244(c)(2) violates the constitutional doctrine of separation of powers.

We granted certiorari....

• • •

III

A

We turn now to the question whether action of one House of Congress under § 244(c)(2) violates strictures of the Constitution. We begin, of course, with the presumption that the challenged statute is valid. Its wisdom is not the concern of the courts; if a challenged action does not violate the Constitution, it must be sustained....

By the same token, the fact that a given law or procedure is efficient, convenient, and useful in facilitating functions of government, standing alone, will not save it if it is contrary to the Constitution. Convenience and efficiency are not the primary objectives—or the hallmarks—of democratic government and our inquiry is sharpened rather than blunted by the fact that congressional veto provisions are appearing with increasing frequency in statutes which delegate authority to executive and independent agencies:

> "Since 1932, when the first veto provision was enacted into law, 295 congressional veto-type procedures have been inserted in 196 different statutes as follows: from 1932 to 1939, five statutes were affected; from 1940–49, nineteen statutes; between 1950–59, thirty-four statutes; and from 1960–69, forty-nine. From the year 1970 through 1975, at least one hundred sixty-three such provisions were included in eighty-nine laws."...

Justice White undertakes to make a case for the proposition that the one-House veto is a useful "political invention," ...[dissent] and we need not challenge that assertion. We can even concede this utilitarian argument although the long-range political wisdom of this "invention" is arguable....But policy arguments supporting even useful "political inventions" are subject to the demands of the Constitution which defines powers and, with respect to this subject, sets out just how those powers are to be exercised.

Explicit and unambiguous provisions of the Constitution prescribe and define the respective functions of the Congress and of the Executive in the legislative process. Since the precise terms of those familiar provisions are critical to the resolution of this case, we set them out verbatim. Article I provides:

> "All legislative Powers herein granted shall be vested in a Congress of the United States, which shall consist of a Senate *and* House of Representatives." Art I, § 1. (Emphasis added.)
>
> "Every Bill which shall have passed the House of Representatives *and* the Senate, *shall*, before it becomes a Law, be presented to the President of the United States...." Art. I, § 7, cl 2. (Emphasis added.)
>
> "*Every* Order, Resolution, or Vote to which the Concurrence of the Senate and House of Representatives may be necessary (except on a question of Adjournment) *shall be* presented to the President of the United States; and before the Same shall take Effect, *shall be* approved by him, or being disapproved by him, *shall be* repassed by two thirds of the Senate and House of Representatives, according to the Rules and Limitations prescribed in the Case of a Bill." Art I, § 7, cl 3. (Emphasis added.)

These provisions of Art I are integral parts of the constitutional design for the separation of powers. We have recently noted that "[t]he principle of separation of powers was not simply an abstract generalization in the minds of the Framers: it was woven into the document that they drafted in Philadelphia in the summer of 1787."...

Just as we relied on the textual provision of Art II, § 2, cl 2, to vindicate the principle of separation of powers in Buckley [v Valeo, 1976] we see that the purposes underlying the Presentment Clauses, Art I, § 7, cls 2, 3, and the bicameral requirement of Art I, § 1, and § 7, cl 2, guide our resolution of the important question presented in these cases. The very structure of the articles delegating and separating powers under Arts I, II, and III exemplifies the concept of separation of powers, and we now turn to Art I.

B
The Presentment Clauses

The records of the Constitutional Convention reveal that the requirement that all legislation be presented to the President before becoming law was uniformly accepted by the Framers. Presentment to the President and the Presidential veto were considered so imperative that the draftsmen took special pains to assure that these requirements could not be circumvented. During the final debate on Art I, § 7, cl 2, James Madison expressed concern that it might easily be evaded by the simple expedient of calling a proposed law a "resolution" or "vote" rather than a "bill."...

As a consequence, Art I, § 7, cl 3...was added....

The decision to provide the President with a limited and qualified power to nullify proposed legislation by veto was based on the profound conviction of the Framers that the powers conferred on Congress were the powers to be most carefully circumscribed. It is beyond doubt that lawmaking was a power to be shared by both Houses and the President. In The Federalist No. 73,...Hamilton focused on the President's role in making laws:

> "If even no propensity had ever discovered itself in the legislative body to invade the rights of the Executive, the rules of just reasoning and theoretic propriety would of themselves teach us that the one ought not to be left to the mercy of the other, but ought to possess a constitutional and effectual power of self-defence...."

The President's role in the lawmaking process also reflects the Framers' careful efforts

to check whatever propensity a particular Congress might have to enact oppressive, improvident, or ill-considered measures. The President's veto role in the legislative process was described later during public debate on ratification:

> "It establishes a salutary check upon the legislative body, calculated to guard the community against the effects of faction, precipitancy, or of any impulse unfriendly to the public good, which may happen to influence a majority of that body.
>
> "...The primary inducement to conferring the power in question upon the Executive is, to enable him to defend himself; the secondary one is to increase the chances in favor of the community against the passing of bad laws, through haste, inadvertence, or design." [Quoting Federalist No. 73]...

The Court also has observed that the Presentment Clauses serve the important purpose of assuring that a "national" perspective is grafted on the legislative process:

> "The President is a representative of the people just as the members of the Senate and of the House are, and it may be, at some times, on some subjects, that the President elected by all the people is rather more representative of them all than are the members of either body of the Legislature whose constituencies are local and not countrywide...." Myers v United States, [1926]....

C
Bicameralism

The bicameral requirement of Art I, §§ 1, 7, was of scarcely less concern to the Framers than was the Presidential veto and indeed the two concepts are interdependent. By providing that no law could take effect without the concurrence of the prescribed majority of the Members of both Houses, the Framers reemphasized their belief, already remarked upon in connection with the Presentment Clauses, that legislation should not be enacted unless it has been carefully and fully considered by the Nation's elected officials. In the Constitutional Convention debates on the need for a bicameral legislature, James Wilson, later to become a Justice of this Court, commented:

> "Despotism comes on mankind in different shapes. Sometimes in an Executive, sometimes in a military, one. Is there danger of a Legislative despotism? Theory & practice both proclaim it. If

the Legislative authority be not restrained, there can be neither liberty nor stability; and it can only be restrained by dividing it within itself, into distinct and independent branches. In a single house there is no check, but the inadequate one, of the virtue & good sense of those who compose it."...

Hamilton argued that a Congress comprised of a single House was antithetical to the very purpose of the Constitution. Were the Nation to adopt a Constitution providing for only one legislative organ, he warned:

"[W]e shall finally accumulate, in a single body, all the most important prerogatives of sovereignty, and thus entail upon our posterity one of the most execrable forms of government that human infatuation ever contrived. Thus we should create in reality that very tyranny which the adversaries of the new Constitution either are, or affect to be, solicitous to avert." The Federalist No. 22....

This view was rooted in a general skepticism regarding the fallibility of human nature later commented on by Joseph Story:

"Public bodies, like private persons, are occasionally under the dominion of strong passions and excitements; impatient, irritable, and impetuous....If [a legislature] feels no check but its own will, it rarely has the firmness to insist upon holding a question long enough under its own view, to see and mark it in all its bearings and relations on society."...

These observations are consistent with what many of the Framers expressed, none more cogently than Madison in pointing up the need to divide and disperse power in order to protect liberty:

"In republican government, the legislative authority necessarily predominates. The remedy for this inconveniency is to divide the legislature into different branches; and to render them, by different modes of election and different principles of action, as little connected with each other as the nature of their common functions and their common dependence on the society will admit." The Federalist No. 51....

However familiar, it is useful to recall that apart from their fear that special interests could be favored at the expense of public needs, the Framers were also concerned, although not of one mind, over the apprehensions of the smaller states. Those states feared a commonality of interest among the larger states would work to their disadvantage; representatives of the larger states, on the other hand, were skeptical of a legislature that could pass laws favoring a minority of the people.... It need hardly be repeated here that the Great Compromise, under which one House was viewed as representing the people and the other the states, allayed the fears of both the large and small states.

We see therefore that the Framers were acutely conscious that the bicameral requirement and the Presentment Clauses would serve essential constitutional functions. The President's participation in the legislative process was to protect the Executive Branch from Congress and to protect the whole people from improvident laws. The division of Congress into two distinctive bodies assures that the legislative power would be exercised only after opportunity for full study and debate in separate settings. The President's unilateral veto power, in turn, was limited by the power of two-thirds of both Houses of Congress to overrule a veto thereby precluding final arbitrary action of one person....It emerges clearly that the prescription for legislative action in Art I, §§ 1, 7, represents the Framers' decision that the legislative power of the Federal Government be exercised in accord with a single, finely wrought and exhaustively considered, procedure.

IV

The Constitution sought to divide the delegated powers of the new Federal Government into three defined categories, Legislative, Executive, and Judicial, to assure, as nearly as possible, that each branch of government would confine itself to its assigned responsibility. The hydraulic pressure inherent within each of the separate Branches to exceed the outer limits of its power, even to accomplish desirable objectives, must be resisted.

• • •

Since it is clear that the action by the House under § 244(c)(2) was not within any of the express constitutional exceptions authorizing one House to act alone, and equally clear that it was an exercise of legislative power, that action was subject to the standards prescribed in Art I. The bicameral requirement, the Presentment Clauses, the President's veto, and Congress' power to override a veto were intended to erect enduring checks on each Branch and to protect the people from the improvident exercise of power by mandating certain prescribed steps. To preserve those checks, and maintain the separation of powers, the carefully defined limits on the power of each Branch must not be eroded. To accomplish what has been attempted by one House of Congress in this case requires action in conformity with the express procedures of the Constitution's prescription for legislative action: passage by a majority of both Houses and presentment to the President.

The veto authorized by § 244(c)(2) doubtless has been in many respects a convenient shortcut; the "sharing" with the Executive by Congress of its authority over aliens in this manner is, on its face, an appealing compromise. In purely practical terms, it is obviously easier for action to be taken by one House without submission to the President; but it is crystal clear from the records of the Convention, contemporaneous writings and debates, that the Framers ranked other values higher than efficiency. The records of the Convention and debates in the States preceding ratification underscore the common desire to define and limit the exercise of the newly created federal powers affecting the states and the people. There is unmistakable expression of a determination that legislation by the national Congress be a step-by-step, deliberate and deliberative process.

The choices we discern as having been made in the Constitutional Convention impose burdens on governmental processes that often seem clumsy, inefficient, even unworkable, but those hard choices were consciously made by men who had lived under a form of government that permitted arbitrary governmental acts to go unchecked. There is no support in the Constitution or decisions of this Court for the proposition that the cumbersomeness and delays often encountered in complying with explicit constitutional standards may be avoided, either by the Congress or by the President....With all the obvious flaws of delay, untidiness, and potential for abuse, we have not yet found a better way to preserve freedom than by making the exercise of power subject to the carefully crafted restraints spelled out in the Constitution.

•   •   •

Discussion Questions

1. In dissent, Justice White wrote: "Without the legislative veto, Congress is faced with a Hobson's choice: either to refrain from delegating the necessary authority, leaving itself with a hopeless task of writing laws with the requisite specificity to cover endless special circumstances across the entire policy landscape, or in the alternative, to abdicate its lawmaking function to the Executive Branch and independent agencies. To choose the former leaves major national problems unresolved; to opt for the latter risks unaccountable policy-making by those not elected to fill that role." Do you think White has properly framed the issue? Are there intermediate courses Congress might take? If so, what are they and what are their advantages and disadvantages?

2. The Court writes that governmental processes based on the Constitution "often seem clumsy, inefficient, even unworkable." Can you think of clear instances in which U.S. government has been "unworkable"? In your view, does the demise of the legislative veto make government more workable or less workable?

3. Administrative doctrine often frowns on duplication and overlap between agencies. Does the bicameralism of Congress differ significantly from such overlaps as are found among agencies such as Interior (national parks) and Agriculture (national forests), the Bureau of Reclamation, the Soil Conservation Service, and the Army Corps of Engineers, or the Equal Employment Opportunity Commission and the Department of Labor's Office of Federal Contract Compliance? If so, how? If not, can we expect to derive benefits from agency overlaps that are similar to those that the Court believes we derive from bicameralism? What would those benefits be?

Case 1.2
Who's in Charge of the Executive Branch?

MORRISON v. OLSON
Argued April 26, 1988
Decided June 29, 1988
487 US 654

REHNQUIST, C.J., delivered the opinion of the Court.

• • •

Briefly stated, Title VI of the Ethics in Government Act (Title VI or the Act)... allows for the appointment of an "independent counsel" to investigate and, if appropriate, prosecute certain high ranking Government officials for violations of federal criminal laws. The Act requires the Attorney General, upon receipt of information that he determines is "sufficient to constitute grounds to investigate whether any person [covered by the Act] may have violated any Federal criminal law," to conduct a preliminary investigation of the matter. When the Attorney General has completed this investigation, or 90 days has elapsed, he is required to report to a special court (the Special Division) created by the Act "for the purpose of appointing independent counsels."...If the Attorney General determines that "there are no reasonable grounds to believe that further investigation is warranted," then he must notify the Special Division of this result. In such a case, "the division of the court shall have no power to appoint an independent counsel."...If, however, the Attorney General has determined that there are "reasonable grounds to believe that further investigation or prosecution is warranted," then he "shall apply to the division of the court for the appointment of an independent counsel." The Attorney General's application to the court

> shall contain sufficient information to assist the [court] in selecting an independent counsel and in defining that independent counsel's prosecutorial jurisdiction.

...Upon receiving this application, the Special Division "shall appoint an appropriate independent counsel and shall define that independent counsel's prosecutorial jurisdiction."...

With respect to all matters within the independent counsel's jurisdiction, the Act grants the counsel

> full power and independent authority to exercise all investigative and prosecutorial functions and powers of the Department of Justice, the Attorney General, and any other officer or employee of the Department of Justice....

[T]he counsel's powers include

> initiating and conducting prosecutions in any court of competent jurisdiction, framing and signing indictments, filing informations, and handling all aspects of any case in the name of the United States.

...In addition, whenever a matter has been referred to an independent counsel under the Act, the Attorney General and the Justice Department are required to suspend all investigations and proceedings regarding the matter....An independent counsel has

> full authority to dismiss matters within [his or her] prosecutorial jurisdiction without conducting an investigation or at any subsequent time before prosecution, if to do so would be consistent

with Department of Justice policy....

Two statutory provisions govern the length of an independent counsel's tenure in office. The first defines the procedure for removing an independent counsel. Section 596(a)(1) provides:

> An independent counsel appointed under this chapter may be removed from office, other than by impeachment and conviction, only by the personal action of the Attorney General and only for good cause, physical disability, mental incapacity, or any other condition that substantially impairs the performance of such independent counsel's duties.

If an independent counsel is removed pursuant to this section, the Attorney General is required to submit a report to both the Special Division and the Judiciary Committees of the Senate and the House "specifying the facts found and the ultimate grounds for such removal."...Under the current version of the Act, an independent counsel can obtain judicial review of the Attorney General's action by filing a civil action in the United States District Court for the District of Columbia....

• • •

Finally, the Act provides for congressional oversight of the activities of independent counsel....

The proceedings in this case provide an example of how the Act works in practice. In 1982, two Subcommittees of the House of Representatives issued subpoenas directing the Environmental Protection Agency (EPA) to produce certain documents relating to the efforts of the EPA and the Land and Natural Resources Division of the Justice Department to enforce the "Superfund Law." At that time, appellee Olson was the Assistant Attorney General for the Office of Legal Counsel (OLC), appellee Schmults was Deputy Attorney General, and appellee Dinkins was the Assistant Attorney General for the Land and Natural Resources Division. Acting on the advice of the Justice Department, the President ordered the Administrator of EPA to invoke executive privilege to withhold certain of the documents on the ground that they contained "enforcement-sensitive information." The Administrator obeyed this order and withheld the documents. In response, the House voted to hold the Administrator in contempt, after which the Administrator and the United States together filed a lawsuit against the House. The conflict abated in March, 1983, when the administration agreed to give the House Committees limited access to the documents.

The following year, the House Judiciary Committee began an investigation into the Justice Department's role in the controversy over the EPA documents. During this investigation, appellee Olson testified before a House Subcommittee on March 10, 1983. Both before and after that testimony, the Department complied with several Committee requests to produce certain documents. Other documents were at first withheld, although these documents were eventually disclosed by the Department after the Committee learned of their existence. In 1985, the majority members of the Judiciary Committee published a lengthy report on the Committee's investigation.... [T]he report not only criticized various officials in the Department of Justice for their role in the EPA executive privilege dispute, but it also suggested that appellee Olson had given false and misleading testimony to the Subcommittee on March 10, 1983, and that appellees Schmults and Dinkins had wrongfully withheld certain documents from the Committee, thus obstructing the Committee's investigation. The Chairman of the Judiciary Committee forwarded a copy of the report to the Attorney General with a request, pursuant to 28 U.S.C. § 592(c), that he seek the appointment of an independent counsel to investigate the allegations against Olson, Schmults, and Dinkins.

The Attorney General directed the Public Integrity Section of the Criminal Division to conduct a preliminary investigation. The Section's report concluded that the appointment of an independent counsel was warranted to investigate the Committee's allegations with respect to all three appellees. After consulting with other Department officials, however, the Attorney General chose to apply to the Special Division for the appointment of an independent counsel solely with respect to appellee Olson. The Attorney General accordingly requested appointment of an independent counsel to investigate whether Olson's March 10, 1983, testimony

> regarding the completeness of [OLC's] response to the Judiciary Committee's request for OLC documents, and regarding his knowledge of EPA's willingness to turn over certain disputed documents to Congress, violated 18 U.S.C. § 1505, § 1001, or any other provision of federal criminal law....

• • •

...[I]n May and June, 1987, [Morrison] caused a grand jury to issue and serve subpoenas *ad testificandum* and *duces tecum* on appellees. All three appellees moved to quash the subpoenas, claiming, among other things, that the independent counsel provisions of the Act were unconstitutional, and that appellant accordingly had no authority to proceed. On July 20, 1987, the District Court upheld the constitutionality of the Act and denied the motions to quash.…

A divided Court of Appeals reversed.…Appellant then sought review by this Court, and we noted probable jurisdiction.…We now reverse.

…We… turn to consider the merits of appellees' constitutional claims.

III

The Appointments Clause of Article II reads as follows:

> [The President] shall nominate, and by and with the Advice and Consent of the Senate, shall appoint Ambassadors, other public Ministers and Consuls, Judges of the supreme Court, and all other Officers of the United States, whose appointments are not herein otherwise provided for, and which shall be established by Law: but the Congress may by Law vest the Appointment of such inferior Officers, as they think proper, in the President alone, in the Courts of Law, or in the Heads of Departments.

U.S. Const., Art. II, § 2, cl. 2. The parties do not dispute that "[t]he Constitution for purposes of appointment…divides all its officers into two classes."… As we stated in *Buckley v. Valeo* [1976],

> Principal officers are selected by the President with the advice and consent of the Senate. Inferior officers Congress may allow to be appointed by the President alone, by the heads of departments, or by the Judiciary.

The initial question is, accordingly, whether appellant is an "inferior" or a "principal" officer. If she is the latter, as the Court of Appeals concluded, then the Act is in violation of the Appointments Clause.

The line between "inferior" and "principal" officers is one that is far from clear, and the Framers provided little guidance into where it should be drawn.… We need not attempt here to decide exactly where the line falls between the two types of officers, because, in our view, appellant clearly falls on the "inferior officer" side of that line.…

…[Her] grant of authority does not include any authority to formulate policy for the Government.…

Unlike other prosecutors, appellant has no ongoing responsibilities that extend beyond the accomplishment of the mission that she was ap-

pointed for and authorized by the Special Division to undertake. In our view, these factors…are sufficient to establish that appellant is an "inferior" officer in the constitutional sense.

• • •

This does not, however, end our inquiry under the Appointments Clause. Appellees argue that, even if appellant is an "inferior" officer, the Clause does not empower Congress to place the power to appoint such an officer outside the Executive Branch. They contend that the Clause does not contemplate congressional authorization of "interbranch appointments," in which an officer of one branch is appointed by officers of another branch. The relevant language of the Appointments Clause is worth repeating. It reads:

> …but the Congress may by Law vest the Appointment of such inferior Officers, as they think proper, in the President alone, in the courts of Law, or in the Heads of Departments.

On its face, the language of this "excepting clause" admits of no limitation on interbranch appointments. Indeed, the inclusion of "as they think proper" seems clearly to give Congress significant discretion to determine whether it is "proper" to vest the appointment of, for example, executive officials in the "courts of Law." We recognized as much in one of our few decisions in this area, *Ex parte Siebold* [1879],… where we stated:

• • •

> But as the Constitution stands, the selection of the appointing power, as between the functionaries named, is a matter resting in the discretion of Congress. And, looking at the subject in a practical light, it is perhaps better that it should rest there than that the country should be harassed by the endless controversies to which a more specific direction on this subject might have given rise.

• • •

IV

Appellees next contend that the powers vested in the Special Division by the Act conflict with Article III of the Constitution. We have long recognized that by the express provision of Article III, the judicial power of the United States

is limited to "Cases" and "Controversies."...
The purpose of this limitation is to help ensure
the independence of the Judicial Branch and
to prevent the judiciary from encroaching into
areas reserved for the other branches....

...In our view, Congress' power under the
Clause to vest the "Appointment" of inferior
officers in the courts may, in certain circumstances, allow Congress to give the courts some
discretion in defining the nature and scope of
the appointed official's authority. Particularly
when, as here, Congress creates a temporary
"office" the nature and duties of which will by
necessity vary with the factual circumstances
giving rise to the need for an appointment in
the first place, it may vest the power to define
the scope of the office in the court as an incident to the appointment of the officer pursuant
to the Appointments Clause. This said, we do
not think that Congress may give the Division
unlimited discretion to determine the independent counsel's jurisdiction. In order for the
Division's definition of the counsel's jurisdiction to be truly "incidental" to its power to appoint, the jurisdiction that the court decides
upon must be demonstrably related to the factual circumstances that gave rise to the Attorney
General's investigation and request for the appointment of the independent counsel in the
particular case.

The Act also vests in the Special Division
various powers and duties in relation to the independent counsel that, because they do not
involve appointing the counsel or defining his
or her jurisdiction, cannot be said to derive
from the Division's Appointments Clause authority....

...[W]e do not think that Article III absolutely prevents Congress from vesting these
other miscellaneous powers in the Special Division pursuant to the Act....

• • •

V

A

...[T]he analysis contained in our removal cases
is designed not to define rigid categories of
those officials who may or may not be removed
at will by the President, but to ensure that Congress does not interfere with the President's exercise of the "executive power" and his

constitutionally appointed duty to "take care
that the laws be faithfully executed" under Article II....

• • •

Nor do we think that the "good cause" removal
provision at issue here impermissibly burdens
the President's power to control or supervise
the independent counsel, as an executive official, in the execution of his or her duties under
the Act. This is not a case in which the power
to remove an executive official has been completely stripped from the President, thus providing no means for the President to ensure the
"faithful execution" of laws. Rather, because
the independent counsel may be terminated for
"good cause," the Executive, through the Attorney General, retains ample authority to assure that the counsel is competently performing
his or her statutory responsibilities....

B

The final question to be addressed is whether
the Act, taken as a whole, violates the principle
of separation of powers by unduly interfering
with the role of the Executive Branch. Time
and again we have reaffirmed the importance in
our constitutional scheme of the separation of
governmental powers into the three coordinate
branches....[T]he system of separated powers
and checks and balances established in the Constitution was regarded by the Framers as "a self-
executing safeguard against the encroachment
or aggrandizement of one branch at the expense of the other."

...We have not hesitated to invalidate provisions of law which violate this principle....On the other hand, we have never held
that the Constitution requires that the three
Branches of Government "operate with absolute independence."...

We observe first that this case does not involve an attempt by Congress to increase its
own powers at the expense of the Executive
Branch.... Indeed, with the exception of the
power of impeachment—which applies to all
officers of the United States—Congress retained for itself no powers of control or supervision over an independent counsel. The Act
does empower certain Members of Congress
to request the Attorney General to apply for
the appointment of an independent counsel,

but the Attorney General has no duty to comply with the request, although he must respond within a certain time limit....Other than that, Congress' role under the Act is limited to receiving reports or other information and oversight of the independent counsel's activities,...functions that we have recognized generally as being incidental to the legislative function of Congress....

Similarly, we do not think that the Act works any judicial usurpation of properly executive functions.... The Act does give a federal court the power to review the Attorney General's decision to remove an independent counsel, but in our view this is a function that is well within the traditional power of the judiciary.

Finally, we do not think that the Act "impermissibly undermine[s]" the powers of the Executive Branch,...or

disrupts the proper balance between the coordinate branches [by] prevent[ing] the Executive Branch from accomplishing its constitutionally assigned functions....

The Act...gives the Executive a degree of control over the power to initiate an investigation by the independent counsel. In addition, the jurisdiction of the independent counsel is defined with reference to the facts submitted by the Attorney General, and once a counsel is appointed, the Act requires that the counsel abide by Justice Department policy unless it is not "possible" to do so. Notwithstanding the fact that the counsel is to some degree "independent" and free from Executive supervision to a greater extent than other federal prosecutors, in our view, these features of the Act give the Executive Branch sufficient control over the independent counsel to ensure that the President is able to perform his constitutionally assigned duties.

Discussion Questions

1. On one level, *Morrison* deals only with the appointment and dismissal of independent counsels. What are the broader implications of the Court's decision for control and direction of federal administration?

2. In dissent, Justice Scalia argued that "[t]here are now no lines" to prevent Congress from restricting the president's authority to dismiss appointees in the executive branch. In the majority's opinion, what type of restrictions on the president's removal powers would be unconstitutional? Do you agree with Scalia that "it is now open season upon the President's removal power for all executive officers"?

3. The law under which Kenneth Starr was appointed independent counsel during the Clinton administration was similar to the one reviewed here. In hindsight, do you agree with the majority that, despite their independence, independent counsels do not have the capacity to "impede the President's ability to perform his constitutional duty"? Why or why not?

Case 1.3
Caught Between the Separation of Powers

LOCAL 2677, THE AMERICAN FEDERATION OF GOVERNMENT
EMPLOYEES v. PHILLIPS
United States District Court, District of Columbia
April 11, 1973
358 F. Supp. 60

Opinion

WILLIAM B. JONES, District Judge. These three consolidated actions have been brought to declare unlawful and enjoin what the plaintiffs alleged to be the unlawful dismantlement of the Office of Economic Opportunity (OEO) by the defendant, Howard J. Phillips, Acting Director of OEO. The plaintiffs in Local 2677, American Federation of Government Employees, et al. v. Phillips, Civil Action No. 371-73 (hereinafter *Local 2677*), by an amended complaint, are the labor organization-bargaining agent for the Washington, D.C. headquarters employees of OEO, and two individual OEO headquarters employees. Suit is brought on behalf of all OEO employees throughout the country who have been or are about to be adversely affected by the alleged unlawful acts of the defendant.

• • •

On January 29, 1973, President Nixon submitted his 1974 Budget Message to Congress. That budget message set forth the administration's plan to transfer responsibility for certain OEO functions to other agencies. The message specifically notes that

> No funds are requested for … [OEO] for 1974. Effective July 1, 1973, new funding for … [CAAs]★ will be at the discretion of local communities….With Community Action concepts now incorporated into ongoing programs and local agencies [if the budget proposals are approved], the continued existence of OEO as a separate Federal agency is no longer necessary….

On January 29, 1973, the defendant issued a memorandum to all OEO regional offices…regarding the "termination of section 221 [CAA] funding." That memorandum, at page two, fur-

ther noted that the cessation of funding would rescind individual designations as CAAs. OEO Instruction 6730-3, issued March 15, 1973, at page two, repeats the same instruction of the defendant that CAA funding will cease and further warns that use of funds by a CAA for any purpose except phasing out its activity or the failure of a CAA to submit an "acceptable" phase-out plan 120 days prior to the termination of section 221 funding will result in summary suspension of OEO funds. The same Instruction 6730-3 sets out 21 pages of guidelines for CAAs to follow in shutting down their section 221 operations, with various deadlines to be met throughout that process.

Thus, …all program evaluations and processing of CAA applications for purposes other than phasing out CAA activities have stopped. CAAs have been instructed to stop purchasing or repairing essential equipment. The day-to-day business operations of CAAs have been hindered if not halted by the unwillingness of third parties to deal with CAAs because of the announcement by the defendant of the termination of funding. The orderly continuation of CAA functions … has been halted or severely disrupted by the requirements imposed by OEO regarding termination. Finally, CAA employees are leaving their jobs in anticipation of the cessation of funding in compliance with OEO directives.

• • •

The defendant contends that because the budget message of the President, as the latest assessment of national needs and priorities, requests no funds for OEO to operate after June 30, 1973, the fiscally responsible course for the defendant to undertake is to phase out the CAA program that will be out of existence on

---

★Community Action Agencies.

July 1, 1973. In support of this theory, the defendant cites the general proposition of the law with which the plaintiffs are in total agreement—that the defendant cannot be forced to spend any funds which have not yet been appropriated. The defendant, however, goes on to argue that once the President has submitted his budget to the Congress, a program administrator must look to that message. If no funds are proposed for his agency, it is his duty to terminate that agency's functions to effect the least "waste" of funds. Because the Court can find no support for this position in the budget act, the OEO act, the history of OEO appropriations, or the Constitution itself, the Court finds for the plaintiffs on this count.

• • •

...Assuming, as the defendant argues, that a fiscally responsible administrator must terminate programs under his supervision in the absence, as here, of either an appropriation or a budget request for funds, any program from OEO to agricultural crop subsidies could be terminated by the Executive by not requesting any funds in the budget to continue its operation. That construction would in effect give the President a veto power through the use of his budget message, a veto power not granted him by Article I, section 7, of the Constitution.

• • •

In effect the defendant argues that by use of the budget message the Executive can force the Congress to legislate to keep an authorized program from terminating. The defendant contends further that he can use the funds appropriated by Congress to run section 221 programs to terminate them and force the Congress to act before the time that it has set for itself (June 30, 1973) to act on appropriating the funds as allowed by the authorization. Thus the Executive would effectively legislate the termination of section 221 programs before Congress has declared that they shall end. Article I, section 1, of the Constitution vests "[a]ll legislative powers" in the Congress. No budget message of the President can alter that power and force the Congress to act to preserve legislative programs from extinction prior to the time Congress has declared that they shall terminate, either by its action or inaction.

• • •

An authorization does not necessarily mean that a program will continue. Congress, of course, may itself decide to terminate a program before its authorization has expired, either indirectly by failing to supply funds through a continuing resolution or appropriation, or by explicitly forbidding the future use of funds for the programs....But Congress has not chosen either of these courses, although it may in the future. Until that time, historical precedent, logic, and the text of the Constitution itself obligate the defendant to continue to operate the section 221 programs as was intended by the Congress, and not terminate them.

• • •

In the present case, the Congress has not directed that funds be granted to any particular CAA. The OEO Director has been granted discretion in the disbursing of funds so as to effectuate the goals of the program....But discretion in the implementation of a program is not the freedom to ignore the standards for its implementation....An administrator's responsibilities to carry out the Congressional objectives of a program does not give him the power to discontinue that program, especially in the face of a Congressional mandate that it shall go on.

• • •

Congress has told the Director of OEO through its authorization that it intends that section 221 programs continue. Until Congress changes that command, the defendant is bound to honor it.

Counsel for the defendant urged at oral argument that unless the defendant ignored that Congressional command and terminated section 221 programs, financial chaos would result on July 1, 1973, if the Congress failed to include OEO in a continuing resolution or pass an appropriation bill. This Court will not presume that Congress will act in such an irresponsible manner, any more than it assumes that the defendant is acting in bad faith in his assertion of the duty to terminate section 221 funding. But Congress has shown how the problem posed by counsel for the defendant would be solved in its past action terminating funding for the SST program....Funds were appropriated "[f]or expenses, not otherwise provided for, necessary for the termination of development of the civil supersonic aircraft and to refund the contractors' cost shares, $97,300,000, to remain available until expended."... Thus when Congress orders that a program go forth and later changes its mind, it is for the Congress in the responsible exercise of its legislative power to make provisions for termination. Until those provisions are made, the function of the Executive is to administer the program in accord with the legislated purposes.

Discussion Questions

1. The defendant, Phillips, appears to have been caught dead-center between the separation of powers. Should he have kept spending funds in routine fashion, including for equipment repairs and new projects, even though there was a substantial possibility that the OEO's Community Action Programs would come to a screeching halt at the end of the fiscal year? If you were in Phillips's position, what might you have done? Would Phillips have been more successful simply to use his discretion to deny additional expenditures on a case-by-case basis as opposed to issuing his across-the-board directives for dismantling the CAA's? If so, does such "fudging" raise additional constitutional issues? Ethical issues?

2. The Court's opinion certainly bespeaks of a great deal of congressional direction of executive branch agencies. Does it suggest that in constitutional theory, Congress has the bulk of authority over administration? Consider all of Congress's powers over executive branch agencies.

3. How can the separation of legislative and executive powers over public administration be coordinated? For instance, can political parties be useful in this context? Can the heads of bureaus in the federal bureaucracy develop political relationships with the members of congressional subcommittees, interest groups, and with presidential appointees in the Executive Office of the President and others that could facilitate coordination? What might such relationships look like?

Case 1.4
Interpreting the Commerce Clause

UNITED STATES v. LOPEZ
Argued November 8, 1994
Decided April 26, 1995
514 US 549

CHIEF JUSTICE REHNQUIST delivered the opinion of the Court.

In the Gun-Free School Zones Act of 1990, Congress made it a federal offense "for any individual knowingly to possess a firearm at a place that the individual knows, or has reasonable cause to believe, is a school zone."... The Act neither regulates a commercial activity nor contains a requirement that the possession be connected in any way to interstate commerce. We hold that the Act exceeds the authority of Congress "[t]o regulate Commerce...among the several States...." U.S. Const., Art. I, § 8, cl. 3.

On March 10, 1992, respondent, who was then a 12th-grade student, arrived at Edison High School in San Antonio, Texas, carrying a concealed .38 caliber handgun and five bullets. Acting upon an anonymous tip, school authorities confronted respondent, who admitted that he was carrying the weapon. He was arrested and charged under Texas law with firearm possession on school premises.... The next day, the state charges were dismissed after federal agents charged respondent by complaint with violating the Gun-Free School Zones Act of 1990. 18 U.S.C. § 922(q)(1)(A) (1988 ed., Supp.V).

A federal grand jury indicted respondent on one count of knowing possession of a firearm at a school zone, in violation of § 922(q). Respondent moved to dismiss his federal indictment on the ground that § 922(q) "is unconstitutional as it is beyond the power of Congress to legislate control over our public schools." The District Court denied the motion, concluding that § 922(q)

> is a constitutional exercise of Congress' well-defined power to regulate activities in and affecting commerce, and the "business" of elementary, middle and high schools...affects interstate commerce.

...Respondent waived his right to a jury trial. The District Court conducted a bench trial, found him guilty..., and sentenced him to six months' imprisonment and two years' supervised release.

On appeal, respondent challenged his conviction based on his claim that § 922(q) exceeded Congress' power to legislate under the Commerce Clause. The Court of Appeals for the Fifth Circuit agreed, and reversed respondent's conviction. It held that, in light of what it characterized as insufficient congressional findings and legislative history, "section 922(q), in the full reach of its terms, is invalid as beyond the power of Congress under the Commerce Clause." 2 F.3d 1342, 1367–1368 (1993). Because of the importance of the issue, we granted certiorari...and we now affirm.

We start with first principles. The Constitution creates a Federal Government of enumerated powers. *See* U.S. Const., Art. I, § 8. As James Madison wrote,

> [t]he powers delegated by the proposed Constitution to the federal government are few and defined. Those which are to remain in the State governments are numerous and indefinite.

The Federalist No. 45, pp. 292–293 (C. Rossiter ed. 1961). This constitutionally mandated division of authority "was adopted by the Framers to ensure protection of our fundamental liberties."...

> Just as the separation and independence of the coordinate branches of the Federal Government serves to prevent the accumulation of excessive power in any one branch, a healthy balance of power between the States and the Federal Government will reduce the risk of tyranny and abuse from either front....

The Constitution delegates to Congress the power "[t]o regulate Commerce with foreign Nations, and among the several States, and with the Indian Tribes." U.S. Const., Art. I, § 8, cl. 3. The Court, through Chief Justice Marshall, first defined the nature of Congress' commerce power in *Gibbons v. Ogden*...(1824):

> Commerce, undoubtedly, is traffic, but it is something more: it is intercourse. It describes the commercial intercourse between nations, and parts of nations, in all its branches, and is regulated by prescribing rules for carrying on that intercourse.

The commerce power

> is the power to regulate; that is, to prescribe the rule by which commerce is to be governed. This power, like all others vested in Congress, is complete in itself, may be exercised to its utmost extent, and acknowledges no limitations, other than are prescribed in the constitution....

The *Gibbons* Court, however, acknowledged that limitations on the commerce power are inherent in the very language of the Commere Clause.

> It is not intended to say that these words comprehend that commerce, which is completely internal, which is carried on between man and man in a State, or between different parts of the same State, and which does not extend to or affect other States. Such a power would be inconvenient, and is certainly unnecessary.
>
> Comprehensive as the word "among" is, it may very properly be restricted to that commerce which concerns more States than one.... The enumeration presupposes something not enumerated; and that something, if we regard the language or the subject of the sentence, must be the exclusively internal commerce of a State....

For nearly a century thereafter, the Court's Commerce Clause decisions dealt but rarely with the extent of Congress' power, and almost entirely with the Commerce Clause as a limit on state legislation that discriminated against interstate commerce....

In 1887, Congress enacted the Interstate Commerce Act...and in 1890, Congress enacted the Sherman Antitrust Act.... These laws ushered in a new era of federal regulation under the commerce power. When cases involving these laws first reached this Court, we imported from our negative Commerce Clause cases the approach that Congress could not regulate activities such as "production," "manufacturing," and "mining."...Simultaneously, however, the Court held that, where the interstate and intrastate aspects of commerce were so mingled together that full regulation of interstate commerce required incidental regulation of intrastate commerce, the Commerce Clause authorized such regulation....

In *A.L.A. Schechter Poultry Corp. v. United States*... (1935), the Court struck down regulations that fixed the hours and wages of individuals employed by an intrastate business because the activity being regulated related to interstate commerce only indirectly. In doing so, the Court characterized the distinction between direct and indirect effects of intrastate transactions upon interstate commerce as "a fundamental one, essential to the maintenance of our constitutional system."...Activities that affected interstate commerce directly were within Congress' power; activities that affected interstate commerce indirectly were beyond Congress' reach....The justification for this formal distinction was rooted in the fear that otherwise "there would be virtually no limit to the federal power and for all practical purposes we should have a completely centralized government."...

Two years later, in the watershed case of *NLRB v. Jones & Laughlin Steel Corp.*...(1937), the Court upheld the National Labor Relations Act against a Commerce Clause challenge, and in the process, departed from the distinction between "direct" and "indirect" effects on interstate commerce....The Court held that intrastate activities that

> have such a close and substantial relation to interstate commerce that their control is essential or appropriate to protect that commerce from burdens and obstructions

are within Congress' power to regulate....

In *United States v. Darby*... (1941), the Court upheld the Fair Labor Standards Act, stating:

> The power of Congress over interstate commerce is not confined to the regulation of commerce among the states. It extends to those activities intrastate which so affect interstate commerce or the exercise of the power of Congress over it as to make regulation of them appropriate means to the attainment of a legitimate end, the exercise of the granted power of Congress to regulate interstate commerce....

In *Wickard v. Filburn* [1942], the Court upheld the application of amendments to the Agricultural Adjustment Act of 1938 to the production and consumption of home-grown wheat....The *Wickard* Court explicitly rejected earlier distinctions between direct and indirect effects on interstate commerce, stating:

> [E]ven if appellee's activity be local and though it may not be regarded as commerce, it may still, whatever its nature, be reached by Congress if it exerts a substantial economic effect on interstate commerce, and this irrespective of whether such effect is what might at some earlier time have been defined as "direct" or "indirect."...

The *Wickard* Court emphasized that although Filburn's own contribution to the demand for wheat may have been trivial by itself, that was not

> enough to remove him from the scope of federal regulation where, as here, his contribution, taken together with that of many others similarly situated, is far from trivial....

Jones & Laughlin Steel, Darby, and *Wickard* ushered in an era of Commerce Clause jurisprudence that greatly expanded the previously defined authority of Congress under that Clause. In part, this was a recognition of the great changes that had occurred in the way business was carried on in this country. Enterprises that had once been local or at most regional in nature had become national in scope. But the doctrinal change also reflected a view that earlier Commerce Clause cases artificially had constrained the authority of Congress to regulate interstate commerce.

But even these modern-era precedents which have expanded congressional power under the Commerce Clause confirm that this power is subject to outer limits....Since [these precedents] the Court has...undertaken to decide whether a rational basis existed for concluding that a regulated activity sufficiently affected interstate commerce....

• • •

Consistent with this structure, we have identified three broad categories of activity that Congress may regulate under its commerce power....First, Congress may regulate the use of the channels of interstate commerce.... ("'[T]he authority of Congress to keep the channels of interstate commerce free from immoral and injurious uses has been frequently sustained, and is no longer open to question.'"...). Second, Congress is empowered to regulate and protect the instrumentalities of interstate commerce, or persons or things in interstate commerce, even though the threat may come only from intrastate activities....Finally, Congress' commerce authority includes the power to regulate those activities having a substantial relation to interstate commerce..., *i.e.,* those activities that substantially affect interstate commerce....

We now turn to consider the power of Congress, in the light of this framework, to enact § 922(q). The first two categories of authority may be quickly disposed of: § 922(q) is not a regulation of the use of the channels of interstate commerce, nor is it an attempt to prohibit the interstate transportation of a commodity through the channels of commerce; nor can 922(q) be justified as a regulation by which Congress has sought to protect an instrumentality of interstate commerce or a thing in interstate commerce. Thus, if § 922(q) is to be sustained, it must be under the third category as a regulation of an activity that substantially affects interstate commerce.

. . .

Section 922(q) is a criminal statute that, by its terms, has nothing to do with "commerce" or any sort of economic enterprise, however broadly one might define those terms. Section 922(q) is not an essential part of a larger regulation of economic activity, in which the regulatory scheme could be undercut unless the intrastate activity were regulated. It cannot, therefore, be sustained under our cases upholding regulations of activities that arise out of or are connected with a commercial transaction, which viewed in the aggregate, substantially affects interstate commerce.

. . .

Although as part of our independent evaluation of constitutionality under the Commerce Clause we of course consider legislative findings, and indeed even congressional committee findings, regarding effect on interstate commerce..., the Government concedes that

[n]either the statute nor its legislative history contain[s] express congressional findings regarding the effects upon interstate commerce of gun possession in a school zone....

. . .

The Government's essential contention, *in fine,* is that we may determine here that § 922(q) is valid because possession of a firearm in a local school zone does indeed substantially affect interstate commerce....The Government argues that possession of a firearm in a school zone may result in violent crime and that violent crime can be expected to affect the functioning of the national economy in two ways. First, the costs of violent crime are substantial, and, through the mechanism of insurance, those costs are spread throughout the population....Second, violent crime reduces the willingness of individuals to travel to areas within the country that are perceived to be unsafe....The Government also argues that the presence of guns in schools poses a substantial threat to the educational process by threatening the learning environment. A handicapped educational process, in turn, will result in a less productive citizenry. That, in turn, would have an adverse effect on the Nation's economic well-being. As a result, the Government argues that Congress could rationally have concluded that § 922(q) substantially affects interstate commerce.

We pause to consider the implications of the Government's arguments. The Government admits, under its "costs of crime" reasoning, that Congress could regulate not only all violent crime, but all activities that might lead to violent crime, regardless of how tenuously they relate to interstate commerce.... Similarly, under the Government's "national productivity" reasoning, Congress could regulate any activity that it found was related to the economic productivity of individual citizens: family law (including marriage, divorce, and child custody), for example. Under the theories that the Government presents in support of § 922(q), it is difficult to perceive any limitation on federal power, even in areas such as criminal law enforcement or education where States historically have been sovereign. Thus, if we were to accept the Government's arguments, we are hard-pressed to posit any activity by an individual that Congress is without power to regulate.

• • •

Admittedly, a determination whether an intrastate activity is commercial or noncommercial may in some cases result in legal uncertainty. But, so long as Congress' authority is limited to those powers enumerated in the Constitution, and so long as those enumerated powers are interpreted as having judicially enforceable outer limits, congressional legislation

under the Commerce Clause always will engender "legal uncertainty."…

• • •

These are not precise formulations, and in the nature of things they cannot be. But we think they point the way to a correct decision of this case. The possession of a gun in a local school zone is in no sense an economic activity that might, through repetition elsewhere, substantially affect any sort of interstate commerce.…

Discussion Questions

1. According to the majority, what categories of activity may Congress regulate under the Commerce Clause? Give an example of each. Why doesn't the Gun-Free School Zones Act fit into one or more of these categories?

2. The majority suggests that if Congress could regulate guns in school zones it might be able to regulate any activity by an individual. Can you think of an activity, other than one protected by a clear constitutional right (such as free speech), that Congress would not be able to regulate?

3. Congress represents the people, but it sits in Washington, D.C., where guns in school zones may be a problem. Are they a problem where you are now? Where you grew up? As a matter of public policy, is it desirable to have a national standard prohibiting guns in school zones? Why or why not?

Case 1.5
The Tenth Amendment

PRINTZ v. UNITED STATES
Argued December 3, 1996
Decided June 27, 1997
117 S. Ct. 2365

JUSTICE SCALIA delivered the opinion of the Court.

The question presented in these cases is whether certain interim provisions of the Brady Handgun Violence Prevention Act, Pub.L. 103-159, 107 Stat. 1536, commanding state and local law enforcement officers to conduct background checks on prospective handgun purchasers and to perform certain related tasks, violate the Constitution.

I

The Gun Control Act of 1968 (GCA), 18 U.S.C. § 921 *et seq.,* establishes a detailed federal scheme governing the distribution of firearms. It prohibits firearms dealers from transferring handguns to any person under 21, not resident in the dealer's State, or prohibited by state or local law from purchasing or possessing firearms…It also forbids possession of a firearm by, and transfer of a firearm to, convicted felons, fugitives from justice, unlawful users of controlled substances, persons adjudicated as mentally defective or committed to mental institutions, aliens unlawfully present in the United States, persons dishonorably discharged from the Armed Forces, persons who have renounced their citizenship, and persons who have been subjected to certain restraining orders or been convicted of a misdemeanor offense involving domestic violence....

In 1993, Congress amended the GCA by enacting the Brady Act. The Act requires the Attorney General to establish a national instant background check system by November 30, 1998...and immediately puts in place certain interim provisions until that system becomes operative. Under the interim provisions, a firearms dealer who proposes to transfer a handgun must first: (1) receive from the transferee a statement (the Brady Form)... containing the name, address and date of birth of the proposed transferee along with a sworn statement that the transferee is not among any of the classes of prohibited purchasers...; (2) verify the identity of the transferee by examining an identification document...; and (3) provide the "chief law enforcement officer" (CLEO) of the transferee's residence with notice of the contents (and a copy) of the Brady Form.... With some exceptions, the dealer must then wait five business days before consummating the sale, unless the CLEO earlier notifies the dealer that he has no reason to believe the transfer would be illegal....

The Brady Act creates two significant alternatives to the foregoing scheme. A dealer may sell a handgun immediately if the purchaser possesses a state handgun permit issued after a background check..., or if state law provides for an instant background check....In States that have not rendered one of these alternatives applicable to all gun purchasers, CLEOs are required to perform certain duties. When a CLEO receives the required notice of a proposed transfer from the firearms dealer, the CLEO must

> make a reasonable effort to ascertain within 5 business days whether receipt or possession would be in violation of the law, including research in whatever State and local recordkeeping systems are available and in a national system designated by the Attorney General....

The Act does not require the CLEO to take any particular action if he determines that a pending transaction would be unlawful; he may notify the firearms dealer to that effect, but is not required to do so. If, however, the CLEO notifies a gun dealer that a prospective purchaser is ineligible to receive a handgun, he must, upon request, provide the would-be purchaser with a written statement of the reasons for that determination....Moreover, if the CLEO does not discover any basis for objecting to the sale, he must destroy any records in his possession relating to the transfer, including his copy of the Brady Form....Under a separate provision of the GCA, any person who

> knowingly violates [the section of the GCA amended by the Brady Act] shall be fined under this title, imprisoned for no more than 1 year, or both....

Petitioners Jay Printz and Richard Mack, the CLEOs for Ravalli County, Montana, and Graham County, Arizona, respectively, filed separate actions challenging the constitutionality of the Brady Act's interim provisions. In each case, the District Court held that the provision requiring CLEOs to perform background checks was unconstitutional, but concluded that that provision was severable from the remainder of the Act, effectively leaving a voluntary background check system in place....A divided panel of the Court of Appeals for the Ninth Circuit reversed, finding none of the Brady Act's interim provisions to be unconstitutional....We granted certiorari....

II

From the description set forth above, it is apparent that the Brady Act purports to direct state law enforcement officers to participate, albeit only temporarily, in the administration of a federally enacted regulatory scheme. Regulated firearms dealers are required to forward Brady Forms not to a federal officer or employee, but to the CLEOs, whose obligation to accept those forms is implicit in the duty imposed upon them to make "reasonable efforts" within five days to determine whether the sales reflected in the forms are lawful. While the CLEOs are subjected to no federal requirement that they prevent the sales determined to be unlawful (it is perhaps assumed that their state law duties will require prevention or apprehension), they are empowered to grant, in effect, waivers of the federally prescribed 5-day waiting period for handgun purchases by notifying the gun dealers that they have no reason to believe the transactions would be illegal.

The petitioners here object to being pressed into federal service, and contend that congressional action compelling state officers to execute federal laws is unconstitutional. Because there is no constitutional text speaking to this precise question, the answer to the CLEOs challenge must be sought in historical understanding and practice, in the structure of the Constitution, and in the jurisprudence of this Court. We treat those three sources, in that order, in this and the next two sections of this opinion

• • •

...[E]arly laws establish at most, that the Constitution was originally understood to permit imposition of an obligation on state *judges* to enforce federal prescriptions, insofar as those prescriptions related to matters appropriate for the judicial power....

...[W]e do not think the early statutes imposing obligations on state courts imply a power of Congress to impress the state executive into its service....

• • •

In addition to early legislation, the Government also appeals to other sources we have usually regarded as indicative of the original understanding of the Constitution. It points to portions of The Federalist which reply to criticisms that Congress's power to tax will produce two sets of revenue officers....

• • •

III

A

It is incontestible that the Constitution established a system of "dual sovereignty."...Although the States surrendered many of their powers to the new Federal Government, they retained a "residuary and inviolable sovereignty," The Federalist No. 39....Residual state sovereignty was also implicit, of course, in the Constitution's conferral upon Congress of not all

governmental powers, but only discrete, enumerated ones....

The Framers' experience under the Articles of Confederation had persuaded them that using the States as the instruments of federal governance was both ineffectual and provocative of federal-state conflict. *See* The Federalist No. 15. Preservation of the States as independent political entities being the price of union, and "[t]he practicality of making laws, with coercive sanctions, for the States as political bodies" having been, in Madison's words, "exploded on all hands"..., the Framers rejected the concept of a central government that would act upon and through the States, and instead designed a system in which the state and federal governments would exercise concurrent authority over the people—who were, in Hamilton's words, "the only proper objects of government".... "The Framers explicitly chose a Constitution that confers upon Congress the power to regulate individuals, not States."...The great innovation of this design was that "our citizens would have two political capacities, one state and one federal, each protected from incursion by the other" —

> a legal system unprecedented in form and design, establishing two orders of government, each with its own direct relationship, its own privity, its own set of mutual rights and obligations to the people who sustain it and are governed by it....

The Constitution thus contemplates that a State's government will represent and remain accountable to its own citizens....

• • •

IV

When we were at last confronted squarely with a federal statute that unambiguously required the States to enact or administer a federal regulatory program, our decision should have come as no surprise. At issue in *New York v. United States* (1992), were the so-called "take title" provisions of the Low-Level Radioactive Waste Policy Amendments Act of 1985, which required States either to enact legislation providing for the disposal of radioactive waste generated within their borders, or to take title to, and possession of the waste—effectively requiring the States either to legislate pursuant to Congress's directions or to implement an administrative solution.…We concluded that Congress could constitutionally require the States to do neither.… "The Federal Government," we held, "may not compel the States to enact or administer a federal regulatory program."…

The Government contends that *New York* is distinguishable on the following ground: unlike the "take title" provisions invalidated there, the background check provision of the Brady Act does not require state legislative or executive officials to make policy, but instead issues a final directive to state CLEOs.…

The Government's distinction between "making" law and merely "enforcing" it, between "policymaking" and mere "implementation," is an interesting one.…We are doubtful that the new line the Government proposes would be any more distinct. Executive action that has utterly no policymaking component is rare, particularly at an executive level as high as a jurisdiction's chief law enforcement officer. Is it really true that there is no policymaking involved in deciding, for example, what "reasonable efforts" shall be expended to conduct a background check?

• • •

The Government also maintains that requiring state officers to perform discrete, ministerial tasks specified by Congress does not violate the principle of *New York* because it does not diminish the accountability of state or federal officials. This argument fails even on its own terms. By forcing state governments to absorb the financial burden of implementing a federal regulatory program, Members of Congress can take credit for "solving" problems without having to ask their constituents to pay for the solutions with higher federal taxes. And even when the States are not forced to absorb the costs of implementing a federal program, they are still put in the position of taking the blame for its burdensomeness and for its defects.…Under the present law, for example, it will be the CLEO and not some federal official who stands between the gun purchaser and immediate possession of his gun. And it will likely be the CLEO, not some federal official, who will be blamed for any error (even one in the designated federal database) that causes a purchaser to be mistakenly rejected.

The dissent makes no attempt to defend the Government's basis for distinguishing *New York*, but instead advances what seems to us an even more implausible theory. The Brady Act, the dissent asserts, is different from the "take title" provisions invalidated in *New York* because the former is addressed to individuals—namely CLEOs—while the latter were directed to the State itself. That is certainly a difference, but it cannot be a constitutionally significant one. While the Brady Act is directed to "individuals," it is directed to them in their official capacities as state officers; it controls their actions, not as private citizens, but as the agents of the State.…

Finally, the Government puts forward a cluster of arguments that can be grouped under the heading:

> The Brady Act serves very important purposes, is most efficiently administered by CLEOs during the interim period, and places a minimal and only temporary burden upon state officers.

There is considerable disagreement over the extent of the burden, but we need not pause over that detail. Assuming *all* the mentioned factors were true, they might be relevant if we were evaluating whether the incidental application to the States of a federal law of general applicability excessively interfered with the functioning of state governments.…But where, as here, it is the whole *object* of the law to direct the functioning of the state executive, and hence to compromise the structural framework of dual sovereignty, such a "balancing" analysis is inappropriate.… We adhere to that principle [dual sovereignty] today, and conclude categorically, as we concluded categorically in *New York:* "The Federal Government may not compel the States to enact or administer a federal regulatory program."…The mandatory obligation imposed on CLEOs to perform background checks on prospective handgun purchasers plainly runs afoul of that rule.

• • •

V

We held in *New York* that Congress cannot compel the States to enact or enforce a federal regulatory program. Today we hold that Congress cannot circumvent that prohibition by conscripting the State's officers directly. The

Federal Government may neither issue directives requiring the States to address particular problems, nor command the States' officers, or those of their political subdivisions, to administer or enforce a federal regulatory program. It matters not whether policymaking is involved, and no case-by-case weighing of the burdens or benefits is necessary; such commands are fundamentally incompatible with our constitutional system of dual sovereignty....

• • •

Discussion Questions

1. Why does the majority think that a balancing of interests would be inappropriate?

2. In arguing the case, the government tried to draw a distinction between policymaking and implementing. Based on your knowledge of public administration, how useful or tenable is such a distinction?

3. *Printz* holds that Congress cannot "conscript" state and local administrators into the service of the federal government. What alternative means were available to Congress to achieve its purposes regarding the aspects of the Brady Act at issue in the case? How do these means compare with "conscription" in terms of cost-effectiveness?

Case 1.6
The "Dormant" Commerce Clause

C & A CARBONE, INC. v. TOWN OF CLARKSTOWN
Argued December 7, 1993
Decided May 16, 1994
511 US 383

JUSTICE KENNEDY delivered the opinion of the Court.

As solid waste output continues apace and landfill capacity becomes more costly and scarce, state and local governments are expending significant resources to develop trash control systems that are efficient, lawful, and protective of the environment. The difficulty of their task is evident from the number of recent cases that we have heard involving waste transfer and treatment....

We consider a so-called flow control ordinance, which requires all solid waste to be processed at a designated transfer station before leaving the municipality. The avowed purpose of the ordinance is to retain the processing fees charged at the transfer station to amortize the cost of the facility. Because it attains this goal by depriving competitors, including out-of-state firms, of access to a local market, we hold that the flow control ordinance violates the Commerce Clause.

The town of Clarkstown, New York, lies in the lower Hudson River valley, just upstream from the Tappan Zee Bridge and by highway minutes from New Jersey. Within the town limits are the village of Nyack and the hamlet of West Nyack. In August, 1989, Clarkstown entered into a consent decree with New York State Department of Environmental Conservation. The town agreed to close its landfill located on Route 303 in West Nyack and build a new solid waste transfer station on the same site. The station would receive bulk solid waste and separate recyclable from nonrecyclable items. Recyclable waste would be baled for shipment to a recycling facility; nonrecyclable waste, to a suitable landfill or incinerator.

The cost of building the transfer station was estimated at $1.4 million. A local private contractor agreed to construct the facility and operate it for five years, after which the town would buy it for one dollar. During those five years, the town guaranteed a minimum waste flow of 120,000 tons per year, for which the contractor could charge the hauler a so-called tipping fee of $81 per ton. If the station received less that 120,000 tons in a year, the town promised to make up the tipping fee deficit. The object of this arrangement was to amortize the cost of the transfer station: the town would finance its new facility with the income generated by the tipping fees.

• • •

At the outset, we confirm that the flow control ordinance does regulate interstate commerce, despite the town's position to the contrary. The town says that its ordinance reaches only waste within its jurisdiction, and is, in practical effect, a quarantine: it prevents garbage from entering the stream of interstate commerce until it is made safe. This reasoning is premised, however, on an outdated and mistaken concept of what constitutes interstate commerce.

While the immediate effect of the ordinance is to direct local transport of solid waste to a designated site within the local jurisdiction, its economic effects are interstate in reach. The Carbone facility in Clarkstown receives and processes waste from places other than Clarkstown, including from out of State. By requiring Carbone to send the nonrecyclable portion of this waste to the Route 303 transfer station at an additional cost, the flow control ordinance drives up the cost for out-of-state interests to dispose of their solid waste. Furthermore, even as to waste originant in Clarkstown, the ordinance prevents everyone except the favored local operator from performing the initial processing step. The ordinance thus deprives out-of-state businesses of access to a local market. These economic effects are more than enough to bring the Clarkstown ordinance within the purview of the Commerce Clause. It is well settled that actions are within the domain of the Commerce Clause if they burden interstate commerce or impede its free flow....

The real question is whether the flow control ordinance is valid despite its undoubted effect on interstate commerce. For this inquiry, our case law yields two lines of analysis: first, whether the ordinance discriminates against interstate commerce...and second, whether the ordinance imposes a burden on interstate commerce that is "clearly excessive in relation to the putative local benefits".... As we find that the ordinance discriminates against interstate commerce, we need not resort to the [other test].

The central rationale for the rule against discrimination is to prohibit state or municipal laws whose object is local economic protectionism, laws that would excite those jealousies and retaliatory measures the Constitution was designed to prevent....We have interpreted the Commerce Clause to invalidate local laws that impose commercial barriers or discriminate against an article of commerce by reason of its origin or destination out of state....

Clarkstown protests that its ordinance does not discriminate, because it does not differentiate solid waste on the basis of its geographic origin. All solid waste, regardless of origin, must be processed at the designated transfer station before it leaves the town.... [The town says] the ordinance erects no barrier to the import or export of any solid waste, but requires only that the waste be channeled through the designated facility.

Our initial discussion of the effects of the ordinance on interstate commerce goes far toward refuting the town's contention that there is no discrimination in its regulatory scheme. The town's own arguments go the rest of the way. As the town itself points out, what makes garbage a profitable business is not its own worth but the fact that its possessor must pay to get rid of it. In other words, the article of commerce is not so much the solid waste itself, but rather the service of processing and disposing of it.

With respect to this stream of commerce, the flow control ordinance discriminates, for it allows only the favored operator to process waste that is within the limits of the town. The ordinance is no less discriminatory because in-state or in-town processors are also covered by the prohibition....

• • •

Discrimination against interstate commerce in favor of local business or investment is *per se* invalid, save in a narrow class of cases in which the municipality can demonstrate, under rigorous scrutiny, that it has no other means to advance a legitimate local interest....

...The Commerce Clause presumes a national market free from local legislation that discriminates in favor of local interests. Here Clarkstown has any number of nondiscriminatory alternatives for addressing the health and environmental problems alleged to justify the ordinance in question. The most obvious would be uniform safety regulations enacted without the object to discriminate....

Nor may Clarkstown justify the flow control ordinance as a way to steer solid waste away from out-of-town disposal sites that it might deem harmful to the environment. To do so would extend the town's police power beyond its jurisdictional bounds. States and localities may not attach restrictions to exports or imports in order to control commerce in other states....

• • •

Clarkstown maintains that special financing is necessary to ensure the long-term survival of the designated facility. If so, the town may subsidize the facility through general taxes or municipal bonds.... But having elected to use the open market to earn revenues for its project, the town may not employ discriminatory regulation to give that project an advantage over rival businesses from out of state.

Though the Clarkstown ordinance may not in explicit terms seek to regulate interstate commerce, it does so nonetheless by its practical effect and design....

State and local governments may not use their regulatory power to favor local enterprise by prohibiting patronage of out-of-state competitors or their facilities....

Discussion Questions

1. What are the two tests used to assess alleged violations of the Dormant Commerce Clause? Give a few examples of what each would prohibit.

2. In the previous case, *Printz v. United States,* the Supreme Court emphasizes "dual sovereignty." What are the full implications of the Dormant Commerce Clause for a state's ability to regulate its natural resources for the benefit of its citizens? To adopt regulations intended to protect its citizens' way of life?

TWO

At Your Own Risk!
Public Administrators' Liability
for Violating Individuals'
Constitutional Rights

The previous chapter shows that constitutional law is of fundamental importance to American public administration. The separation of powers and federalism have powerful impacts on public administrative organization and practice at all levels of government. But the Constitution can be of much more immediate personal concern to public administrators as they go about their jobs on a day-to-day basis.

Public administrators must know how the Constitution constrains their own official activities. To be successful, they not only have to live within these constraints, but they must efficiently and effectively integrate them into the performance of their jobs. This is obviously true in terms of law enforcement, but today relationships with customers, contractors, and coworkers are also regulated by constitutional law.

The administrator who lacks constitutional competence—that is, adequate knowledge of what the Constitution requires of him or her—runs a real risk of violating an individual's constitutional rights and being sued personally in return. Such lawsuits for "constitutional torts" can even be brought against public administrators who unintentionally or unknowingly infringe upon someone's constitutional rights. Administrators who lose or settle suits of this kind may be held *personally* responsible for whatever sums of money are due to the injured individual. There may be better reasons for public administrators to gain constitutional competence, but perhaps none creates a greater incentive than trying to avoid being sued and paying damages.

This chapter explains how constitutional rights became central to public administrative practice, as well as the logic and scope of administrative liability for constitutional torts. The cases clearly set forth the contemporary legal standards that govern personal and municipal liability.

Making Constitutional Rights Relevant
to Administrative Practice

In the 1880s, Woodrow Wilson could write that public administration, "at most points stands apart even from the debatable ground of constitutional study."[1] In

1926, Leonard D. White, author of the first American textbook on public administration, could share the same general perspective: "the study of administration should start from the base of management rather than the foundation of law, and is therefore more absorbed in the affairs of the American Management Association than in the decisions of the courts."[2] No longer! Today, the practice of public administration is infused with constitutional constraints and values.

Since the 1950s, the federal judiciary, including the Supreme Court, has developed a vast array of constitutional rights and protections for individuals in their encounters with public administrators. The rationales, doctrinal shifts, and incremental growth of the case law varied widely, but the net result is that doing public administration without being aware of individuals' constitutional rights is now unthinkable.[3] The decisions of the courts matter a great deal to public managers and administrators who deal with clients, customers, coworkers, contractors, inmates in prisons, patients in public mental health facilities, and individuals involved in "street-level" law enforcement actions.

Much of the continuing expansion of individual constitutional rights in the context of public administration results from fundamental changes in three constitutional doctrines. First, in the famous case of *Brown v. Board of Education* (1954),[4] the Supreme Court held that the Equal Protection Clause of the Fourteenth Amendment prohibits governments from mandating or promoting racial segregation in public schools. A total demise of the older doctrine, which allowed "separate but equal" treatment based on race or ethnicity, soon followed. In truth, the emphasis had been on the "separate," not the "equal," and the older doctrine allowed rampant governmental discrimination against racial minorities.

By the 1970s, equal protection could also be effectively used to challenge discrimination based on gender. Public policies based on gender stereotypes were increasingly tested in the courts. For example, in *Craig v. Boren* (1976), Case 4.3, the Supreme Court held that Oklahoma's policy of permitting females, but not males, to buy "3.2% beer" at age 18 was unconstitutional. The relevance of contemporary equal protection doctrine to public administrative practice is illustrated by several of the cases in the following chapters. (See Case 4.4, *Hawkins v. Town of Shaw*, 1971; Case 5.3, *Adarand Constructors, Inc. v. Pena*, 1995; Case 7.3, *United States v. Virginia*, 1996; Case 7.4, *Zobel v. Williams*, 1982.)

A second fundamental change in constitutional doctrines concerned the legal status of government benefits such as contracts, public employment, licenses, public housing, and welfare payments. Historically, these had been defined as "privileges" to which individuals had no "right." Therefore, the government could award or withdraw them on its own terms and conditions. Beginning in the 1960s, these benefits were reconceptualized as a form of "new property."[5] As such, they enjoy constitutional protection because, under the Fifth and Fourteenth Amendments, governments are not permitted to deprive anyone of "life, liberty, or property without due process of law." The impact of this change has been very dramatic in public personnel management, where hearings and appeals from adverse actions are now common, and in social service administration[6] (e.g., see Case 6.1, *Cleveland Board of Education v. Loudermill*, 1985).

In a third fundamental shift during the same period, the federal judiciary dusted off its long-standing "unconstitutional conditions" doctrine and began applying it to mainstream public administrative operations.[7] Today, even though one may not have a legal entitlement to a benefit, the doctrine can prevent government from withholding it on a basis that impairs constitutionally protected rights. For example, a local government cannot terminate a contractor's commercial relationship with it solely in retaliation for his or her outspoken political opposition to its elected officials. (See Case 3.3, *Board of County Commissioners, Wabaunsee County v. Umbehr*, 1996.) In recent years, the doctrine has also been used to prevent governments from infringing on property rights by attaching unconstitutional conditions to building permits (Case 8.4, *Dolan v. City of Tigard*, 1994).

In addition to these far-reaching doctrinal changes, the constitutional rights of prisoners and individuals confined to public mental health facilities were greatly expanded.[8] In the 1970s, the Eighth Amendment's protection against cruel and unusual punishment was applied to conditions in prison, apparently for the first time, and the Fourteenth Amendment's Due Process Clause was interpreted to incorporate a right to treatment or habilitation for the publicly confined mentally ill and disabled (see Cases 3.4 and 8.1, *Richardson v. McKnight*, 1997 and *Wyatt v. Stickney*, 1971). Prisoners also have a constitutional right to adequate medical care, as well as some rights to free exercise of religion, to marry, and to due process in disciplinary matters.[9] Finally, the Fourth Amendment gained wide application to street-level encounters[10] (e.g., Case 4.1, *Delaware v. Prouse*, 1979).

If these doctrinal changes are abstract, it is in legal theory only. Their administrative consequences have been tangible in terms of operating procedures, staffing, budgets, and authority. No public personnel system has been unaffected. Corrections, public mental health, public education, public housing, street-level law enforcement, and several aspects of social services have been deeply affected. It is emblematic of the judicial impact on public administration that, in 1981, 48 percent of Boston's budgetary appropriations were "presided" over by state and federal judges seeking to protect individuals' constitutional rights against administrative encroachments.[11]

Recent Supreme Court cases continue the historical trend of placing constitutional constraints on public administration. In the 1990s, the Court complicated privatization by holding that, in some circumstances, contractors' First Amendment rights are very similar to those of public employees (e.g., see *Umbehr*). The Court also made it clear that governments cannot circumvent their constitutional obligations by structuring their agencies like private corporations, or as public–private hybrids (see Case 3.1, *Lebron v. National Railroad Passenger Corporation*, 1995). Private contractors engaged in public functions, such as incarceration, may be subject to the same constitutional constraints as government agencies. And, their employees may actually face greater liability than public employees for constitutional torts (see *Richardson*).

Enforcement: From Absolute to Qualified Immunity

It is axiomatic that constitutional rights must be enforceable. Otherwise they are hollow, and the Constitution loses some of its status as the supreme law of the land. By the mid-1970s, the federal courts had created two major enforcement mechanisms by which individuals could vindicate their constitutional rights vis-à-vis public administrators.

One was the judiciary's development of a new type of suit that makes it easier for the courts to impose thoroughgoing reforms on public administrative systems. Variously called "remedial law" or "public law litigation," such suits can involve entire administrative systems, including personnel, corrections, public mental health, and public education. Unlike conventional suits, they are not resolved by the immediate termination of a specific practice or a one-shot transfer of property or money. Nor are they "bipolar," involving a single plaintiff and defendant with fixed, diametrically opposed interests. Instead, they engulf broad areas of public policy and spending. The interests of the parties are less clear-cut and may even overlap. For instance, the superintendent of a prison and the prisoners may both want more funding from the state legislature. Nor does the court's involvement with the suit end with its decision. Rather, in order to vindicate the violated rights, the court may have to exercise ongoing supervision of institutional reforms for a decade or more (see *Wyatt* and Case 9.2, *Missouri v. Jenkins,* 1995).

Remedial lawsuits are powerful enforcement tools. They enable judges to supervise administrators and to regulate administration for the protection of individual rights. However, they are also cumbersome and expensive. Sometimes they have unintended detrimental consequences as well. For example, as judicial efforts to protect the constitutional rights of patients in public mental health facilities raised costs, deinstitutionalization and greater homelessness followed.[12] Moreover, even though they are part of the complex administrative operations that are attacked in remedial law suits, few, if any, public managers and employees can reasonably be held personally responsible for institutionalized violations of individual rights. It is not a prison guard's fault that a facility is unconstitutionally overcrowded or understaffed. Effective enforcement requires some complementary approach that gives public administrators a personal stake in protecting the constitutional rights of the people on whom they act in the course of their jobs.

The Supreme Court personalized administrator's responsibility for constitutional competence by revising the immunity doctrines that shield public employees and officials from civil law suits. Prior to the 1970s, the courts generally presumed that most public administrators had *absolute immunity* from being sued personally for compensatory or punitive damages for violating individuals' constitutional rights in the course of their official actions.[13] Absolute immunity is immunity from suit, not just from having to pay damages. It enables public employees and officials to exercise necessary discretion without fear of being sued personally, it guards against harassment by suits or threats of them, it protects government's ability to recruit talented individuals, and it reduces private parties' opportunity to disrupt program implementation by bringing lawsuits.

Absolute immunity still applies to federal, state, and local judges when they perform judicial functions, and to legislators at all levels when they are involved in legislative activities. By extension it also applies to public administrators who are engaged in some aspects of adjudication, such as prosecuting or serving as hearing examiners. Similarly, executive officials have absolute immunity when they undertake legislative functions, as in the case of a mayor working with a city council to form an annual operating budget.[14]

It is important to remember that absolute immunity goes by *function,* not position title. A judge or legislator does not have absolute immunity when hiring staff or performing some other executive function. To date, the sole exception is the

U.S. President, who has absolute immunity for his official actions as president, but not for personal acts taken prior to entering that office.[15]

For the most part, other public employees exercising discretionary functions have *qualified immunity*. As Case 2.1, *Harlow v. Fitzgerald* (1982), explains, this means they "generally are shielded from liability for civil damages insofar as their conduct does not violate clearly established statutory or constitutional rights of which a reasonable person would have known." Typically, qualified immunity enables public administrators to defend themselves by asserting that they could not reasonably have known that their official actions could constitute a violation of constitutional rights because the rights in question were (or are) not clearly established.

Public administrators can raise this defense in a federal court proceeding called a "summary judgment," which takes place before a judge (without a jury). The questions at this stage are purely legal. Were the constitutional rights at issue clearly established? Would a reasonable person have been aware of them? The district court judge's decision to grant or deny summary judgment can be appealed. However, only after a denial of summary judgment becomes final can the suit proceed to the more burdensome aspects of legal procedure: deposition, discovery, and trial.

From the public administrator's perspective the great virtue of qualified immunity is that it allows summary judgment, which is relatively efficient and inexpensive (at least in comparison to a jury trial). The major risk is that judges, who are specialists in law, will be more prone than administrators to believe that reasonable people would know that some constitutional rights are clearly established even when the case law is not highly developed. Consequently, as a general rule it may be best for "officials who may harbor doubts about the lawfulness of their intended actions to err on the side of protecting citizens' constitutional rights."[16]

Most state and local employees, as well as municipal governments, are sued for constitutional torts under provisions of the Civil Rights Act of 1871, which is now codified at 42 U.S. Code, Section 1983. The key provision reads:

> Every person who, under color of any statute, ordinance, regulation, custom, usage, of any State or Territory or the District of Columbia, subjects, or causes to be subjected, any citizen of the United States or any other person within the jurisdiction thereof to the deprivation of any rights, privileges, or immunities secured by the Constitution and laws, shall be liable to the party injured in an action at law, suit in equity, or other proper proceeding for redress. For the purposes of this section, any Act of Congress applicable exclusively to the District of Columbia shall be considered to be a statute of the District of Columbia.

The original purpose of the act was to enable former slaves to protect their rights in federal court against violations by the Ku Klux Klan, whose actions were apparently sanctioned by state law enforcement officials and judges. (For a time the act was known as the Ku Klux Klan Act.)

However, despite the act's comprehensive wording, it was pretty much a dead letter for almost a century. First, its application to "every person who" was limited by the widespread absolute immunity available to government employees and officials. The courts interpreted it to mean every person who acted under color of state law, and so forth *and* did not enjoy absolute immunity under common law doctrines. This turned out to be very few indeed. Second, the scope of the Fourteenth Amendment's proscription against state and local governmental deprivation of liberty without due process of law was very limited. The term "liberty" had not yet come to "incorporate" much of the Constitution's Bill of Rights. As a result, individuals could not use the act to assert many civil rights or liberties, such as free speech or free exercise of religion, against curtailment by state or local jurisdictions. Third, as noted earlier, people did not yet have significant equal protection or other federal constitutional rights in the context of administration.

By the time the current standard for qualified immunity was established in the *Harlow* case, the picture had completely changed. The general presumption under "Section 1983" was against absolute immunity, much of the Bill of Rights had been applied to the states through the Fourteenth Amendment, and individuals had a wide array of rights. In fact, as the Supreme Court explains in *Harlow*, the point of switching from absolute to qualified immunity was to protect those rights.

Following *Harlow*, public administrative liability for constitutional torts expanded in a variety of ways. Municipalities are considered persons within the scope of "every person who." As Case 2.2, *Pembaur v. Cincinnati* (1986), explains, they can only be held liable if their policies cause violations of constitutional rights. They are not "vicariously" responsible for the unauthorized or wayward acts of their employees. However, they can be held liable for unwritten policies and even one-time, on-the-spot decisions by administrators who have final authority for a policy area.

Case 2.3, *City of Canton v. Harris* (1989) holds that municipalities can also be held liable for failing to train their employees to protect individuals' constitutional rights. At least in policy and program areas where constitutional rights are of obvious importance, *Canton* virtually mandates constitutional competence for public managers at the local governmental level.

The selection of cases is rounded out by Case 2.4, *Harley v. Schuylkill County* (1979), which declares that public employees have a constitutional right to disobey unconstitutional orders, commands, or directives precisely because they potentially face personal liability for violating individuals' constitutional rights. Although *Harley* was decided by a federal district court, rather than the Supreme Court, it remains settled law. But the public administrator who would assert the right to disobey should be careful. Success requires that the administrator sincerely believe he or she is being asked to do something unconstitutional, and he or she must be correct that it is unconstitutional. One hardly expects such a right to be asserted frequently, but it does provide another illustration of why constitutional competence is so desirable.

Before presenting the cases, a few additional points should be made for clarity's sake. There are some technical differences in how state level and local level employees can be sued under Section 1983, though in practice both face identical personal liabilities.[17] However, the Eleventh Amendment prevents using the federal courts to bring constitutional tort actions seeking money damages against state governments or state agencies. If such suits are possible, it is only under state law, in state courts. Nevertheless states and their agencies can be sued under Section 1983 for other types of relief.

Section 1983 does not apply to federal employees. Their liability grows directly out of the Constitution—the First, Fourth, Fifth, and Eighth Amendments to be precise.[18] This is largely a distinction without a difference. Precedents involving federal and nonfederal public administrators are interchangeable. Both face compensatory and punitive damages. The latter may be assessed when the administrator is either callously indifferent to federally protected constitutional rights or violates them with a malicious motive or intent to injure.[19] Punitive damages can be established by a judge or jury not only to punish the offending administrator, but also to set an example that may deter others from treading on protected rights. Like state agencies, federal agencies cannot be sued for money damages for their constitutional torts.[20]

The cumulative number of constitutional tort suits against public employees at all levels of government since the 1970s is unknown. A reasonable estimate is that the federal district courts handle upwards of 425 constitutional tort claims against public employees and local governments per year.[21] The damages awarded in individual cases are often in the hundreds of thousands of dollars, and sometimes in the millions.[22] However, many cases are settled for less and never go to trial.[23]

Governments and agencies may reduce the risk public employees face by providing them with legal representation and indemnification. The U.S. Department of Justice will generally represent federal employees under two conditions: (1) it is in the interest of the government to do so, and (2) the employee acted within the scope of his or her duties.[24] Of the 7,000 federal employees who requested representation from 1993 to 1998, it was denied to only 150.[25] Indemnification is at the discretion of federal agencies. State and local policies vary. Private insurance is also available. Nevertheless, as a Department of Justice official notes, "The key piece of bad news about these lawsuits is, they're personal."[26] One way or another, the individual employee has to deal with them—and the anxiety, paperwork, and diversion of energy they produce. Better to gain constitutional competence and avoid them altogether!

Notes

1. Woodrow Wilson, "The Study of Administration," in Jay Shafritz and Albert Hyde, eds., *Classics of Public Administration*, 3rd ed. (Pacific Grove, CA: Brooks/Cole, 1992), p. 18. (Wilson's essay was written in 1887.)

2. Leonard D. White, "Introduction to the Study of Public Administration," in Shafritz and Hyde, *Classics of Public Administration*, p. 57. (White's book by the same title was originally published in 1926.)

3. For a comprehensive discussion see David H. Rosenbloom and Rosemary O'Leary, *Public Administration and Law*, 2nd ed. (New York: Marcel Dekker, 1997).

4. *Brown v. Board of Education*, 347 U.S. 483 (1954).

5. Charles Reich, "The New Property," *Yale Law Journal*, 73 (1964): 733; Rosenbloom and O'Leary, *Public Administration and Law*, Chapter 4.

6. Rosenbloom and O'Leary, *Public Administration and Law*, Chapters 4 and 6.

7. In *Frost and Frost Trucking Co. v. Railroad Commission*, 271 U.S. 583, 593–594 (1926), the Supreme Court explained that "It would be a palpable incongruity to strike down an act of state legislation which, by words of express divestment, seeks to strip the citizen of rights guaranteed by the federal Constitution, but to uphold an act by which the same result is accomplished under the guise of a surrender of a right in exchange for a valuable privilege which the state threatens otherwise to withhold....If the State may compel the surrender of one constitutional right as a condition of its favor, it may, in like manner, compel a surrender of all. It is inconceivable that guarantees embedded in the Constitution of the United States may thus be manipulated out of existence."

8. Rosenbloom and O'Leary, *Public Administration and Law*, Chapter 7.

9. Ibid.

10. Ibid., Chapter 5.

11. Robert Turner, "Governing From The Bench," *Boston Globe Magazine*, November 8, 1981, pp. 12ff.

12. John LaFond and Mary Durham, *Back to the Asylum* (New York: Oxford University Press, 1992); Christopher Jencks, *The Homeless* (Cambridge, MA: Harvard University Press, 1994).

13. Rosenbloom and O'Leary, *Public Administration and Law*, Chapter 8. The classic discussion is "Section

1983 and Federalism," *Harvard Law Review,* 90 (1977): 1133–1361 (author not identified).

14. *Bogan v. Scott-Harris,* U.S. Supreme Court, No. 96-1569 (1998).

15. *William Jefferson Clinton v. Paula Corbin Jones,* 117 S.Ct. 1636 (1997).

16. *Owen v. City of Independence,* 445 U.S. 622, 652 (1980).

17. *Hafer v. Melo,* 502 U.S. 21 (1997), held that state employees can be sued in their *personal* capacities for constitutional torts committed by their use of governmental authority. Under *Will v. Michigan Department of State Police,* 491 U.S. 58 (1989), state employees cannot be sued in federal court for money damages under Section 1983 in their *official* capacities. The *Will* ruling prevents suits against state employees as surrogates for the states, which cannot be sued in federal court in this type of case because they enjoy sovereign immunity under the Eleventh Amendment.

18. In principle, *Bush v. Lucas,* 462 U.S. 367 (1983), establishes the availability of constitutional tort actions for money damages under the First Amendment. The actual ruling is that such suits arising in the context of federal personnel administration are not generally allowed because Congress provided a different remedy, that of appeal to the Merit Systems Protection Board. *Bivens v. Six Unknown Named Agents,* 403 U.S. 388 (1971), established the principle that constitutional tort suits for damages are a remedy for violations of Fourth Amendment rights. *Davis v. Passman,* 422 U.S. 228 (1979), authorizes constitutional tort actions under the Fifth Amendment; *Carl-*son v. Green, 446 U.S. 14 (1980), under the Eighth Amendment.

19. *Smith v. Wade,* 461 U.S. 30 (1983).

20. *FDIC v. Meyer,* 510 U.S. 471 (1994).

21. Yong S. Lee, "Civil Liability of State and Local Governments: Myth and Reality," *Public Administration Review,* 47 (March/April 1987): 160–170; Public Risk Management Association, *Public Official Liability: Decisions in Federal Court,* 1 (January–March 1989): 5–6.

22. Public Risk Management Association, *Public Official Liability,* p. 7. See also, Andrew Blum, "Lawsuits Put Strain on City Budgets," *National Law Journal,* 10 (May 1988), pp. 1ff.

23. Systematic information on cases settled out of court is not available. From 1993 to 1998, 7,000 federal employees sought legal representation by the Department of Justice, but only 14 were found personally liable in court. Coupled with the cost of litigation, which deters frivolous actions, the disparity in numbers suggests that many actions are settled out of court. See Brian Friel, "Managers Rarely Found Liable in Lawsuits," *Government Executive (The Daily Fed),* May 19, 1998, p. 1.

24. Ibid.; Leigh Rivenbark, "Protection Needed Against Lawsuits," *Federal Times,* July 20, 1998, p. 3.

25. Friel, "Managers Rarely Found Liable in Lawsuits," p. 1.

26. Rivenbark, "Protection Needed Against Lawsuits," p. 3, quoting John Euler, Deputy Director of the Department of Justice's tort branch and Chairman of the federal Senior Executives Association.

Additional Reading

Harvard Law Review. "Section 1983 and Federalism," 90 (1977): 1133–1361 (authors not identified).

Nahmod, Sheldon. *Constitutional Torts.* Cincinnati: Anderson Publishing, 1995.

Rosenbloom, David, and Rosemary O'Leary. *Public Administration and Law.* 2nd ed. Chapter 8. New York: Marcel Dekker, 1997.

Case 2.1
Qualified Immunity

HARLOW v. FITZGERALD
Argued November 30, 1981
Decided June 24, 1982
457 US 800

JUSTICE POWELL delivered the opinion of the Court.

The issue in this case is the scope of the immunity available to the senior aides and advisers of the President of the United States in a suit for damages based upon their official acts.

I

In this suit for civil damages petitioners Bryce Harlow and Alexander Butterfield are alleged to have participated in a conspiracy to violate the constitutional and statutory rights of the respondent A. Ernest Fitzgerald....

• • •

...As evidence of Harlow's conspiratorial activity respondent relies heavily on a series of conversations in which Harlow discussed Fitzgerald's dismissal with Air Force Secretary Robert Seamans. The other evidence most supportive of Fitzgerald's claims consists of a recorded conversation in which the President later voiced a tentative recollection that Harlow was "all for canning" Fitzgerald.

• • •

Petitioner Butterfield also is alleged to have entered the conspiracy not later than May 1969. Employed as Deputy Assistant to the President and Deputy Chief of Staff to H. R. Haldeman, Butterfield circulated a White House memorandum in that month in which he claimed to have learned that Fitzgerald planned to "blow the whistle" on some "shoddy purchasing practices" by exposing these practices to public view. Fitzgerald characterizes this memorandum as evidence that Butterfield had commenced efforts to secure Fitzgerald's retaliatory dismissal.

• • •

II

...[O]ur decisions consistently have held that Government officials are entitled to some form of immunity from suits for damages. As recognized at common law, public officers require this protection to shield them from undue interference with their duties and from potentially disabling threats of liability.

Our decisions have recognized immunity defenses of two kinds. For officials whose special functions or constitutional status requires complete protection from suit, we have recognized the defense of "absolute immunity." The absolute immunity of legislators, in their legislative functions...and of judges, in their judicial functions...now is well settled. Our decisions also have extended absolute immunity to certain officials of the Executive Branch. These include prosecutors and similar officials,...executive officers engaged in adjudicative functions...and the President of the United States....

For executive officials in general, however, our cases make plain that qualified immunity represents the norm. In Scheuer v Rhodes [1974]...we acknowledged that high officials require greater protection than those with less complex discretionary responsibilities. Nonetheless, we held that a governor and his aides could receive the requisite protection from qualified or good-faith immunity....

In Butz v Economou [1978] we extended the approach of Scheuer to high federal officials of the Executive Branch. Discussing in detail the considerations that also had underlain our decision in Scheuer, we explained that the recognition of a qualified immunity defense for high executives reflected an attempt to balance competing values: not only the importance of a damages remedy to protect the rights of citizens,…but also "the need to protect officials who are required to exercise their discretion and the related public interest in encouraging the vigorous exercise of official authority.…"

Butz continued to acknowledge that the special functions of some officials might require absolute immunity. But the Court held that "federal officials who seek absolute exemption from personal liability for unconstitutional conduct must bear the burden of showing that public policy requires an exemption of that scope."

• • •

III

C

• • •

…In order to establish entitlement to absolute immunity a Presidential aide first must show that the responsibilities of his office embraced a function so sensitive as to require a total shield from liability. He then must demonstrate that he was discharging the protected function when performing the act for which liability is asserted.

Applying these standards to the claims advanced by petitioners Harlow and Butterfield, we cannot conclude on the record before us that either has shown that "public policy requires [for any of the functions of his office] an exemption of [absolute] scope."…Nor, assuming that petitioners did have functions for which absolute immunity would be warranted, could we now conclude that the acts charged in this lawsuit—if taken at all—would lie within the protected area.…

Even if they cannot establish that their official functions require absolute immunity, petitioners assert that public policy at least mandates an application of the qualified immunity standard that would permit the defeat of insubstantial claims without resort to trial. We agree.

A

The resolution of immunity questions inherently requires a balance between the evils inevitable in any available alternative. In situations of abuse of office, an action for damages may offer the only realistic avenue for vindication of constitutional guarantees.…

It is this recognition that has required the denial of absolute immunity to most public officers. At the same time, however, it cannot be disputed seriously that claims frequently run against the innocent as well as the guilty—at a cost not only to the defendant officials, but to the society as a whole. These social costs include the expenses of litigation, the diversion of official energy from pressing public issues, and the deterrence of able citizens from acceptance of public office. Finally, there is the danger that fear of being sued will "dampen the ardor of all but the most resolute, or the most irresponsible [public officials], in the unflinching discharge of their duties."

In identifying qualified immunity as the best attainable accommodation of competing values, in Butz,…as in Scheuer…we relied on the assumption that this standard would permit "[i]nsubstantial lawsuits [to] be quickly terminated."…

• • •

Consistently with the balance at which we aimed in Butz, we conclude today that bare allegations of malice should not suffice to subject government officials either to the costs of trial or to the burdens of broad-reaching discovery. We therefore hold that government officials performing discretionary functions generally are shielded from liability for civil damages insofar as their conduct does not violate clearly established statutory or constitutional rights of which a reasonable person would have known.…

Reliance on the objective reasonableness of an official's conduct, as measured by reference to clearly established law, should avoid excessive disruption of government and permit the resolution of many insubstantial claims on summary judgment. On summary judgment, the judge appropriately may determine, not only the currently applicable law, but whether that law was clearly established at the time an action occurred. If the law at that time was not clearly established, an official could not reasonably be expected to anticipate subsequent legal developments, nor could he fairly be said to "know" that the law forbade conduct not previously identified as unlawful. Until this threshold immunity question is resolved, discovery should not be allowed. If the law was clearly established, the immunity defense ordinarily should fail, since a reasonably competent public official should know the law governing his conduct. Nevertheless, if the official pleading the defense claims extraordinary circumstances and can prove that he neither knew nor should have known of the relevant legal standard, the defense should be sustained. But again, the defense would turn primarily on objective factors.

By defining the limits of qualified immunity essentially in objective terms, we provide no license to lawless conduct. The public interest in deterrence of unlawful conduct and in compensation of victims remains protected by a test that focuses on the objective legal reasonableness of an official's acts. Where an official could be expected to know that certain conduct would violate statutory or constitutional rights, he should be made to hesitate; and a person who suffers injury caused by such conduct may have a cause of action. But where an official's duties legitimately require action in which clearly established rights are not implicated, the public interest may be better served by action taken "with independence and without fear of consequences."...

Discussion Questions

1. In *Harlow*, the Court tries to establish a balance that will protect public administrators from frivolous suits or harassment by litigation and at the same time enable individuals whose constitutional rights have been abridged to recover. What problems, if any, do you see with the balance the Court strikes? Can you think of other ways of essentially achieving the same purposes?

2. Most public administrators are not shielded from liability if their conduct violates clearly established constitutional rights of which a reasonable person would have known. One can fairly infer that the "reasonable person" to which the Court refers would be assessed in the context of the particular public administrative job he or she holds. For instance, a "reasonable" police officer would be expected to know more about the constitutional rights of those involved in arrests or stops-and-frisks than would a budget analyst in the State Department. Does this mean that the "reasonable person" standard is really one of administrative competence, as assessed by judges? How can an administrator develop reasonable knowledge of the constitutional rights that bear on his or her job? How can a judge determine what "reasonable" knowledge of this kind an administrator should have? Do you think that judges are likely to understand public administration well enough to make sound decisions in this regard?

Case 2.2
Municipal Liability

PEMBAUR v. CITY OF CINCINNATI et al.
Argued December 2, 1985
Decided March 25, 1986
475 US 469

JUSTICE BRENNAN delivered the opinion of the Court, except as to Part II-B.

In Monell v New York City Dept. of Social Services...(1978), the Court concluded that municipal liability under 42 USC § 1983 [42 USCS § 1983] is limited to deprivations of federally protected rights caused by action taken "pursuant to official municipal policy of some nature...."

• • •

The question presented is whether, and in what circumstances, a decision by municipal policymakers on a single occasion may satisfy this requirement.

I

Bertold Pembaur is a licensed Ohio physician and the sole proprietor of the Rockdale Medical Center, located in the city of Cincinnati in Hamilton County. Most of Pembaur's patients are welfare recipients who rely on government assistance to pay for medical care. During the spring of 1977, Simon Leis, the Hamilton County Prosecutor, began investigating charges that Pembaur fraudulently had accepted payments from state welfare agencies for services not actually provided to patients. A grand jury was convened, and the case was assigned to Assistant Prosecutor William Whalen. In April, the grand jury charged Pembaur in a six-count indictment.

During the investigation, the grand jury issued subpoenas for the appearance of two of Pembaur's employees. When these employees failed to appear as directed, the Prosecutor obtained capiases* for their arrest and detention from the Court of Common Pleas of Hamilton County.

On May 19, 1977, two Hamilton County Deputy Sheriffs attempted to serve the capiases at Pembaur's clinic. Although the reception area is open to the public, the rest of the clinic may be entered only through a door next to the receptionist's window. Upon arriving, the Deputy Sheriffs identified themselves to the receptionist and sought to pass through this door, which was apparently open. The receptionist blocked their way and asked them to wait for the doctor. When Pembaur appeared a moment later, he and the receptionist closed the door, which automatically locked from the inside, and wedged a piece of wood between it and the wall. Returning to the receptionist's window, the Deputy Sheriffs identified themselves to Pembaur, showed him the capiases and explained why they were there. Pembaur refused to let them enter, claiming that the police had no legal authority to be there and requesting that they leave. He told them that he had called the Cincinnati police,

the local media, and his lawyer. The Deputy Sheriffs decided not to take further action until the Cincinnati police arrived.

Shortly thereafter, several Cincinnati police officers appeared. The Deputy Sheriffs explained the situation to them and asked that they speak to Pembaur. The Cincinnati police told Pembaur that the papers were lawful and that he should allow the Deputy Sheriffs to enter. When Pembaur refused, the Cincinnati police called for a superior officer. When he too failed to persuade Pembaur to open the door, the Deputy Sheriffs decided to call their supervisor for further instructions. Their supervisor told them to call Assistant Prosecutor Whalen and to follow his instructions. The Deputy Sheriffs then telephoned Whalen and informed him of the situation. Whalen conferred with County Prosecutor Leis, who told Whalen to instruct the Deputy Sheriffs to "go in and get [the witnesses]." Whalen in turn passed these instructions along to the Deputy Sheriffs.

After a final attempt to persuade Pembaur voluntarily to allow them to enter, the Deputy sheriffs tried unsuccessfully to force the door. City police officers, who had been advised of the County Prosecutor's instructions to "go in and get" the witnesses, obtained an axe and chopped down the door. The Deputy Sheriffs then entered and searched the clinic. Two individuals who fit descriptions of the witnesses sought were detained, but turned out not to be the right persons.

• • •

On April 20, 1981, Pembaur filed the present action in the United States District Court for the Southern District of Ohio against the city of Cincinnati, the county of Hamilton, the Cincinnati Police Chief, the Hamilton County Sheriff, the members of the Hamilton Board of County Commissioners (in their official capacities only), Assistant Prosecutor Whalen, and nine city and county police officers. Pembaur sought damages under 42 USC § 1983, alleging that the county and city police had violated his rights under the Fourth and Fourteenth Amendments. His theory was that, absent exigent circumstances, the Fourth Amendment prohibits police from searching an individual's home or business without a search warrant even to execute an arrest warrant for a third person.

---

*A capias is a writ of attachment commanding a county official to bring a subpoenaed witness who has failed to appear before the court to testify and to answer for civil contempt.

We agreed with that proposition in Steagald v United States ... (1981), decided the day after Pembaur filed this lawsuit. Pembaur sought $10 million in actual and $10 million in punitive damages, plus costs and attorney's fees.

• • •

II

A

Our analysis must begin with the proposition that "Congress did not intend municipalities to be held liable unless action pursuant to official municipal policy of some nature caused a constitutional tort." ...As we read its opinion, the Court of Appeals held that a single decision to take particular action, although made by municipal policymakers, cannot establish the kind of "official policy" required by Monell as a predicate to municipal liability under § 1983. The Court of Appeals reached this conclusion without referring to Monell—indeed, without any explanation at all. However, examination of the opinion in Monell clearly demonstrates that the Court of Appeals misinterpreted its holding.

Monell is a case about responsibility. In the first part of the opinion, we held that local government units could be made liable under § 1983 for deprivations of federal rights....In the second part of the opinion, we recognized a limitation on this liability and concluded that a municipality cannot be made liable by application of the doctrine of *respondeat superior*....

The conclusion that tortious conduct, to be the basis for municipal liability under § 1983, must be pursuant to a municipality's "official policy" is contained in this discussion. The "official policy" requirement was intended to distinguish acts of the *municipality* from acts of *employees* of the municipality, and thereby make clear that municipal liability is limited to action for which the municipality is actually responsible. Monell reasoned that recovery from a municipality is limited to acts that are, properly speaking, acts "of the municipality"—that is, acts which the municipality has officially sanctioned or ordered.

With this understanding, it is plain that municipal liability may be imposed for a single decision by municipal policymakers under appropriate circumstances. No one has ever doubted, for an instance, that a municipality may be liable under § 1983 for a single decision by its properly constituted legislative body— whether or not that body had taken similar action in the past or intended to do so in the future—because even a single decision by such a body unquestionably constitutes an act of official government policy.... But the power to establish policy is no more the exclusive province of the legislature at the local level than at the state or national level. Monell's language makes clear that it expressly envisioned other officials "whose acts or edicts may fairly be said to represent official policy,"...and whose decisions therefore may give rise to municipal liability under § 1983.

Indeed, any other conclusion would be inconsistent with the principles underlying § 1983. To be sure, "official policy" often refers to formal rules or understandings—often but not always committed to writing—that are intended to, and do, establish fixed plans of action to be followed under similar circumstances consistently and over time. That was the case in Monell itself, which involved a written rule requiring pregnant employees to take unpaid leaves of absence before such leaves were medically necessary. However,...a government frequently chooses a course of action tailored to a particular situation and not intended to control decisions in later situations. If the decision to adopt that particular course of action is properly made by that government's authorized decisionmakers, it surely represents an act of official government "policy" as that term is commonly understood. More importantly, where action is directed by those who establish governmental policy, the municipality is equally responsible whether that action is to be taken only once or to be taken repeatedly. To deny compensation to the victim would therefore be contrary to the fundamental purpose of § 1983.

B

Having said this much, we hasten to emphasize that not every decision by municipal officers automatically subjects the municipality to § 1983 liability. Municipal liability attaches only where the decisionmaker possesses final authority to establish municipal policy with respect to the action ordered. The fact that a particular official —even a policymaking official—has discretion in the exercise of particular functions does not, without more, give rise to municipal liability based on an exercise of that discretion....The official must also be responsible for establishing final government policy respecting such activity before the municipality can be held liable. Authority to make municipal policy may be granted directly by a legislative enactment or may be delegated by an official who possesses such authority, and of course, whether an official had final policymaking authority is a question of state law. However, like other governmental entities, municipalities often spread policymaking authority among various officers and official bodies. As a result, particular officers may have authority to establish binding county policy respecting particular matters and to adjust that policy for the county in changing circumstances....We hold that municipal liability under § 1983 attaches where—and only where—a deliberate choice to follow a course of action is made from among various alternatives by the official

responsible for establishing final policy with respect to the subject matter in question....

C

Applying this standard to the case before us, we have little difficulty concluding that the Court of Appeals erred in dismissing petitioner's claim against the county. The Deputy Sheriffs who attempted to serve the capiases at petitioner's clinic found themselves in a difficult situation. Unsure of the proper course of action to follow, they sought instructions from their supervisors. The instructions they received were to follow the orders of the County Prosecutor. The Prosecutor made a considered decision based on his understanding of the law and commanded the officers forcibly to enter petitioner's clinic. That decision directly caused the violation of petitioner's Fourth Amendment rights.

• • •

Discussion Questions

1. What are the implications of treating the statement by the prosecutor, "to go in and get" the witnesses, as official governmental policy? Do you think the prosecutor foresaw that it would lead the police to chop down Pembaur's door? Would a reasonable administrator foresee such a consequence?

2. In a concurring opinion, Justice White emphasized that, at the time it occurred, "the forcible entry made in this case was not...illegal under federal, state, or local law." But later, in *Steagald v. U.S.,* 451 U.S. 204 (1981), such an entry was found unconstitutional. Justice Stevens's concurring opinion stated, "In my view, it is not at all surprising that [Cincinnati]...'conceded' the retroactivity of Steagald. For Steagald plainly presented its holding as compelled by and presaged in, well-established precedent."Thus, Pembaur points to a very fundamental question: If a type of administrative action has never been directly challenged in court as unconstitutional, can a reasonable public administrator know, nevertheless, that the action is in fact unconstitutional? If so, what kind of knowledge of constitutional law and values must an administrator have?

Case 2.3
Failure to Train

CITY OF CANTON, OHIO v. HARRIS
Argued November 8, 1988
Decided February 28, 1989
489 US 378

JUSTICE WHITE delivered the opinion of the Court.

In this case, we are asked to determine if a municipality can ever be liable under 42 U.S.C.

§ 1983 for constitutional violations resulting from its failure to train municipal employees. We hold that, under certain circumstances, such liability is permitted by the statute.

I

In April, 1978, respondent Geraldine Harris was arrested by officers of the Canton Police Department. Mrs. Harris was brought to the police station in a patrol wagon.

When she arrived at the station, Mrs. Harris was found sitting on the floor of the wagon. She was asked if she needed medical attention, and responded with an incoherent remark. After she was brought inside the station for processing, Mrs. Harris slumped to the floor on two occasions. Eventually, the police officers left Mrs. Harris lying on the floor to prevent her from falling again. No medical attention was ever summoned for Mrs. Harris. After about an hour, Mrs. Harris was released from custody, and taken by an ambulance (provided by her family) to a nearby hospital. There, Mrs. Harris was diagnosed as suffering from several emotional ailments; she was hospitalized for one week and received subsequent outpatient treatment for an additional year.

Some time later, Mrs. Harris commenced this action, alleging many state law and constitutional claims against the city of Canton and its officials. Among these claims was one seeking to hold the city liable under 42 U.S.C. § 1983 for its violation of Mrs. Harris' right, under the Due Process Clause of the Fourteenth Amendment, to receive necessary medical attention while in police custody.

A jury trial was held on Mrs. Harris' claims. Evidence was presented that indicated that, pursuant to a municipal regulation, shift commanders were authorized to determine, in their sole discretion, whether a detainee required medical care.... In addition, testimony also suggested that Canton shift commanders were not provided with any special training (beyond first-aid training) to make a determination as to when to summon medical care for an injured detainee....

At the close of the evidence, the District Court submitted the case to the jury, which rejected all of Mrs. Harris' claims except one: her § 1983 claim against the city resulting from its failure to provide her with medical treatment while in custody. In rejecting the city's subsequent motion for judgment notwithstanding the verdict, the District Court explained the theory of liability as follows:

> The evidence, construed in a manner most favorable to Mrs. Harris, could be found by a jury to demonstrate that the City of Canton had a custom or policy of vesting complete authority with the police supervisor of when medical treatment would be administered to prisoners. Further, the jury could find from the evidence that the vesting of such *carte blanche* authority with the police supervisor, without adequate training to recognize when medical treatment is needed, was grossly negligent, or so reckless that future police misconduct was almost inevitable or substantially certain to result....

On appeal, the Sixth Circuit affirmed this aspect of the District Court's analysis, holding that

> a municipality is liable for failure to train its police force, [where] the plaintiff... prove[s] that the municipality acted recklessly, intentionally, or with gross negligence....

The Court of Appeals also stated that an additional prerequisite of this theory of liability was that the plaintiff must prove

> that the lack of training was so reckless or grossly negligent that deprivations of persons's constitutional rights were substantially certain to result....

Thus, the Court of Appeals found that there had been no error in submitting Mrs. Harris' "failure to train" claim to the jury. However, the Court of Appeals reversed the judgment for respondent and remanded this case for a new trial, because it found that certain aspects of the District Court's jury instructions might have led the jury to believe that it could find against the city on a mere *respondeat superior* theory. Because the jury's verdict did not state the basis on which it had ruled for Mrs. Harris on her § 1983 claim, a new trial was ordered.

• • •

III

In *Monell v. New York City Dept. of Social Services*... (1978), we decided that a municipality can be found liable under § 1983 only where the municipality itself causes the constitutional violation at issue....

Thus, our first inquiry in any case alleging municipal liability under § 1983 is the question whether there is a direct causal link between a municipal policy or custom and the alleged constitutional deprivation. The inquiry is a difficult one; one that has left this Court deeply divided in a series of cases that have followed *Monell;* one that is the principal focus of our decision again today.

• • •

B

Though we agree with the court below that a city can be liable under § 1983 for inadequate training of its employees, we cannot agree that the District Court's jury instructions on this issue were proper, for we conclude that the Court of Appeals provided an overly broad rule for when a municipality can be held liable under the "failure to train" theory....

Monell's rule that a city is not liable under § 1983 unless a municipal policy causes a constitutional deprivation will not be satisfied by merely alleging that the existing training program for a class of employees, such as police officers, represents a policy for which the city is responsible. That much may be true. The issue in a case like this one, however, is whether that training program is adequate; and if it is not, the question becomes whether such inadequate training can justifiably be said to represent "city policy." It may seem contrary to common sense to assert that a municipality will actually have a policy of not taking reasonable steps to train its employees. But it may happen that, in light of the duties assigned to specific officers or employees the need for more or different training is so obvious, and the inadequacy so likely to result in the violation of constitutional rights, that the policymakers of the city can reasonably be said to have been deliberately indifferent to the need. In that event, the failure to provide proper training may fairly be said to represent a policy for which the city is responsible, and for which the city may be held liable if it actually causes injury.

In resolving the issue of a city's liability, the focus must be on adequacy of the training program in relation to the tasks the particular officers must perform. That a particular officer may be unsatisfactorily trained will not alone suffice to fasten liability on the city, for the officer's shortcomings may have resulted from factors other than a faulty training program....It may be, for example, that an otherwise sound program has occasionally been negligently administered. Neither will it suffice to prove that an injury or accident could have been avoided if an officer had had better or more training, sufficient to equip him to avoid the particular injury-causing conduct. Such a claim could be made about almost any encounter resulting in injury, yet not condemn the adequacy of the program to enable officers to respond properly to the usual and recurring situations with which they must deal. And plainly, adequately trained officers occasionally make mistakes; the fact that they do says little about the training program or the legal basis for holding the city liable.

Moreover, for liability to attach in this circumstance, the identified deficiency in a city's training program must be closely related to the ultimate injury. Thus, in the case at hand, respondent must still prove that the deficiency in training actually caused the police officers' indifference to her medical needs. Would the injury have been avoided had the employee been trained under a program that was not deficient in the identified respect? Predicting how a hypothetically well-trained officer would have acted under the circumstances may not be an easy task for the factfinder, particularly since matters of judgment may be involved, and since officers who are well trained are not free from error, and perhaps might react very much like the untrained officer in similar circumstances. But judge and jury, doing their respective jobs, will be adequate to the task.

To adopt lesser standards of fault and causation would open municipalities to unprecedented liability under § 1983. In virtually every instance where a person has had his or her constitutional rights violated by a city employee, a § 1983 plaintiff will be able to point to something the city "could have done" to prevent the unfortunate incident....Thus, permitting cases against cities for their "failure to train" employees to go forward under § 1983 on a lesser standard of fault would result in *de facto respondeat superior* liability on municipalities—a result we rejected in *Monell*.... It would also engage the federal courts in an endless exercise of second-guessing municipal employee training programs. This is an exercise we believe the federal courts are ill-suited to undertake, as well as one that would implicate serious questions of federalism....

Consequently, while claims such as respondent's—alleging that the city's failure to pro-vide training to municipal employees resulted in the constitutional deprivation she suffered—are cognizable under § 1983, they can only yield liability against a municipality where that city's failure to train reflects deliberate indifference to the constitutional rights of its inhabitants.

Discussion Questions

1. Restate the standard under which municipalities may be held liable for failure to train. Are you personally aware of a failure to train in your local government that could trigger liability?

2. If a municipality has a "policy" of failure to train because it lacks sufficient funds, should it be potentially liable for constitutional torts caused by that failure? Why or why not?

Case 2.4
Public Administrators' Constitutional Right to Disobey

HARLEY v. SCHUYLKILL COUNTY et al.
United States District Court
E.D. Pennsylvania
Aug. 23, 1979
476 F. Supp. 191

Opinion

HUYETT, District Judge.
Plaintiff John R. Harley has brought this civil rights action, raising a variety of theories in support of his request for relief....

There now remain[s] before us...[the] issue [ ] for decision:...whether the right to refuse to perform an unconstitutional act is a "right, privilege, or immunity secured by the Constitution and laws" within the meaning of 42 U.S.C. § 1983;...

I

As this is a motion to dismiss, we must take plaintiff's factual allegations as true and construe them in a light most favorable to plaintiff....The complaint alleges that plaintiff John Harley was employed by the Schuylkill County Prison as a prison guard. On February 28, 1976, plaintiff reported to work on the second shift and was informed by the Acting Deputy of the First Shift that defendant Joseph Dooley, at that time the Acting Warden of Schuylkill County Prison, had left orders that inmate Kenneth Hennessey was to "stand check" in front of his cell, even if he had to be dragged from his cell....Upon examining Hennessey, plaintiff discovered that the inmate had previously been beaten and, in fact, Hennessey informed plaintiff that he had been dragged from his cell and beaten because he refused to stand check....

Hennessey further informed plaintiff that he had refused to stand check because of his religious beliefs....

Plaintiff determined that Hennessey intended to refuse to stand check again, and that at that time, under the circumstances, the only way that the "check could be effectuated would have been to use unwarranted force, which would aggravate Hennessey's injuries."... Plaintiff then proceeded, at the time of the first check, to secure Hennessey's cell and file a conduct report instead of forcing Hennessey to stand check....

Later that evening, plaintiff informed Dooley of these events and stated that in plaintiff's opinion further physical abuse of Hennessey would be illegal and improper under the circumstances....Dooley stated that he wanted Hennessey to stand check no matter what the circumstances and insisted that Hennessey be dragged from his cell....Plaintiff continued to refuse to obey this order because he felt that it was immoral and illegal. The complaint further alleged that the orders given by Dooley were unconstitutional, and that "their effectuation deprived Hennessey of his Fourth, Eighth, and Fourteenth Amendment Rights under the Constitution of the United States, and such orders, if carried out by plaintiff, would have subjected plaintiff to liability for such unconstitutional acts."...

Subsequently, plaintiff and other guards met with the Schuylkill County Commissioners to discuss this incident. The meeting ended without resolution of the issues; however, the Commissioners stated that they would investigate the incident and notify plaintiff and the other guards of the results of the investigation....

However, the Commissioners' reasons for discharging plaintiff were widely reported in area newspaper articles. According to those reports, plaintiff was discharged for causing dissension between Dooley and the guards in the second shift....One of the defendants also appeared on a radio talk show and stated that plaintiff was dismissed for insubordination....

II

Plaintiff seeks relief pursuant to 42 U.S.C. § 1983 on the grounds that he was discharged for refusing to perform an unconstitutional act. In connection with this claim, it is important to note that plaintiff is *not* seeking to vindicate prisoner Hennessey's constitutional rights. Rather, plaintiff is asserting a right personal to him; the right to refuse an order which would result in the violation of another's constitutional rights. The question presented here is whether this "right" is a "right[s], privilege[s], or immunit[y] secured by the Constitution and laws" as required by 42 U.S.C. § 1983.

At first blush, this question would appear to be one for which there is a simple answer, buttressed by a plethora of authority. In fact, there are surprisingly few authorities on this issue, and we could locate no case which discusses the matter in any great depth. See, e.g., *Parrish v. Civil Service Commission of County of Alame-*

*da,...*425 P.2d 223 (1967) (holds that there is a right to refuse to obey an unconstitutional order; however, it is not clear from this case whether this right is secured by the United State Constitution);...Despite the absence of authority, however, we are confident that the right to refuse to violate another's federal constitutional rights is a right secured by the constitution.

• • •

Under the facts as alleged in the complaint, plaintiff would have been liable for a deprivation of Hennessey's constitutional rights if he had proceeded to obey the order given to him....To put the matter another way, plaintiff had a clear duty under the constitution to refrain from acting in a manner that would deprive Hennessey of his constitutional rights. If plaintiff is under a *duty* to refrain from performing an act, then we believe that he has the concurrent *right* to so act. To hold otherwise would create an unconscionable burden upon one charged with the duty to uphold another's constitutional rights.

The issue remaining is whether that right is one "secured by the Constitution." The *duty* to refrain from acting in a manner which would deprive another of constitutional rights is a duty created and imposed by the constitution itself. It is logical to believe that the concurrent *right* is also one which is created and secured by the constitution. Therefore, we hold that the right to refuse to perform an unconstitutional act is a right "secured by the Constitution" within the meaning of § 1983.

We believe that our conclusion is supported by strong policy considerations. Parties such as plaintiff, who are acting in the capacities of prison administrators, policemen and the like, may daily be faced with situations where they are required to act in a manner which is consonant with the constitutional rights of others who are subject to their authority. The potential for abuse in these situations scarcely needs to be mentioned. If such persons are to be *encouraged* to respect the constitutional rights of others, they must at least have the minimal assurance that their actions are also protected by the constitution in those cases where they are confronted with the difficult choice of obeying an official order or violating another's constitutional rights.

Discussion Questions

1. How might public administrators' right to disobey unconstitutional orders affect hierarchical control and accountability in public agencies?

2. Assuming that the right to disobey is constitutionally protected, how would you deal with a subordinate who (a) correctly asserted that one of your orders was unconstitutional, and (b) incorrectly so asserted and refused to obey?

3. Suppose you were a police officer in the *Pembaur* case (Case 2.2) and were ordered to chop down the door. Suppose, in addition, that you knew such an action in those circumstances would be an unconstitutional breach of the Fourth Amendment, even though it had never actually been declared so by a court. What would you do?

THREE

Privatization and Outsourcing

The New Public Management

In the early 1990s, a "New Public Management" (NPM) crystallized in several English-speaking democracies.[1] Generally called "reinventing government" in the United States, NPM concepts underlie Vice President Al Gore's National Performance Review and a great deal of contemporary public administrative reform at the state and local levels.[2] The NPM's core tenets add to the constitutional competence required of public managers.

The NPM calls on government to "steer," rather than "row." In other words, the basic responsibility of public managers is to arrange for the provision of governmental services to the public, not necessarily to provide them directly. The decision of whether to outsource government work to contractors, not-for-profits, or other third parties depends primarily on two factors.

First, a jurisdiction may view some activities as inherently governmental functions that should never be outsourced. However, there are few, if any, bright lines, or clear distinctions, differentiating these activities from others, and what is considered inherently governmental varies among governments. Generally, such functions involve policymaking or other activities for which democratic theory is thought to require direct accountability to the electorate. For example, the Government Performance and Results Act (1993) requires federal agencies to develop their strategic plans in-house.[3] They may consult with outsiders, but the task of formulating the plans cannot be outsourced. By contrast, when engaging in rulemaking, agencies sometimes rely on third parties to write the initial proposed rules.

The second consideration is cost-effectiveness. Will outsourcing serve customers as well or better at the same or less cost? Part of the NPM focus is on making government highly competitive with the private sector. If government can do something better-faster-cheaper than a contractor or other organization, there is obviously no point in outsourcing. Reinventing initiatives along these lines include making agencies customer driven and entrepreneurial, reorganizing them to operate more like private corporations, and transforming them into "performance-based organizations" that are given great flexibility to achieve well defined business objectives.

Similarly, there is no point in keeping a function that is not inherently governmental in-house if third parties can perform it more cost-effectively.

Outsourcing relieves the government of expensive and complex overhead functions, such as personnel and building maintenance. It also facilitates adjustment to surges and declines in the volume of work.

Where cost-effectiveness is about equal, current thinking holds that the government should provide the service itself because there are advantages to maintaining direct control.[4] Outsourcing often involves imponderables. Third parties may be more difficult to monitor, they may fall short of the government's expectations, and sometimes they resist governmental steering aimed at making midcourse corrections. The government may also face a problem if bidding for contracts becomes uncompetitive.

Privatization and outsourcing can take many forms. Contracts may be with for-profits, not-for-profits, or other governments. Agencies or their subunits can be turned into private corporations. Some government operations, such as providing electricity or disposing of solid waste, may be sold to private firms. A number of hybrid arrangements, including public–private partnerships, can be developed. Governments can provide grants to subsidize desired services, research, or other work. Likewise, they may supply individuals with vouchers or scrip, such as food stamps, to make services more affordable or to promote their policy objectives.

There are so many possibilities for letting third parties do the rowing that, for many arrangements, "alternative service delivery" is really a better, if clumsier, term than privatization or outsourcing. Today, it encompasses a very wide range of activity, including public works, transportation, health and human services, corrections, recreation, trash collection, building inspections, fire and police communication, landscaping, building and vehicle maintenance, and payroll and other support functions.

Alternative service delivery presents three main concerns for constitutional competence: the doctrine of "state action"; the liability of private entities for constitutional torts; and constitutional constraints on dealing with contractors. During the late 1980s and mid-1990s, the Supreme Court made it clear that, under some circumstances, outsourcing will be very much regulated by constitutional law.

The Doctrine of "State Action"

Traditionally, U.S. constitutional law posits a clear distinction between private and governmental action. The latter is inaptly called "state action" in constitutional law, regardless of the level of government that undertakes it. Government is thoroughly regulated by the Constitution. However, with the exception of the Thirteenth Amendment's prohibition of slavery and involuntary servitude, private action is not ordinarily controlled by constitutional law. This may have seemingly odd consequences, such as the fact that a state university typically has less freedom than a private one to regulate its students' conduct and to discipline them. For instance, it is much easier for private universities than public ones to ban racist, misogynistic, or homophobic "hate" speech. As the Supreme Court starkly explained in 1988, "embedded within our Fourteenth Amendment jurisprudence is a dichotomy between state action, which is subject to strict scrutiny under the Amendment's Due Process Clause, and private conduct, against which the Amendment affords no shield, no matter how unfair that conduct may be."[5]

The NPM puts considerable pressure on the public–private dichotomy and makes it very difficult to sustain. Privatization, public–private partnerships, and other hybrid arrangements can span traditional boundaries. Cases 3.1 and 3.2, *Lebron v. National Railroad Passenger Corporation* (1995) and *West v. Atkins* (1988), explain the Supreme Court's concern that constitutional rights not be lost in the blurring of sectors. The Court makes it clear that hybrids and even clearly private parties can sometimes be considered state actors for constitutional purposes. In other words, though they are nongovernmental in an organizational sense, their actions are subject to constitutional constraints.

As *Lebron* illustrates, the case law concerning the transformation of private parties into state actors is not particularly clear or consistent. This makes gaining constitutional competence regarding privatizing and outsourcing more difficult. But it is nevertheless necessary for both governments and private parties when designing alternative service delivery. Three imperfect tests are used to determine whether a private entity is engaged in state action.

First, as *West* explains, private individuals or organizations become state actors when they are engaged in "public functions." *West* pertains to the provision of adequate medical care to prisoners, which is indisputably a public function under the Eighth Amendment. Other services provided by third parties may be less clear-cut, but as the Supreme Court suggests in *Lebron,* it will ultimately be the judiciary's call as to what constitutes a public function for the purposes of state action doctrine. Some *possibilities* include doing security investigations or drug tests on civil servants.

Second, a private organization or hybrid may become a state actor when it is so enmeshed with the government that it is difficult or impossible to tell where one begins and the other ends. Public–private partnerships are a prime concern here. Note that, as in *Lebron,* it is possible for an organization to be regarded as a nongovernmental entity for commercial purposes but as governmental when consitutional rights are at issue.

Third, and of far less importance to contemporary public administration, private individuals or organizations can be treated as state actors when the government somehow authorizes or encourages them to violate constitutional rights. In these circumstances, the private party is "clothed with the authority of state law" and its actions may be "fairly attributable to the State."[6] No constitutionally competent public administrator will knowingly become involved in such a relationship. However, it is possible for old laws to authorize private actions, such as seizing disputed assets, which turn out to be unconstitutional under contemporary standards.[7]

It is also important to note what these three tests do not include. Generally speaking, private entities will not be engaged in state action simply because they are heavily regulated or subsidized by the government. Nor will governmental subsidization of their clientele make them state actors. Under current law, therefore, neither the persons receiving vouchers from the government nor the organizations in which they expend them are automatically considered state actors.

There is no doubt that state action doctrine complicates privatization and outsourcing. To the extent that private entities become state actors, privatization and outsourcing are likely to cost more and become less attractive to businesses, not-for-profits, and other third parties. Complying with some constitutional rights, including procedural due process and the Eighth Amendment's protections against cruel and unusual punishment, adds directly to expenses. But even where compliance costs are minimal, as is often the case with equal protection, engaging in state action makes individuals and organizations vulnerable to lawsuits for constitutional torts. Moreover, for most private entities, the need to comply with constitutional restrictions imposes new requirements that must be learned and integrated into organizational cultures. Additionally, if a wider variety of administrative functions are privatized or outsourced in the future, the subjective character of state action criteria is likely to tempt injured individuals and their attorneys to file potentially expensive and distracting litigation.

Private State Actors' Liability for Constitutional Torts

When private parties engage in state action, they take on constitutional obligations and may accordingly incur considerable liabilities for violating individuals' constitutional rights. This poses a serious threat to privatization and outsourcing in some program areas. Private entities or hybrids may consider the risk of liability or the costs of training their employees in constitutional competence to be greater than the potential benefits of performing public functions or becoming enmeshed with government. Likewise, governments and public managers may be reluctant to privatize functions that typically generate liability suits or to entangle third parties in performing them. Implementation is bound to be disrupted if those doing the rowing are subject to numerous suits or required to pay large sums in damages. Costs will also rise, which makes contracting out less attractive.

In Case 3.4, *Richardson v. McKnight* (1997), the Supreme Court made the outlook much worse for the privatization of public functions involving human services. Its 5-4 decision denied guards working in a privatized prison the same qualified immunity that is available to similar personnel employed by government-run correctional facilities. As explained in the previous chapter, qualified immunity makes public employees immune from suit unless they violate clearly established constitutional or federal statutory rights of which a reasonable person would have known. Under *Richardson v. McKnight,* the privately employed guards are potentially liable if they violate any constitutional rights, regardless of how clearly they are established or what a reasonable person might know about them.

Without qualified immunity it is difficult for private entities engaged in state action to defend themselves in constitutional tort suits. They face a considerably greater risk than public employees of facing high litigation costs and being assessed with damages. At present, their only argument seems to be that they have not, in fact, infringed on anyone's constitutional rights—which offers no protection if a court finds that they have. The Supreme Court has raised the possibility that private state actors may be able to raise a "good faith" defense of some kind under common law. But whether it will be available and, if so, what form it may take, has yet to be determined by the courts.

The central holding in *Richardson v. McKnight* is not confined to corrections.[8] It presumably applies to all private parties engaged in state action who tread on individuals' constitutional rights. *Richardson v. McKnight* simply explains the reasons why a majority of the Supreme Court does not think it is appropriate to extend qualified immunity to private employees. The potential problem for private state actors is great because constitutional law "is what the courts say it is,"[9] and they may not have said it clearly or even at all. It is perfectly possible for a private party engaged in state action to be found liable even though the conduct at issue was authorized by law and never previously declared unconstitutional![10]

Constitutional Constraints on Dealing with Contractors

Flexibility is a key administrative value in privatizing and outsourcing. Government's relationship with its own employees is often encumbered by civil service procedures and constitutional law. Comprehensive regulations for entering into contracts are also common. Often contracts must be let to the lowest competent bidder. However, the termination of contracts is generally subject to a good deal more administrative discretion. Some contracts can be terminated "at will," with no reason given; others for poor performance. Prior notice of the government's intent to terminate a contract may be required, but typically the lead time will not be burdensome.

From the NPM's perspective, placing constitutional constraints on contracting out undercuts the logic of privatizing or outsourcing in the first place. Contracting out is a business decision. A lot of procedural checks are both unnecessary and cost-ineffective because, as Gore explains, "people—in government or out—are, for the most part, neither crooked nor stupid. Most people want to do the right thing, so long as the right thing makes sense."[11] But in viewing administration as business, the reinventers neglect a political side of contracting out. In Justice Antonin Scalia's words, "There can be no dispute that, like rewarding one's allies, the correlative act of refusing to reward one's opponents…is an American political tradition as old as the Republic. This is true not only with regard to employment matters…but also in the area of government contracts…."[12]

In Case 3.3, *Board of County Commissioners, Wabaunsee County v. Umbehr* (1996), the Supreme Court placed important First Amendment constraints on government's freedom to terminate its relationships with private contractors. Relying on the unconstitutional conditions doctrine discussed in Chapter 2, the court explains why following a political tradition that Scalia views as venerable may now violate an individual's constitutionally protected freedom of speech. The Court also sets forth an elaborate balancing procedure for determining when the termination of a contract with a private party will unconstitutionally abridge his or her free speech rights.

But there is no reason to stop at free speech. The First Amendment protects political association and free exercise of religion as well. Contractors also have privacy rights under the Fourth Amendment. Those who are not engaged in public safety or sensitive work cannot be compelled to submit to drug tests as a condition of keeping their contracts with the government.[13] The Fourteenth Amendment's Equal Protection Clause clearly protects contractors from being terminated because of their race or ethnicity.[14] With very few exceptions the same would be true for terminations based on gender.[15]

Not only does *Umbehr* place constitutional constraints on contracting out, like state action doctrine it also invites litigation. Public managers can reduce the likelihood of suits by being constitutionally competent and understanding how to balance all the factors involved. But they cannot be heartened in the Court's admission that the constitutional analysis must be "fact-sensitive" and "nuanced."[16] As is often the case, the best stategy may be to "err on the side of protecting citizens' constitutional rights."[17]

Conclusion

The Supreme Court has given public managers much to consider when seeking to privatize or outsource a function. What may seem to be a relatively straightforward decision based on cost-effectiveness is complicated by considerations of state action, liability, and constitutional constraints on contracting out. There is an ever-present possibility that implementation will be disrupted or resources will be drained by lawsuits against third parties or, in the case of alleged unconstitutional conditions, litigation by them. Understanding the cases that follow will enable public managers to build the constitutional competence to recognize the constitutional issues in privatizing, outsourcing, and terminating contracts. As the Court's holding in *Richardson v. McKnight* suggests, constitutional competence also requires ensuring that when public managers rely on nongovernmental state actors to do the rowing, those private entities are well versed in their constitutional obligations.

Notes

1. R.C. Mascarenhaus, "Building An Enterprise Culture in the Public Sector: Reform of the Public Sector in Australia, Britain, and New Zealand," *Public Administration Review*, vol. 53 (July/August 1993): 319; B. Guy Peters and Donald Savoie, "Civil Service Reform," *Public Administration Review*, vol. 54 (September/October 1994): 418.

2. Al Gore, *From Red Tape to Results: Creating a Government That Works Better & Costs Less* (Washington, DC: U.S. Government Printing Office, 1993); Al Gore, *Common Sense Government Works Better & Costs Less* (Washington, DC: U.S. Government Printing Office, 1995); David Osborne and Ted Gaebler, *Reinventing Government* (Reading, MA: Addison-Wesley, 1992).

3. Public Law 103-62, 107 Stat. 285, section 306 (e) (August 3, 1993).

4. Rowan Miranda and Allan Lerner, "Bureaucracy, Organizational Redundancy, and the Privatization of Public Services," *Public Administration Review*, vol. 55 (March/April 1995): 193; Jonas Prager, "Contracting Out Government Services: Lessons from the Private Sector," *Public Administration Review*, vol. 54 (March/April 1994): 176.

5. *National Collegiate Athletic Association v. Tarkanian*, 488 U.S. 179, 191 (1988).

6. *West v. Atkins,* 487 U.S. 42, 55 (1988); *Lugar v. Edmonston Oil Company,* 457 U.S. 922, 937 (1982).

7. *Wyatt v. Cole,* 504 U.S. 158 (1992).

8. Ibid.

9. *Owen v. City of Independence,* 445 U.S. 622, 669 (1980).

10. *Wyatt v. Cole,* 504 U.S. 158 (1992).

11. Gore, *Common Sense Government,* p. 33.

12. *O'Hare Truck Service, Inc. v. City of Northlake,* 116 S.Ct. 2353, 2362 (1996) (dissenting opinion).

13. See *Skinner v. Railway Labor Executives' Association,* 489 U.S. 602 (1989).

14. *Adarand Constructors, Inc. v. Pena,* 515 U.S. 200 (1995), Case 5.3.

15. See *United States v. Virginia,* 518 U.S. 515 (1996), Case 7.3. The gender of service providers could be related to the achievement of the government's objectives in some therapeutic settings, such as rape crisis centers.

16. *Board of County Commissioners, Wabaunsee County v. Umbehr,* 116 S.Ct. 2342, 2348, 2349 (1996). See also *O'Hare Truck,* which extends constitutional protection to persons having a preexisting commercial relationship with a government, though no actual contract.

17. *Owen v. City of Independence,* 445 U.S. 622, 652 (1980).

Additional Reading

Donahue, John D. *The Privatization Decision: Public Ends, Private Means.* New York: Basic Books, 1989.

Esper, Dilan. "Some Thoughts on the Puzzle of State Action." *Southern California Law Review,* 62 (1995): 663–717.

Gilmour, Robert, and Laura Jensen. "Reinventing Government Accountability: Public Functions, Privatization, and the Meaning of 'State Action.'" *Public Administration Review,* 58 (May/June 1998): 247–258.

Gore, Al. *Common Sense Government Works Better & Costs Less.* Washington, DC: U.S. Government Printing Office, 1995.

Rosenbloom, David. "Constitutional Problems for the New Public Management in the United States." In Khi Thai and Rosalyn Carter, eds., *Current Public Policy Issues: The 1998 Annals.* Boca Raton, FL: PrAcademics Press, 1999.

Case 3.1
State Action

LEBRON v. NATIONAL RAILROAD PASSENGER CORPORATION
Argued November 7, 1994
Decided February 21, 1995
513 US 374

JUSTICE SCALIA delivered the opinion of the Court.

In this case, we consider whether actions of the National Railroad Passenger Corporation, commonly known as Amtrak, are subject to constraints of the Constitution.

I

Petitioner, Michael A. Lebron, creates billboard displays that involve commentary on public issues, and that seemingly propel him into litigation....In August, 1991, he contacted Transportation Displays, Incorporated (TDI), which manages the leasing of the billboards in Amtrak's Pennsylvania Station in New York City, seeking to display an advertisement on a billboard of colossal proportions, known to New Yorkers (or at least to the more Damon Runyonesque among them) as "the Spectacular." The Spectacular is a curved, illuminated billboard, approximately 103 feet long and 10 feet high, which dominates the main entrance to Penn Station's waiting room and ticket area.

On November 30, 1992, Lebron signed a contract with TDI to display an advertisement on the Spectacular for two months beginning in January, 1993. The contract provided that "[a]ll advertising copy is subject to approval of TDI and [Amtrak] as to character, text, illustration, design and operation."...Lebron declined to disclose the specific content of his advertisement throughout his negotiations with TDI, although he did explain to TDI that it was generally political. On December 2, he submitted to TDI (and TDI later forwarded to Amtrak) an advertisement described by the District Court as follows:

> The work is a photomontage, accompanied by considerable text. Taking off on a widely circulated Coors beer advertisement which proclaims Coors to be the "Right Beer," Lebron's piece is captioned "Is it the Right's Beer Now?" It includes photographic images of convivial drinkers

of Coors beer, juxtaposed with a Nicaraguan village scene in which peasants are menaced by a can of Coors that hurtles towards them, leaving behind a trail of fire, as if it were a missile. The accompanying text, appearing on either end of the montage, criticizes the Coors family for its support of right-wing causes, particularly the contras in Nicaragua. Again taking off on Coors' advertising which uses the slogan of "Silver Bullet" for its beer cans, the text proclaims that Coors is "The Silver Bullet that aims The Far Right's political agenda at the heart of America."...

Amtrak's vice president disapproved the advertisement, invoking Amtrak's policy, inherited from its predecessor as landlord of Penn Station, the Pennsylvania Railroad Company, "that it will not allow political advertising on the [S]pectacular advertising sign."...

Lebron then filed suit against Amtrak and TDI, claiming, *inter alia,* that the refusal to place his advertisement on the Spectacular had violated his First and Fifth Amendment rights.... [T]he District Court ruled that Amtrak, because of its close ties to the Federal Government, was a Government actor at least for First Amendment purposes, and that its rejection of Lebron's proposed advertisement as unsuitable for display in Penn Station had violated the First Amendment. The court granted Lebron an injuction and ordered Amtrak and TDI to display Lebron's advertisement on the Spectacular.

The United States Court of Appeals for the Second Circuit reversed....The panel's opinion first noted that Amtrak was, by the terms of the legislation that created it, not a Government entity...; and then concluded that the Federal Government was not so involved with Amtrak that the latter's decisions could be considered federal action....

II

We have held once..., and said many times, that actions of private entities can sometimes be regarded as governmental action for constitutional purposes.…It is fair to say that "our cases deciding when private action might be deemed that of the state have not been a model of consistency."…

• • •

III

Before proceeding to consider Lebron's contention that Amtrak, though nominally a private corporation, must be regarded as a Government entity for First Amendment purposes, we examine the nature and history of Amtrak.…

A

Congress established Amtrak in order to avert the threatened extinction of passenger trains in the United States. The statute that created it begins with the congressional finding, redolent of provisions of the Interstate Commerce Act…, that "the *public convenience and necessity* require the continuance and improvement" of railroad passenger service. …In the current version of the RPSA [Rail Passenger Service Act of 1970],…the congressional findings are followed by a section entitled "Goals," which begins "The Congress hereby establishes the following goals for Amtrak."…

…The President appoints three…directors with the advice and consent of the Senate…, selecting one from a list of individuals recommended by the Railway Labor Executives Association…, one "from among the Govenors of States with an interest in rail transportation,"… and one as a "representative of business with an interest in rail transportation,"… These directors serve 4-year terms.… The President appoints two additional directors without the involvement of the Senate, choosing them from a list of names submitted by various commuter rail authorities.…These directors serve 2-year terms.…

• • •

IV

Amtrak claims that, whatever its relationship with the Federal Government, its charter's disclaimer of agency status prevents it from being considered a Government entity in the present case.…

But it is not for Congress to make the final determination of Amtrak's status as a government entity for purposes of determining the

constitutional rights of citizens affected by its actions. If Amtrak is, by its very nature, what the Constitution regards as the Government, congressional pronouncement that it is not such can no more relieve it of its First Amendment restrictions than a similar pronouncement could exempt the Federal Bureau of Investigation from the Fourth Amendment. The Constitution constrains governmental action "by whatever instruments or in whatever modes that action may be taken."…

• • •

V

The question before us today is unanswered, therefore, by governing statutory text or by binding precedent of this Court. Facing the question of Amtrak's status for the first time, we conclude that it is an agency or instrumentality of the United States for the purpose of individual rights guaranteed against the Government by the Constitution.

This conclusion seems to us in accord with public and judicial understanding of the nature of Government-created and -controlled corporations over the years. A remarkable feature of the heyday of those corporations…was that, even while they were praised for their status

> as agencies separate and distinct, administratively and financially and legally, from the government itself, [which] has facilitated their adoption of commercial methods of accounting and financing, avoidance of political controls, and utilization of regular procedures of business management,

it was fully acknowledged that they were a "device" of "government," and constituted "federal corporate agencies" apart from "regular government departments."…

• • •

That Government-created and -controlled corporations are (for many purposes at least) part of the Government itself has a strong basis not merely in past practice and understanding, but in reason itself. It surely cannot be that government, state or federal, is able to evade the most solemn obligations imposed in the Constitution by simply resorting to the corporate form.…

Amtrak was created by a special statute, explicitly for the furtherance of federal governmental goals. As we have described, six of the corporation's eight externally named directors (the ninth is named by a majority of the board itself) are appointed directly by the President of the United States—four of them (including the Secretary of Transportation) with the advice and consent of the Senate....Although the statute restricts most of the President's choices to persons suggested by certain organizations or persons having certain qualifications, those restrictions have been tailor-made by Congress for this entity alone. They do not, in our view, establish an absence of control by the Government as a whole, but rather constitute a restriction imposed by one of the political branches upon the other. Moreover, Amtrak is not merely in the temporary control of the Government (as a private corporation whose stock comes into federal ownership might be); it is established and organized under federal law for the very purpose of pursuing federal governmental objectives, under the direction and control of federal governmental appointees. It is, in that respect, no different from the so-called independent regulatory agencies such as the Federal Communications Commission or the Securities Exchange Commission, which are run by Presidential appointees with fixed terms. It is true that the directors of Amtrak, unlike commissioners of independent regulatory agencies, are not, by the explicit terms of the statute, removable by the President for cause, and are not impeachable by Congress. But any reduction in the immediacy of accountability for Amtrak directors vis-à-vis regulatory commissioners seems to us of minor consequence for present purposes—especially since, by the very terms of the chartering Act, Congress's "right to repeal, alter, or amend this chapter at any time is expressly reserved."...

• • •

We hold that where, as here, the Government creates a corporation by special law, for the furtherance of governmental objectives, and retains for itself permanent authority to appoint a majority of the directors of that corporation, the corporation is part of the Government for purposes of the First Amendment.

Discussion Questions

1. Why does it matter to Lebron whether Amtrak is considered a governmental agency or not?

2. If Amtrak is governmental for First Amendment purposes when dealing with clients, would the Constitution also apply to Amtrak's treatment of its own employees? Why or why not? If so, what are the implications?

3. The Court admits that its application of state action doctrine has not been particularly consistent. How might its difficulty in defining state actors affect government outsourcing?

Case 3.2
Contractors as State Actors

WEST v. ATKINS
Argued March 28, 1988
Decided June 20, 1988
487 US 42

JUSTICE BLACKMUN delivered the opinion of the Court.

This case presents the question whether a physician who is under contract with the State to provide medical services to inmates at a state prison hospital on a part-time basis acts "under color of state law," within the meaning of 42 U.S.C. § 1983, when he treats an inmate.

I

Petitioner, Quincy West, tore his left Achilles tendon in 1983 while playing volleyball at Odom Correctional Center, the Jackson, N.C., state prison at which he was incarcerated. A physician under contract to provide medical care to Odom inmates examined petitioner and directed that he be transferred to Raleigh for orthopedic consultation at Central Prison Hospital, the acute care medical facility operated by the State for its more than 17,500 inmates. Central Prison Hospital has one full-time staff physician, and obtains additional medical assistance under "Contracts for Professional Services" between the State and area physicians.

Respondent, Samuel Atkins, M.D., a private physician, provided orthopedic services to inmates pursuant to one such contract. Under it, Doctor Atkins was paid approximately $52,000 annually to operate two "clinics" each week at Central Prison Hospital, with additional amounts for surgery. Over a period of several months, he treated West's injury by placing his leg in a series of casts. West alleges that, although the doctor acknowledged that surgery would be necessary, he refused to schedule it, and that he eventually discharged West while his ankle was still swollen and painful, and his movement still impeded. Because West was a prisoner in "close custody," he was not free to employ or elect to see a different physician of his own choosing.

Pursuant to 42 U.S.C. § 1983, West, proceeding *pro se,* commenced this action against Doctor Atkins in the United States District Court for the Eastern District of North Carolina for violation of his Eighth Amendment right to be free from cruel and unusual punishment. West alleged that Atkins was deliberately indifferent to his serious medical needs, by failing to provide adequate treatment.

• • •

To state a claim under § 1983, a plaintiff must allege the violation of a right secured by the Constitution and laws of the United States, and must show that the alleged deprivation was committed by a person acting under color of state law....Petitioner West sought to fulfill the first requirement by alleging a violation of his rights secured by the Eighth Amendment under *Estelle v. Gamble*...(1976). There the Court held

that deliberate indifference to a prisoner's serious medical needs, whether by a prison doctor or a prison guard, is prohibited by the Eighth Amendment....The adequacy of West's allegation and the sufficiency of his showing on this element of his § 1983 cause of action are not contested here. The only issue before us is whether petitioner has established the second essential element—that respondent acted under color of state law in treating West's injury.

A

The traditional definition of acting under color of state law requires that the defendant in a § 1983 action have exercised power "possessed by virtue of state law and made possible only because the wrongdoer is clothed with the authority of state law."...

To constitute state action,

> the deprivation must be caused by the exercise of some right or privilege created by the State...or by a person for whom the State is responsible,

and "the party charged with the deprivation must be a person who may fairly be said to be a state actor."... "[S]tate employment is generally sufficient to render the defendant a state actor."...It is firmly established that a defendant in a § 1983 suit acts under color of state law when he abuses the position given to him by the State....Thus, generally, a public employee acts under color of state law while acting in his official capacity or while exercising his responsibilities pursuant to state law....

• • •

C

We now make explicit what was implicit in our holding in *Estelle*: respondent, as a physician employed by North Carolina to provide medical services to state prison inmates, acted under color of state law for purposes of § 1983 when undertaking his duties in treating petitioner's injury. Such conduct is fairly attributed to the State.

The Court recognized in *Estelle*: "An inmate must rely on prison authorities to treat his medical needs; if the authorities fail to do so, those needs will not be met."...In light of this, the Court held that the State has a constitutional obligation, under the Eighth Amendment, to provide adequate medical care to those whom it has incarcerated....North Carolina employs physicians, such as respondent, and defers to their professional judgment, in order to fulfill this obligation. By virtue of this relationship, effected by state law, Doctor Atkins is authorized and obliged to treat prison inmates, such as West. He does so "clothed with the authority of state law."...He is "a person who may fairly be said to be a state actor."...It is only those physicians authorized by the State to whom the inmate may turn. Under state law, the only medical care West could receive for his injury was that provided by the State. If Doctor Atkins misused his power by demonstrating deliberate indifference to West's serious medical needs, the resultant deprivation was caused, in the sense relevant for state action inquiry, by the State's exercise of its right to punish West by incarceration and to deny him a venue independent of the State to obtain needed medical care.

The fact that the State employed respondent pursuant to a contractual arrangement that did not generate the same benefits or obligations applicable to other "state employees" does not alter the analysis. It is the physician's function within the state system, not the precise terms of his employment, that determines whether his actions can fairly be attributed to the State. Whether a physician is on the state payroll or is paid by contract, the dispositive issue concerns the relationship among the State, the physician, and the prisoner. Contracting out prison medical care does not relieve the State of its constitutional duty to provide adequate medical treatment to those in its custody, and it does not deprive the State's prisoners of the means to vindicate their Eighth Amendment rights. The State bore an affirmative obligation to provide adequate medical care to West; the State delegated that function to respondent Atkins; and respondent voluntarily assumed that obligation by contract.

Nor does the fact that Doctor Atkins' employment contract did not require him to work exclusively for the prison make him any less a state actor than if he performed those duties as a full-time, permanent member of the state prison medical staff. It is the physician's function while working for the State, not the amount of time he spends in performance of those duties or the fact that he may be employed by others to perform similar duties, that determines whether he is acting under color of state law. In the State's employ, respondent worked as a physician at the prison hospital fully vested with state authority to fulfill essential aspects of the duty, placed on the State by the Eighth Amendment and state law, to provide essential medical care to those the State had incarcerated. Doctor Atkins must be considered to be a state actor.

III

For the reasons stated above, we conclude that respondent's delivery of medical treatment to West was state action fairly attributable to the State, and that respondent therefore acted under color of state law for purposes of § 1983....

Discussion Questions

1. Why is Dr. Atkins a "state actor"? Public defenders under contract with the government to provide legal assistance to indigent defendants or appellants are not considered state actors because they retain professional independence and act in opposition to the state (see *Polk County v. Dodson,* 454 U.S. 312, 1981). List some categories of persons under contract with the government to provide public services who might be considered state actors under the Court's ruling in *West.* Explain why.

2. If you were responsible for prisoners' health in a facility that relied on contracted physicians, such as Dr. Atkins, what steps would you take to ensure that the prisoners received adequate medical attention?

3. As a matter of public policy, what are the advantages and disadvantages of permitting prisoners to bring constitutional tort suits for violations of the Eighth Amendment's requirement that they receive adequate medical care, as opposed to allowing them to sue specific health care workers for malpractice only?

Case 3.3
Contractors' First Amendment Rights

BOARD OF COUNTY COMMISSIONERS, WABAUNSEE COUNTY,
KANSAS v. UMBEHR
Argued November 28, 1995
Decided June 28, 1996
518 US 668

O'CONNOR, J., delivered the opinion of the Court with respect to Parts I, II-A, II-B-2, and III, in which Rehnquist, C.J., and Stevens, Kennedy, Souter, Ginsburg, and Breyer, JJ., joined, and the opinion of the Court with respect to Part II-B-1, in which Stevens, Kennedy, Souter, Ginsburg, and Breyer, JJ., joined. Scalia, J., filed a dissenting opinion, in which Thomas, J., joined.

This case requires us to decide whether, and to what extent, the First Amendment protects independent contractors from the termination of at-will government contracts in retaliation for their exercise of the freedom of speech.

I

Under state law, Wabaunsee County, Kansas (County) is obliged to provide for the disposal of solid waste generated within its borders. In 1981, and, after renegotiation, in 1985, the County contracted with respondent Umbehr for him to be the exclusive hauler of trash for cities in the county at a rate specified in the contract. Each city was free to reject or, on 90 days' notice, to opt out of, the contract. By its terms, the contract between Umbehr and the County was automatically renewed annually unless either party terminated it by giving notice at least 60 days before the end of the year or a renegotiation was instituted on 90 days' notice. Pursuant to the contract, Umbehr hauled trash for six of the County's seven cities from 1985 to 1991 on an exclusive and uninterrupted basis.

During the term of his contract, Umbehr was an outspoken critic of petitioner, the Board of County Commissioners of Wabaunsee County (Board), the three-member governing body of the County. Umbehr spoke at the Board's meetings, and wrote critical letters and editorials in local newspapers regarding the County's landfill user rates, the cost of obtaining official documents from the County, alleged violations by the Board of the Kansas Open Meetings Act, the County's alleged mismanagement of taxpayers' money, and other topics. His allegations of violation of the Kansas Open Meetings Act were vindicated in a consent decree signed by the Board's members....

The Board's members allegedly took Umbehr's criticism badly, threatening the official county newspaper with censorship for publishing his writings. In 1990, they voted, 2-to-1, to terminate (or prevent the automatic renewal of) Umbehr's contract with the County. That attempt at termination failed because of a technical defect, but in 1991, the Board succeeded in terminating Umbehr's contract, again by a 2-to-1 vote. Umbehr subsequently negotiated new contracts with five of the six cities that he had previously served.

• • •

IIA

• • •

[P]recedents have long since rejected Justice Holmes' famous dictum, that a policeman "may have a constitutional right to talk politics, but he has no constitutional right to be a policeman."...Recognizing that

> constitutional violations may arise from the deterrent, or "chilling," effect of governmental [efforts] that fall short of a direct prohibition against the exercise of First Amendment rights,

...our modern "unconstitutional conditions" doctrine holds that the government "may not deny a benefit to a person on a basis that infringes his constitutionally protected...freedom of speech" even if he has no entitlement to that benefit....We have held that government workers are constitutionally protected from dismissal for refusing to take an oath regarding their political affiliation..., for publicly or privately criticizing their employer's policies..., for expressing hostility to prominent political figures..., or, except where political affiliation may reasonably be considered an appropriate job qualification, for supporting or affiliating with a particular political party....

While protecting First Amendment freedoms, we have, however, acknowledged that the First Amendment does not create property or tenure rights, and does not guarantee absolute freedom of speech.... We have, therefore, "consistently given greater deference to government predictions of harm used to justify restriction of employee speech than to predictions of harm used to justify restrictions on the speech of the public at large."...

The parties each invite us to differentiate between independent contractors and employees. The Board urges us not to "extend" the First Amendment rights of government employees to contractors. Umbehr, joined by the Solicitor General as *amicus curiae*, contends that, on proof of viewpoint-based retaliation for contractors' political speech, the government should be required to justify its actions as narrowly tailored to serve a compelling state interest.

Both parties observe that independent contractors in general, and Umbehr in particular, work at a greater remove from government officials than do most government employees. In the Board's view, the key feature of an independent contractor's contract is that it does not give the government the right to supervise and control the details of how work is done. The Board argues that the lack of day-to-day control accentuates the government's need to have the work done by someone it trusts.... Umbehr, on the other hand, argues that the government interests in maintaining harmonious working environments and relationships recognized in our government employee cases are attenuated where the contractor does not work at the government's workplace and does not interact daily with government officers and employees. He also points out that to the extent that he is publicly perceived as an *independent* contractor, any government concern that his political statements will be confused with the government's political positions is mitigated....

• • •

Umbehr's claim that speech threatens the government's interests as contractor less than its interests as employer will also inform the application of the *Pickering*★ test. Umbehr is correct that if the Board had exercised sovereign power against him as a citizen in response to his political speech, it would be required to demonstrate that its action was narrowly tailored to serve a compelling governmental interest. But in this case, as in government employment cases, the Board exercised contractual power, and its interests as a public service provider, including its interest in being free from intensive judicial supervision of its daily management functions, are potentially implicated. Deference is therefore due to the government's reasonable assessments of its interests *as contractor.*

We therefore see no reason to believe that proper application of the *Pickering* balancing test cannot accommodate the differences between employees and independent contractors. There is ample reason to believe that such a nuanced approach, which recognizes the variety of interests that may arise in independent contractor cases, is superior to a brightline rule distinguishing independent contractors from employees. The brightline rule proposed by the Board and the dissent would give the government *carte blanche* to terminate independent contractors for exercising First Amendment rights. And that brightline rule would leave First Amendment rights unduly dependent on whether state law labels a government service provider's contract as a contract of employment or a contract for services, a distinction which is at best a very poor proxy for the interests at stake....

• • •

B2

In sum, neither the Board nor Umbehr have persuaded us that there is a "difference of constitutional magnitude"...between independent contractors and employees in this context.

★Editors' note: *Pickering v. Board of Education,* 391 U.S. 563 (1968), held that the interests of a public employee in commenting on matters of public concern must be balanced with the interests of the government in providing efficient public services.

Independent government contractors are similar in most relevant respects to government employees, although both the speaker's and the government's interests are typically—though not always—somewhat less strong in the independent contractor case. We therefore conclude that the same form of balancing analysis should apply to each.

III

Because the courts below assumed that Umbehr's termination (or nonrenewal) was in retaliation for his protected speech activities, and because they did not pass on the balance between the government's interests and the free speech interests at stake, our conclusion that independent contractors do enjoy some First Amendment protection requires that we affirm the Tenth Circuit's decision to remand the case. To prevail, Umbehr must show that the termination of his contract was motivated by his speech on a matter of public concern, an initial showing that requires him to prove more than the mere fact that he criticized the Board members before they terminated him. If he can make that showing, the Board will have a valid defense if it can show, by a preponderance of

the evidence, that, in light of their knowledge, perceptions and policies at the time of the termination, the Board members would have terminated the contract regardless of his speech.... The Board will also prevail if it can persuade the District Court that the County's legitimate interests as contractor, deferentially viewed, outweigh the free speech interests at stake. And, if Umbehr prevails, evidence that the Board members discovered facts after termination that would have led to a later termination anyway, and evidence of mitigation of his loss by means of his subsequent contracts with the cities, would be relevant in assessing what remedy is appropriate.

Finally, we emphasize the limited nature of our decision today. Because Umbehr's suit concerns the termination of a preexisting commercial relationship with the government, we need not address the possibility of suits by bidders or applicants for new government contracts who cannot rely on such a relationship.

Subject to these limitations and caveats, however, we recognize the right of independent government contractors not to be terminated for exercising their First Amendment rights....

Discussion Questions

1. In a companion case to *Umbehr, O'Hare Truck, Inc. v. City of Northlake,* 518 U.S. 712 (1996), the Court extended First Amendment protection to a tow truck operator who had a preexisting commercial relationship with the city, but no contract. (The city used a "rotation list" for calling tow trucks as needed to clear vehicles from its roadways.) Do you think similar protection will be available to ordinary suppliers and/or bidders on government contracts? Why? What would the implications of such an extension be?

2. Can you think of an explanation that the Board could use to prevail in its contest with Umbehr?

3. One of the reasons for privatizing is to gain flexibility in dealing with service providers. How does the *Umbehr* decision affect governmental flexibility in terminating contractors?

Case 3.4
Private State Actors' Liability for Constitutional Torts

RICHARDSON v. McKNIGHT
Argued March 19, 1997
Decided June 23, 1997
117 S. Ct. 2100

JUSTICE BREYER delivered the opinion of the Court.

The issue before us is whether prison guards who are employees of a private prison management firm are entitled to a qualified immunity from suit by prisoners charging a violation of 42 U.S.C. § 1983. We hold that they are not.

I

Ronnie Lee McKnight, a prisoner at Tennessee's South Central Correctional Center (SCCC), brought this federal constitutional tort action against two prison guards, Darryl Richardson and John Walker. He says the guards injured him by placing upon him extremely tight physical restraints, thereby unlawfully "subject[ing]" him "to the deprivation of" a right "secured by the Constitution" of the United States....Richardson and Walker asserted a qualified immunity from § 1983 lawsuits...and moved to dismiss the action. The District Court noted that Tennessee had "privatized" the management of a number of its correctional facilities, and that consequently a private firm, not the state government, employed the guards....The court held that, because they worked for a private company, rather than the government, the law did not grant the guards immunity from suit. It therefore denied the guards' motion to dismiss....

• • •

II

B

History does *not* reveal a "firmly rooted" tradition of immunity applicable to privately employed prison guards....*Government*-employed prison guards may have enjoyed a kind of immunity defense arising out of their status as public employees at common law.

• • •

Our research, including the sources that the parties have cited, reveals that, in the 19th century (and earlier), sometimes private contractors and sometimes government itself carried on prison management activities. And we have...found no conclusive evidence of an historical tradition of immunity for private parties carrying out these functions. History therefore does not provide significant support for the immunity claim....

C

Whether the immunity doctrine's *purposes* warrant immunity for private prison guards presents a closer question. *Wyatt* [*v. Cole*, 1992], consistent with earlier precedent, described the doctrine's purposes as protecting "government's ability to perform its traditional functions" by providing immunity where "necessary to preserve" the ability of government officials

> to serve the public good or to ensure that talented candidates were not deterred by the threat of damages suits from entering public service.

...Earlier precedent described immunity as protecting the public from unwarranted timidity on the part of public officials by, for example, "encouraging the vigorous exercise of official authority,"...by contributing to "'principled and fearless decisionmaking,'"...and by responding to the concern that threatened liability would, in Judge Hand's words, "'dampen the ardour of all but the most resolute, or the most irresponsible'" public officials....

The guards argue that those purposes support immunity whether their employer is private or public....

[This Court] never has held that the mere performance of a governmental function could make the difference between unlimited § 1983 liability and qualified immunity..., especially for a private person who performs a job without government supervision or direction. Indeed a purely functional approach bristles with difficulty, particularly since, in many areas, government and private industry may engage in fundamentally similar activities, ranging from electricity production, to waste disposal, to even mail delivery.

Petitioners' argument also overlook[s] certain important differences that, from an immunity perspective, are critical. First, the most important special government immunity-producing concern—unwarranted timidity—is less likely present, or at least is not special, when a private company subject to competitive market pressures operates a prison. Competitive pressures mean not only that a firm whose guards are too aggressive will face damages that raise costs, thereby threatening its replacement, but also that a firm whose guards are too timid will face threats of replacement by other firms with records that demonstrate their ability to do both a safer and a more effective job.

These ordinary marketplace pressures are present here. The private prison guards before us work for a large, multistate private prison management firm....

In other words, marketplace pressures provide the private firm with strong incentives to avoid overly timid, insufficiently vigorous, unduly fearful, or "nonarduous" employee job performance. And the contract's provisions—including those that might permit employee indemnification and avoid many civil service restrictions—grant this private firm freedom to respond to those market pressures through rewards and penalties that operate directly upon its employees....To this extent, the employees before us resemble those of other private firms and differ from government employees.

This is not to say that government employees, in their efforts to act within constitutional limits, will always, or often, sacrifice the otherwise effective performance of their duties. Rather, it is to say that government employees typically act within a *different* system. They work within a system that is responsible through elected officials to voters who, when they vote, rarely consider the performance of individual subdepartments or civil servants specifically and in detail. And that system is often characterized by multi-department civil service rules that, while providing employee security, may limit the incentives or the ability of individual departments or supervisors flexibly to reward, or to punish, individual employees. Hence, a judicial determination that "effectiveness" concerns warrant special immunity-type protection in respect to this latter (governmental) system does not prove its need in respect to the former. Consequently, we can find no *special* immunity-related need to encourage vigorous performance.

Second, "privatization" helps to meet the immunity-related need "to ensure that talented candidates" are "not deterred by the threat of damages suits from entering public service."...It does so in part because of the comprehensive insurance coverage requirements just mentioned. The insurance increases the likelihood of employee indemnification, and, to that extent, reduces the employment-discouraging fear of unwarranted liability potential applicants face. Because privatization law also frees the private prison management firm from many civil service law restraints..., it permits the private firm, unlike a government department, to offset any increased employee liability risk with higher pay or extra benefits. In respect to this second government immunity-related purpose then, it is difficult to find a *special* need for immunity, for the guards' employer can operate like other private firms; it need not operate like a typical government department.

Third, lawsuits may well "'distrac[t]'" these employees "'from their...duties'"..., but the risk of "distraction" alone cannot be sufficient grounds for an immunity. Our qualified immunity cases do not contemplate the complete elimination of lawsuit-based distractions....And it is significant that, here, Tennessee law reserves certain important discretionary tasks—those related to prison discipline, to parole, and to good time—for state officials....Given a continual and conceded need for deterring constitutional violations and our sense that the firm's tasks are not enormously different in respect to their importance from various other publicly important tasks carried out by private firms, we are not persuaded that the threat of distracting workers from their duties is enough virtually by itself to justify providing an immunity....

D

Our examination of history and purpose thus reveals nothing special enough about the job or about its organizational structure that would warrant providing these private prison guards with a governmental immunity. The job is one that private industry might, or might not, perform, and which history shows private firms did sometimes perform without relevant immunities. The organizational structure is one subject to the ordinary competitive pressures that normally help private firms adjust their behavior in response to the incentives that tort suits provide—pressures not necessarily present in government departments....

III

. . .

[W]e have answered the immunity question narrowly, in the context in which it arose. That context is one in which a private firm, systematically organized to assume a major lengthy administrative task (managing an institution) with limited direct supervision by the government, undertakes that task for profit and potentially in competition with other firms. The case does not involve a private individual briefly associated with a government body, serving as an adjunct to government in an essential government activity, or acting under close official supervision.

. . .

Justice Scalia, with whom the Chief Justice, Justice Kennedy and Justice Thomas join, dissenting.

. . .

Today's decision says that two sets of prison guards who are indistinguishable in the ultimate source of their authority over prisoners, indistinguishable in the powers that they possess over prisoners, and indistinguishable in the duties that they owe towards prisoners, are to be treated quite differently in the matter of their financial liability. The only sure effect of today's decision—and the only purpose, as far as I can tell—is that it will artificially raise the cost of privatizing prisons. Whether this will cause privatization to be prohibitively expensive, or instead simply divert state funds that could have been saved or spent on additional prison services, it is likely that taxpayers and prisoners will suffer as a consequence. Neither our precedent, nor the historical foundations of § 1983, nor the policies underlying § 1983, support this result.

I respectfully dissent.

Discussion Questions

1. What are the implications of the Court's decision for privatization of public functions? If you were managing a private prison, how would you respond to the Court's decision?

2. If public employees are responsible to political appointees and the electorate, why are the private guards, whose contracts are subject to renewal, not equally responsible?

3. The dissent claims that the Court's decision will raise the cost of privatizing prisons. Why might privatized, for-profit prisons be less expensive to operate than governmental ones? Based on your answer, do you agree with the Court that qualified immunity should not be extended to private prison guards?

FOUR

Decisionmaking

Decisionmaking is a central administrative activity. It has been the focus of systematic study at least since the 1940s, when Herbert Simon wrote, in his classic work *Administrative Behavior*, that "The task of 'deciding' pervades the entire administrative organization...."[1] It is difficult to think of public administrative activities that do not require decisionmaking of some sort. Budgeting, strategic planning, personnel administration, and organizing administrative structures and work processes are completely infused with the need to make decisions. At a broader level, public administrators must make decisions regarding the interpretations of statutes and court rulings. Many agencies are charged with rulemaking and adjudication, both of which are decisionmaking processes. The implementation of agency missions also requires a great deal of decisionmaking: How should broad legal mandates or objectives be applied to specific cases? How strictly should a regulation be enforced? Where should a field office or a military base be located? To whom should a contract be let? When should the agency pursue its objectives through litigation? When should it settle out of court? Which of the multitude of private organizations subject to agency jurisdiction should be inspected or audited? More problematically, if the agency lacks the resources to enforce its regulations universally—as so many do—on what basis should selective enforcement and nonenforcement occur? These are some of the kinds of decisions administrators face daily.

Because public administration requires decisionmaking, administrators *must* exercise considerable discretion, whether in formulating public policies, developing the means to achieve their objectives, or implementing them. A particularly vivid example of exercising discretion occurs when officials decide not to enforce a law in a specific instance or not to pursue a case. Decisions not to act are often difficult or impossible to challenge.[2]

The exercise of administrative discretion is in general tension with the Constitution's firm commitment to the rule of law. In fact, as the fledgling American administrative state grew during the early part of the twentieth century, a very influential legal scholar, Roscoe Pound, thought that administrative adjudication was "one of those reversions to justice *without* law."[3] More recently, Theodore Lowi, a leading political scientist, has argued that the administrative state is essentially lawless.[4] He advocates a new regime of "juridical democracy"—that is, lawmaking by the legislature and an end to broad delegations of legislative authority to administrative agencies.

This chapter focuses on three major types of administrative decisionmaking and how the dynamic of each is constrained by constitutional requirements. It notes how the New Public Management's effort to reinvent public administration embraces all three. The cases presented illustrate constitutional pitfalls inherent in each of the decisionmaking models. The specific areas of law with which they deal are important to constitutional competence as well, but the primary focus should be on the shortcomings of *how* the administrative decisions were made. Much of the rest of the book deals more directly with the substantive conflicts between administrative values and contemporary constitutional law.

Model I: Intuition

Intuition can be defined as the "direct perception of the truth or fact, independent of any reasoning process" or "a keen and quick insight."[5] Everyone relies on intuition on occasion, especially when dealing with other people. We often reach quick judgments or feel as though we "just know" something, even though we cannot explain how in rational or logical terms. Of course, sometimes intuitive judgments are wrong, just as may be the most formally reasoned deductive or inductive conclusions.[6] Although public administrators in a wide variety of settings may use intuition from time to time, those who are engaged in "street-level" administration must rely on it constantly in order to do their jobs properly.

In *Terry v. Ohio* (1968), Chief Justice Earl Warren considered "the role of the Fourth Amendment in the confrontation on the street between the citizen and the policeman...."[7] Later, in 1980, Michael Lipsky's *Street-Level Bureaucracy* formalized the "street-level" concept and brought it to the forefront of public administrative study.[8] Lipsky defines street-level bureaucrats in the following terms:

> public service workers who interact directly with citizens in the course of their jobs, and who have substantial discretion in the execution of their work....Typical street-level bureaucrats are teachers, police officers and other law enforcement personnel, social workers, [trial] judges, public lawyers, and other court officers, health workers, and many other public employees who grant access to government programs and provide services within them.[9]

He emphasizes the importance of street-level administrators' decisions, arguing that

> when taken together the individual decisions of these workers become, or add up to, agency policy. Whether government policy is to deliver "goods"—such as welfare or public housing—or to confer status—such as "criminal" or "mentally ill"—the discretionary actions of public employees are the benefits and sanctions of government programs or determine access to government rights and benefits.[10]

Among the major characteristics of street-level bureaucrats are that they (a) constantly interact with members of the public in face-to-face encounters; (b) have considerable independence, as they often work in the absence of direct visual or close proximate supervision and because a great deal of information about their conduct is supplied by the street-level personnel themselves; (c) are in a position to have a great impact on the individuals on whom they act, or choose not to act; (d) tend to interact with "clients" or "customers" who would prefer not to have to go through the encounter even though they may want a benefit, such as public housing or food stamps, that might result from it; (e) work with heavy case-loads in an environment of scarce resources and, sometimes, one in which physical and psychological threats are common; (f) have limited control over their involuntary clients, such as prisoners or mental health patients, who may not be well socialized to accept administrative authority or to deal effectively with administrative processes; and (g) face difficulties in adequately measuring their performance.

Street-level administrators often rely almost entirely on intuition in exercising discretion. The following illustration is from the testimony in court of a police officer who stopped a car at a roadblock because he thought it was being used to transport marihuana:

Q   Would you tell the Court, would you describe to the Court what their appearance was on the day in question that led you to believe that they were dope haulers....

A   Well, they just look like dope haulers.

Q   Okay.

A   I got my own way of telling...

Q   ...When in your State Police School did they tell you how to identify dope hualers?

A   No, like I said, it comes with experience.

Q   I see. Was it their age?

A   No, I didn't know how old they was.

Q   Okay, was it the length of their hair?

A   No.

Q   Was it the clothes they were wearing?

A   No. It was the way they acted. Like I said, I got my own way of telling which you wouldn't have.

Q   Okay.

A   You know, I can't explain it to you.[11]

Even though the officer could not explain why he thought the car was carrying marihuana, he was correct in his assessment. But was he constitutional?

There is perhaps no proposition more fundamental to democratic constitutionalism in the United States than that government will be based on and subordinate to the rule of law. Under Article VI, the Constitution is the "supreme Law of the Land." Governmental officials at all levels are required to swear or affirm their allegiance to it. All officials, including the president and his closest aides, are subject to constitutional and legal restrictions. Nobody is in any sense considered to be "above the law." This is why so many Americans consider events such as Watergate, the Iran-Contra affair, and allegations of presidential obstruction of justice to constitute serious threats to American governance. But it is not always easy to square the rule of law with the exercise of unbridled discretion by public administrators or other government officials. Their actions should be directed by laws and rules, not personal judgments, prejudices, or intuition. As Justice William O. Douglas once expressed it, "if the individual is no longer to be sovereign, if the police can pick him up whenever they do not like the cut of his jib, if they can 'seize' and 'search' him in their discretion, we enter a new regime."[12]

The dilemma is that on the one hand, in order to do their jobs—indeed, sometimes to survive—street-level personnel must rely on their intuition (and they often are correct in so doing); while on the other hand, intuition, by its very nature, entails very broad discretion that cannot be assessed in rational terms by higher-level officials or the courts. For every car hauling marihuana that is stopped by a particular police officer, an unknown number of others escape his or her detection. Others are mistakenly stopped, possibly in violation of their occupants' rights. *Delaware v. Prouse* (1979), Case 4.1, analyzes the constitutional problem with intuitive decision making that infringes an individual's protected rights.

Model II: Rational Comprehensiveness

The rational-comprehensive decisionmaking model stands almost diametrically opposed to the exercise of intuition. It assumes that public administrators have the time, resources, and wherewithal to analyze logically and comprehensively when making decisions. Rational comprehensiveness is the preferred model of orthodox and managerially oriented public administration. It relies on theory and organizational features, such as specialization and formalization, to enhance the rationality of administrative decisions.[13]

Some version of rational-comprehensiveness is implicit or explicit in much of the policy analysis or policy science on which public managers rely. Large-scale social experiments may be the most scientific or pure form of rational-comprehensiveness in decisionmaking, since they are modeled to the extent feasible on the physical and biological sciences. Many social scientists view natural science as the appropriate model or paradigm for building strong prescriptive capability in the field of management.[14] However, the opportunities for social experiments are frequently circumscribed by their cost and the privacy, equal protection, and other constitutional and legal rights of the human subjects involved.[15] Consequently, rational-comprehensiveness often employs nonexperimental or quasi-experimental research designs.

Rational-comprehensive approaches emphasize finding and applying the right methods and techniques for problem solving and implementing solutions.[16] Performance measurement and program evaluations are particularly important tools for rational-comprehensive decisionmaking.[17] In 1993, Congress enacted the Government Performance and Results Act (GPRA), committing federal management to a form of rational-comprehensiveness in strategic planning, budgeting, implementation, and annual performance evaluation.[18] The act is a very large-scale effort to shift managerial attention from procedures to results. However, the implementation of many specific programs and systems, such as income maintenance and personnel, will necessarily continue to be informed by constitutional due process, equal protection, and other procedural safeguards.

In simplified form, the rational-comprehensive model involves the following steps. First, in making decisions the public manager must specify the objectives or ends of the public policy with which he or she is concerned. If the objectives are unclear, they should be clarified and expressed in operational terms—that is, in ways that can be observed and measured. For example, a policy that seeks to equalize employment opportunity is less operational than one that takes affirmative steps toward changing the social composition of a workforce because "opportunity" does not lend itself to precise observation or measurement. Of course, public managers do not have a free hand in determining policy objectives. They are constrained by culture, socialization, training, law, administrative regulations, hierarchical authority, jurisdictional specialization, and political factors, including constitutional checks and balances.

Second, once the objectives of public policy are established, various means for accomplishing them must be considered. In order to achieve the requisite comprehensiveness, virtually all the potential means that can be identified must be analyzed. Rational-comprehensiveness demands that the public manager try to project *all* the consequences of each of the alternative means under consideration. This may require heavy reliance on theory, since it is highly unlikely that all the potential means have at one time or another been tested and evaluated in practice. Analysis will often involve formulating fundamental assumptions about how people behave. It may also use simulations.

Third, the most appropriate means to the desired ends are chosen. Traditional public administrative theory favors the maximization of efficiency, economy, and effectiveness in the choice of means. When these core administrative values are not fully in harmony with one another, then some balance among them will be selected. The New Public Management (NPM) shares these values, but adds responsiveness to customers and the creation of valued services for them. Because public management is a governmental endeavor, attention must also be paid to political and legal values, such as representativeness and the protection of individual civil rights and liberties.

There has been a long-standing debate over whether the rational-comprehensive model can be widely used in American public administration.[19] The separation of powers and federalism create multiple power centers that are apt to promote different perspectives on any complex policy issue. In many cases, policy objectives are too unclear to be expressed in operational terms without losing significant political support for a program. Is the food stamp program for producers (farmers, food companies), transporters (trucking companies and railroads), retailers (supermarkets), consumers (recipients), or all of these interests? Nor do public managers necessarily have the time and resources to approach decisions in a dispassionate way and to engage in thorough analysis of the relative appropriateness of alternative means. More fundamentally, if one agrees with Simon that administrative rationality is "bounded," then the prospects for being fully, or even highly, rational are limited.[20]

The rational-comprehensive model can also run into problems from a constitutional perspective. Its reliance on theory, particularly social scientific theory, leads to the use of categories, such as female and male, as a means of understanding and predicting how people behave. Such categories are common in political analysis, where familiar terms include the "gender gap," and the "labor," "farm," "black," and "Hispanic" votes. But the Constitution looks toward the individual, not the group to which he or she belongs, in determining rights and liberties. Broad social scientific generalizations may be constitutionally problematic as a basis for public policy, because by their very nature they are not intended to apply equally to each individual. By definition, they do not attempt to treat individuals on their own merits (see Case 6.2, *Cleveland Board of Education v. LaFleur,* 1974). Moreover, equal protection analysis under the Fourteenth and Fifth Amendments is skeptical of governmental action that treats members of different social groups disparately. Case 4.3, *Craig v. Boren* (1976), even asserts that "proving broad sociological propositions by statistics is dubious business, and one that inevitably is in tension with the normative philosophy that underlies the Equal Protection Clause."[21]

Another difference between the rational-comprehensive model and constitutional law concerns the standard of rationality that makes a decision permissible. Here, rational-comprehensiveness may exceed the threshold for constitutionality. It implies that there is "one best way" to determine and implement any policy. That approach matches the "least restrictive alternative" and "narrow tailoring" requirements in the structure of substantive and equal protection rights, as discussed in Chapter 1. But as the Supreme Court explains in Case 4.2, *New Jersey v. T.L.O.* (1985), a much weaker standard of reasonableness is used for Fourth Amendment privacy (see also Case 6.4, *Vernonia School District 47 J v. Acton,* 1995). Similarly, reasonableness rather than rational-comprehensiveness is required by contemporary procedural due process and the "rough proportionality" standard under the Fifth Amendment's "takings" clause (see Chapter 1 and Cases 6.1 and 8.4, *Cleveland Board of Education v. Loudermill,* 1985, and *Dolan v. City of Tigard,* 1994). The reasonableness approach is very much in keeping with the NPM's effort to empower front line service providers to solve customer's problems.

Model III: Incrementalism

Incrementalism is a third common model of public managerial decisionmaking. It differs radically from the rational-comprehensive approach in its fundamental outlook. It assumes that the question for public administrators is more likely to be, "What should we do next?" rather than, "How should we maximize the attainment of our objectives?" Incrementalism proceeds step by step, often without a very clear or agreed-on objective, in an effort to use whatever resources are available to further a program's general mission. It recognizes that in a pluralistic political system characterized by fragmented power, the objectives of public policy must often necessarily be stated in vague and politically appealing terms in order to win sufficient support for a program or course of action. Lack of specificity is frequently the price of compromise and coalition building.

Examples abound. The Federal Communication Commission is charged with regulating the nation's airwaves in "the public convenience, interest, or necessity."[22] None of these terms has been precisely defined comprehensively, and each may conflict with the others on occasion. But such language enables a broad majority of legislators and interested parties to support governmental regulation of radio and television broadcasting without having to agree on specific regulatory standards. Instead, the overall content of regulatory policy is the outgrowth of numerous decisions by the FCC.

Likewise, the federal Occupational Safety and Health Act of 1970 calls on the Secretary of Labor to set a standard for toxic materials or harmful physical agents in the workplace "which most adequately assures, to the extent feasible" that no employee's health or functional capacity will be materially impaired.[23] After studying the act's legislative history, Justice William Rehnquist concluded that the feasibility standard "is a legislative mirage, appearing to some Members [of Congress] but not to others, and assuming any form desired by the beholder."[24] Not defined by Congress, the term's meaning develops incrementally as the product of Occupational Safety and Health Administration regulations weighing workers' well-being against the costs to industry, as well as subsequent litigation reviewing the agency's decisions.[25] At the first stage of an incremental decision, ends and means are treated as a package rather than as distinct from one another. Since the ends of public policies are viewed as ill-defined and sometimes cannot be defined without jeopardizing political support, the decisionmaker considers some plausible steps that might be taken to improve the conditions for which the program under his or her jurisdiction bears responsibility. The decisionmaker recognizes that alternative steps may ultimately lead to different definitions of what the general policy will be.

After a few possible courses of action are identified and considered, one is selected. The main criterion is likely to be agreement or consensus among those concerned that the proposed step is desirable. Since the incremental approach is generally sensitive to politics, a decision that generates support will be viewed as "good," whereas one that begets substantial opposition will typically be avoided. Again, the model enables concerned interests to agree on the next move even though they may differ significantly in their understandings of the overall policy's proper objectives.

Analysis tends to be more limited in the incremental approach than in the rational-comprehensive model. A few means-ends packages are considered. One that is *satisfactory* is chosen. Little or no effort is made to reach an optimal decision that maximizes all the pertinent values. Moreover, in practice, reliance on theory is downgraded because incrementalism does not seek to be comprehensive, to maximize, or to predict the long-term consequences of decisions. Policy grows out of a succession of choices among limited means-ends packages that can usually be corrected whenever it appears to be on the wrong course.

Like the intuitive and rational-comprehensive models, the incremental approach has some political and constitutional pitfalls. By definition, it is conservative because its effort to change the status quo is incremental. Consequently, it is not suited to decisions regarding the adoption of fundamentally new policy directions or large-scale innovations. Since it is not comprehensive, it may neglect important political values and policy alternatives. Proceeding step by step, without a map, can lead decisionmakers to an unexpected (and undesirable) place.

Moreover, if an incremental decisionmaking process fails to take constitutional values into account in selecting its steps, the resulting policy may be unconstitutional. This possibility is illustrated by Case 4.4, *Hawkins v. Town of Shaw* (1971), the last case presented in this chapter. It deals with a pattern of incrementalism in which each individual decision the town made in developing its infrastructure and economic base *might* have been constitutional and sensible on its own merits. But, taken together, the net result of a series of the town's decisions was such a broad disparity in public spending between the town's white and African American neighborhoods as to violate the Equal Protection Clause of the Fourteenth Amendment. Similarly, it is easy to conceive of a series of incremental decisions maintaining de facto racial segregation in public schools and constitutionally inadequate conditions in public mental health facilities and prisons.[26]

New Public Management Decisionmaking

The NPM makes use of all three types of decisionmaking. Because it is results oriented, the NPM leans toward rational-comprehensiveness in the establishment of objectives and missions for public programs that are clear, coherent, and subject to performance measurement. Ill-defined missions like the FCC's or OSHA's are anathema to the NPM. When it is difficult to specify results, administrative activity will often focus on inputs and procedures rather than outcomes.

Once clear objectives are set, the NPM favors the use of marketlike dynamics to achieve them. Agencies should be run in a businesslike fashion. They should sometimes compete with one another or with private firms. Where practical, they should generate at least some of their revenues through user fees, vouchers, or other means. Agencies should identify their customers and be responsive to them. For the NPM, customer satisfaction is a generic performance measure.

Acting like firms in a market requires both rational-comprehensive and incremental decisionmaking. Rational-comprehensiveness is manifested in strategic planning and goal setting aimed at achieving results and enhancing cost-effectiveness. It is also a component of NPM entrepreneurship that leads agencies continually to enhance their value to society. At the same time, being customer-driven requires incremental adjustments to satisfy customers' expectations and demands. In sum,

> Effective, entrepreneurial governments insist on customer satisfaction. They listen carefully to their customers—using surveys, focus groups, and the like. They restructure their basic operations to meet customers' needs. And they use market dynamics such as competition and customer choice to create incentives that drive their employees to put customers first.[27]

At the level of frontline service provision, the NPM seeks to empower employees "to use their creative judgment as they offer service to customers and solve problems."[28] Empowered employees can also help redesign work flows and processes. Presumably, empowerment entails both incremental and intuitive decisionmaking. Much of the organizational change that flows from it will be in the form of incremental adjustments. But, as noted in the discussion of street-level administration, intuition is sometimes a key factor in successfully dealing with customers. Embracing empowerment should increase its acceptability as a basis for decisionmaking in public administration.

Conclusion

Public management involves matters of art, science, and craft.[29] Each places greater reliance on a different mix of the three decisionmaking models. Management typically prefers science; art embraces intuition; craft relies heavily on incrementalism and intuition, but is also informed by science.

The cases that follow add another level of complexity. When making decisions, public managers must also be sensitive to constitutional standards and values. *Delaware v. Prouse* explains why intuition alone will almost always be an unconstitutional basis for taking action that infringes on an individual's constitutional rights. Meaningful judicial review of alleged violations of the Constitution requires that administrators provide reasons for their actions. *New Jersey v. T.L.O.* defines a minimal threshold of rationality for constitutional purposes. When rights are at stake decisions must be based on common sense, if not more, rather than "an inchoate and unparticularized suspicion or 'hunch.'"[30] *Craig v. Boren* shows the difficulties that broad social scientific generalizations about group behavior can present in terms of the Constitution's guarantee of equal protection of the laws. *Hawkins v. Town of Shaw* illustrates how unchecked incrementalism can lead to unconstitutional results.

In considering these cases, it is useful to think about other ways in which the administrative decisions they involve could have been made. Each case is followed by a series of discussion questions intended to facilitate a deeper exploration of each of the decisionmaking models and the constitutional constraints on them. The next chapter, on administrative effectiveness, augments the analysis of decisionmaking by considering the problem of selecting constitutional administrative means for implementing objectives.

Notes

1. Herbert Simon, *Administrative Behavior,* 2nd ed. (New York: Free Press, 1957), p. 1. (Originally copyrighted in 1945.)

2. *Armstrong v. United States,* 116 S.Ct. 1480 (1996); *Heckler v. Chaney,* 476 U.S. 821 (1985).

3. Roscoe Pound, "Justice According to Law," *Columbia Law Review,* vol. 14 (1914):1, at p. 18.

4. Theodore Lowi, *The End of Liberalism,* 2nd ed. (New York: W.W. Norton, 1979).

5. *Random House Dictionary* (New York: Random House, 1980).

6. Jonathan Baron, *Judgment Misguided: Intuition and Error in Public Decision Making* (Cambridge, U.K.: Oxford University Press, 1998).

7. *Terry v. Ohio,* 392 U.S. 1, 4 (1968).

8. Michael Lipsky, *Street-Level Bureaucracy* (New York: Russell Sage, 1980).

9. Ibid., p. 3.

10. Ibid.

11. *New Mexico v. Bloom,* 561 P.2d 925, 930 (1976).

12. *Terry v. Ohio,* 392 U.S. 1, 39 (1968), dissent.

13. See Charles Perrow, *Complex Organizations,* 3rd ed. (New York: Random House, 1986).

14. See Jay Shafritz, ed., *The International Encyclopedia of Public Policy and Administration* (Boulder, CO: Westview Press, 1997).

15. See David H. Greenberg and Mark Shroder, *The Digest of Social Experiments* (Washington, DC: Urban Institute, 1997).

16. Peter J. Haas and J. Fred Springer, *Applied Policy Research* (New York: Garland, 1998).

17. Evert Vedung, *Public Policy and Program Evaluation* (New Brunswick, NJ: Transaction Publishers, 1997).

18. U.S. General Accounting Office, *Managing for Results: The Statutory Framework for Improving Federal Management and Effectiveness* (Washington, DC: U.S. General Accounting Office, 1997).

19. See Charles Lindblom, "The Science of 'Muddling Through,'" *Public Administration Review,* vol. 19 (Spring 1959): 79. See also Deborah Stone, *Policy Paradox: The Art of Political Decision Making,* 2nd ed. (New York: W.W. Norton, 1997).

20. Herbert Simon, *Models of Man* (New York: Wiley, 1957).

21. *Craig v. Boren,* 429 U.S. 190, 204 (1976).

22. Federal Communications Act of 1934, 47 U.S.C. 151.

23. Stat. 1590, 1594 (1970).

24. *Industrial Union Department, AFL-CIO v. American Petroleum Institute,* 448 U.S. 607, 681 (1980), concurring opinion.

25. Ibid., and *American Textile Manufacturers Institute v. Donovan,* 452 U.S. 490 (1981).

26. See *Swann v. Charlotte-Mecklenburg Board of Education*, 403 U.S. 912 (1971); *Wyatt v. Stickney* 325 F. Supp. 781 (1971) (Case 8.1); *Rhodes v. Chapman*, 452 U.S. 337 (1981).

27. Al Gore, *From Red Tape to Results: Creating a Government That Works Better & Costs Less* (Washington, DC: U.S. Government Printing Office, 1993), p. 6.

28. Ibid., p. 71.

29. Lawrence E. Lynn, Jr., *Public Management As Art, Science, and Profession* (Chatham, NJ: Chatham House, 1996); George Berkley, *The Craft of Public Administration*, 4th ed. (Dubuque, IA: William C. Brown, 1988).

30. *New Jersey v. T.L.O.*, 469 U.S. 325, 346 (1985).

Additional Reading

Baron, Jonathan. *Judgment Misguided: Intuition and Error in Public Decision Making.* Cambridge, U.K.: Oxford University Press, 1998.

Lindblom, Charles E. "The Science of 'Muddling Through,'" *Public Administration Review,* 19 (Spring 1959), 79–88.

Simon, Herbert. *Administrative Behavior.* 3rd ed. New York: Free Press, 1976.

Stone, Deborah. *The Policy Paradox: The Art of Political Decision Making.* 2nd ed. New York: W.W. Norton, 1997.

Case 4.1
Administrative Intuition

DELAWARE v. PROUSE
Argued January 17, 1979
Decided March 27, 1979
440 US 648

MR. JUSTICE WHITE delivered the opinion of the Court.

The question is whether it is unreasonable seizure under the Fourth and Fourteenth Amendments to stop an automobile, being driven on a public highway, for the purpose of checking the driving license of the operator and the registration of the car, where there is neither probable cause to believe nor reasonable suspicion that the car is being driven contrary to the laws governing the operation of motor vehicles or that either the car or any of its occupants is subject to seizure or detention in connection with the violation of other applicable law.

I

At 7:20 p.m. on November 30, 1976, a New Castle County, Del., patrolman in a police cruiser stopped the automobile occupied by respondent. The patrolman smelled marihuana smoke as he was walking toward the stopped vehicle, and he seized marihuana in plain view on the car floor. Respondent was subsequently indicted for illegal possession of a controlled substance. At a hearing on respondent's motion to suppress the marihuana seized as a result of the stop, the patrolman testified that prior to stopping the vehicle he had observed neither traffic or equipment violations nor any suspicious activity, and that he made the stop only in order to check the driver's license and registration. The patrolman was not acting pursuant to any standards, guidelines or procedures pertaining to document spot checks, promulgated by either his department or the State Attorney General. Characterizing the stop as "routine," the patrolman explained, "I saw the car in the area and wasn't answering any complaints, so I decided to pull them off."...The trial court granted the motion to suppress, finding the stop and detention to have been wholly capricious and therefore violative of the Fourth Amendment.

The Delaware Supreme Court affirmed, noting first that "[t]he issue of the legal validity of systematic, roadblock-type stops of a number of vehicles for license and vehicle registration check is *not* now before the Court,"...The court held that "a random stop of a motorist in the absence of specific articulable facts which justify the stop by indicating a reasonable suspicion that a violation of the law has occurred is constitutionally impermissible and violative of the Fourth and Fourteenth Amendments to the United States Constitution."...We granted certiorari to resolve the conflict between this decision, which is in accord with decisions in five other jurisdictions, and the contrary determination in six jurisdictions that the Fourth Amendment does not prohibit the kind of automobile stop that occurred here....

• • •

III

The Fourth and Fourteenth Amendments are implicated in this case because stopping an automobile and detaining its occupants constitute a "seizure" within the meaning of those Amendments, even though the purpose of the stop is limited and the resulting detention quite brief....The essential purpose of the proscriptions in the Fourth Amendment is to impose a standard of "reasonableness" upon the exercise of discretion by government officials, including law enforcement agents, in order "'to safeguard the privacy and security of individuals against arbitrary invasions....'" ...Thus, the permissibility of a particular law enforcement practice is judged by balancing its intrusion on the individual's Fourth Amendment interests against its promotion of legitimate governmental interests. Implemented in this manner, the reasonableness standard usually requires, at a minimum, that the facts upon which an intrusion is based be capable of measurement against "an objective standard," whether this be probable cause or a less stringent test. In those situations in which the balance of interests precludes insistence upon "some quantum of individualized suspicion," other safeguards are generally relied upon to assure that the individual's reasonable expectation of privacy is not "subject to the discretion of the official in the field.".…

In this case, however, the State of Delaware urges that patrol officers be subject to no constraints in deciding which automobiles shall be stopped for a license and registration check because the State's interest in discretionary spot checks as a means of ensuring the safety of its roadways outweighs the resulting intrusion on the privacy and security of the persons detained.

• • •

V

But the State of Delaware urges that even if discretionary spot checks such as occurred in this case intrude upon motorists as much as or more than do the roving patrols held impermissible in Brignoni-Ponce,* these stops are reasonable under the Fourth Amendment because the State's interest in the practice as a means of promoting public safety upon its roads more than outweighs the intrusion entailed. Although the record discloses no statistics concerning the extent of the problem of lack of highway safety, in Delaware or in the Nation as a whole, we are aware of the danger to life and property posed by vehicular traffic and of the difficulties that even a cautious and an experienced driver may encounter. We agree that the States have a vital interest in ensuring that only those qualified to do so are permitted to operate motor vehicles, that these vehicles are fit for safe operation, and hence that licensing, registration, and vehicle inspection requirements are being observed. Automobile licenses are issued periodically to evidence that the drivers holding them are sufficiently familiar with the rules of the road and are physically qualified to operate a motor vehicle. The registration requirement and, more pointedly, the related annual inspection requirement in Delaware are designed to keep dangerous automobiles off the road. Unques-

tionably, these provisions, properly administered, are essential elements in a highway safety program. Furthermore, we note that the State of Delaware requires a minimum amount of insurance coverage as a condition to automobile registration, implementing its legitimate interest in seeing to it that its citizens have protection when involved in a motor vehicle accident.

The question remains, however, whether in the service of these important ends the discretionary spot check is a sufficiently productive mechanism to justify the intrusion upon Fourth Amendment interests which such stops entail. On the record before us, that question must be answered in the negative. Given the alternative mechanisms available, both those in use and those that might be adopted, we are unconvinced that the incremental contribution to highway safety of the random spot check justifies the practice under the Fourth Amendment.

The foremost method of enforcing traffic and vehicle safety regulations, it must be recalled, is acting upon observed violations. Vehicle stops for traffic violations occur countless times each day; and on these occasions, licenses and registration papers are subject to inspection and drivers without them will be ascertained. Furthermore, drivers without licenses are presumably the less safe drivers whose propensities may well exhibit themselves. Absent some empirical data to the contrary, it must be assumed that finding an unlicensed driver among those who commit traffic violations is a much more likely event than finding an unlicensed driver by choosing randomly from the entire universe of drivers. If this were not so, licensing of drivers would hardly be an effective means of promoting roadway safety. It seems common sense that the percentage of all drivers on the road who are driving without a license is very small and that the number of licensed drivers who will be stopped in order to find one unlicensed operator will be large indeed. The contribution to highway safety made by discretionary stops selected from among drivers generally will therefore be marginal at best. Furthermore, and again absent something more than mere assertion to the contrary, we find it difficult to believe that the unlicensed driver would not be deterred by the possibility of being involved in a traffic violation or having some other experience calling for proof of his

*U.S. v. Brignoni-Ponce, 422 U.S. 873 (1975)—editors' note.

entitlement to drive but that he would be deterred by the possibility that he would be one of those chosen for a spot check. In terms of actually discovering unlicensed drivers or deterring them from driving, the spot check does not appear sufficiently productive to qualify as a reasonable law enforcement practice under the Fourth Amendment.

Much the same can be said about the safety aspects of automobiles as distinguished from drivers. Many violations of minimum vehicle-safety requirements are observable, and something can be done about them by the observing officer, directly and immediately. Furthermore, in Delaware, as elsewhere, vehicles must carry and display current license plates, which themselves evidence that the vehicle is properly registered; and, under Delaware law, to qualify for annual registration a vehicle must pass the annual safety inspection and be properly insured. It does not appear, therefore, that a stop of a Delaware-registered vehicle is necessary in order to ascertain compliance with the State's registration requirements; and because there is nothing to show that a significant percentage of automobiles from other States do not also require license plates indicating current registration, there is no basis for concluding that stopping even out-of-state cars for document checks substantially promotes the State's interest.

The marginal contribution to roadway safety possibly resulting from a system of spot checks cannot justify subjecting every occupant of every vehicle on the roads to a seizure—limited in magnitude compared to other intrusions but nonetheless constitutionally cognizable—at the unbridled discretion of law enforcement officials. To insist neither upon an appropriate factual basis for suspicion directed at a particular automobile nor upon some other substantial and objective standard or rule to govern the exercise of discretion "would invite intrusions upon constitutionally guaranteed rights based on nothing more substantial than inarticulate hunches...."...By hypothesis, stopping apparently safe drivers is necessary only because the danger presented by some drivers is not observable at the time of the stop. When there is not probable cause to believe that a driver is violating any one of the multitude of applicable traffic and equipment regulations—or other articulable basis amounting to reasonable suspi-

cion that the driver is unlicensed or his vehicle unregistered—we cannot conceive of any legitimate basis upon which a patrolman could decide that stopping a particular driver for a spot check would be more productive than stopping any other driver. This kind of standardless and unconstrained discretion is the evil the Court has discerned when in previous cases it has insisted that the discretion of the official in the field be circumscribed, at least to some extent....

VI

The "grave danger" of abuse of discretion... does not disappear simply because the automobile is subject to state regulation resulting in numerous instances of police-citizen contact....Only last Term we pointed out that "if the government intrudes...the privacy interest suffers whether the government's motivation is to investigate violations of criminal laws or breaches of other statutory or regulatory standards."...There are certain "relatively unique circumstances,"...in which consent to regulatory restrictions is presumptively concurrent with participation in the regulated enterprise.... Otherwise, regulatory inspections unaccompanied by any quantum of individualized, articulable suspicion must be undertaken pursuant to previously specified "neutral criteria."...

An individual operating or traveling in an automobile does not lose all reasonable expectation of privacy simply because the automobile and its use are subject to government regulation. Automobile travel is a basic, pervasive, and often necessary mode of transportation to and from one's home, workplace, and leisure activities. Many people spend more hours each day traveling in cars than walking on the streets. Undoubtedly, many find a greater sense of security and privacy in traveling in an automobile than they do in exposing themselves by pedestrian or other modes of travel. Were the individual subject to unfettered governmental intrusion every time he entered an automobile, the security guaranteed by the Fourth Amendment would be seriously circumscribed.... [P]eople are not shorn of all Fourth Amendment protection when they step from their homes onto the public sidewalks. Nor are they shorn of those interests when they step from the sidewalks into their automobiles.

VII

Accordingly, we hold that except in those situations in which there is at least articulable and reasonable suspicion that a motorist is unlicensed or that an automobile is not registered, or that either the vehicle or an occupant is otherwise subject to seizure for violation of law, stopping an automobile and detaining the driver in order to check his driver's license and the registration of the automobile are unreasonable under the Fourth Amendment. This holding does not preclude the State of Delaware or other States from developing methods for spot checks that involve less intrusion or that do not involve the unconstrained exercise of discretion. Questioning of all oncoming traffic at roadblock type stops is one possible alternative. We hold only that persons in automobiles on public roadways may not for that reason alone have their travel and privacy interfered with at the unbridled discretion of police officers....

Discussion Questions

1. It is difficult to ignore the fact that in *Prouse*, the police officer stopped a car in which a crime was occurring. In this sense, he was doing his job properly. The chances of randomly stopping someone smoking marihauna in a moving vehicle in Delaware must be extremely remote. Since the officer was unable to provide even an articulable suspicion that such a crime was taking place, it appears that his decision to stop Prouse was intuitive. Thus, the facts of the case suggest that the patrolman's intuition worked well. Yet, the Supreme Court's opinion prohibits sole reliance on intuition in such circumstances because it is neither articulable nor, by definition, reasonable. Do you think street-level administrators can do their jobs properly without relying on intuition? Under what circumstances would intuition seem most important? Least important? If you were the administrative supervisor of officers, such as the one in *Prouse*, how would you recommend that your subordinates become "constitutionally competent" while doing their jobs well?

2. In dissent, Justice Rehnquist pointed out that because Justice White's opinion would allow the States to stop *all* cars at roadblocks for license and registration checks, the majority's fundamental concern was with the exercise of discretionary authority by police, rather than the intrusiveness of the stops themselves. Indeed, in some ways stopping all motorists is more intrusive than stopping only some. Why does the majority have greater difficulty with discretionary stops than it does with comprehensive stops? Do you find its argument convincing?

3. Suppose the officer had decided to stop Prouse on the basis of a written profile of a motorist likely to be smoking marihuana. What questions would you raise in addressing the administrative utility and constitutionality of reliance on such a profile? As a place to start your analysis, consider the practice at issue in *U.S. v. Brignoni-Ponce* of roving vehicle stops made by the U.S. Border Patrol partly on the basis that those being stopped "looked Mexican." See also the discussion of "driving while black" in Chapter 7.

Case 4.2
Reasonableness

NEW JERSEY v. T.L.O.
Argued March 28, 1984
Reargued October 2, 1984
Decided January 15, 1985
469 US 325

JUSTICE WHITE delivered the opinion of the Court.

We granted certiorari in this case to examine the appropriateness of the exclusionary rule as a remedy for searches carried out in violation of the Fourth Amendment by public school authorities. Our consideration of the proper application of the Fourth Amendment to the public schools, however, has led us to conclude that the search that gave rise to the case now before us did not violate the Fourth Amendment. Accordingly, we here address only the questions of the proper standard for assessing the legality of searches conducted by public school officials and the application of that standard to the facts of this case.

I

On March 7, 1980, a teacher at Piscataway High School in Middlesex County, N.J. discovered two girls smoking in a lavatory. One of the two girls was the respondent T.L.O., who at the time was a 14-year-old high school freshman. Because smoking in the lavatory was a violation of a school rule, the teacher took the two girls to the Principal's office, where they met with Assistant Vice Principal Theodore Choplick. In response to questioning by Mr. Choplick, T.L.O.'s companion admitted that she had violated the rule. T.L.O., however, denied that she had been smoking in the lavatory and claimed that she did not smoke at all.

Mr. Choplick asked T.L.O. to come into his private office and demanded to see her purse. Opening the purse, he found a pack of cigarettes, which he removed from the purse and held before T.L.O. as he accused her of having lied to him. As he reached into the purse for the cigarettes, Mr. Choplick also noticed a package of cigarette rolling papers. In his experience, possession of rolling papers by high school students was closely associate with the

use of marihuana. Suspecting that a closer examination of the purse might yield further evidence of drug use, Mr. Choplick proceeded to search the purse thoroughly. The search revealed a small amount of marihuana, a pipe, a number of empty plastic bags, a substantial quantity of money in one-dollar bills, an index card that appeared to be a list of students who owed T.L.O. money, and two letters that implicated T.L.O. in marihuana dealing.

Mr. Choplick notified T.L.O.'s mother and the police, and turned the evidence of drug dealing over to the police. At the request of the police, T.L.O.'s mother took her daughter to police headquarters, where T.L.O. confessed that she had been selling marihuana at the high school. On the basis of the confession and the evidence seized by Mr. Choplick, the State brought delinquency charges against T.L.O. in the Juvenile and Domestic Relations Court of Middlesex County. Contending that Mr. Choplick's search of her purse violated the Fourth Amendment, T.L.O. moved to suppress the evidence found in her purse as well as her confession, which, she argued, was tainted by the allegedly unlawful search. The Juvenile Court denied the motion to suppress....Although the court concluded that the Fourth Amendment did apply to searches carried out by school officials, it held that

> a school official may properly conduct a search of a student's person if the official has a reasonable suspicion that a crime has been or is in the process of being committed, *or* reasonable cause to believe that the search is necessary to maintain school discipline or enforce school policies....

Applying this standard, the court concluded that the search conducted by Mr. Choplick was a reasonable one. The initial decision to open the purse was justified by Mr. Choplick's well-founded suspicion that T.L.O. had violated the rule forbidding smoking in the lavatory. Once the purse was open, evidence of marihuana violations was in plain view, and Mr. Choplick was entitled to conduct a thorough search to determine the nature and extent of T.L.O.'s drug-related activities.… Having denied the motion to suppress, the court on March 23, 1981, found T.L.O. to be a delinquent and on January 8, 1982, sentenced her to a year's probation.

• • •

The New Jersey Supreme Court agreed with the lower courts that the Fourth Amendment applies to searches conducted by school officials.…

With respect to the question of the legality of the search before it, the court agreed with the Juvenile Court that a warrantless search by a school official does not violate the Fourth Amendment so long as the official

> has reasonable grounds to believe that a student possesses evidence of illegal activity or activity that would interfere with school discipline and order.…

However, the court, with two justices dissenting, sharply disagreed with the Juvenile Court's conclusion that the search of the purse was reasonable. According to the majority, the contents of T.L.O.'s purse had no bearing on the accusation against T.L.O., for possession of cigarettes (as opposed to smoking them in the lavatory), did not violate school rules, and a mere desire for evidence that would impeach T.L.O.'s claim that she did not smoke cigarettes could not justify the search. Moreover, even if a reasonable suspicion that T.L.O. had cigarettes in her purse would justify a search, Mr. Choplick had no such suspicion, as no one had furnished him with any specific information that there were cigarettes in the purse. Finally, leaving aside the question whether Mr. Choplick was justified in opening the purse, the court held that the evidence of drug use that he saw inside did not justify the extensive "rummaging" through T.L.O.'s papers and effects that followed.…

• • •

In determining whether the search at issue in this case violated the Fourth Amendment, we are faced initially with the question whether that Amendment's prohibition on unreasonable searches and seizures applies to searches conducted by public school officials. We hold that it does.

• • •

To hold that the Fourth Amendment applies to searches conducted by school authorities is only to begin the inquiry into the standards governing such searches. Although the underlying command of the Fourth Amendment is always that searches and seizures be reasonable, what is reasonable depends on the context within which a search takes place. The determination of the standard of reasonableness governing any specific class of searches requires "balancing the need to search against the invasion which the search entails."…On one side of the balance are arrayed the individual's legitimate expectations of privacy and personal security; on the other, the government's need for effective methods to deal with breaches of public order.

• • •

Although this Court may take notice of the difficulty of maintaining discipline in the public schools today, the situation is not so dire that students in the schools may claim no legitimate expectations of privacy.…

Nor does the State's suggestion that children have no legitimate need to bring personal property into the schools seem well anchored in reality. Students at a minimum must bring to school not only the supplies needed for their studies, but also keys, money, and the necessaries of personal hygiene and grooming. In addition, students may carry on their persons or in purses or wallets such nondisruptive yet highly personal items as photographs, letters, and diaries. Finally, students may have perfectly legitimate reasons to carry with them articles of property needed in connection with extracurricular or recreational activities. In short, schoolchildren may find it necessary to carry with them a variety of legitimate, noncontraband items, and there is no reason to conclude that they have necessarily waived all rights to privacy in such items merely by bringing them onto school grounds.

Against the child's interest in privacy must be set the substantial interest of teachers and administrators in maintaining discipline in the classroom and on school grounds. Maintaining order in the classroom has never been easy, but in recent years, school disorder has often taken particularly ugly forms: drug use and violent crime in the schools have become major social problems....Even in schools that have been spared the most severe disciplinary problems, the preservation of order and a proper educational environment requires close supervision of schoolchildren, as well as the enforcement of rules against conduct that would be perfectly permissible if undertaken by an adult. "Events calling for discipline are frequent occurrences and sometimes require immediate, effective action."...Accordingly, we have recognized that maintaining security and order in the schools requires a certain degree of flexibility in school disciplinary procedures, and we have respected the value of preserving the informality of the student-teacher relationship....

How, then, should we strike the balance between the schoolchild's legitimate expectations of privacy and the school's equally legitimate need to maintain an environment in which learning can take place? It is evident that the school setting requires some easing of the restrictions to which searches by public authorities are ordinarily subject....

• • •

...[T]he legality of a search of a student should depend simply on the reasonableness, under all the circumstances, of the search. Determining the reasonableness of any search involves a twofold inquiry: first, one must consider "whether the...action was justified at its inception," ...second, one must determine whether the search as actually conducted "was reasonably related in scope to the circumstances which justified the interference in the first place...." Under ordinary circumstances, a search of a student by a teacher or other school official will be "justified at its inception" when there are reasonable grounds for suspecting that the search will turn up evidence that the student has violated or is violating either the law or the rules of the school. Such a search will be permissible in its scope when the measures adopted are reasonably related to the objectives of the search and not excessively intrusive in light of the age and sex of the student and the nature of the infraction.

This standard will, we trust, neither unduly burden the efforts of school authorities to maintain order in their schools nor authorize unrestrained intrusions upon the privacy of schoolchildren. By focusing attention on the question of reasonableness, the standard will spare teachers and school administrators the necessity of schooling themselves in the niceties of probable cause and permit them to regulate their conduct according to the dictates of reason and common sense. At the same time, the reasonableness standard should ensure that the interest of students will be invaded no more than is necessary to achieve the legitimate end of preserving order in the schools.

There remains the question of the legality of the search in this case. We recognize that the "reasonable grounds" standard applied by the New Jersey Supreme Court in its consideration of this question is not substantially different from the standard that we have adopted today. Nonetheless, we believe that the New Jersey court's application of that standard to strike down the search of T.L.O.'s purse reflects a somewhat crabbed notion of reasonableness. Our review of the facts surrounding the search leads us to conclude that the search was in no sense unreasonable for Fourth Amendment purposes.

The incident that gave rise to this case actually involved two separate searches, with the first—the search for cigarettes—providing the suspicion that gave rise to the second—the search for marihuana. Although it is the fruits of the second search that are at issue here, the validity of the search for marihuana must depend on the reasonableness of the initial search for cigarettes, as there would have been no reason to suspect that T.L.O. possessed marihuana had the first search not taken place. Accordingly, it is to the search for cigarettes that we first turn our attention.

The New Jersey Supreme Court pointed to two grounds for its holding that the search for cigarettes was unreasonable. First, the court observed that possession of cigarettes was not in itself illegal or a violation of school rules. Because the contents of T.L.O.'s purse would therefore have "no direct bearing on the infraction" of which she was accused (smoking in a lavatory where smoking was prohibited), there was no reason to search her purse. Second, even assuming that a search of T.L.O.'s purse might under some circumstances be reasonable in light of the accusation made against T.L.O., the New Jersey court concluded that Mr. Choplick in this particular case had no reasonable grounds to suspect that T.L.O. had cigarettes in her purse. At best, according to the court, Mr. Choplick had "a good hunch."...

Both these conclusions are implausible. T.L.O. had been accused of smoking, and had denied the accusation in the strongest possible terms when she stated that she did not smoke at all. Surely it cannot be said that under these circumstances, T.L.O.'s possession of cigarettes would be irrelevant to the charges against her or to her response to those charges. T.L.O.'s possession of cigarettes, once it was discovered, would both corroborate the report that she had been smoking and undermine the credibility of her defense to the charge of smoking. To be sure, the discovery of the cigarettes would not prove that T.L.O. had been smoking in the lavatory; nor would it, strictly speaking, necessarily be inconsistent with her claim that she did not smoke at all. But it is universally recognized that evidence, to be relevant to an inquiry, need not conclusively prove the ultimate fact in issue, but only have

> any tendency to make the existence of any fact that is of consequence to the determination of the action more probable or less probable than it would be without the evidence....

The relevance of T.L.O.'s possession of cigarettes to the question whether she had been smoking and to the credibility of her denial that she smoked supplied the necessary "nexus" between the item searched for and the infraction under investigation.... Thus, if Mr. Choplick in fact had a reasonable suspicion that T.L.O. had cigarettes in her purse, the search was justified despite the fact that the cigarettes, if found, would constitute "mere evidence" of a violation....

Of course, the New Jersey Supreme Court also held that Mr. Choplick had no reasonable suspicion that the purse would contain cigarettes. This conclusion is puzzling. A teacher had reported that T.L.O. was smoking in the lavatory. Certainly this report gave Mr. Choplick reason to suspect that T.L.O. was carrying cigarettes with her, and if she did have cigarettes, her purse was the obvious place in which to find them. Mr. Choplick's suspicion that

there were cigarettes in the purse was not an "inchoate and unparticularized suspicion or 'hunch,'"...rather, it was sort of "common-sense conclusio[n] about human behavior" upon which "practical people"—including government officials—are entitled to rely. Of course, even if the teacher's report were true, T.L.O. *might* not have had a pack of cigarettes with her; she might have borrowed a cigarette from someone else or have been sharing a cigarette with another student. But the requirement of reasonable suspicion is not a requirement of absolute certainty: "sufficient probability, not certainty, is the touchstone of reasonableness under the Fourth Amendment...." Because the hypothesis that T.L.O. was carrying cigarettes in her purse was itself not unreasonable, it is irrelevant that other hypotheses were also consistent with the teacher's accusation. Accordingly, it cannot be said that Mr. Choplick acted unreasonably when he examined T.L.O.'s purse to see if it contained cigarettes.

Our conclusion that Mr. Choplick's decision to open T.L.O.'s purse was reasonable brings us to the question of the further search for marihuana once the pack of cigarettes was located. The suspicion upon which the search for marihuana was founded was provided when Mr. Choplick observed a package of rolling papers in the purse as he removed the pack of cigarettes. Although T.L.O. does not dispute the reasonableness of Mr. Choplick's belief that the rolling papers indicated the presence of marihuana, she does contend that the scope of the search Mr. Choplick conducted exceeded permissible bounds when he seized and read certain letters that implicated T.L.O. in drug dealing. This argument, too, is unpersuasive. The discovery of the rolling papers concededly gave rise to a reasonable suspicion that T.L.O. was carrying marihuana as well as cigarettes in her purse. This suspicion justified further exploration of T.L.O.'s purse, which turned up more evidence of drug-related activities: a pipe, a number of plastic bags of the type commonly used to store marihuana, a small quantity of marihuana, and a fairly substantial amount of money. Under these circumstances, it was not unreasonable to extend the search to a separate zippered compartment of the purse; and when a search of that compartment revealed an index card containing a list of "people who owe me money" as well as two letters, the inference that T.L.O. was involved in marihuana trafficking was substantial enough to justify Mr. Choplick in examining the letters to determine whether they contained any further evidence. In short, we cannot conclude that the search for marihuana was unreasonable in any respect.

Because the search resulting in the discovery of the evidence of marihuana dealing by T.L.O. was reasonable, the New Jersey Supreme Court's decision to exclude that evidence from T.L.O.'s juvenile delinquency proceedings on Fourth Amendment grounds was erroneous....

Discussion Questions

1. We often hear state and local officials complain about the federal government's intrusiveness. Yet in *T.L.O.* and *Delaware v. Prouse* each state appealed the decision of its Supreme Court to the U.S. Supreme Court. In your view, does such a practice comport with the core ideas of U.S. federalism? Can you think of guidelines as to when states should appeal decisions of their highest courts to the U.S. Supreme Court?

2. The Fourth Amendment protects against "unreasonable searches and seizures." Reasonableness is obviously subjective at the margins. Judges and public managers may disagree on what is reasonable. Do you think Choplick's search of T.L.O.'s purse was reasonable in its inception? Scope?

3. The "exclusionary rule" generally prohibits the use of illegally seized material as evidence in criminal trials and in some administrative contexts. Its purpose is to deter violations of Fourth Amendment rights by taking away any incentive the police might have to engage in illegal searches. It was constructed by the courts before contemporary qualified immunity doctrine was established (see Chapter 2). What would be the advantages and disadvantages of relying on constitutional tort suits alone to protect Fourth Amendment rights?

Case 4.3
Rational-Comprehensive Decisions: Social Scientific Generalization Versus Equal Protection

CRAIG et al. v. BOREN, GOVERNOR OF OKLAHOMA, et al.
Argued October 5, 1976
Decided December 20, 1976
429 US 190

Opinion

MR. JUSTICE BRENNAN delivered the opinion of the Court.

The interaction of two sections of an Oklahoma statute, Okla. Stat., Tit. 37, §§ 241 and 245 (1958 and Supp. 1976), prohibits the sale of "nonintoxicating" 3.2% beer to males under the age of 21 and to females under the age of 18. The question to be decided is whether such a gender-based differential constitutes a denial to males 18–20 years of age of the equal protection of the laws in violation of the Fourteenth Amendment.

• • •

[II] C

We accept for purposes of discussion the District Court's identification of the objective underlying §§ 241 and 245 as the enhancement of traffic safety. Clearly, the protection of public health and safety represents an important function of state and local governments. However, appellees' statistics in our view cannot support the conclusion that the gender-based distinction closely serves to achieve that objective and therefore the distinction cannot...withstand equal protection challenge.

The appellees introduced a variety of statistical surveys. First, an analysis of arrest statistics for 1973 demonstrated that 18–20-year-old male arrests for "driving under the influence" and "drunkenness" substantially exceeded female arrests for that same age period. Similarly, youths aged 17–21 were found to be overrepresented among those killed or injured in traffic accidents, with males again numerically exceeding females in this regard. Third, a random roadside survey in Oklahoma City revealed that young males were more inclined to drive and drink beer than were their female counterparts. Fourth, Federal Bureau of Investigation nationwide statistics exhibited a notable increase in arrests for "driving under the influence." Finally, statistical evidence gathered in other jurisdictions, particularly Minnesota and Michigan, was offered to corroborate Oklahoma's experience by indicating the pervasiveness of youthful participation in motor vehicle accidents following the imbibing of alcohol. Conceding that "the case is not free from doubt,"...the District Court nonetheless concluded that this statistical showing substantiated "a rational basis for the legislative judgment underlying the challenged classification."...

Even were this statistical evidence accepted as accurate, it nevertheless offers only a weak answer to the equal protection question presented here. The most focused and relevant of the statistical surveys, arrests of 18–20-year-olds for alcohol-related driving offenses, exemplifies the ultimate unpersuasiveness of this evidentiary record. Viewed in terms of the correlation between sex and the actual activity that Oklahoma seeks to regulate—driving while under the influence of alcohol—the statistics broadly establish that .18% of females and 2% of males in that age group were arrested for that offense. While such a disparity is not trivial in a statistical sense, it hardly can form the basis for employment of a gender line as a classifying device. Certainly if maleness is to serve as a proxy for drinking and driving, a correlation of 2% must be considered

an unduly tenuous "fit." Indeed, prior cases have consistently rejected the use of sex as a decisionmaking factor even though the statutes in question certainly rested on far more predictive empirical relationships than this.

Moreover, the statistics exhibit a variety of other shortcomings that seriously impugn their value to equal protection analysis. Setting aside the obvious methodological problems, the surveys do not adequately justify the salient features of Oklahoma's gender-based traffic-safety law. None purports to measure the use and dangerousness of 3.2% beer as opposed to alcohol generally, a detail that is of particular importance since, in light of its low alcohol level, Oklahoma apparently considers the 3.2% beverage to be "nonintoxicating."...Moreover, many of the studies, while graphically documenting the unfortunate increase in driving while under the influence of alcohol, make no effort to relate their findings to age-sex differentials as involved here. Indeed, the only survey that explicitly centered its attention upon young drivers and their use of beer—albeit apparently not of the diluted 3.2% variety—reached results that hardly can be viewed as impressive in justifying either a gender or age classification.

There is no reason to belabor this line of analysis. It is unrealistic to expect either members of the judiciary or state officials to be well versed in the rigors of experimental or statistical technique. But this merely illustrates that proving broad sociological propositions by statistics is dubious business, and one that inevitably is in tension with the normative philosophy that underlies the Equal Protection Clause. Suffice to say that the showing offered by the appellees does not satisfy us that sex represents a legitimate accurate proxy for the regulation of drinking and driving. In fact, when it is further recognized that Oklahoma's statute prohibits only the selling of 3.2% beer to young males and not their drinking the beverage once acquired (even after purchase by their 18–20-year-old female companions), the relationship between gender and traffic safety becomes far to tenuous to satisfy...[the] requirement that the gender-based difference be substantially related to achievement of statutory objective.

We hold, therefore, that...Oklahoma's 3.2% beer statute invidiously discriminates against males 18–20 years of age.

Discussion Questions

1. The Court reasoned that "proving broad sociological propositions by statistics…that inevitably is in tension with the normative philosophy that underlies the Equal Protection Clause." What is that philosophy and how is it related to the use of categories, such as female and male or white and black, in social scientific analysis? What are the implications of the tension of which the Court speaks for the use of social science in public policymaking and implementation?

2. In a concurring opinion, Justice Stevens argued that "…the empirical data submitted by the State accentuate the unfairness of treating all 18–20-year-old males as inferior to their female counterparts. The legislation imposes a restraint on 100% of the males in the class allegedly because about 2% of them have probably violated one or more laws relating to the consumption of alcholic [sic] beverages. It is unlikely that this law will have a significant deterrent effect either on that 2% or on the law-abiding 98%. But even assuming some such slight benefit, it does not seem to me that an insult to all of the young men of the State can be justified by visiting the sins of the 2% on the 98%." How does this rejection of the classification by sex differ from that of the Court's majority opinion? What are the implications of Stevens's position for the use of social scientific generalizations in public policy?

3. In dissent, Justice Rehnquist maintained that "[t]he rationality of a statutory classification for equal protection purposes does not depend upon the statistical 'fit' between the class and the trait sought to be singled out. It turns on whether there may be a sufficiently higher incidence of the trait within the included class than in the excluded class to justify different treatment." How does this dissenting position differ from those of the majority and Justice Stevens?

4. Assess the compatibility of each of the positions noted in the foregoing question with rational-comprehensive decisionmaking.

Case 4.4
Incrementalism: Neglecting Important Constitutional Values Without a Master Plan

HAWKINS v. TOWN OF SHAW, MISSISSIPPI
United States Court of Appeals
Fifth Circuit
Jan. 23, 1971
437 F. 2d 1286

Opinion

TUTTLE, Circuit Judge:

Referring to a portion of town or a segment of society as being "on the other side of the tracks" has for too long been a familiar expression to most Americans. Such a phrase immediately conjures up an area characterized by poor housing, overcrowded conditions and, in short, overall deterioration. While there may be many reasons why such areas exist in nearly all of our cities, one reason that cannot be accepted is the discriminatory provision of municipal services based on race. It is such a reason that is alleged as the basis of this action.

Appellants are Negro citizens of the Town of Shaw, Mississippi. They alleged that the town has provided various municipal services including street paving and street lighting, sanitary sewers, surface water drainage as well as water mains and fire hydrants in a discriminatory manner based on race. Appellants brought a class action seeking injunctive relief under 42

U.S.C. § 1983 against the town, the town's mayor, clerk and five aldermen....

Facts

The Town of Shaw, Mississippi, was incorporated in 1886 and is located in the Mississippi Delta. Its population, which has undergone little change since 1930, consists of about 2,500 people—1,500 black and 1,000 white residents. Residential racial segregation is almost total. There are 451 dwelling units occupied by blacks in town, and, of these, 97% (439) are located in neighborhoods in which no whites reside. That the town's policies in administering various municipal services have led to substantially less attention being paid to the black portion of town is clear.

• • •

Street Paving

The undisputed evidence is that 97% of all those who live in homes fronting on unpaved streets are black. In attempting to justify this, the trial court stated:

> "Initially, concrete paving was afforded to those streets serving commercial and industrial interests and to the areas nearest the town's center. In some cases this resulted in more street paving in white than Negro neighborhoods, but the paving actually done in the municipality was on the basis of general usage, traffic needs and other objective criteria. Residential neighborhoods not facing principal streets or thoroughfares long remained unpaved, regardless of their character as white or black neighborhoods."

The record simply does not support the justification that streets were built according to traffic needs and usage. The town's one engineer who made recommendation to defendants as to the priority of street paving projects testified that he had never surveyed the town to determine which streets were used the most. Nor did he compare the usage of streets in black neighborhoods. He even admitted that he was not familiar with the usage of streets in the Promised Land Addition, which is one of the oldest and largest black neighborhoods in Shaw.

The finding that many streets were paved in the business areas and that this resulted, "in some cases," in providing more paving in white

rather than black neighborhoods, also fails to justify the existing disparities. As appellants point out, in 1956 when the first residential streets in black neighborhoods were paved, 96% of the white residents of Shaw already lived on paved streets, most of which had been paved during the 1930's. Many of these streets, however, were solely residential, and could not possibly serve commercial, industrial or any public buildings.

The trial court also found that many of the streets on which blacks live were too narrow to pave. The town engineer had testified that streets in black neighborhoods had not been paved because they did not have the fifty foot right-of-way he considered necessary. However, as appellants point out, most of the streets in Shaw, in both black and white neighborhoods, have platted rights of way that range from 30 to 40 feet. Further, while most streets *under* 50 feet in white neighborhoods are paved, those in the black areas are not.

In short, even if we assume that such criteria as traffic usage, need and width constitute compelling state interests, they were not applied equally to both black and white neighborhoods. We are led to the inevitable conclusion that Shaw's policies, which have resulted in such significant disparities between the black and white portions of town, are, in no way justifiable.

Street Lights

The record clearly shows that absolutely no high power mercury vapor street lights have been installed in black residential areas. Only the much weaker bare bulb fixtures are to be found. The trial court stated that there was no showing that the lighting was inadequate and, in any event:

> "The brighter lights are provided for those streets forming either a state highway, or serving commercial, industrial or special school needs, or otherwise carrying the heaviest traffic load."

The fact that there was no specific showing that lighting was not adequate is not significant. What is significant is that it is clear that all of the *better* lighting that exists in Shaw can be found *only* in the white parts of town. Surely, this cannot be justified merely on the ground that the bare bulb fixtures are not shown to be inadequate. One might readily assume, it seems, that the modern high intensity lights are *more* adequate from the fact of their use by the city. *Improvements* to existing facilities provided in a discriminatory manner may also constitute a violation of equal protection.

The other justifications accepted by the trial court again fail, for if the "special needs" criteria were applied equally for the benefit of both black and white citizens, all the high intensity lights would not be in only the white areas of town. For example, while streets with heavy traffic serving commercial and public centers, such as Gale Street, in black areas have only bare bulb fixtures, many little traveled streets in white neighborhoods have the high intensity variety. In short, we are again convinced that as with the paving of streets, the placement of new light fixtures only in the white portion of town cannot be justified.

Sanitary Sewers

While 99% of white residents are served by a sanitary sewer system, nearly 20% of the black population is not so served. The trial court thought this was justified by noting that:

> "Part of the problem in reaching all older un-served areas has been the necessity for bringing this service into newer subdivisions developed for both races and brought into the town, as it is the town's firm policy to make sewer installations for all such new areas."

It is not at all clear from the record that such a "firm policy" exists. However, even assuming that it does, the fact that extensions are now made to new areas in a non-discriminatory manner is not sufficient when the effect of such a policy is to "freeze in" the results of past discrimination. As this court stated [previously]... "a relationship otherwise rational may be insufficient in itself to meet constitutional standards—if its effect is to freeze-in past discrimination." We find that since over one-third of the black population was not served when the original sewer system was constructed and nearly twenty percent of this population remains unserved, a policy of serving only new areas would freeze in the results of past discrimination.

The trial court, however, also stated that:

> "While the complaint about less than 100% sanitary sewage for all residences is certainly a real one, that condition arises basically from the fact that local law does not yet require indoor plumbing. The lack of sanitary sewers in certain areas of the town is not the result of racial discrimination in withholding a vital service: rather it is a consequence of *not* requiring through a proper housing code, certain minimal conditions for inhabited housing."

While we recognize that a proper housing code would help this situation, it is circular reasoning to argue that because indoor plumbing is not required, sewers are not provided. If sewers were provided, indoor plumbing could be more easily installed. Indeed, without it, black residents desiring such facilities are forced to incur the extra expense of installing individual sewage disposal apparatus. In short, the justifications offered for the disparities that exist in the town's sewerage system are not valid.

Surface Water Drainage

We do not doubt that as the trial court notes: "Having flat nonporous soil with slow run-off conditions, Shaw suffers from drainage problems common to the Delta area." Indeed, there are serious drainage problems in both the black and white sections of town. However, the record reveals that the problems of the black community are far more serious. Whereas, the white community has been provided with either underground storm sewers or a continuous system of drainage ditches, the black neighborhoods have been provided with a poorly maintained system of drainage ditches and, on many streets, none at all....

Appellees point to various impediments to justify this disparity including haphazard subdividing, the absence of zoning regulations and rights of way of insufficient width. We have already dealt with the claim that roads in the black area are of insufficient width. Regarding the other impediments, we only note that they have been substantially overcome in white neighborhoods. We see no acceptable reason why they should not have been overcome in the black community as well.

Water Mains, Fire Hydrants and Traffic Control Signs

Although water is supplied to all residents of the town, the trial court found that "at all times water pressure is inadquate in certain localities, irrespective of their racial character." We agree that the record discloses inadequate water pressure, but disagree that it is not related to the racial make-up of the locality.

The record reveals that the two areas where water pressure is most inadequate are black and constitute 63% of the town's black population. As appellants note, in the Gale Street area, 211 homes are served by 4" water mains while in the Promised Land, most of the 74 homes are served by 2" or 1¼" mains. Most of the white community is served by 6" mains. The 4" mains that do exist in the white portion of town serve, however, far fewer homes than the 4" mains in the black section. In short, as with the previously examined municipal services, the town's policies have again created a situa-tion in which the black portion of town is se-verely disadvantaged. An examination of the record regarding the placement of fire hydrants as well as the placement of any traffic control signs in black neighborhoods leads us to the same conclusion.

Intent

Yet, despite the fact that we conclude that no compelling state interests can justify the dispar-ities that exist in the black and white portions of town, it may be argued that this result was not intended. That is to say, the record contains no direct evidence aimed at establishing bad faith, ill will or an evil motive on the part of the Town of Shaw and its public officials.... Having determined that no compelling state interests can possibly justify the discriminatory *results* of Shaw's administration of municipal ser-vices, we conclude that a violation of equal pro-tection has occurred.

Discussion Questions

1. One of the outstanding aspects of the *Hawkins* case was that the disparities between the white and African-American neighborhoods developed in the absence of comprehensive zoning plans and housing codes. Step by step, the town demonstrated a marked preference for whites in the allocation of street, lighting, sewer, drainage, and water improvements. Each step was ac-companied by somewhat different rationales and/or rationalizations. Consequently, there was clearly a process of incremental discrimination, though, as the court noted, no comprehensive plan to treat whites favorably was found in the case. In a subsequent ruling, *Washington v. Davis* (1976),* the Supreme Court rejected "...the proposition that a law or other official act, with-out regard to whether it reflects a racially discriminatory pupose, is unconstitutional *solely* be-cause it has a racially disproportionate impact." It went on to hold that "[n]ecessarily, an invidious [racially] discriminatory purpose may often be inferred from the totality of the rel-evant facts, including the fact, if it is true, that the law bears more heavily on one race than an-other. It is also not infrequently true that the discriminatory impact...may for all practical purposes demonstrate unconstitutionality because in various circumstances the discrimination is difficult to explain on nonracial grounds." Based on your reading of the facts in the *Hawkins* case, do you think it can be inferred that the town's actions reflected an underlying invidious discriminatory purpose? Why or why not? What kinds of additional information, if any, would help you decide? Did the incremental decisionmaking described in *Hawkins* have any clear pur-poses? Consider the testimony of the town's engineer regarding street paving in addressing this question.

2. In a concurring opinion, Judge Bell noted that "since the Negro citizens obtained the right to vote some four years ago under the Voting Rights Act of 1965 and under the present govern-ment which took office in 1965, there has been a considerable improvement in most of the ser-vices rendered them by the city." This fact suggests that incremental decisionmaking is less

*426 U.S. 229.

likely to neglect important values when all major interests are represented in the policymaking process. Consider concrete ways in which public administrators can enhance their ability to recognize salient values and interests when engaging in incremental decisionmaking. For instance, would public opinion surveys or mechanisms for public participation be useful in this regard?

3. Beyond the *Hawkins* case, can you think of instances in which incremental decisionmaking has neglected important political and/or constitutional values? Would zoning regulations in your city or town be an example?

FIVE

Administrative Effectiveness

Traditionally, public management in the United States has been concerned primarily with the means of carrying out governmental action. Woodrow Wilson's classic call for "The Study of Administration" explained that

> Public administration is detailed and systematic execution of public law. Every particular application of general law is an act of administration. The assessment and raising of taxes, for instance, the hanging of a criminal, the transportation and delivery of the mails, the equipment and recruiting of the army and navy, etc., are all obvious acts of administration; but the general laws which direct these things to be done are as obviously outside and above administration. The broad plans of governmental action are not administrative; the detailed execution of such plans is administrative.[1]

Wilson even argued that "the weightier debates of constitutional principle ... are no longer of more immediate practical moment than questions of administration. It is getting to be harder to *run* a constitution than to frame one."[2] Following this perspective, much of the field's historical thrust has been to build the capacity to implement public policy effectively by finding the best ways of organizing, managing human resources, and budgeting.

The New Public Management (NPM) and the "reinventing government" movement also focus on means rather than substantive policy objectives.[3] Their main disagreement with traditional administration is over how to achieve high performance and effective implementation. Should the emphasis be placed on overhead and inputs, as traditionally thought, or on outputs and outcomes? Vice President Al Gore embraces the NPM's instrumental approach to public administration in his National Performance Review: "[w]e want to make improving the way government does business a permanent part of how government works, regardless of which party is in power."[4]

What has frequently been neglected from Wilson to Gore, however, is that the Constitution places constraints on the means available to public administrators for implementing public policy. This distinguishes public management from the private sector, where only the Thirteenth Amendment applies. "Running" the Constitution is not divorced from debates—even weighty ones, at that—over constitutional principles. And it presents public management with opportunities to promote vitally important values.[5]

At a minimum, constitutionally competent public administrators must be aware of how the Constitution limits the means available for implementing public poli-   **105** cy. More broadly, though, as Constance Horner, former director of the federal Office of Personnel Management, noted, public administrators should be constitutionally competent so that they can effectively engage in discussions over both means and ends. In her words, "I am calling … for a commitment to what might be termed *constitutional literacy*" because "…one antidote to growing specialization within the Federal executive service is to reinvigorate *constitutional* discourse, so we can meet once again on common ground. As Professor John Rohr puts it, we must 'create within the bureaucracy a community of moral discourse centered on fundamental constitutional values.'"[6]

Constitutional Means: A Brief History of Judicial Approaches

In some ways it is obvious that the Constitution constrains the choice of means for achieving legitimate governmental ends. In principle, democratic constitutionalism must reject the premise that even laudable ends can justify unconstitutional means. In fact, Chief Justice John Marshall made this very point in one of the most famous passages in United States constitutional law. In *McCulloch v. Maryland* (1819), he wrote for the Court, "Let the end be legitimate, let it be within the scope of the Constitution, and all means which are appropriate, which are plainly adapted to that end, which are not prohibited, but consistent with the letter and spirit of the Constitution, are constitutional."[7] Conversely, means not meeting these tests would be unconstitutional. But precisely which administrative means are contrary to the letter or the spirit of the Constitution is not always clear.

Over the past century, the federal judiciary adopted three successive general stances in assessing the constitutionality of public administrative means. First, from the 1880s to the mid-1930s, it tended to oppose two types of administrative means—one on substantive grounds and the other for procedural reasons. Substantively, the judiciary was highly skeptical of any governmental interference in the functioning of free markets, such as wage and hour laws. Procedurally, the courts frowned on administrative adjudication, and to a lesser extent, rulemaking on the grounds that both processes violated the constitutional separation of powers. Judges also tended to view the adjudicatory activities of public agencies as an infringement on constitutional due process. During this period, the judiciary generally paid little deference to administrative expertise. In fact, in 1890, the Supreme Court declared that "investigation by judicial machinery," as opposed to administrative procedure, was required for rate-setting.[8] In general, the judiciary's approach placed a heavy burden of persuasion on public administrators who sought to defend the constitutionality of the means chosen to implement even those policies that the courts considered legitimate.

The period of judicial opposition came to a head during the New Deal. In response to the Great Depression, Congress delegated vast legislative authority to the executive branch. It sought to enable the president and federal agencies to intervene more readily in the economy in an effort to bring about a recovery. The judiciary resisted the blurring of the separation of powers and the government's increasingly deep involvement in the free market. According to Robert Jackson, a former Supreme Court Justice, in 1935–1936, "'hell broke loose' in the lower [federal] courts. Sixteen hundred injunctions restraining officers of the Federal Government from carrying out acts of Congress were granted by federal judges."[9] In 1935, the Supreme Court undercut a major New Deal initiative, the National Industrial Recovery Act of 1933, by ruling, among other problems, that it involved an unconstitutional delegation of legislative power to the executive branch.[10] Earlier in the same year, the Court had overturned a scheme granting the president authority to regulate practices in the petroleum industry.[11] In 1936, the Court found major constitutional defects with another New Deal measure, the Bituminous Coal Conservation Act of 1935.[12]

In early 1937, following his landslide reelection in 1936, President Franklin D. Roosevelt responded to these judicial defeats by asking Congress to increase the size of the Supreme Court so that he could appoint enough additional justices to create a solid majority in favor of New Deal policies. The "Court Packing" plan was never enacted.[13] From the president's perspective, it was soon unnecessary. First, Justice Owen Roberts became more supportive of New Deal initiatives, thereby transforming a minority of four justices into a majority of five. Second, the crisis abated over time as Roosevelt appointed a number of new Supreme Court justices and other federal judges who were sympathetic toward the exercise of national power through administrative agencies.

A second judicial stance on administrative means grew out of Roosevelt's ability to defeat the opposition to New Deal measures and eventually to reconstitute the federal bench through a large number of appointments. From the late 1930s to the mid-1950s, the judiciary acquiesced to administrative action. During this period, the courts did not simply rubber-stamp administrative activities, but they did pay great deference to administrators' expertise and they seldom found administrative means to be unconstitutional. What C. Herman Pritchett wrote of the Supreme Court's record from 1941 to 1946 characterized the judicial mood generally: "A basic assumption of the Roosevelt Court has been that administrative agencies possess an expertness and a competence in economic and social fields which the Court does not share, and that consequently in areas where this expertness is relevant the Court will not disturb or contradict administrative conclusions."[14] The Court also remained committed to constitutional doctrines that effectively allowed administrative agencies to infringe on individuals' constitutional rights in the course of providing them with public services and benefits.[15] Consequently, even into the 1960s, relations between courts and agencies were generally harmonious. As Martin Shapiro explained with reference to the federal courts:

> Judicial review of administrative decision making is…marginal in the sense that… policy differences are unlikely to arise in most instances in which review is theoretically possible. Thus most of the relations between agencies and courts are relations of acquiescence, consent, or compromise arrived at by anticipation of the other participant's position before even a tremor of conflict arises.[16]

However, by the 1950s, a major constitutional change was beginning and the current judicial perspective on administrative means was developing. As noted in Chapter 2, over the past several decades the judiciary has handed down many decisions and fashioned several doctrines that have greatly expanded the constitutional rights of individuals as they come into contact with public administration. Consequently, today public administrators are more constrained by the Constitution than ever before when dealing with clients, customers, contractors, subordinate employees and applicants for civil service jobs, patients in public mental health facilities, inmates in prisons, property owners, and individuals involved in street-level administrative encounters.[17] This is precisely why public administrators must now have constitutional competence.

The contemporary judicial approach to public administration emerged in response to a variety of actions. During the "red scare"[18] of the late 1940s and early 1950s, some public employees were labeled disloyal and dismissed partly on the basis of activities such as favoring peace and civil liberties, racial equality, and desegregation. Such abuses led the courts to reassess and to reject the historic concept that governmental benefits were "privileges" that could be terminated without procedural due process and to which almost any conditions could be attached without violating the Constitution.[19] Eventually, agency clients, customers, and employees gained considerable procedural and substantive constitutional protections against the erosion of their rights through their dependency on the government for benefits or jobs.[20] By 1954, the Supreme Court unanimously concluded that legally enforced racial segregation in public schools was an unconstitutional denial of equal protection of the laws.[21] Thereafter, equal protection was applied to the distribution of public services generally. Prisons and other public institutions were also desegregated and subsequently became the object of broad, constitutionally based reforms.[22]

General Constitutional Restrictions on Administrative Means Today

The vast expansion of individuals' rights vis-à-vis public administration since the 1950s has been accompanied by the formulation of constitutional doctrines and judicial approaches that place broad constraints on administrators' choices of means for implementing public policies. The two most general limitations of this kind are (a) procedural due process as a protection against arbitrary or capricious administrative actions and (b) requiring that infringements on individuals' constitutional rights for permissible governmental purposes satisfy the least restrictive alternative test or be narrowly tailored.

Due Process

It is axiomatic, as Chief Justice Marshall indicated in *McCulloch v. Maryland,* that administrative means or actions must bear a direct and strong relationship to the achievement of legitimate governmental objectives. Means that are not logically related to the policy objectives being sought and those based on inaccurate premises or conclusions are vulnerable to successful legal challenges in court.[23] Similarly, by definition, means that are arbitrary or capricious do not connect administrative actions to their intended purposes. The Due Process Clause of the Fifth and Fourteenth Amendments is a generalized check on the use of arbitrary or capricious administrative means that infringe on individuals' constitutionally protected rights.

At a minimum, procedural due process usually requires that an individual be notified of administrative decisions that will abridge his or her liberty or property interests and that he or she be afforded an opportunity to respond to the adverse in-formation, charges, and rationale for the action. More elaborately, it may require trial-like hearings. Case 5.1, *Kolender v. Lawson* (1983), illustrates that at a very broad level, even a law or regulation that encourages arbitrary or capricious administrative implementation may be considered an unconstitutional violation of due process.

The Least Restrictive Alternative and Narrow Tailoring

The least restrictive alternative and narrow tailoring tests place constraints on ad-ministrative means that infringe on individuals' substantive constitutional rights. Al-though rights such as freedom of speech, association, and religion are not absolute, contemporary constitutional law prohibits their gratuitous or unnecessary abridge-ment. In order to infringe on these rights constitutionally, the government must have a compelling interest *and* it must choose the method for achieving its purpose that is either the least restrictive of the individual's opportunity to exercise his or her constitutional rights, or is narrowly tailored to limit the damage to them.

As discussed in Chapter 1, these tests focus on the extent to which alternative means abridge protected rights, rather than on their economic or administrative costs. Sometimes this can lead to startling conclusions. For instance, in a case in-volving Eighth Amendment rights, a court explained that "inadequate resources can never be an adequate justification for the state's depriving any person of his con-stitutional rights. If the state cannot obtain the resources to detain persons awaiting trial in accordance with minimum constitutional standards, then the state simply will not be permitted to detain such persons."[24]

The vigor with which the courts apply the least restrictive alternative tests varies with the scope of administrative infringement on individuals' rights. How-ever, as discussed in *Elrod v. Burns* (1976), Case 5.2, the test is a necessary guide for administrators seeking to be constitutionally competent.

Narrow tailoring offers somewhat more flexibility. It is used primarily in cases dealing with equal protection or time, place, and manner restrictions on First Amendment freedoms. It allows the use of means that are narrowly drawn rather than only those that are *least* restrictive. The concept of narrow tailoring is inher-ently subjective. However, as noted in Chapter 1, there are some general guidelines. The courts will consider the relative efficacy of alternative means, including a rough gauging of their costs. Means are more likely to be viewed as narrowly tai-lored if they have a fixed duration or logical stopping point and if they do not completely foreclose the exercise of a right. (Case 5.3, *Adarand Constructors, Inc. v. Pena*, 1995, calls for narrow tailoring when using classifications that are suspect under equal protection analysis; Case 7.2, *Church of Lukumi Babalu Aye, Inc. v. City of Hialeah*, 1993, addresses narrow tailoring in the context of religious freedom.)

Impact on Public Administration

The constitutional limits on the means available to public managers can be frus-trating. They sometimes make effective implementation difficult or impossible even when policies enjoy broad public or legislative support. *Adarand* provides a good illustration of this problem.

The federal Department of Transportation (DOT) sought to help equalize competition for federal highway funds by providing contractors with an incentive to subcontract firms controlled by socially and economically disadvantaged individuals. But how would a contractor know which potential subcontractors were socially and economically disadvantaged? DOT could have constructed an index of disadvantage and maintained a list of eligible firms. That would have required gathering and analyzing a lot of information, some of it personal and potentially difficult to obtain. Updating would also be necessary as firms changed hands. Inevitably, such an approach would have been administratively cumbersome and perhaps costly. Instead, federal regulations instructed contractors to presume that "Black Americans, Hispanic Americans, Native Americans, Asian Pacific Americans, and other minorities" were disadvantaged.[25] Using these categories as surrogates for disadvantage may have been effective, but it suffered from two constitutional infirmities.

First, it shifted the level of review. Ordinarily classifications based on disadvantage would be subject to mere rationality review (see Chapter 1). Prior to the Supreme Court's holding in *Adarand,* benign federal racial and ethnic classifications, such as minority business set-asides, faced middle-level review. The latter is a considerably tougher standard than mere rationality. However, in *Adarand,* the Court raised the bar even higher by holding that all racial or ethnic classifications, whether intended to be benign or invidious, are subject to strict scrutiny. They can be supported only by a compelling governmental interest.

Second, suspect classifications must also be narrowly tailored. Although the Court did not reach the issue, race and ethnicity are not narrowly tailored indicators of disadvantage. The presumptions that *all* minorities who head businesses are disadvantaged is far too broad, as is the counterassumption that, in general, nonminorities should not be considered disadvantaged.[26] However, in practice, using race and ethnicity as a proxy for disadvantage could be cost-effective because disadvantage is disproportionately concentrated among members of some minority groups.

The *Kolender* case is another example of the potential difficulty of finding constitutional means to a legitimate governmental purpose. A California statute required that, upon proper request by the police, an individual provide credible and reliable identification and account for his or her presence in any particular place. The Supreme Court found the law to be unconstitutionally vague. The law's lack of clear standards for determining what was credible and reliable identification created two problems. It inadequately notified individuals about how to comply and also failed to establish minimal guidelines to limit arbitrary enforcement by the police. But try drafting an effective and constitutional antivagrancy or antiloitering regulation.

In *Papachristou v. City of Jacksonville* (1972),[27] eight defendants were convicted of violating a Jacksonville, Florida, ordinance that provided:

> Rogues and vagabonds, or dissolute persons who go about begging, common gamblers, persons who use juggling or unlawful games or plays, common drunkards, common night walkers, thieves, pilferers or pickpockets, traders in stolen property, lewd, wanton and lascivious persons, keepers of gambling places, common railers and brawlers, persons wandering or strolling around from place to place without any lawful purpose or object, habitual loafers, disorderly persons, persons neglecting all lawful business and ha-

bitually spending their time by frequenting houses of ill fame, gaming houses, or places where alcoholic beverages are sold or served, [and] persons able to work but habitually living upon the earnings of their wives or minor children shall be deemed vagrants and, upon conviction in the Municipal Court shall be punished [by 90 days' imprisonment, a $500 fine, or both].[28]

The Supreme Court held the ordinance void for vagueness. Ever since the *Papachristou* case, municipalities and states have struggled to balance the constitutional rights of people to move in public space and to travel freely, with the need for public order. To what extent is the right to stand on the sidewalk and talk to friends the right to block the path of others? When does exercising a right become a wrong?

The effort to regulate the use of public space constitutionally continues to confound local governments. It takes many forms—including a concern with loitering,[29] drug sales,[30] street gangs,[31] aggressive begging,[32] and homelessness.[33] In all cases, the problem has been maintaining one of the most fundamental of rights—the right to travel in the public space—while controlling obstructive behavior in a way that provides specific notice of what is prohibited. Relying on constitutional interpretation, the courts insist that regulations not be so vague as to leave the determination of what is illegal solely to the judgment of the police. From an administrative perspective, however, effective law enforcement necessarily requires that professionally trained police have considerable discretion to determine what constitutes a threat to public order and safety.

Conclusion: Complexity and Change in Public Management

Civil service jobs were once stereotyped as dull havens for the security minded. No more! Today, the public service is widely recognized as highly demanding, even impossible.[34] The complexity of many governmental objectives, the often chronic underfunding of public agencies, the need to balance competing values, media attention, the requisites of political accountability, and the openness with which much of the public sector operates all contribute to the challenges that public managers face. The discussion and cases in this chapter highlight another dimension, and one that has traditionally been neglected in public managerial education. Constitutional limits on the means available to public managers add greatly to the complexity of achieving results in public programs.

In each of the following cases, the government was pursuing constitutionally legitimate ends that many citizens would consider quite worthy. In finding constitutional defects with the means chosen in these cases, the Supreme Court claims that it is not foreclosing the ends. But when one considers seriously the administrative feasibility of alternative means, the complexity of doing public administration effectively *and* constitutionally becomes wholly evident. There is certainly no simple—and perhaps no more cost-effective—way to achieve the governmental purposes sought in these cases.

Moreover, the constitutional limits on administrative means are not fixed or static. They change over time. No case illustrates this better than *Elrod v. Burns,* in which patronage dismissals, "a practice as old as the Republic," as Justice Lewis Powell noted in dissent, were declared unconstitutional.[35] *Adarand* also broke new constitutional ground by treating a benign federal racial and ethnic classification as suspect and subject to strict scrutiny.

Although constitutional change is real, it need not come as a surprise. *Elrod* was presaged by earlier Supreme Court decisions.[36] *Adarand* shifted the level of review for the classification involved, but it did not eliminate the contemporary three-tier framework for equal protection analysis. Due process, the least restrictive alternative test, and narrow tailoring provide a durable foundation for assessing the constitutionality of administrative means. Understanding what they require will help enable public managers to assimilate constitutional change and to adjust their administrative practice accordingly.

Notes

1. Woodrow Wilson, "The Study of Administration," in Jay Shafritz and A. Hyde, eds., *Classics of Public Administration,* 2nd ed. (Chicago: Dorsey Press, 1987), p. 19. (Originally published in 1887.)

2. Ibid., p. 12.

3. David Osborne and Ted Gaebler, *Reinventing Government* (Reading, MA: Addison-Wesley, 1992); Al Gore, *From Red Tape to Results: Creating a Government That Works Better & Costs Less* (Washington, DC: U.S. Government Printing Office, 1993); Ewan Ferlie, ed., *The New Public Management in Action* (Cambridge, UK: Oxford University Press, 1996); Kieron Walsh, *The Public Services and Market Mechanisms: Competition, Contracting, and the New Public Management* (New York: St. Martin's Press, 1995); "Forum: 'Reinventing' Public Administration," *Public Administration Review,* vol. 56 (May/June 1996): 245; U.S. General Accounting Office, *Managing for Results: The Statutory Framework for Improving Federal Management and Effectiveness* (Washington, DC: U.S. General Accounting Office, 1997).

4. Gore, *From Red Tape to Results,* p. iv.

5. See John A. Rohr, *To Run a Constitution* (Lawrence KS: University Press of Kansas, 1986).

6. Constance Horner, "Remarks to FEI's [Federal Executive Institute's] 20th Anniversary Dinner," Charlottesville, Virginia, October 14, 1988, pp. 13–14.

7. *McCulloch v. Maryland,* 4 Wheaton 316, 420 (1819).

8. *Chicago, Milwaukee and St. Paul Railway Co. v. Minnesota,* 134 U.S. 418, 458 (1890).

9. Robert H. Jackson, *The Struggle for Judicial Supremacy* (New York: Knopf, 1941), p. 115.

10. *Schechter Poultry Corp. v. United States,* 295 U.S. 495 (1935).

11. *Panama Refining Co. v. Ryan,* 292 U.S. 388 (1935).

12. *Carter v. Carter Coal Co.,* 298 U.S. 238 (1936).

13. See Gerald Gunther, *Cases and Materials on Constitutional Law* (Mineola, NY: Foundation Press, 1975), pp. 167–171.

14. C. Herman Pritchett, *The Roosevelt Court* (New York: Macmillan, 1948), p. 172.

15. See David Rosenbloom and Rosemary O'Leary, *Public Administration and Law,* 2nd ed. (New York: Marcel Dekker, 1997), Chapters 4, 6, and 7.

16. Martin Shapiro, *The Supreme Court and Administrative Agencies* (New York: Free Press, 1968), p. 268.

17. Rosenbloom and O'Leary, *Public Administration and Law,* Chapters 4–7.

18. The "red scare," also called the "McCarthy period," after Republican Senator Joseph McCarthy of Wisconsin, was characterized by a widespread belief that Communists had infiltrated the governmental and cultural institutions of the United States and that they were subverting public policy and promoting communistic values. The federal government and many states and localities established loyalty-security programs to screen out employees and applicants who might advance communist causes. Communism was viewed as a threat to the American family structure, which led some to believe that rejection of marriage and engaging in premarital sex were symptoms of communist leanings. See David Rosenbloom, *Federal Service and the Constitution* (Ithaca, NY: Cornell University Press, 1971), Chapter 6.

19. See William Van Alstyne, "The Demise of the Right-Privilege Distinction in Constitutional Law," *Harvard Law Review,* vol. 81 (1968): 1439; and Rosenbloom, *Federal Service and the Constitution,* Chapter 7.

20. Rosenbloom and O'Leary, *Public Administration and Law,* Chapters 4 and 6.

21. *Brown v. Board of Education of Topeka,* 347 U.S. 483 (1954).

22. Rosenbloom and O'Leary, *Public Administration and Law,* Chapter 7.

23. *Federal Trade Commission v. Sperry & Hutchinson,* 405 U.S. 233 (1972); *Industrial Union Department, AFL-CIO v. American Petroleum Institute,* 448 U.S. 607 (1980); *Motor Vehicle Manufacturers Association v. State Farm,* 463 U.S. 29 (1983).

24. *Hamilton v. Love,* 328 F. Supp. 1182. 1194 (1971).

25. *Adarand Constructors v. Pena,* 515 U.S. 200, 205 (1995).

26. The regulation also applied to any individual found disadvantaged by the Small Business Administration under the Small Business Act. See *Adarand*.

27. *Papachristou v. City of Jacksonville*, 405 U.S. 156 (1972).

28. Ibid., footnote 1.

29. Peter W. Porilos, "Chicago's Ban on Gang Loitering: Making Sense of Vagueness and Overbreadth in Loitering Laws," *California Law Review*, vol. 83 (1995): 379. See *Chicago v. Morales*, U.S. Supreme Court, No. 97-1121 (1999).

30. William Trosch, "The Third Generation of Loitering Laws Goes to Court: Do Laws That Criminalize Loitering with the Intent to Sell Drugs Pass Constitutional Muster?" *North Carolina Law Review*, vol. 71 (1993): 513.

31. Terrence R. Boga, "Turf Wars: Street Gangs, Local Governments, and the Battle for Public Space," *Harvard Civil Rights-Civil Liberties Law Review*, vol. 29 (1993): 477.

32. Robert Teir, "Maintaining Safety and Civility in Public Spaces: A Constitutional Approach to Aggressive Begging," *Louisiana Law Review*, vol. 54 (1993): 285.

33. Harry Simon, "Towns Without Pity: A Constitutional and Historical Analysis of Official Efforts to Drive Homeless Persons from American Cities," *Tulane Law Review*, vol. 66 (1992): 631; Nancy A. Millich, "Compassion Fatigue and the First Amendment: Are the Homeless Constitutional Castaways?" *University of Davis Law Review*, vol. 27 (1994): 255; Robert C. McConkey III, "'Camping Ordinances' and the Homeless: Constitutional and Moral Issues Raised by Ordinances Prohibiting Sleeping in Public Areas," *Cumberland Law Review*, vol. 26 (1996): 633.

34. E. Hargrove and J. Glidewell, eds., *Impossible Jobs in Public Management* (Lawrence, KS: University Press of Kansas, 1990).

35. *Elrod v. Burns*, 427 U.S. 347, 376 (1976).

36. See Rosenbloom, *Federal Service and the Constitution*, Chapters 7 and 8.

Additional Reading

Ban, Carolyn. *How Do Public Managers Manage?* San Francisco: Jossey-Bass, 1995.

Cohen, Steven, and William Eimicke. *The New Effective Public Manager.* San Francisco: Jossey-Bass, 1995.

Hargrove, E., and J. Glidewell, eds. *Impossible Jobs in Public Management.* Lawrence, KS: University Press of Kansas, 1990.

Case 5.1
Due Process Versus Arbitrary Means

KOLENDER, CHIEF OF POLICE OF SAN DIEGO, et al. v. LAWSON
Argued November 8, 1982
Decided May 2, 1983
461 US 352

JUSTICE O'CONNOR delivered the opinion of the Court.

This appeal presents a facial challenge to a criminal statute that requires persons who loiter or wander on the streets to provide a "credible and reliable" identification and to account for their presence when requested by a peace officer under circumstances that would justify a stop under the standards of *Terry v. Ohio,* 392 U.S. 1 (1968). We conclude that the statute as it has been construed is unconstitutionally vague within the meaning of the Due Process Clause of the Fourteenth Amendment by failing to clarify what is contemplated by the requirement that a suspect provide a "credible and reliable" identification. Accordingly, we affirm the judgment of the court below.

I

Appellee Edward Lawson was detained or arrested on approximately 15 occasions between March 1975 and January 1977 pursuant to Cal. Penal Code Ann. § 647(e) (West 1970). Lawson was prosecuted only twice, and was convicted once. The second charge was dismissed.

Lawson then brought a civil action in the District Court for the Southern District of California seeking a declaratory judgment that § 647(e) is unconstitutional, a mandatory injunction to restrain enforcement of the statute, and compensatory and punitive damages against the various officers who detained him. The District Court found that § 647(e) was overbroad because "a person who is stopped on less than probable cause cannot be punished for failing to identify himself." ... The District Court enjoined enforcement of the statute....

... The Court of Appeals affirmed the District Court determination as to the unconstitutionality of § 647(e).... The appellate court determined that the statute was unconstitu-

tional in that it violates the Fourth Amendment's proscription against unreasonable searches and seizures, it contains a vague enforcement standard that is susceptible to arbitrary enforcement, and it fails to give fair and adequate notice of the type of conduct prohibited....

The officers appealed to this Court....

• • •

II

Our Constitution is designed to maximize individual freedoms within a framework of ordered liberty. Statutory limitations on those freedoms are examined for substantive authority and contents as well as for definiteness or certainty of expression....

As generally stated, the void-for-vagueness doctrine requires that a penal statute define the criminal offense with sufficient definiteness that ordinary people can understand what conduct is prohibited and in a manner that does not encourage arbitrary and discriminatory enforcement.... Although the doctrine focuses both on actual notice to citizens and arbitrary enforcement, we have recognized recently that the more important aspect of the vagueness doctrine "is not actual notice, but the other principal element of the doctrine—the requirement that a legislature establish minimal guidelines to govern law enforcement." ... Where the legislature fails to provide such minimal guidelines, a criminal statute may permit "a standardless sweep [that] allows policemen, prosecutors, and juries to pursue their personal predilections." ...

Section 647(e), as presently drafted and as construed by the state courts, contains no standard for determining what a suspect has to do in order to satisfy the requirement to provide a "credible and reliable" identification. As such, the statute vests virtually complete discretion in the hands of the police to determine whether the suspect has satisfied the statute and must be permitted to go on his way in the absence of probable cause to arrest. An individual, who police may think is suspicious but do not have probable cause to believe has committed a crime, is entitled to continue to walk the public streets "only at the whim of any police officer" who happens to stop that individual under § 647(e).... Our concern here is based upon the "potential for arbitrarily suppressing First Amendment liberties...." ...In addition, § 647(e) implicates consideration of the constitutional right to freedom of movement....

Section 647(e) is not simply a "stop-and-identify" statute. Rather, the statute requires that the individual provide a "credible and reliable" identification that carries a "reasonable assurance" of its authenticity, and that provides "means for later getting in touch with the person who has identified himself." ...

In addition, the suspect may also have to account for his presence "to the extent it assists in producing credible and reliable identification."...

At oral argument, the appellants confirmed that a suspect violates § 647(e) unless "the officer [is] satisfied that the identification is reliable." ... In giving examples of how suspects would satisfy the requirement, appellants explained that a jogger, who was not carrying identification, could, depending on the particular officer, be required to answer a series of questions concerning the route that he followed to arrive at the place where the officers detained him, or could satisfy the identification requirement simply by reciting his name and address....

It is clear that the full discretion accorded to the police to determine whether the suspect has provided a "credible and reliable" identification necessarily "entrust[s] lawmaking 'to the moment-to-moment judgment of the policeman on his beat.'" ... Section 647(e) "furnishes a convenient tool for 'harsh and discriminatory enforcement by local prosecuting officials, against particular groups deemed to merit their displeasure,'" ... and "confers on police a virtually unrestrained power to arrest and charge persons with a violation." ... In providing that a detention under § 647(e) may occur only where there is the level of suspicion sufficient to justify a *Terry* stop, the State ensures the existence of "neutral limitations on the conduct of individual officers." ...

Although the initial detention is justified, the State fails to establish standards by which the officers may determine whether the suspect has complied with the subsequent identification requirement.

Appellants stress the need for strengthened law enforcement tools to combat the epidemic of crime that plagues our Nation. The concern of our citizens with curbing criminal activity is certainly a matter requiring the attention of all branches of government. As weighty as this concern is, however, it cannot justify legislation that would otherwise fail to meet constitutional standards for definiteness and clarity.... Section 647(e), as presently construed, requires that "suspicious" persons satisfy some undefined identification requirement, or face criminal punishment. Although due process does not require "impossible standards" of clarity, this is not a case where further precision in the statutory language is either impossible or impractical.

Discussion Questions

1. There is more to *Kolender v. Lawson* than meets the eye. In part, the majority opinion holds the regulation unconstitutional because it encourages arbitrary enforcement. But it is possible to apply the regulation in nonarbitrary ways as well. For instance, Justice White speculated in dissent that an individual might answer, "Who I am is just none of your business." Would an arrest for failing to comply with the regulation be arbitrary under such circumstances? According to the Court's logic, does the constitutional requirement that a criminal statute be definite and clear rule out even the nonarbitrary application of vague statutes? What does the *Kolender* ruling suggest in terms of enforcing administrative rules?

2. The Court maintains that "... this is not a case where further precision in the statutory language is either impossible or impractical." Try to draft a statute that would accomplish the purposes sought by California while meeting the constitutional standards for definiteness and clarity.

3. Accounting for one's presence creates a logical difficulty, since everyone must always be *someplace*. Can you think of times when your answer to a police officer's question, "Why are you here?" might "inadequately" account for your presence? Does the legitimacy of one's presence depend on the time and circumstances? In short, does the statute demand a high degree of social conformity in order to assure compliance at all times?

4. In a concurring opinion, Justice Brennan noted that failure to comply with the California regulations might "... subject [a pedestrian] to arrest and all that goes with it: new acquaintances among jailers, lawyers, prisoners, and bail bondsmen, firsthand knowledge of local jail conditions, a 'search incident to arrest,' and the expense of defending against a possible prosecution." Do you think that, in practical terms, such penalties are disproportionate to the offense of failing to provide adequate identification or an account of one's presence?

Case 5.2
The Least Restrictive Alternative

ELROD, SHERIFF, et al. v. BURNS et al.
Argued April 19, 1976
Decided June 28, 1976
427 US 347

MR. JUSTICE BRENNAN announced the judgment of the Court and delivered an opinion in which Mr. Justice White and Mr. Justice Marshall joined.

This case presents the question whether public employees who allege that they were discharged or threatened with discharge solely because of their partisan political affiliation or nonaffiliation state a claim for deprivation of constitutional rights secured by the First and Fourteenth Amendments.

• • •

II

In December 1970, the Sheriff of Cook County, a Republican, was replaced by Richard Elrod, a Democrat. At that time, respondents, all Republicans, were employees of the Cook County Sheriff's Office. They were non–civil-service employees and, therefore, not covered by any statute, ordinance, or regulation protecting them from arbitrary discharge. One respondent, John Burns, was Chief Deputy of the Process Division and supervised all Depart-

ments of the Sheriff's Office working on the seventh floor of the building housing that office. Frank Vargas was a bailiff and security guard at the Juvenile Court of Cook County. Fred L. Buckley was employed as a process server in the office. Joseph Dennard was an employee in the office.

It has been the practice of the Sheriff of Cook County, when he assumes office from a Sheriff of a different political party, to replace non–civil-service employees of the Sheriff's Office with members of his own party when the existing employees lack or fail to obtain requisite support from, or fail to affiliate with, that party. Consequently, subsequent to Sheriff Elrod's assumption of office, respondents, with the exception of Buckley, were discharged from their employment solely because they did not support and were not members of the Democratic Party and had failed to obtain the sponsorship of one of its leaders. Buckley is in imminent danger of being discharged solely for the same reasons. Respondents allege that the discharges were ordered by Sheriff Elrod under the direction of the codefendants in this suit.

• • •

IV

The Cook County Sheriff's practice of dismissing employees on a partisan basis is but one form of the general practice of political patronage. The practice also includes placing loyal supporters in government jobs that may or may not have been made available by political discharges. Nonofficeholders may be the beneficiaries of lucrative government contracts for highway construction, buildings, and supplies. Favored wards may receive improved public services. Members of the judiciary may even engage in the practice through the appointment of receiverships, trusteeships, and refereeships. Although political patronage comprises a broad range of activities, we are here concerned only with the constitutionality of dismissing public employees for partisan reasons.

Patronage practice is not new to American politics. It has existed at the federal level at least since the Presidency of Thomas Jefferson, although its popularization and legitimation primarily occurred later, in the Presidency of Andrew Jackson. The practice is not unique to American politics. It has been used in many European countries, and in darker times, it played a significant role in the Nazi rise to power in Germany and other totalitarian states. More recent times have witnessed a strong decline in its use, particularly with respect to public employment. Indeed, only a few decades after Andrew Jackson's administration, strong discontent with the corruption and inefficiency of the patronage system of public employment eventuated in the Pendleton Act, the foundation of modern civil service. And on the state and local levels, merit systems have increasingly displaced the practice. This trend led the Court to observe in *CSC v. Letter Carriers* ... (1973), that "the judgment of Congress, the Executive, and the country appears to have been that partisan political activities by federal employees must be limited if the Government is to operate effectively and fairly, elections are to play their proper part in representative government, and employees themselves are to be sufficiently free from improper influences."

The decline of patronage employment is not, of course, relevant to the question of its constitutionality. It is the practice itself, not the magnitude of its occurrence, the constitutionality of which must be determined. Nor for that matter does any unacceptability of the practice signified by its decline indicate its unconstitutionality. Our inquiry does not begin with the judgment of history, though the actual operation of a practice viewed in retrospect may help to assess its workings with respect to constitutional limitations.... Rather, inquiry must commence with identification of the constitutional limitations implicated by a challenged governmental practice.

V

The cost of the practice of patronage is the restraint it places on freedoms of belief and association. In order to maintain their jobs, respondents were required to pledge their political allegiance to the Democratic Party, work for the election of other candidates of the Democratic Party, contribute a portion of their wages to the Party, or obtain the sponsorship of a member of the Party, usually at the price of one of the first three alternatives. Regardless of the incumbent party's identity, Democratic or otherwise, the consequences for association and belief are the same. An individual who is a member of the out-party maintains affiliation with his own party at the risk of losing his job. He works for the election of his party's candidates and espouses its policies at the same risk. The financial and campaign assistance that he is induced to provide to another party furthers the advancement of that party's policies to the detriment of his party's views and ultimately his own beliefs, and any assessment of his salary is tantamount to coerced belief.

Even a pledge of allegiance to another party, however ostensible, only serves to compromise the individual's true beliefs. Since the average public employee is hardly in the financial position to support his party and another, or to lend his time to two parties, the individual's ability to act according to his beliefs and to associate with others of his political persuasion is constrained, and support for his party is diminished.

It is not only belief and association which are restricted where political patronage is the practice. The free functioning of the electoral process also suffers. Conditioning public employment on partisan support prevents support of competing political interests. Existing employees are deterred from such support, as well as the multitude seeking jobs. As government employment, state or federal, becomes more pervasive, the greater the dependence on it becomes, and therefore the greater becomes the power to starve political opposition by commanding partisan support, financial and otherwise. Patronage thus tips the electoral process in favor of the incumbent party, and where the practice's scope is substantial relative to the size of the electorate, the impact on the process can be significant.

Our concern with the impact of patronage on political belief and association does not occur in the abstract, for political belief and association constitute the core of those activities protected by the First Amendment. Regardless of the nature of the inducement, whether it be by the denial of public employment or, as in *Board of Education v. Barnette...* (1943), by the influence of a teacher over students, "[i]f there is any fixed star in our constitutional constellation, it is that no official, high or petty, can prescribe what shall be orthodox in politics, nationalism, religion, or other matters of opinion or force citizens to confess by word or act their faith therein." ... And, though freedom of belief is central, "[t]he First Amendment protects political association as well as political expression." ... "There can no longer be any doubt that freedom to associate with others for the common advancement of political beliefs and ideas is a form of 'orderly group activity' protected by the First and Fourteenth Amendments.... The right to associate with the political party of one's choice is an integral part of this basic constitutional freedom."

These protections reflect our "profound national commitment to the principle that debate on public issues should be uninhibited, robust, and wide-open," ... a principle itself reflective of the fundamental understanding that "[c]ompetition in ideas and governmental policies is at the core of our electoral process...." ... Patronage, therefore, to the extent it compels or restrains belief and association, is inimical to the process which undergirds our system of government and is "at war with the deeper traditions of democracy embodied in the First Amendment."

• • •

VI

Although the practice of patronage dismissals clearly infringes First Amendment interests, our inquiry is not at an end, for the prohibition on encroachment of First Amendment protections is not an absolute. Restraints are permitted for appropriate reasons....

• • •

...It is firmly established that a significant impairment of First Amendment rights must survive exacting scrutiny.... "This type of scrutiny is necessary even if any deterrent effect on the exercise of First Amendment rights arises, not through direct government action, but indirectly as an unintended but inevitable result of the government's conduct...." ... Thus encroachment "cannot be justified upon a mere showing of a legitimate state interest." ...

The interest advanced must be paramount, one of vital importance, and the burden is on the government to show the existence of such an interest.... In the instant case, care must be taken not to confuse the interest of partisan organizations with governmental interests. Only the latter will suffice. Moreover, it not enough that the means chosen in furtherance of the interest be rationally related to that end.... The gain to the subordinating interest provided by the means must outweigh the incurred loss of protected rights ... and the government must "emplo[y] means closely drawn to avoid unnecessary abridgment...." ..."[A] State may not choose means that unnecessarily restrict constitutionally protected liberty. 'Precision of regulation must be the touchstone in an area so closely touching our most precious freedoms.' If the State has open to it a less drastic way of satisfying its legitimate interests, it may not choose a legislative scheme that broadly stifles the exercise of fundamental personal liberties." ... In short, if conditioning the retention of public employment on the employee's support of the in-party is to survive constitutional challenge, it must further some vital government end by a means that is least restrictive of freedom of belief and association in achieving that end, and the benefit gained must outweigh the loss of constitutionally protected rights.

One interest which has been offered in justification of patronage is the need to insure effective government and the efficiency of public employees. It is argued that employees of political persuasions not the same as that of the party in control of public office will not have the incentive to work effectively and may even be motivated to subvert the incumbent administration's efforts to govern effectively. We are not persuaded. The inefficiency resulting from the wholesale replacement of large numbers of public employees every time political office changes hands belies this justification. And the prospect of dismissal after an election in which the incumbent party has lost is only a disincentive to good work. Further, it is not clear that dismissal in order to make room for a patronage appointment will result in replacement by a person more qualified to do the job since appointment often occurs in exchange for the delivery of votes, or other party service, not job capability. More fundamentally, however, the argument does not succeed because it is doubtful that the mere difference of political persuasion motivates poor performance; nor do we think it legitimately may be used as a basis for imputing such behavior. The Court has consistently recognized that mere political association is an inadaquate basis for imputing disposition to ill-willed conduct....

Even if the first argument that patronage serves effectiveness and efficiency be rejected, it still may be argued that patronage serves those interests by giving the employees of an incumbent party the incentive to perform well in order to insure their party's incumbency and thereby their jobs. Patronage, according to the argument, thus makes employees highly accountable to the public. But the ability of officials more directly accountable to the electorate to discharge employees for cause and the availability of merit systems, growth in the use of which has been quite significant, convince us that means less intrusive than patronage still exist for achieving accountability in the public work force and, thereby, effective and efficient government. The greater effectiveness of patronage over these less drastic means, if any, is at best marginal, a gain outweighed by the absence of intrusion on protected interests under the alternatives....

A second interest advanced in support of patronage is the need for political loyalty of employees, not to the end that effectiveness and efficiency be insured, but to the end that representative government not be undercut by tactics obstructing the implementation of policies of the new administration, policies presumably sanctioned by the electorate. The justification is not without force, but is nevertheless inadequate to validate patronage wholesale. Limiting patronage dismissals to policymaking positions is sufficient to achieve this governmental end. Nonpolicymaking individuals usually have only limited responsibility and are therefore not in a position to thwart the goals of the in-party....

It is argued that a third interest supporting patronage dismissals is the preservation of the democratic process. According to petitioners, "'we have contrived no system for the support of party that does not place considerable reliance on patronage. The party organization makes a democratic government work and charges a price for its services.'" The argument is thus premised on the centrality of partisan politics to the democratic process.

Preservation of the democratic process is certainly an interest protection of which may in some instances justify limitations on First Amendment freedoms.... But however important preservation of the two-party system or any system involving a fixed number of parties may or may not be, we are not persuaded that the elimination of patronage practice or, as is specifically involved here, the interdiction of patronage dismissals, will bring about the demise of party politics. Political parties existed in the absence of active patronage practice prior to the administration of Andrew Jackson, and they have survived substantial reduction in their patronage power through the establishment of merit systems.

Patronage dismissals thus are not the least restrictive alternative to achieving the contribution they may make to the democratic process. The process functions as well without the practice, perhaps even better, for patronage dismissals clearly also retard that process. Patronage can result in the entrenchment of one or a few parties to the exclusion of others. And most indisputably, as we recognized at the outset, patronage is a very effective impediment to the associational and speech freedoms which are essential to a meaningful system of democratic government. Thus, if patronage contributes at all to the elective process, that contribution is diminished by the practice's impairment of the same....

• • •

In summary, patronage dismissals severely restrict political belief and association. Though there is a vital need for government efficiency and effectiveness, such dismissals are on balance not the least restrictive means for fostering that end. There is also a need to insure that policies which the electorate has sanctioned are effectively implemented. That interest can be fully satisfied by limiting patronage dismissals to policymaking positions. Finally, patronage dismissals cannot be justified by their contribution to the proper functioning of our democratic process through their assistance to partisan politics since political parties are nurtured by other, less intrusive and equally effective methods. More fundamentally, however, any contribution of patronage dismissals to the democratic process does not suffice to override their severe encroachment on First Amendment freedoms. We hold, therefore, that the practice of patronage dismissals is unconstitutional under the First and Fourteenth Amendments, and that respondents thus stated a valid claim for relief.

Discussion Questions

1. Justice Brennan's plurality opinion identifies three governmental objectives allegedly served by patronage dismissals and concludes that such dismissals are not the means least restrictive of constitutional rights for achieving any of them. Consider each of the objectives mentioned and less restrictive means that could be employed to promote them. Are the means you choose more or less effective than patronage dismissals?

2. Justice Powell dissented in an opinion joined by Chief Justice Burger and Justice Rehnquist. He noted that "The Court holds unconstitutional a practice as old as the Republic...." Does the *Elrod* decision suggest (a) that the judiciary is free to declare any practice implicating constitutional rights to which it is opposed to be unconstitutional regardless of the history of that practice; (b) that the Constitution is continually being adapted to changing political, economic, and social circumstances; and/or (c) that the constitutional requirements are constant and the courts simply articulate them when the opportunity and need arises (in other words, patronage was always unconstitutional, but the Court was never presented with the opportunity to rule on it prior to the *Elrod* case)? What are the full implications of each of these three possible interpretations for choosing administrative means that are constitutional? For achieving constitutional competence generally?

3. In *Branti v. Finkel,* 445 U.S. 506 (1980), the Supreme Court modified the constitutional barrier to patronage dismissals by indicating that "... the ultimate inquiry is not whether the label 'policymaker' or 'confidential' fits a particular position; rather, the question is whether the hiring authority can demonstrate that party affiliation is an appropriate requirement for the effective performance of the public office involved." Can you think of an administrative position for which patronage dismissals could be successfully defended under this standard? Under the least restrictive alternative test? Would a department head or budget director fill such a position? A city manager? The U.S. Secretary of State? What criteria, if any exist, would such a position have to meet? See also *Rutan v. Republican Party of Illinois,* 497 U.S. 62 (1990), which extends the *Branti* standard to almost all personnel practices.

Case 5.3
Racial and Ethnic Classifications

ADARAND CONSTRUCTORS, INC. v. PENA
Argued January 17, 1995
Decided June 12, 1995
515 US 200

JUSTICE O'CONNOR announced the judgment of the Court and delivered an opinion
with respect to Parts I, II, III-A, III-B, III-D,
and IV, which is for the Court except insofar as
it might be inconsistent with the views expressed in Justice Scalia's concurrence, an opinion with respect to Part III-C in which Justice
Kennedy joins.

Petitioner Adarand Constructors, Inc., claims
that the Federal Government's practice of giving general contractors on government projects
a financial incentive to hire subcontractors controlled by "socially and economically disadvantaged individuals," and, in particular, the
Government's use of race-based presumptions
in identifying such individuals, violates the
equal protection component of the Fifth
Amendment's Due Process Clause. The Court
of Appeals rejected Adarand's claim. We conclude, however, that courts should analyze cases
of this kind under a different standard of review than the one the Court of Appeals applied. We therefore vacate the Court of Appeals'
judgment and remand the case for further proceedings.

I

In 1989, the Central Federal Lands Highway
Division (CFLHD), which is part of the United States Department of Transportation (DOT),
awarded the prime contract for a highway construction project in Colorado to Mountain
Gravel & Construction Company. Mountain
Gravel then solicited bids from subcontractors
for the guardrail portion of the contract.
Adarand, a Colorado-based highway construction company specializing in guardrail work,
submitted the low bid. Gonzales Construction
Company also submitted a bid.

The prime contract's terms provide that
Mountain Gravel would receive additional
compensation if it hired subcontractors certified as small businesses controlled by "socially

and economically disadvantaged individuals."
... Gonzales is certified as such a business;
Adarand is not. Mountain Gravel awarded the
subcontract to Gonzales, despite Adarand's low
bid, and Mountain Gravel's Chief Estimator has
submitted an affidavit stating that Mountain
Gravel would have accepted Adarand's bid had
it not been for the additional payment it received by hiring Gonzales instead.... Federal
law requires that a subcontracting clause similar
to the one used here must appear in most federal agency contracts, and it also requires the
clause to state that

> [t]he contractor shall presume that socially and
> economically disadvantaged individuals include
> Black Americans, Hispanic Americans, Native
> Americans, Asian Pacific Americans, and other
> minorities, or any other individual found to be
> disadvantaged by the [Small Business] Adminis-
> tration pursuant to section 8(a) of the Small Busi-
> ness Act....

Adarand claims that the presumption set forth
in that statute discriminates on the basis of race
in violation of the Federal Government's Fifth
Amendment obligation not to deny anyone
equal protection of the laws.

These fairly straightforward facts implicate
a complex scheme of federal statutes and regulations....

• • •

III

A

The Government urges that "[t]he Subcontracting Compensation Clause program is...a
program based on *disadvantage*, not on race," and
thus that it is subject only to "the most relaxed
judicial scrutiny."... To the extent that the
statutes and regulations involved in this case are
race-neutral, we agree. The Government concedes, however, that "the race-based rebuttable

presumption used in some certification determinations under the Subcontracting Compensation Clause" is subject to some heightened level of scrutiny…. (We note, incidentally, that this case concerns only classifications based explicitly on race, and presents none of the additional difficulties posed by laws that, although facially race neutral, result in racially disproportionate impact and are motivated by a racially discriminatory purpose.)…

Adarand's claim arises under the Fifth Amendment to the Constitution, which provides that "No person shall…be deprived of life, liberty, or property, without due process of law." Although this Court has always understood that Clause to provide some measure of protection against *arbitrary* treatment by the Federal Government, it is not as explicit a guarantee of *equal* treatment as the Fourteenth Amendment, which provides that "No *State* shall…deny to any person within its jurisdiction the equal protection of the laws" (emphasis added). Our cases have accorded varying degrees of significance to the difference in the language of those two Clauses. We think it necessary to revisit the issue here.

• • •

B

• • •

Despite lingering uncertainty in the details,… the Court's cases…had established three general propositions with respect to governmental racial classifications. First, skepticism: "'[a]ny preference based on racial or ethnic criteria must necessarily receive a most searching examination'";… "[A]ny official action that treats a person differently on account of his race or ethnic origin is inherently suspect";… "[R]acial classifications [are] 'constitutionally suspect'"… "Distinctions between citizens solely because of their ancestry are by their very nature odious to a free people." Second, consistency: "the standard of review under the Equal Protection Clause is not dependent on the race of those burdened or benefited by a particular classification,"…*i.e.,* all racial classifications reviewable under the Equal Protection Clause must be strictly scrutinized. And third, congruence: "[e]qual protection analysis in the Fifth Amendment area is the same as that under the

Fourteenth Amendment."… Taken together, these three propositions lead to the conclusion that any person, of whatever race, has the right to demand that any governmental actor subject to the Constitution justify any racial classification subjecting that person to unequal treatment under the strictest judicial scrutiny….

• • •

By adopting intermediate scrutiny as the standard of review for congressionally mandated "benign" racial classifications, *Metro Broadcasting,* [*Inc. v. FCC,* 1990] departed from prior cases in two significant respects. First, it turned its back on [the previous] explanation of why strict scrutiny of all governmental racial classifications is essential:

> Absent searching judicial inquiry into the justification for such race-based measures, there is simply no way of determining what classifications are "benign" or "remedial" and what classifications are in fact motivated by illegitimate notions of racial inferiority or simple racial politics. Indeed, the purpose of strict scrutiny is to "smoke out" illegitimate uses of race by assuring that the legislative body is pursuing a goal important enough to warrant use of a highly suspect tool. The test also ensures that the means chosen "fit" this compelling goal so closely that there is little or no possibility that the motive for the classification was illegitimate racial prejudice or stereotype….

We adhere to that view today, despite the surface appeal of holding "benign" racial classifications to a lower standard, because "it may not always be clear that a so-called preference is in fact benign."…

> [M]ore than good motives should be required when government seeks to allocate its resources by way of an explicit racial classification system….

• • •

Accordingly, we hold today that all racial classifications, imposed by whatever federal, state, or local governmental actor, must be analyzed by a reviewing court under strict scrutiny. In other words, such classifications are constitutional only if they are narrowly tailored measures that further compelling governmental interests. To the extent that *Metro Broadcasting* is inconsistent with that holding, it is overruled.

• • •

Justice Stevens concurs in our view that courts should take a skeptical view of all governmental racial classifications.... He also allows that

> [n]othing is inherently wrong with applying a single standard to fundamentally different situations, as long as that standard takes relevant differences into account....

...What he fails to recognize is that strict scrutiny *does* take "relevant differences" into account—indeed, that is its fundamental purpose. The point of carefully examining the interest asserted by the government in support of a racial classification, and the evidence offered to show that the classification is needed, is precisely to distinguish legitimate from illegitimate uses of race in governmental decisionmaking....

• • •

Justice Stevens chides us for our "supposed inability to differentiate between 'invidious' and 'benign' discrimination," because it is in his view sufficient that "people understand the difference between good intentions and bad."... But, as we have just explained, the point of strict scrutiny is to "differentiate between" permissible and impermissible governmental use of race. And Justice Stevens himself has already explained...why "good intentions" alone are not enough to sustain a supposedly "benign" racial classification:

> [E]ven though it is not the actual predicate for this legislation, a statute of this kind [giving preference to minority businesses] inevitably is perceived by many as resting on an assumption that those who are granted this special preference are less qualified in some respect that is identified purely by their race. Because that perception—*especially when fostered by the Congress of the United States*—can only exacerbate rather than reduce racial prejudice, it will delay the time when race will become a truly irrelevant, or at least insignificant, factor. *Unless Congress clearly articulates the need and basis* for a racial classification, *and also tailors the classification to its justification,* the Court should not uphold this kind of statute....

• • •

D

Our action today makes explicit [that]... federal racial classifications, like those of a State, must serve a compelling governmental interest, and must be narrowly tailored to further that interest....

• • •

Finally, we wish to dispel the notion that strict scrutiny is "strict in theory, but fatal in fact."... The unhappy persistence of both the practice and the lingering effects of racial discrimination against minority groups in this country is an unfortunate reality, and government is not disqualified from acting in response to it. As recently as 1987, for example, every Justice of this Court agreed that the Alabama Department of Public Safety's "pervasive, systematic, and obstinate discriminatory conduct" justified a narrowly tailored race-based remedy....When race-based action is necessary to further a compelling interest, such action is within constitutional constraints if it satisfies the "narrow tailoring" test this Court has set out in previous cases.

IV

...The Court of Appeals did not decide the question whether the interests served by the use of subcontractor compensation clauses are properly described as "compelling." It also did not address the question of narrow tailoring in terms of our strict scrutiny cases, by asking, for example, whether there was "any consideration of the use of race-neutral means to increase minority business participation" in government contracting..., or whether the program was appropriately limited such that it "will not last longer than the discriminatory effects it is designed to eliminate."...

• • •

Accordingly, the judgment of the Court of Appeals is vacated, and the case is remanded for further proceedings consistent with this opinion.

Discussion Questions

1. The majority notes that strict scrutiny is *not* "strict in theory but fatal in fact." What might be a compelling governmental interest that would justify racial or ethnic classifications?

2. Is a distinction between "benign" and "invidious" racial classifications useful? Before answering, consider the following passages from Justice Clarence Thomas's concurring opinion:

… there can be no doubt that racial paternalism and its unintended consequences can be as poisonous and pernicious as any other form of discrimination. So-called "benign" discrimination teaches many that because of chronic and apparently immutable handicaps, minorities cannot compete with them without their patronizing indulgence. Inevitably, such programs engender attitudes of superiority or, alternatively, provoke resentment among those who believe that they have been wronged by the government's use of race. These programs stamp minorities with a badge of inferiority that may cause them to develop dependencies or to adopt an attitude that they are "entitled" to preferences.…

In my mind, government-sponsored racial discrimination based on benign prejudice is just as noxious as discrimination inspired by malicious prejudice. In each instance, it is racial discrimination, plain and simple.

3. Assume that a government or state university wants to bring more minorities into its workforce or student body. What constitutional tests would the use of affirmative action techniques face? Can you think of other approaches that would be both constitutional and effective?

SIX

Efficiency

According to the orthodox approach to public administration, "The fundamental objective of the science of administration is the accomplishment of the work in hand with the least expenditure of man-power and materials ˉ ficiency is thus axiom number one in the value scale of administration."[1] ˉ   ˙rtance of administrative efficiency is almost self-evident. As the ˊ   ˙ninistrative state grew, the potential impact of waste through iˉ   ˙mendous. For example, today, if each federal employee ˉ   ˊ workday in the year, the total lost time would   ˋoying 125,000 workers for a year—more than thɛ   ˋe-partments of State, Labor, Energy, Housing ʐ   ʌ, and Commerce combined. However, like otĥ   ˍy must often be subordinated to constitutional valuɛ   ˍpetent public administrator can no longer assume that eɦ.   ˳ood'"[2] of his or her work.

Efficiency Defined Traditionally

Administrative efficiency is traditionally defined analogously to mechanical efficiency. It is a ratio of outputs to inputs. The outputs can be any units of service or constraints delivered or applied through public administrative operations. The number of tons of garbage collected, miles of streets snowplowed, square miles patrolled by police, and restaurants inspected are examples of outputs. The inputs include personnel, equipment, supplies, materials, buildings, and the overhead administrative activities used to obtain and/or maintain them. The greater the outputs, relative to the inputs, the more efficient public administration is considered to be.

Although the concept of administrative efficiency is related to economy, it is analytically distinct. Efficiency seeks to use a given level of inputs to produce more outputs. It looks toward better management, training, organization of work, and technology as means of obtaining more output with the same (or less) input. Economy, which is the subject of Chapter 8, by contrast, is concerned with operational expenses, such as the cost per unit of output. Economy seeks to reduce the cost of the output, rather than the effort, energy, and time required to produce it. Of **125** course, efficiency and economy may overlap, but the distinction between the two is illustrated by any number of technologies that are both more efficient and more expensive. For instance, a faster modem that uses the same or less energy than a slower one is more efficient. But it may also be more expensive, depending on initial price and utilization. Because public administrative operations are often underfunded, public managers frequently face a trade-off between efficiency and economy.

Administrative organization generally places a high premium on efficiency. Agencies rely on specialization, or a division of labor, because it promotes efficiency. As Adam Smith observed in *The Wealth of Nations* (1776),[3] the same number of workers can produce more pins or other products per unit of time when each specializes in the creation of part of the item rather than if each worker is expected to produce it entirely by himself or herself. Assembly-line production is an embodiment of this idea. Administrative organizations typically use hierarchy to coordinate the specialized functions so that the desired outputs are produced. Further, these organizations emphasize hiring and promoting the most capable workers.

It is important to bear in mind that the traditional concept of efficiency does not directly concern the value of the outputs. Efficiency is not a ratio of benefits to inputs: administrative "... efficiency takes the output you intend to produce as given; it does not question the output's benefit."[4] Therefore, the emphasis on efficiency may beg the larger question of what public administrative activity actually achieves. This is a point of departure for the New Public Management (NPM), for which results are paramount.

Efficiency and the New Public Management (NPM)

The NPM places the value of efficiency in a much broader context. First, it assesses efficiency from the perspective of attaining governmental objectives or *outcomes* rather than generating outputs. In the NPM, efficiency is closely related to effectiveness. A program with a high ratio of outputs to inputs will not be considered efficient if it fails to achieve the results for which it was designed. For instance, whereas traditional public administration might measure the inputs necessary to produce an output such as "annually inspect 3,200 grain elevators," the NPM will be concerned with the outcome: "Through periodic grain and elevator inspection, reduce the incidence of grain dust explosions resulting in catastrophic loss or fatalities to zero."[5] In practice, this difference is fundamental because it tends to shift an organization's focus and culture from concentrating on inputs and overhead to measuring results.

Second, the NPM makes something of an exception to its outcome orientation where customers are concerned. It places a very high premium on efficiency in customer service. Ideally, for the NPM, administrative organizations should be "customer driven," that is, organized and operated to "delight" the customer.[6] Where possible, programs should operate according to "market dynamics," that is, based on competition for customers among government agencies as well as between them and private organizations.[7] If marketlike arrangements are inappropriate, then the NPM relies heavily on customer satisfaction standards to make public management more efficient. These standards often reflect the NPM's results orientation. For example, the Postal Service pledges that "Your local First Class Mail will be delivered overnight."[8] Sometimes, however, the standards look more toward outputs, as in the case of the Occupational Safety and Health Administration's promise to "Be respectful and professional during inspections."[9] In either event, meeting these standards is a key measure of agency performance, and the fewer inputs consumed, the more efficient the organization is.

Third, the NPM largely rejects hierarchy and centralization as means of promoting administrative efficiency. According to the federal National Performance Review (NPR), as a result of traditional public management, "The federal government is filled with good people trapped in bad systems: budget systems, personnel systems, procurement systems, financial management systems, information systems."[10] In response to stifling hierarchical and centralized controls, "… many employees have simply given up. They do everything by the book—whether it makes sense or not."[11] Unfortunately, therefore, "In the name of controlling waste, we have created paralyzing inefficiency. It's time we found a way to get rid of waste and encourage efficiency."[12]

The NPM's strategy is to deregulate the public service and empower its employees. The NPR insists that "all federal agencies will delegate, decentralize, and empower employees to make decisions. This will let front-line and front-office workers use their creative judgment as they offer service to customers and solve problems."[13] Empowerment, coupled with accountability for results, is both efficient and safe because

> … people—in government or out—are, for the most part, neither crooked nor stupid. Most people want to do the right thing, so long as the right thing makes sense. Perhaps the most important thing about the reinvention initiative, and its regulatory reform work in particular, is that it is based on a new assumption: that people are honest and that if you tell people what needs to be done, and let them get on with doing it, the chances are it will be done better—and more cheaply—than if you tell them how.[14]

Whether this view of human nature is correct is a moot question. However, it clearly runs against the underlying premises of the Constitution and the received political culture in the United States. For the Framers, as James Madison explained in *Federalist No. 51,*

> If men were angels, no government would be necessary. If angels were to govern men, neither external nor internal controls on government would be necessary. In framing a government which is to be administered by men over men, the great difficulty lies in this: you must first enable the government to control the governed; and in the next place oblige it to control itself. A dependence on the people is, no doubt, the primary control on the government; but experience has taught mankind the necessity of auxiliary precautions.[15]

Since one person's "auxiliary precautions" are another's "red tape," extensive deregulation and employee empowerment would inevitably create tension with some aspects of constitutional structure and procedure—especially the separation of powers and due process.[16] Constitutionally competent public managers will want to remain especially alert to this area in the future.

Efficiency as a Moral Value

Efficiency is instrumental because it is not concerned with the ultimate purposes or objectives of public administration. However, it is frequently treated as an end in itself. Because it is the antithesis of waste, which is viewed by many to be immoral, efficiency can be considered a moral good. As Robert Simmons and Eugene Dvorin note, according to orthodox administrative theory,

> The "goodness" or "badness" of a particular organizational pattern was a mathematical relationship of "inputs" to "outputs." Where the latter was maximized and the former minimized, a moral "good" resulted. Where the situation was reversed, a moral "bad" resulted. Virtue or "goodness" was therefore equated with the relationship of these two factors, that is, "efficiency" or "inefficiency." Mathematics was transformed into ethics.[17]

The NPM also broadly thinks of efficiency as a moral good, but for different reasons. In its view, administrative performance is the key to developing citizens' trust in government—and, "Democracy stands or falls on trust."[18] The NPR starkly makes the case that efficient administration is a moral imperative for self-government:

> When we are not trusted, when nothing we say or do seems to make a difference, we feel powerless. Elections alone do not restore that power. The power that matters in a self-governing democracy is the power we can exercise "over-the-counter," on a daily basis, whenever we interact with our government, whenever we seek to make our needs known. Someone must be listening. Someone must act.[19]

However, despite the importance of efficiency and the moral value many attach to it, constitutional competence demands that efficiency not be treated as an end in itself. As Dwight Waldo, a major critic of the traditional approach, argued in his classic book, *The Administrative State*, "… efficiency cannot *itself* be a 'value.' … Things are not simply 'efficient' or 'inefficient.' They are efficient or inefficient for given purposes, and efficiency for one purpose may mean inefficiency for another."[20] For example, consider the question of whether the bicameral legislatures used in the federal government and 49 of the 50 states (Nebraska being the sole exception) are efficient. Certainly, the two legislative chambers have overlapping responsibilities. They could even be considered redundant, especially at the state level, where the upper and lower houses are both apportioned on the basis of population. The legislative process is generally slow, cumbersome, and vulnerable to numerous veto points. It is stalemated unless both houses agree, by majority vote, to pass a bill. Consequently, on the surface, and from an organizational perspective, bicameralism looks inefficient as a means of processing proposals for legislation. However, as a structural arrangement for representing constituencies, deliberating over public policy, and placing checks and balances on elected legislators, bicameralism may be highly efficient.

Moreover, seeking efficiency with regard to some governmental purposes may be of secondary concern. Although a lot of lip and media service is paid to governmental efficiency, American political culture does not place the highest premium on it. As Chief Justice Burger wrote in *Immigration and Naturalization Service v. Chadha* (1983), Case 1.1, "with all the obvious flaws of delay, untidiness, and potential for abuse, we have not yet found a better way to preserve freedom than by making the exercise of power subject to the carefully crafted restraints spelled out in the Constitution."[21] To the extent that public administration is intertwined or infused with constitutionalism and politics, it may be inappropriate to view efficiency as "axiom number one." Even Luther Gulick, who believed that efficiency could be the basis of a science of administration, noted that "There are ... highly inefficient arrangements like citizen boards and small local governments which *may* be necessary in a democracy...."[22]

One of the most common disparities between democratic constitutionalism and administrative efficiency centers on accountability. Accountability requires *red tape*—vouchers, forms, approvals, and oversight by inspectors general, legislatures, courts, and others—which clearly militates against administrative efficiency.[23] Similarly, arrangements for citizen participation, interest group representation, open meetings, and freedom of information may also detract from the efficient application of administrative expertise.[24]

Efficiency Within the Constitutional Framework

Public administrators must be aware of at least four broad constitutional values that help to determine the appropriateness of efforts to maximize efficiency. Already outlined in Chapter 1, these are constitutional integrity; procedural due process; robust individual civil rights and liberties; and equal protection of the laws. Together, these concerns provide a framework that can guide constitutionally competent public managers in their pursuit of efficiency.

The Fifth and Fourteenth Amendments provide that the government shall not deprive any person of "life, liberty, or property, without due process of law." The essence of procedural due process is fairness. In the public administrative context, it often requires procedures, such as hearings, that are at odds with managerial efficiency.

The importance of procedural due process in public management is heightened by the treatment of some governmental benefits as "property interests." These include public employment and welfare benefits to which one has a legal right or entitlement, whether for a fixed or indefinite duration. Procedural due process applies when the government seeks to terminate such a property interest during the term for which it was offered, though not ordinarily upon its expiration.

Case 6.1, *Cleveland Board of Education v. Loudermill* (1985), well illustrates the application of procedural due process to routine public management. In considering the constitutionality of an employee's dismissal, the Supreme Court assesses the three standard factors, first established in *Mathews v. Eldridge* (1976),[25] which must be taken into account when public administrators deprive individuals of governmental benefits in which liberty or property interests are implicated. These are "... first, the private interest that will be affected by the official action; second, the risk of an erroneous deprivation of such interest through the procedures used, and the probable value, if any, of additional or substitute procedural safeguards; and finally, the Government's interest, including the function involved and the fiscal and administrative burdens that the additional or substitute procedural requirement would entail."[26]

The *Loudermill* case also discusses the constitutional importance of providing individuals, who stand to be deprived of liberty or property interests, notice of the impending action and an opportunity to respond to the information on which it is based. Although the decision applies specifically to dismissal from civil service employment, the Court's discussion of due process is broad enough to encompass other administrative actions as well.

Case 6.2, *Cleveland Board of Education v. LaFleur* (1974), illustrates two additional aspects of procedural due process's commitment to fundamental fairness: (a) the Constitution's distaste for conclusive, or irrebuttable, harmful presumptions about individuals, and (b) its strong preference for individualized treatment of persons whose liberty or property interests may be abridged by administrative action. However, avoiding generalized presumptions—such as that a school teacher will be unfit to continue in the classroom after the fourth or fifth month of her normal pregnancy—and assessing each case on its own merits may sometimes interfere with efficiency, as the school boards claimed in *LaFleur.*

LaFleur is also a good example of substantive due process, which was explained in Chapter 1. Note that the Supreme Court is primarily concerned with the teachers' substantive due process liberty interests to make choices regarding marriage and childbearing. The potential deprivation of these liberty interests is what triggers the need for procedural due process as well as the Court's concern with irrebuttable presumptions and its preference for individualized determinations.

The potential conflict between administrative efficiency and the Constitution's strong commitment to individual civil rights and liberties is nicely illustrated by Case 6.3, *Rankin v. McPherson* (1987). *Rankin* deals with a relatively common, but complex administrative issue: When can public employees' remarks be the basis for adverse actions intended to promote the efficiency of the civil service? The Supreme Court reached the startling conclusion that McPherson, a probationary employee in a constable's office, had a constitutionally protected right to say to a coworker on the job that if there were another assassination attempt on President Ronald Reagan, "… I hope they get him."[27] The Court broadly explains how the government's concern with efficiency must be balanced against public employees' countervailing interests in freedom of speech.

The Court noted that there is a basic tension between the government's responsibility to conduct its business effectively and efficiently and the rights of millions of public employees to speak out about administrative wrongdoing, dangers to public health or safety, and general inefficiency. The public's interest in receiving information about how government operates is also a key concern.[28]

Once a public employee says something that is damaging to administrative operations, the first question is whether the remark is on a matter of public concern. A statement on a subject far removed from the kind of information the public needs to assess governmental performance is not of public concern and does not enjoy constitutional protection. However, the context of the remarks can be important. Everyday complaints about internal workplace matters are not protected, even though they might be elements of a matter of "public concern" in an investigation or broader context. The Court was divided over whether McPherson's comment passed the threshold for constitutional protection, but a majority found it of public concern because it was uttered during a general discussion of Reagan's policies toward minorities. Even incorrect statements on matters of public concern will be protected, unless the employee knew they were false or did not care if they were truthful.[29]

Remarks on matters of public concern are protected, but the government can still take action based on them. This is because

> ... the extra power the government has in this area comes from the nature of the government's mission as [an] employer.... The key to First Amendment analysis of government employment decisions, then, is this: The government's interest in achieving its goals as effectively and efficiently as possible is elevated from a relatively subordinate interest when it acts as sovereign to a significant one when it acts as an employer. The government cannot restrict the speech of the public at large just in the name of efficiency. But where the government is employing someone for the very purpose of effectively achieving its goals, such restrictions may well be appropriate.[30]

In general, to prevail, the employee must prove that the protected speech was a motivating factor in the government's adverse action against him or her. Then the government must demonstrate that, on balance, the public value of the speech did not outweigh the governmental interest in efficient or effective administration. Among the factors to be balanced are the nature of the employee's position; the time, place, and manner in which the remarks were made; and their impact on discipline, workplace harmony, confidentiality, normal administrative operations, and the employee's ability to do his or her job. When there is a dispute about what the employee actually said, the employer must take reasonable steps to find out before disciplining him or her.[31]

In passing, it should be noted that employee speech cases may be complicated by statutes that specifically protect whistleblowing. For example, in the federal government, public employee free speech cases often arise under the Whistleblower Protection Act of 1978, as amended.[32] The Act defines whistleblowing as

> any disclosure of information...which the employee or applicant reasonably believes evidences—(i) a violation of any law, rule, or regulation, or (ii) gross mismanagement, a gross waste of funds, an abuse of authority, or a substantial and specific danger to public health or safety....[33]

Additional federal statutes protect employee and others in speaking out on specific matters.[34] Consequently, many federal employee cases involving freedom of speech are decided on statutory rather than constitutional grounds.[35] By contrast, in states without whistleblower protection of public employees, state and local government workers typically rely on the First Amendment to protect their speech.[36]

Case 6.4, *Vernonia School District 47J v. Acton* (1995), illustrates a broad tension between Fourth Amendment privacy and administrative efficiency. *Vernonia* is one of four major drug testing cases decided by the Supreme Court since 1989. It is settled that the Fourth Amendment regulates drug testing in the public sector. However, its scope is at issue. When does the Fourth Amendment's protection against unreasonable searches require the government to have an individualized or particularized suspicion that the person being tested uses illegal drugs? It can clearly be more efficient to test randomly the target population—such as a group of civil servants or public school students—than to require that the government have probable cause or a reasonable suspicion for each person tested. Well-organized random testing is less cumbersome and may have a greater deterrent effect.

In *Skinner v. Railway Executives' Association* (1989),[37] the Court upheld suspicionless drug testing of railroad employees. It said that specific evidence of probable cause is unnecessary when privacy interests are limited, public safety is at stake, and a substantial government interest would be jeopardized by requiring individualized suspicion.

In a second case, *National Treasury Employees Union v. Von Raab*,[38] also decided in 1989, the Court upheld a drug testing program that applied to United States Customs Service Employees seeking promotion to positions that required carrying firearms and involvement in drug interdiction. *Vernonia* upheld a urinalysis requirement for public school students engaging in interscholastic athletics. However, in *Chandler v. Miller* (1997),[39] the Court struck down a Georgia statute requiring candidates for state office to submit to and pass a drug test in order to qualify for state office. *Vernonia* provides a very clear analysis of how to analyze the tension between the Fourth Amendment and administrative efficiency.

Conclusion

After analyzing the cases in this chapter and responding to the discussion questions, the full challenge of constitutional competence should be clear. Public managers are almost under siege by elected officials, the media, and the vocal populace to be more efficient. They often lack the resources and technologies to produce the desired levels of outputs. Elected officials may have given their programs unclear, contradictory, or impossible goals. Outcomes are hard to measure, and in many policy areas very difficult to control or even significantly influence. Unlike the private sector, public managers can rarely choose their customers or freely write off problem cases. And they are under constitutional constraints in their effort to promote administration that "works better and costs less," as the NPR puts it.[40] Still, as Chief Justice Burger explained in *Chadha* and as the cases in this chapter illustrate, there is no real choice. The job must be done within the framework of the Constitution. Constitutional competence is a prerequisite and a guide to integrating constitutional values and requirements into on-the-job performance, but does not offer a comprehensive blueprint. As you contemplate *Loudermill, LaFleur,* and *Rankin,* consider how the administrators might have pursued efficiency more consistently with constitutional values. With respect to *Vernonia,* consider whether even a constitutional means—the suspicionless drug test of a seventh grader—is the most efficient way of achieving the government's purpose.

Notes

1. Luther Gulick and L. Urwick, eds., *Papers on the Science of Administration* (New York: Institute of Public Administration, 1937), p. 192.

2. Ibid.

3. Adam Smith, *An Inquiry Into The Nature and Causes of the Wealth of Nations* (New York: Modern Library, 1937). (Originally published in 1776.)

4. George Downs and Patrick Larkey, *The Search for Government Efficiency* (New York: Random House, 1986), p. 6.

5. U.S. Office of Management and Budget, "Primer on Performance Measurement," September 23, 1994, p. 4.7. (Unpublished; see David H. Rosenbloom, *Public Administration: Understanding Management, Politics, and Law in the Public Sector,* 4th ed. [New York: McGraw-Hill, 1998], p. 386.)

6. National Performance Review, *Putting Customers First: Serving the American Public: Best Practices in Telephone Service* (Washington, DC: National Performance Review, 1995), p. 34.

7. Al Gore, *From Red Tape to Results: Creating a Government That Works Better & Costs Less* (Washington, DC: U.S. Government Printing Office, 1993), p. 60.

8. Bill Clinton and Al Gore, *Putting Customers First: Standards for Serving the American People* (Washington, DC: U.S. Government Printing Office, 1994), p. 25.

9. Ibid., p. 83.

10. Gore, *From Red Tape to Results*, p. 2.

11. Ibid., p. 3.

12. Ibid.

13. Ibid., p. 71.

14. Al Gore, *Common Sense Government Works Better & Costs Less* (Washington, DC: U.S. Government Printing Office, 1995), p. 33.

15. *Federalist Papers* (1787–1788), Clinton Rossiter, ed. (New York: New American Library, 1961), No. 51, p. 322.

16. Gore, *From Red Tape to Results*, calls for much less congressional oversight of federal administration. See pp. 16–17, 20, 34. Tension with procedural due process can be found in the recommendation to "reduce by half the time required to terminate federal managers and employees for cause and improve the system for dealing with poor performers" (p. 25). Overall, the National Performance Review pays very little attention the Administrative Procedure Act of 1946, which is the basic regulatory statute for federal administration.

17. Robert Simmons and Eugene Dvorin, *Public Administration* (Port Washington, NY: Alfred Publishers, 1977), p. 217.

18. Gore, *Common Sense Government Works Better & Costs Less*, p. 92.

19. Ibid., p. 93.

20. Dwight Waldo, *The Administrative State*, 2nd ed. (New York: Holmes and Meier, 1984), p. 193.

21. *Immigration and Naturalization Service v. Chadha*, 462 U.S. 919, 959 (1983).

22. Gulick and Urwick, eds., *Papers on the Science of Administration*, p. 193 (emphasis in the original). See Waldo, *The Administrative State*, Chapter 10, for a strong critique of orthodox administration on these points.

23. See Herbert Kaufman, *Red Tape* (Washington, DC: Brookings Institution, 1977).

24. David H. Rosenbloom and Richard D. Schwartz, eds., *Handbook of Regulation and Administrative Law* (New York: Marcel Dekker, 1994), Chapters 1, 10, 13, 16, 19, 20.

25. *Mathews v. Eldridge*, 424 U.S. 319 (1976).

26. Ibid., p. 335.

27. *Rankin v. McPherson*, 483 U.S. 378 (1987).

28. See *Connick v. Myers*, 461 U.S. 138 (1983); Kermit Roosevelt, "The Costs of Agencies: *Waters v. Churchill* and the First Amendment in the Administrative State," *Yale Law Journal*, vol. 106 (1993): 1233.

29. *Pickering v. Board of Education*, 391 U.S. 563 (1968).

30. *Waters v. Churchill*, 114 S.Ct. 1878, 1887–1888 (1994). Justice Byron White similarly commented in *Connick v. Myers*, 461 U.S. 138, 154 (1983), that the courts must balance the First Amendment aim of "full protection of speech upon issues of public concern" against "the practical realities involved in the administration of a government office."

31. *Waters v. Churchill*, 114 S.Ct. 1878 (1994).

32. See Whistleblower Protection Act of 1989, Public Law No. 101–102, 5 U.S. Code 1201–1222.

33. U.S. Code 2302 (b)(8)(A) (1994).

34. Approximately 20 additional federal statutes protect employees' and others' speech on specific matters, such as protection of those who report violations of environmental protection laws.

35. For a survey of federal cases see Charles M. Hemingway, "A Closer Look at *Waters v. Churchill* and *United States v. National Treasury Employees Union*: Constitutional Tensions Between the Government as Employer and the Citizen as a Federal Employee," *American Law Review*, vol. 44 (1995): 2231.

36. See Marsha Miceli and Janet Near, *Blowing the Whistle* (Lexington, MA: Lexington Books, 1992). See also Rosalie Berger Levinson, "Silencing Government Employee Whistleblowers in the Name of Efficiency," *Ohio Northern University Law Review*, vol. 23 (1996): 17.

37. *Skinner v. Railway Executives' Association*, 489 U.S. 20 (1989).

38. *National Treasury Employees Union v. Von Raab*, 489 U.S. 656 (1989).

39. *Chandler v. Miller*, 117 S.Ct. 1295 (1997). See also Nathan Brown, "Reining the National Drug Testing Epidemic: *Chandler v. Miller*, 117 S.Ct. 1295," *Harvard Civil Rights–Civil Liberties Law Review*, vol. 33 (1998), 253.

40. Gore, *From Red Tape to Results* and *Common Sense Government Works Better & Costs Less*.

Additional Reading

Downs, George, and Patrick Larkey. *The Search for Government Efficiency*. New York: Random House, 1986.

Linden, Russell. *Seamless Government*. San Francisco: Jossey-Bass, 1994.

Waldo, Dwight. *The Administrative State*. 2nd ed. New York: Holmes and Meier, 1984.

Case 6.1
Due Process and Efficient Process

CLEVELAND BOARD OF EDUCATION v. LOUDERMILL et al.
Argued December 3, 1984
Decided March 19, 1985
470 US 532

JUSTICE WHITE delivered the opinion of the Court.

In these cases we consider what pretermination process must be accorded a public employee who can be discharged only for cause.

I

In 1979 the Cleveland Board of Education, petitioner in No. 83-1362, hired respondent James Loudermill as a security guard. On his job application, Loudermill stated that he had never been convicted of a felony. Eleven months later, as part of a routine examination of his employment records, the Board discovered that in fact Loudermill had been convicted of grand larceny in 1968. By letter dated November 3, 1980, the Board's Business Manager informed Loudermill that he had been dismissed because of his dishonesty in filling out the employment application. Loudermill was not afforded an opportunity to respond to the charge of dishonesty or to challenge his dismissal. On November 13, the Board adopted a resolution officially approving the discharge.

Under Ohio law, Loudermill was a "classified civil servant."... Such employees can be terminated only for cause, and may obtain administrative review if discharged.... Pursuant to this provision, Loudermill filed an appeal with the Cleveland Civil Service Commission on November 12. The Commission appointed a referee, who held a hearing on January 29, 1981. Loudermill argued that he had thought that his 1968 larceny conviction was for a misdemeanor rather than a felony. The referee recommended reinstatement. On July 20, 1981, the full Commission heard argument and orally announced that it would uphold the dismissal. Proposed findings of fact and conclusions of law followed on August 10, and Loudermill's attorneys were advised of the result by mail on August 21.

• • •

The other case before us arises on similar facts and followed a similar course. Respondent Richard Donnelly was a bus mechanic for the Parma Board of Education. In August 1977, Donnelly was fired because he had failed an eye examination. He was offered a chance to retake the examination but did not do so. Like Loudermill, Donnelly appealed to the Civil Service Commission. After a year of wrangling about the timeliness of his appeal, the Commission heard the case. It ordered Donnelly reinstated, though without back-pay. In a complaint essentially identical to Loudermill's, Donnelly challenged the constitutionality of the dismissal procedures.

• • •

II

Respondents' federal constitutional claim depends on their having had a property right in continued employment.... If they did, the State could not deprive them of this property without due process....

Property interests are not created by the Constitution, "they are created and their dimensions are defined by existing rules or understandings that stem from an independent source such as state law...." ... The Ohio statute plainly creates such an interest. Respondents were "classified civil service employees," entitled to retain their positions "during good behavior and efficient service," who could not be dismissed "except ... for ... misfeasance, malfeasance, or nonfeasance in office."... The statute plainly supports the conclusion, reached by both lower courts, that respondents possessed property rights in continued employment. Indeed, this question does not seem to have been disputed below.

The Parma Board argues, however, that the property right is defined by, and conditioned on, the legislature's choice of procedures for its deprivation.... The Board stresses that in addition to specifying the grounds for termination, the statute sets out procedures by which termination may take place. The procedures were adhered to in these cases. According to petitioner, "[t]o require additional procedures would in effect expand the scope of the property interest itself."...

• • •

...[I]t is settled that the "bitter with the sweet" approach [argued by the Parma Board] misconceives the constitutional guarantee. If a clearer holding is needed, we provide it today. The point is straightforward: the Due Process Clause provides that certain substantive rights—life, liberty, and property—cannot be deprived except pursuant to constitutionally adequate procedures. The categories of substance and procedure are distinct. Were the rule otherwise, the Clause would be reduced to a mere tautology. "Property" cannot be defined by the procedures provided for its deprivation any more than can life or liberty. The right to due process "is conferred, not by legislative grace, but by constitutional guarantee. While the legislature may elect not to confer a property interest in [public] employment, it may not constitutionally authorize the deprivation of such an interest, once conferred, without appropriate procedural safeguards."...

In short, once it is determined that the Due Process Clause applies, "the question remains what process is due."... The answer to that question is not to be found in the Ohio statute.

III

An essential principle of due process is that a deprivation of life, liberty, or property "be preceded by notice and opportunity for hearing appropriate to the nature of the case."... We have described "the root requirement" of the Due Process Clause as being "that an individual be given an opportunity for a hearing *before* he is deprived of any significant property interest."... This principle requires "some kind of a hearing" prior to the discharge of an employee who has a constitutionally protected property interest in his employment.... Even decisions finding no constitutional violation in termination procedures have relied on the existence of

some pretermination opportunity to respond....

The need for some form of pretermination hearing...is evident from a balancing of the competing interests at stake. These are the private interest in retaining employment, the governmental interest in the expeditious removal of unsatisfactory employees and the avoidance of administrative burdens, and the risk of an erroneous termination. See *Mathews v. Eldridge,* 424 U.S. 319, 335 (1976).

First, the significance of the private interest in retaining employment cannot be gainsaid. We have frequently recognized the severity of depriving a person of the means of livelihood.... While a fired worker may find employment elsewhere, doing so will take some time and is likely to be burdened by the questionable circumstances under which he left his previous job....

Second, some opportunity for the employee to present his side of the case is recurringly of obvious value in reaching an accurate decision. Dismissals for cause will often involve factual disputes.... Even where the facts are clear, the appropriateness or necessity of the discharge may not be; in such cases, the only meaningful opportunity to invoke the discretion of the decisionmaker is likely to be before the termination takes effect....

The cases before us illustrate these considerations. Both respondents had plausible arguments to make that might have prevented their discharge. The fact that the Commission saw fit to reinstate Donnelly suggests that an error might have been avoided had he been provided an opportunity to make his case to the Board. As for Loudermill, given the Commission's ruling we cannot say that the discharge was mistaken. Nonetheless, in light of the referee's recommendation, neither can we say that a fully informed decisionmaker might not have exercised its discretion and decided not to dismiss him, notwithstanding its authority to do so. In any event, the termination involved arguable issues, and the right to a hearing does not depend on a demonstration of certain success....

The governmental interest in immediate termination does not outweigh these interests. As we shall explain, affording the employee an opportunity to respond prior to termination would impose neither a significant administrative burden nor intolerable delays. Furthermore, the employer shares the employee's interest in avoiding disruption and erroneous decisions; and until the matter is settled, the employer would continue to receive the benefit of the employee's labors. It is preferable to keep a qualified employee on than to train a new one. A governmental employer also has an interest in keeping citizens usefully employed rather than taking the possibly erroneous and counterproductive step of forcing its employees onto the welfare rolls. Finally, in those situations where the employer perceives a significant hazard in keeping the employee on the job, it can avoid the problem by suspending with pay.

IV

The foregoing considerations indicate that the pretermination "hearing," though necessary, need not be elaborate. We have pointed out that "[t]he formality and procedural requisites for the hearing can vary, depending upon the importance of the interests involved and the nature of the subsequent proceedings."... In general, "something less" than a full evidentiary hearing is sufficient prior to adverse administrative action.... Under state law, respondents were later entitled to a full administrative hearing and judicial review. The only question is what steps were required before the termination took effect.

In only one case, *Goldberg v. Kelly*...(1970), has the court required a full adversarial evidentiary hearing prior to adverse governmental action. However, ...that case presented significantly different considerations than are present in the context of public employment.* Here, the pretermination hearing need not definitively resolve the propriety of the discharge. It should be an initial check against mistaken decisions—essentially, a determination of whether there are reasonable grounds to believe that the charges against the employee are true and support the proposed action....

The essential requirements of due process, and all that respondents seek or the Court of Appeals required, are notice and an opportunity to respond. The opportunity to present reasons, either in person or in writing, why proposed action should not be taken is a fundamental due process requirement.

The tenured public employee is entitled to oral or written notice of the charges against him, an explanation of the employer's evidence, and an opportunity to present his side of the story.... To require more than this prior to termination would intrude to an unwarranted extent on the government interest in quickly removing an unsatisfactory employee.

V

Our holding rests in part on the provisions in Ohio law for a full post-termination hearing....

VI

We conclude that all the process that is due is provided by a pretermination opportunity to respond, coupled with post-termination administrative procedures as provided by the Ohio statute....

*Editors' note: Goldberg involved the termination of a welfare benefit, upon which the individual allegedly depended for his immediate survival.

Discussion Questions

1. Consider the extent to which administrative efficiency may be compromised by the due process requirement that those public employees who have a property interest in their jobs be afforded notice and an opportunity to respond to information against them prior to termination. For instance, will agency lawyers ordinarily review the wording of the information prior to its transmission to the employee? Will higher-level administrators have to sign off on the information? Does the right to respond implicitly include a right to have the response considered seriously?

2. The Court's decision clearly rests, in part, on the availability of a post-termination hearing procedure. Presumably, such a hearing would be before an impartial examiner, referee, or administrative law judge, and the employee would have the right to bring counsel as well as to confront and cross-examine adverse witnesses. Would such hearings undercut administrative efficiency? Would pretermination hearings be significantly more burdensome to efficient ad-

ministration? Consider the interest of the government, the employee, and the employee's supervisor in responding to these questions.

3. In a dissenting opinion, Justice Rehnquist stated:

This customary "balancing" inquiry conducted by the Court in these cases reaches a result that is quite unobjectionable, but it seems to me that it is devoid of any principles which will either instruct or endure. The balance is simply an ad hoc weighing which depends to a great extent upon how the Court subjectively views the underlying interests at stake.

Do you think that the three-factor test prescribed by *Mathews v. Eldridge,* as elaborated on in *Loudermill,* provides public administrators with sufficient guidance regarding the applicability and requirements of due process? Can you suggest a better test?

Case 6.2
Presumptions, Individualized Determinations, and Efficiency

CLEVELAND BOARD OF EDUCATION et al. v. LaFLEUR et al.
Argued October 15, 1973
Decided January 21, 1974
414 US 632

MR. JUSTICE STEWART delivered the opinion of the Court.

The respondents in No. 72-777 and the petitioner in No. 72-1129 are female public school teachers. During the 1970–1971 school year, each informed her local school board that she was pregnant; each was compelled by a mandatory maternity leave rule to quit her job without pay several months before the expected birth of her child. These cases call upon us to decide the constitutionality of the school boards' rules.

I

Joe Carol LaFleur and Ann Elizabeth Nelson, the respondents in No. 72-777, are junior high school teachers employed by the Board of Education of Cleveland, Ohio. Pursuant to a rule first adopted in 1952, the school board requires every pregnant school teacher to take maternity leave without pay, beginning five months before the expected birth of her child. Application for such leave must be made no later than two weeks prior to the date of departure. A teacher on maternity leave is not allowed to return to work until the beginning of the next regular school semester which follows the date when her child attains the age of three months. A doctor's certificate attesting to the health of the teacher is a prerequisite to return; an additional physical examination may be required. The teacher on maternity leave is not promised reemployment after the birth of the child; she is merely given priority in reassignment to a position for which she is qualified. Failure to comply with the mandatory maternity leave provisions is ground for dismissal.

Neither Mrs. LaFleur nor Mrs. Nelson wished to take an unpaid maternity leave; each wanted to continue teaching until the end of the school year. Because of the mandatory maternity leave rule, however, each was required to leave her job in March 1971. The two women then filed separate suits in the United States District Court for the Northern District of Ohio under 42 U.S.C. § 1983, challenging the constitutionality of the maternity leave rule. The District Court tried the cases together, and rejected the plaintiffs' arguments.... A divided panel of the United States Court of Appeals for the Sixth Circuit reversed, finding the Cleveland rule in violation of the Equal

Protection Clause of the Fourteenth Amendment....

The petitioner in No. 72-1129, Susan Cohen, was employed by the School Board of Chesterfield County, Virginia. That school board's maternity leave regulation requires that a pregnant teacher leave work at least four months prior to the expected birth of her child. Notice in writing must be given to the school board at least six months prior to the expected birth date. A teacher on maternity leave is declared re-eligible for employment when she submits written notice from a physician that she is physically fit for re-employment, and when she can give assurance that care of the child will cause only minimal interference with her job responsibilities. The teacher is guaranteed re-employment no later than the first day of the school year following the date upon which she is declared re-eligible.

Mrs. Cohen informed the Chesterfield County School Board in November 1970, that she was pregnant and expected the birth of her child about April 28, 1971. She initially requested that she be permitted to continue teaching until April 1, 1971. The school board rejected the request, as it did Mrs. Cohen's subsequent suggestion that she be allowed to teach until January 21, 1971, the end of the first school semester. Instead, she was required to leave her teaching job on December 18, 1970. She subsequently filed this suit under 42 U.S.C. § 1983 in the United States District Court for the Eastern District of Virginia. The District Court held that the school board regulation violates the Equal Protection Clause, and granted appropriate relief.... A divided panel of the Fourth Circuit affirmed, but, on rehearing en banc* the Court of Appeals upheld the constitutionality of the challenged regulation in a 4–3 decision....

We granted certiorari in both cases...in order to resolve the conflict between the Courts of Appeals regarding the constitutionality of such mandatory maternity leave rules for public school teachers.

*Editors' note: A rehearing *en banc* is one in which all the judges of a Circuit Court of Appeals are eligible to participate. The procedure is generally used sparingly and only in cases of extraordinary importance.

II

This Court has long recognized that freedom of personal choice in matters of marriage and family life is one of the liberties protected by the Due Process Clause of the Fourteenth Amendment....

[T]here is a right "to be free from unwarranted governmental intrusion into matters so fundamentally affecting a person as the decision whether to bear or beget a child."

By acting to penalize the pregnant teacher for deciding to bear a child, overly restrictive maternity leave regulations can constitute a heavy burden on the exercise of these protected freedoms. Because public school maternity leave rules directly affect "one of the basic civil rights of man," the Due Process Clause of the Fourteenth Amendment requires that such rules must not needlessly, arbitrarily, or capriciously impinge upon this vital area of a teacher's constitutional liberty. The question before us in these cases is whether the interests advanced in support of the rules of the Cleveland and Chesterfield County School boards can justify the particular procedures they have adopted.

The school boards in these cases have offered two essentially overlapping explanations for their mandatory maternity leave rules. First, they contend that the firm cutoff dates are necessary to maintain continuity of classroom instruction, since advance knowledge of when a pregnant teacher must leave facilitates the finding and hiring of a qualified substitute. Secondly, the school boards seek to justify their maternity rules by arguing that at least some teachers become physically incapable of adequately performing certain of their duties during the latter part of pregnancy. By keeping the pregnant teacher out of the classroom during these final months, the maternity leave rules are said to protect the health of the teacher and her unborn child, while at the same time assuring that students have a physically capable instructor in the classroom at all times.

It cannot be denied that continuity of instruction is a significant and legitimate educational goal. Regulations requiring pregnant teachers to provide early notice of their condition to school authorities undoubtedly facilitate administrative planning toward the important objective of continuity. But, as the

Court of Appeals for the Second Circuit noted in *Green v. Waterford Board of Education,* ...

"Where a pregnant teacher provides the Board with a date certain for commencement of leave... that value [continuity] [sic] is preserved; an arbitrary leave date set at the end of the fifth month is no more calculated to facilitate a planned and orderly transition between the teacher and a substitute than is a date fixed closer to confinement. Indeed, the latter... would afford the Board more, not less, time to procure a satisfactory long-term substitute."...

Thus, while the advance-notice provisions in the Cleveland and Chesterfield County rules are wholly rational and may well be necessary to serve the objective of continuity of instruction, the absolute requirements of termination at the end of the fourth or fifth month of pregnancy are not. Were continuity the only goal, cutoff dates much later during pregnancy would serve as well as or better than the challenged rules, providing that ample advance notice requirements were retained. Indeed, continuity would seem just as well attained if the teacher herself were allowed to choose the date upon which to commence her leave, at least so long as the decision were required to be made and notice given of it well in advance of the date selected.

In fact, since the fifth or sixth month of pregnancy will obviously begin at different times in the school year for different teachers, the present Cleveland and Chesterfield County rules may serve to hinder attainment of the very continuity objectives that they are purportedly designed to promote. For example, the beginning of the fifth month of pregnancy for both Mrs. LaFleur and Mrs. Nelson occurred during March of 1971. Both were thus required to leave work with only a few months left in the school year, even though both were fully willing to serve through the end of the term. Similarly, if continuity were the only goal, it seems ironic that the Chesterfield County rule forced Mrs. Cohen to leave work in mid-December 1970 rather than at the end of the semester in January, as she requested.

We thus conclude that the arbitrary cutoff dates embodied in the mandatory leave rules before us have no rational relationship to the valid state interest of preserving continuity of instruction. As long as the teachers are required

to give substantial advance notice of their condition, the choice of firm dates later in pregnancy would serve the boards' objectives just as well, while imposing a far lesser burden on the women's exercise of constitutionally protected freedom.

The question remains as to whether the cutoff dates at the beginning of the fifth and sixth months can be justified on the other ground advanced by the school boards—the necessity of keeping physically unfit teachers out of the classroom. There can be no doubt that such an objective is perfectly legitimate, both on educational and safety grounds. And, despite the plethora of conflicting medical testimony in these cases, we can assume, *arguendo,* that at least some teachers become physically disabled from effectively performing their duties during the latter stages of pregnancy.

The mandatory termination provisions of the Cleveland and Chesterfield County rules surely operate to insulate the classroom from the presence of potentially incapacitated pregnant teachers. But the question is whether the rules sweep too broadly.... That question must be answered in the affirmative, for the provisions amount to a conclusive presumption that every pregnant teacher who reaches the fifth or sixth month of pregnancy is physically incapable of continuing. There is no individualized determination by the teacher's doctor—or the school board's—as to any particular teacher's ability to continue at her job. The rules contain an irrebuttable presumption of physical incompetency, and that presumption applies even when the medical evidence as to an individual woman's physical status might be wholly to the contrary.

As the Court noted last Term... "permanent irrebuttable presumptions have long been disfavored under the Due Process Clauses of the Fifth and Fourteenth Amendments."

• • •

While the medical experts in these cases differed on many points, they unanimously agreed on one—the ability of any particular pregnant woman to continue at work past any fixed time in her pregnancy is very much an individual matter. Even assuming, *arguendo,* that there are some women who would be physically unable to work past the particular cutoff dates embodied in the challenged rules, it is evident that there are large numbers of teachers who are fully capable of continuing work for longer than the Cleveland and Chesterfield County regulations will allow. Thus, the conclusive presumption embodied in these rules is neither "necessarily [nor] universally true," and is violative of the Due Process Clause.

The school boards have argued that the mandatory termination dates serve the interest of administrative convenience, since there are many instances of teacher pregnancy, and the rules obviate the necessity for case-by-case determinations. Certainly, the boards have an interest in devising prompt and efficient procedures to achieve their legitimate objectives in this area. But, as the Court stated in *Stanley v. Illinois* [1972],

> "[T]he Constitution recognizes higher values than speed and efficiency. Indeed, one might fairly say of the Bill of Rights in general, and the Due Process Clause in particular, that they were designed to protect the fragile values of a vulnerable citizenry from the overbearing concern for efficiency and efficacy that may characterize praiseworthy government officials no less, and perhaps more, than mediocre ones."...

While it might be easier for the school boards to conclusively presume that all pregnant women are unfit to teach past the fourth or fifth month or even the first month, of pregnancy, administrative convenience alone is insufficient to make valid what otherwise is a violation of due process of law. The Fourteenth Amendment requires the school boards to employ alternative administrative means, which do not so broadly infringe upon basic constitutional liberty, in support of their legitimate goals.

We conclude, therefore, that neither the necessity for continuity of instruction nor the state interest in keeping physically unfit teachers out of the classroom can justify the sweeping mandatory leave regulations that the Cleveland and Chesterfield County School Boards have adopted. While the regulations no doubt represent a good-faith attempt to achieve a laudable goal, they cannot pass muster under the Due Process Clause of the Fourteenth Amendment, because they employ irrebuttable presumptions that unduly penalize a female teacher for deciding to bear a child.

Discussion Questions

1. Does the Court's opinion fully identify all the administrative interests of the school boards in enforcing the mandatory maternity leave policies at issue? For instance, would it be more efficient and effective to be able to hire a long-term replacement for a pregnant teacher as of a particular date, known in advance, rather than as of the day the teacher is no longer able to continue in her job based on an individualized medical determination? What other administrative interests might be involved? Do you think the Court's opinion deals with these adequately?

2. The lower courts decided these cases under the Equal Protection Clause. In a concurring opinion, Justice Powell argued that the Supreme Court should have done the same. Discuss how you would decide the cases under equal protection. What might be the advantages for public administrators if equal protection analysis, rather than that of irrebuttable presumptions, were used? Consider how administrative (or legislative) classifications are treated by each approach.

3. Aside from the issue raised in Question 1, would the individualized medical determinations called for by the Court reduce efficiency? How and/or how not?

4. Freedom of personal choice in matters of marriage and family is not mentioned in the Constitution, but the Court held that it is protected by the Due Process Clause. What other unnamed rights or freedoms might that clause protect? How should one decide?

Case 6.3
Public Employees' Freedom of Speech and Administrative Efficiency

RANKIN, etc., et al. v. McPHERSON
Argued March 23, 1987
Decided June 24, 1987
483 US 378

JUSTICE MARSHALL delivered the opinion of the Court.

The issue in this case is whether a clerical employee in a county constable's office was properly discharged for remarking, after hearing of an attempt on the life of the President, "If they go for him again, I hope they get him."

I

On January 12, 1981, respondent Ardith McPherson was appointed a deputy in the office of the constable of Harris County, Texas. The constable is an elected official who functions as a law enforcement officer. At the time of her appointment, McPherson, a black woman, was 19 years old and had attended college for a year, studying secretarial science. Her appointment was conditional for a 90-day probationary period.

Although McPherson's title was "deputy constable," this was the case only because all employees of the constable's office, regardless of job function, were deputy constables.... She was not a commissioned peace officer, did not wear a uniform, and was not authorized to make arrests or permitted to carry a gun. McPherson's duties were purely clerical. Her work station was a desk at which there was no telephone, in a room to which the public did not have ready access. Her job was to type data from court papers into a computer that maintained an automated record of the status of civil process in the county. Her training consisted of two days of instruction in the operation of her computer terminal.

On March 30, 1981, McPherson and some fellow employees heard on an office radio that there had been an attempt to assassinate the President of the United States. Upon hearing that report, McPherson engaged a co-worker, Lawrence Jackson, who was apparently her boyfriend, in a brief conversation, which ac-

cording to McPherson's uncontroverted testimony went as follows:

"Q: What did you say?
"A: I said I felt that that would happen sooner or later.
"Q: Okay. And what did Lawrence say?
"A: Lawrence said, yeah, agreeing with me.
"Q: Okay. Now, when you—after Lawrence spoke, then what was your next comment?
"A: Well, we were talking—it's a wonder why they did that. I felt like it would be a black person that did that, because I feel like most of my kind is on welfare and CETA, and they use medicaid, and at the time, I was thinking that's what it was.
"...But then after I said that, and then Lawrence said, yeah, he's cutting back medicaid and food stamps. And I said, yeah, welfare and CETA. I said, shoot, if they go for him again, I hope they get him."

McPherson's last remark was overheard by another deputy constable, who unbeknownst to McPherson, was in the room at the time. The remark was reported to Constable Rankin, who summoned McPherson. McPherson readily admitted that she had made the statement, but testified that she told Rankin, upon being asked if she made the statement, "Yes, but I didn't mean anything by it."...After their discussion, Rankin fired McPherson.

McPherson brought suit in the United States District Court for the Southern District of Texas under 42 U.S.C. § 1983, alleging that petitioner Rankin, in discharging her, had violated her constitutional rights under color of state law. She sought reinstatement, back pay, costs and fees, and other equitable relief.

• • •

II

It is clearly established that a State may not discharge an employee on a basis that infringes that employee's constitutionally protected interest in freedom of speech....Even though McPherson was merely a probationary employee, and even if she could have been discharged for any reason or for no reason at all, she may nonetheless be entitled to reinstatement if she was discharged for exercising her constitutional right to freedom of expression....

The determination whether a public employer has properly discharged an employee for engaging in speech requires "a balance between the interests of the [employee], [*sic*] as a citizen, in commenting upon matters of public concern and the interest of the State, as an employer, in promoting the efficiency of the public services it performs through its employees."...This balancing is necessary in order to accommodate the dual role of the public employer as a provider of public services and as a government entity operating under the constraints of the First Amendment. On one hand, public employers are *employers,* concerned with the efficient function of their operations: review of every personnel decision made by a public employer could, in the long run, hamper the performance of public functions. On the other hand, "the threat of dismissal from public employment is...a potent means of inhibiting speech."... Vigilance is necessary to ensure that public employers do not use authority over employees to silence discourse, not because it hampers public functions but simply because superiors disagree with the content of employees' speech.

A

The threshold question in applying this balancing test is whether McPherson's speech may be "fairly characterized as constituting speech on a matter of public concern."... "Whether an employee's speech addresses a matter of public concern must be determined by the content, form, and context of a given statement, as revealed by the whole record."...The District Court apparently found that McPherson's speech did not address a matter of public concern. The Court of Appeals rejected this conclusion, finding that "the life and death of the President are obviously matters of public concern."...

Considering the statement in context...discloses that it plainly dealt with a matter of public concern. The statement was made in the course of a conversation addressing the policies of the President's administration. It came on the heels of a news bulletin regarding what is certainly a matter of heightened public attention: an attempt on the life of the President. While a statement that amounted to a threat to kill the President would not be protected by the First Amendment, the District Court concluded, and we agree, that McPherson's statement did not amount to a threat....The inappropriate or controversial character of a statement is irrelevant to the question whether it deals with a matter of public concern. "[D]ebate on public issues should be uninhibited, robust, and wide-open, and...may well include vehement, caustic, and sometimes unpleasantly sharp attacks on government and public officials."...

"Just as erroneous statements must be protected to give freedom of expression the breathing space it needs to survive, so statements criticizing public policy and the implementation of it must be similarly protected."

B

Because McPherson's statement addressed a matter of public concern, [precedent] next requires that we balance McPherson's interest in making her statement against "the interest of the State, as an employer, in promoting the efficiency of the public services it performs through its employees."... The State bears a burden of justifying the discharge on legitimate grounds....

In performing the balancing, the statement will not be considered in a vacuum; the manner, time, and place of the employee's expression are relevant, as is the context in which the dispute arose....

We have previously recognized as pertinent considerations whether the statement impairs discipline by superiors or harmony among coworkers, has a detrimental impact on close working relationships for which personal loyalty and confidence are necessary, or impedes the performance of the speaker's duties or interferes with the regular operation of the enterprise....

These considerations, and indeed the very nature of the balancing test, make apparent that the state interest element of the test focuses on the effective functioning of the public employer's enterprise. Interference with work, personnel relationships, or the speaker's job performance can detract from the public employer's function; avoiding such interference can be a strong state interest. From this perspective, however, petitioner fails to demonstrate a state interest that outweighs McPherson's First Amendment rights. While McPherson's statement was made at the workplace, there is no evidence that it interfered with the efficient functioning of the office. The constable was evidently not afraid that McPherson had disturbed or interrupted other employees—he did not inquire to whom respondent had made the remark and testified that he "was not concerned who she had made it to,"...In fact, Constable Rankin testified that the possibility of interference with the functions of the Constable's office had *not* been a consideration in his discharge of respondent and that he did not even inquire whether the remark had disrupted the work of the office.

Nor was there any danger that McPherson had discredited the office by making her statement in public. McPherson's speech took place in an area to which there was ordinarily no public access; her remark was evidently made in a private conversation with another employee. There is no suggestion that any member of the general public was present or heard McPherson's statement. Nor is there any evidence that employees other than Jackson who worked in the room even heard the remark. Not only was McPherson's discharge unrelated to the functioning of the office, it was not based on any assessment by the constable that the remark demonstrated a character trait that made respondent unfit to perform her work.

While the facts underlying Rankin's discharge of McPherson are, despite extensive proceedings in the District Court, still somewhat unclear, it is undisputed that he fired McPherson based on the *content* of her speech. Evidently because McPherson had made the

statement and because the Constable believed that she "meant it," he decided that she was not a suitable employee to have in a law enforcement agency. But in weighing the State's interest in discharging an employee based on any claim that the content of a statement made by the employee somehow undermines the mission of the public employer, some attention must be paid to the responsibilities of the employee within the agency. The burden of caution employees bear with respect to the words they speak will vary with the extent of authority and public accountability the employee's role entails. Where, as here, an employee serves no confidential, policymaking, or public contact role, the danger to the agency's successful function from that employee's private speech is minimal. We cannot believe that every employee in Constable Rankin's office, whether computer operator, electrician, or file clerk, is equally required, on pain of discharge, to avoid any statement susceptible of being interpreted by the Constable as an indication that the employee may be unworthy of employment in his law enforcement agency. At some point, such concerns are so removed from the effective function of the public employer that they cannot prevail over the free speech rights of the public employee.

This is such a case. McPherson's employment-related interaction with the Constable was apparently negligible. Her duties were purely clerical and were limited solely to the civil process function of the constable's office. There is no indication that she would ever be in a position to further—or indeed to have any involvement with—the minimal law enforcement activity engaged in by the Constable's office. Given the function of the agency, McPherson's position in the office, and the nature of her statement, we are not persuaded that Rankin's interest in discharging her outweighed her rights under the First Amendment.

Discussion Questions

1. In a strongly worded dissent, Justice Scalia, joined by Chief Justice Rehnquist and Justices White and O'Connor, argued that McPherson's speech was not on "a matter of 'public' concern." Do you agree with the majority or the dissent on this point? What guidance does the majority opinion offer public administrators in identifying speech on a matter of public concern? Do you think its guidance is adequate?

2. Even if a public employee's speech is on a matter of public concern, a public employer may be allowed to discipline him or her for it in the interests of government efficiency. What are the factors that must be considered in deciding whether such speech can constitutionally be the basis of an adverse action? Based on these factors, do you think that Rankin should have known that McPherson's speech was protected? Or, do you agree with the dissent that "It boggles the mind to think that she has such a right [of free speech on the job]"?

3. Suppose, on hearing the remark, a fellow employee harshly criticized McPherson for her comment and a great deal of ill-will developed and, in consequence, smooth working relationships were threatened. Based on the Court's reasoning, does the constitutional protection afforded to public employee's speech depend, in part, on how those hearing their remarks react? If so, can you envision any difficulties not considered by the Court?

4. In *Rankin,* a majority of the justices agreed that "…a purely private statement on a matter of public concern will rarely, if ever, justify discharge of a public employee." Can you think of any circumstances in which such remarks might hamper administrative efficiency? For example, suppose an employee at an off-the-job gathering made a racial slur regarding Justice Thomas that was overheard by another employee who subsequently was unable to work with him or her.

Case 6.4
Suspicionless Drug Testing and Fourth Amendment Privacy

VERNONIA SCHOOL DISTRICT 47J v. ACTON
Argued March 28, 1995
Decided June 26, 1995
515 US 646

JUSTICE SCALIA delivered the opinion of the Court.

The Student Athlete Drug Policy adopted by School District 47J in the town of Vernonia, Oregon, authorizes random urinalysis drug testing of students who participate in the District's school athletics programs. We granted certiorari to decide whether this violates the Fourth and Fourteenth Amendments to the United States Constitution.

I

A

Petitioner Vernonia School District 47J (District) operates one high school and three grade schools in the logging community of Vernonia, Oregon. As elsewhere in small-town America, school sports play a prominent role in the town's life, and student athletes are admired in their schools and in the community.

Drugs had not been a major problem in Vernonia schools. In the mid-to-late 1980's, however, teachers and administrators observed a sharp increase in drug use. Students began to speak out about their attraction to the drug culture, and to boast that there was nothing the school could do about it. Along with more drugs came more disciplinary problems. Between 1988 and 1989 the number of disciplinary referrals in Vernonia schools rose to more than twice the number reported in the early 1980's, and several students were suspended. Students became increasingly rude during class; outbursts of profane language became common.

Not only were student athletes included among the drug users but, as the District Court found, athletes were the leaders of the drug culture.…This caused the District's administrators particular concern, since drug use increases the risk of sports-related injury. Expert testimony at the trial confirmed the deleterious effects of drugs on motivation, memory, judgment, reaction, coordination, and performance. The high school football and wrestling coach witnessed a severe sternum injury suffered by a wrestler, and various omissions of safety procedures and mis-executions by football players, all attributable in his belief to the effects of drug use.

Initially, the District responded to the drug problem by offering special classes, speakers, and presentations designed to deter drug use. It even brought in a specially trained dog to detect drugs, but the drug problem persisted. According to the District Court:

> [T]he administration was at its wits end, and…a large segment of the student body, particularly those involved in interscholastic athletics, was in a state of rebellion. Disciplinary problems had reached "epidemic proportions." The coincidence of an almost three-fold increase in classroom disruptions and disciplinary reports along with the staff's direct observations of students using drugs or glamorizing drug and alcohol use led the administration to the inescapable conclusion that the rebellion was being fueled by alcohol and drug abuse as well as the student's misperceptions about the drug culture.…

At that point, District officials began considering a drug testing program. They held a parent "input night" to discuss the proposed Student Athlete Drug Policy (Policy), and the parents in attendance gave their unanimous approval. The school board approved the Policy for implementation in the fall of 1989. Its expressed purpose is to prevent student athletes from using drugs, to protect their health and safety, and to provide drug users with assistance programs.

B

The Policy applies to all students participating in interscholastic athletics. Students wishing to play sports must sign a form consenting to the testing and must obtain the written consent of their parents. Athletes are tested at the beginning of the season for their sport. In addition, once each week of the season the names of the athletes are placed in a "pool" from which a student, with the supervision of two adults, blindly draws the names of 10% of the athletes for random testing. Those selected are notified and tested the same day, if possible.

The student to be tested completes a specimen control form which bears an assigned number. Prescription medications that the student is taking must be identified by providing a copy of the prescription or a doctor's authorization. The student then enters an empty locker room accompanied by an adult monitor of the same sex. Each boy selected produces a sample at a urinal, remaining fully clothed with his back to the monitor, who stands approximately 12 to 15 feet behind the student. Monitors may (though do not always) watch the student while he produces the sample, and they listen for normal sounds of urination. Girls produce samples in an enclosed bathroom stall, so that they can be heard but not observed. After the sample is produced, it is given to the monitor, who checks it for temperature and tampering and then transfers it to a vial.

The samples are sent to an independent laboratory, which routinely tests them for amphetamines, cocaine, and marijuana. Other drugs, such as LSD, may be screened at the request of the District, but the identity of a particular student does not determine which drugs will be tested. The laboratory's procedures are 99.94% accurate. The District follows strict procedures regarding the chain of custody and access to test results. The laboratory does not know the identity of the students whose samples it tests. It is authorized to mail written test reports only to the superintendent, and to provide test results to District personnel by telephone only after the requesting official recites a code confirming his authority. Only the superintendent, principals, vice-principals, and athletic directors have access to test results, and the results are not kept for more than one year.

If a sample tests positive, a second test is administered as soon as possible to confirm the result. If the second test is negative, no further action is taken. If the second test is positive, the athlete's parents are notified, and the school principal convenes a meeting with the student and his parents at which the student is given the option of (1) participating for six weeks in an assistance program that includes weekly urinalysis, or (2) suffering suspension from athletics for the remainder of the current season and the next athletic season. The student is then retested prior to the start of the next athletic season for which he or she is eligible. The Policy states that a second offense results in automatic imposition of option (2); a third offense in suspension for the remainder of the current season and the next two athletic seasons.

C

In the fall of 1991, respondent James Acton, then a seventh-grader, signed up to play football at one of the District's grade schools. He was denied participation, however, because he and his parents refused to sign the testing consent forms. The Actons filed suit, seeking declaratory and injunctive relief from enforcement of the Policy on the grounds that it violated the Fourth and Fourteenth Amendments to the United States Constitution and Article I, § 9, of the Oregon Constitution. After a bench trial, the District Court entered an order denying the claims on the merits and dismissing the action.... The United States Court of Appeals for the Ninth Circuit reversed, holding that the Policy violated both the Fourth and Fourteenth Amendments and Article I, § 9, of the Oregon Constitution.... We granted certiorari....

II

The Fourth Amendment to the United States Constitution provides that the Federal Government shall not violate "[t]he right of the people to be secure in their persons, houses, papers, and effects, against unreasonable searches and seizures...." We have held that the Fourteenth Amendment extends this constitutional guarantee to searches and seizures by state officers..., including public school officials.... In *Skinner v. Railway Labor Executives' Assn....* (1989), we held that state-compelled collection and testing of urine, such as that required by the Student Athlete Drug Policy, constitutes a "search" subject to the demands of the Fourth Amendment....

As the text of the Fourth Amendment indicates, the ultimate measure of the constitutionality of a governmental search is "reasonableness." At least in a case such as this, where there was no clear practice, either approving or disapproving the type of search at issue at the time the constitutional provision was enacted, whether a particular search meets the reasonableness standard

is judged by balancing its intrusion on the individual's Fourth Amendment interests against its promotion of legitimate governmental interests....

Where a search is undertaken by law enforcement officials to discover evidence of criminal wrongdoing, this Court has said that reasonableness generally requires the obtaining of a judicial warrant.... Warrants cannot be issued, of course, without the showing of probable cause required by the Warrant Clause. But a warrant is not required to establish the reasonableness of *all* government searches; and when a warrant is not required (and the Warrant Clause therefore not applicable), probable cause is not invariably required either. A search unsupported by probable cause can be constitutional, we have said, "when special needs, beyond the normal need for law enforcement, make the warrant and probable-cause requirement impracticable."...

We have found such "special needs" to exist in the public school context. There, the warrant requirement "would unduly interfere with the maintenance of the swift and informal disciplinary procedures [that are] needed," and "strict adherence to the requirement that searches be based upon probable cause" would undercut "the substantial need of teachers and administrators for freedom to maintain order in the schools."... The school search we approved in [*New Jersey v.*] *T.L.O.* [1985] while not based on probable cause, *was* based on individualized *suspicion* of wrongdoing. As we explicitly acknowledged, however, "'the Fourth Amendment imposes no irreducible requirement of such suspicion.'"... We have upheld suspicionless searches and seizures to conduct drug testing of railroad personnel involved in train accidents...; to conduct random drug testing of federal customs officers who carry arms or are involved in drug interdiction...; and to maintain automobile checkpoints looking for illegal immigrants and contraband..., and drunk drivers....

The first factor to be considered is the nature of the privacy interest upon which the search here at issue intrudes. The Fourth Amendment does not protect all subjective expectations of privacy, but only those that society recognizes as "legitimate."... What expectations are legitimate varies, of course, with context..., depending, for example, upon whether the individual asserting the privacy interest is at home, at work, in a car, or in a public park. In addition, the legitimacy of certain privacy expectations *vis-à-vis* the State may depend upon the individual's legal relationship with the State....

Traditionally at common law, and still today, unemancipated minors lack some of the most fundamental rights of self-determination—including even the right of liberty in its narrow sense, *i.e.,* the right to come and go at will. They are subject, even as to their physical freedom, to the control of their parents or guardians....

• • •

Fourth Amendment rights, no less than First and Fourteenth Amendment rights, are different in public schools than elsewhere; the "reasonableness" inquiry cannot disregard the schools' custodial and tutelary responsibility for children. For their own good and that of their classmates, public school children are routinely required to submit to various physical examinations, and to be vaccinated against various diseases....

Legitimate privacy expectations are even less with regard to student athletes. School sports are not for the bashful. They require "suiting up" before each practice or event, and showering and changing afterwards. Public school locker rooms, the usual sites for these activities, are not notable for the privacy they afford. The locker rooms in Vernonia are typical: no individual dressing rooms are provided; shower heads are lined up along a wall, unseparated by any sort of partition or curtain; not even all the toilet stalls have doors. As the United States Court of Appeals for the Seventh Circuit has noted, there is "an element of 'communal undress' inherent in athletic participation."...

There is an additional respect in which school athletes have a reduced expectation of privacy. By choosing to "go out for the team," they voluntarily subject themselves to a degree of regulation even higher than that imposed on students generally....

IV

Having considered the scope of the legitimate expectation of privacy at issue here, we turn next to the character of the intrusion that is complained of. We recognized in *Skinner* that collecting the samples for urinalysis intrudes upon "an excretory function traditionally shielded by great privacy."...We noted, however, that the degree of intrusion depends upon the manner in which production of the urine sample is monitored....Under the District's Policy, male students produce samples at a urinal along a wall. They remain fully clothed and are only observed from behind, if at all. Female students produce samples in an enclosed stall, with a female monitor standing outside listening only for sounds of tampering. These conditions are nearly identical to those typically encountered in public restrooms, which men, women, and especially school children use daily. Under such conditions, the privacy interests compromised by the process of obtaining the urine sample are in our view negligible. The other privacy invasive aspect of urinalysis is, of course, the information it discloses concerning the state of the subject's body, and the materials he has ingested. In this regard it is significant that the tests at issue here look only for drugs, and not for whether the student is, for example, epileptic, pregnant, or diabetic....

Respondents argue, however, that the District's Policy is in fact more intrusive than this suggests, because it requires the students, if they are to avoid sanctions for a falsely positive test, to identify *in advance* prescription medications they are taking. We agree that this raises some cause for concern....On the other hand, we have never indicated that requiring advance disclosure of medications is *per se* unreasonable. Indeed, in *Skinner* we held that it was not "a significant invasion of privacy."...

...It may well be that, if and when James was selected for random testing at a time that he was taking medication, the School District would have permitted him to provide the requested information in a confidential manner—for example, in a sealed envelope delivered to the testing lab. Nothing in the Policy contradicts that, and when respondents choose, in effect, to challenge the Policy on its face, we will not assume the worst. Accordingly, we reach the same conclusion as in *Skinner:* that the invasion of privacy was not significant.

V

Finally, we turn to consider the nature and immediacy of the governmental concern at issue here, and the efficacy of this means for meeting it....It is a mistake...to think that the phrase "compelling state interest," in the Fourth Amendment context, describes a fixed, minimum quantum of governmental concern, so that one can dispose of a case by answering in isolation the question: is there a compelling state interest here? Rather, the phrase describes an interest which appears *important enough* to justify the particular search at hand, in light of other factors which show the search to be relatively intrusive upon a genuine expectation of privacy. Whether that relatively high degree of government concern is necessary in this case or not, we think it is met.

• • •

VI

Taking into account all the factors we have considered above—the decreased expectation of privacy, the relative unobtrusiveness of the search, and the severity of the need met by the search—we conclude Vernonia's Policy is reasonable, and hence constitutional.

We caution against the assumption that suspicionless drug testing will readily pass constitutional muster in other contexts. The most significant element in this case is the first we discussed: that the Policy was undertaken in furtherance of the government's responsibilities, under a public school system, as guardian and tutor of children entrusted to its care. Just as when the government conducts a search in its capacity as employer (a warrantless search of an absent employee's desk to obtain an urgently needed file, for example), the relevant question is whether that intrusion upon privacy is one that a reasonable employer might engage in...; so also when the government acts as guardian and tutor the relevant question is whether the search is one that a reasonable guardian and tutor might undertake. Given the findings of need made by the District Court, we conclude that in the present case it is.

• • •

Discussion Questions

1. Based on the Court's analysis in *Vernonia,* do you think Fourth Amendment protection of personal privacy is adequate or inadequate? Why?

2. In *Vernonia,* the school district was looking for illegal drugs. Would the constitutionality of the search be different if the district were trying to prevent the use of legal, nonprescription performance enhancers?

3. The Court noted that most of the parents of the school athletes agreed with the program. This suggests that it may be viewed as reasonable in Vernonia. But the decision applies nationwide. From a social scientific perspective, how satisfactory is judicial reasoning that produces a general rule based on a specific case that involves facts such as those in *Vernonia?* How would you go about establishing a national standard for "reasonableness" with regard to drug testing public school students? Public employees?

SEVEN

Administrative Standardization

As the head of New York City's Human Resources Administration in 1992, Barbara Sabol tried an experiment. After obtaining an officially created false identity and disguising herself in a wig or scarf, glasses, jeans, and sweatshirt, she spent about 23 days applying for various welfare benefits. She received very poor customer service, but her major complaint was that she felt "depersonalized." "I ceased to be," she explained. "I go to this window. They do not ask me my name. They say 'What is your Zip Code?'" During another transaction a frustrated intake worker exclaimed, "Listen to me! Look at me! You can't get this unless you have a number. They wouldn't have sent you to me if you didn't have a number."[1]

Sabol experienced administrative standardization, which can be defined as the transformation of unique and varied individuals into uniform units for impersonal processing. For administrative purposes the whole person is often reduced to a form and then treated as a case. Like Sabol, many people object to this central feature of public administration. The New Public Management (NPM) rejects it entirely in favor of empowering front-line workers to resolve customers' problems. As this chapter explains, standardization also runs counter to four core constitutional values—diversity, equity, individuation, and equal protection. Accordingly, it sometimes leads to the violation of individual rights. Nevertheless, standardization is strongly supported by orthodox public administrative doctrine and remains common.

Standardization: The Orthodox View

Traditionally, administrative theory has held that standardization enhances efficiency. Max Weber (1864–1921), who is generally considered the foremost analyst of bureaucracy, called standardization, "dehumanization."[2] Today we prefer somewhat softer sounding terms, such as "impersonality" or "depersonalization," for the same phenomenon. For Weber, impersonality was the "special virtue" of bureaucracy because it eliminates "all purely personal, irrational, and emotional elements" from official business.[3] Depersonalization of employees is a chief characteristic of bureaucracy: "...the professional bureaucrat is chained to his activity by his entire material and ideal existence. In the great majority of cases, he is only a single *cog* in an ever-moving mechanism which prescribes to him an essentially fixed route of **149** march."[4] Partly as a result, in terms of efficiency the "bureaucratic mechanism compares with other organizations exactly as does the machine with the non-mechanical modes of production."[5]

Several more recent scholars agree with Weber's assessment. Organizational theorists Peter Blau and Marshall Meyer also claim that "efficiency…suffers when emotions or personal considerations influence administrative decisions."[6] Many public managers will naturally resist the idea that they are merely standardized "cogs." However, public personnel administration in the United States is generally based on positions (or "slots" in terminology suitable to the "cog" theory), rather than built around individual persons. Ever since 1920, the fundamentals of federal position classification have held:

1. Positions and not individuals should be classified;
2. The individual characteristics of an employee occupying a position should have no bearing on the classification of the position; and
3. Persons holding positions in the same class should be considered equally qualified for any other position in that class.[7]

Put differently, rank is usually in the position, not the person. The chief exceptions are services that are organized as a "corps" of some kind, such as the military, police, and the federal Senior Executive Service.

Depersonalization extends beyond administrative personnel to agency clients or customers, who, like Sabol, may also be standardized for the sake of efficiency. Administrative forms elicit only the information that the administrators need to track the person and to decide on his or her status (for example, "eligible" or "ineligible"). Everything about the individual that does not appear on the form is extraneous and irrelevant to the administrative process. Sometimes intake workers help clients or customers to transform themselves into cases for processing by administrators who will never actually see the person involved. The administrative logic of such standardization is well expressed by Ralph Hummel:

> The bureaucrat has no time and no permission to become involved in the personal problems of clients. From his point of view the more he can depersonalize the client into a thing devoid of unique features the more easily and smoothly he will be able to handle the cases before him.[8]

In the not-too-distant past, prior to widespread judicial intervention and administrative reforms,[9] standardization of the "clients" or "customers" of public mental health facilities, jails, and prisons was very extreme. Writing with reference to mental asylums in 1961, Erving Goffman explained

> [A] further set of characteristic problems is found in the constant conflict between humane standards on the one hand and institutional efficiency on the other.…The personal possessions of an individual are an important part of the materials out of which he builds a self, but as an inmate the ease with which he can be managed by staff is likely to increase with the degree to which he is dispossessed. The remarkable efficiency with which a mental-hospital ward can adjust to a daily shift in the number of resident patients is related to the fact that the comers and leavers do not come or leave with any properties but themselves and do not have any right to choose where they will be located. Further, the efficiency with which the clothes of these patients can be kept clean and fresh is related to the fact that everyone's soiled clothing can be redistributed not according to ownership but according to approximate sizes.…

Just as personal possessions may interfere with the smooth running of an institutional operation and be removed for this reason, so parts of the body may conflict with efficient management and the conflict may be resolved in favor of efficiency. If the heads of inmates are to be kept clean, and the possessor easily categorized, then a complete head shave is efficacious, despite the damage this does to appearance. On similar grounds, some mental hospitals have found it useful to extract the teeth of "biters," give hysterectomies to promiscuous female patients, and perform lobotomies on chronic fighters.[10]

Extreme, but recognizable. Organization theorist Victor Thompson notes: "Nearly all administrative organizations...must resort to some of the 'stripping' tactics of the more total institutions."[11]

Orthodox public administration also values standardization because it assures procedural equality. At least in theory, individuals who fall into the same categories will be treated identically by public administrators regardless of their extraneous personal characteristics or of any personal biases the officials may have. For instance, standardization is a barrier to racial discrimination in administration or favoritism based on personal connections.[12] As Thompson puts it in the title of a book, administration should be *Without Sympathy or Enthusiasm* because we "are proud of the fact that modern administration, as compared with administration in the past, is relatively free of... 'particularistic' behavior and is 'universalistic' instead."[13]

The New Public Management and Standardization

The NPM is highly critical of orthodox administration's reliance on standardization. It views standardization as a major, somewhat mindless barrier to serving customers well and solving their problems. The intensity of its disdain for standardization is well conveyed by the federal National Performance Review:

> The federal government...went by the book and demanded that everyone else did too.
> But the price was high. Certainty was achieved, but in a rapidly changing world, "certainty" became inflexibility. Fairness was achieved by treating everyone equally, but in a world full of compelling individual situations, "fairness" became unresponsiveness. Bias was avoided by making sure local officials and front-line federal employees couldn't make discretionary decisions—even though they knew best what needed to be done—and by punishing them when they did. The result was a system that hobbled users and abusers alike, treated adults like children, and made everyone a suspect.
> It also put the government's customers—which is to say, all of us—at the bottom of the priority list. The first priority was the rules; the second was those who checked whether the rules were being followed (such as auditors and inspectors general); the third was those who made the rules in the first place...
> The perverse effect of "rule by rules" is that instead of reducing arbitrariness it appears to increase it; instead of fostering cooperation it destroys it; instead of solving problems it worsens them, creating bitterness and resentment along the way.[14]

Little elaboration is necessary. To the extent that the NPM takes hold, the main question will be whether empowered front-line administrators use their discretion well. Systematic abuse or egregious disparities in the treatment of customers will invite new rules and legal checks. However, for the most part, the NPM is much closer than orthodox administration to the constitutional view of standardization.

Constitutional Values and Standardization

Diversity

Individual political, economic, and social diversity lies at the core of the pluralistic government chartered by the Constitution. Diversity of representation is built into the scheme in which the House of Representatives represents the people by districts within the states, the Senate represents them by state, and in the role of chief of state, the president represents the nation as a whole. The different terms of office for these officials are also intended to ensure that while changing points of view can work their way into the system, no short-lived popular passion will take hold of the entire government in one fell swoop.

In *Federalist No. 10,* James Madison explained that according to the newly drafted Constitution's underlying theory, protection of the diverse and individual "faculties of men" was "the first object of government."[15] He wrote, "From the protection of different and unequal faculties of acquiring property, the possession of different degrees and kinds of property immediately results; and from the influence of these on the sentiments and views of the respective proprietors ensues a division of the society into different interests and parties."[16] Madison viewed such divisions, based on individual diversity, as a strong barrier to the development of a majority faction "…who are united and actuated by some common impulse of passion, or of interest, adverse to the rights of other citizens, or to the permanent and aggregate interests of the community."[17]

The Bill of Rights specifically protects personal diversity in matters of religion, speech, and property. Its protections of privacy have been interpreted to provide individuals with a sphere of autonomy, within which they can develop their personalities and make personal choices, free of governmental intrusion.[18] The Equal Protection Clause of the Fourteenth Amendment also protects diversity by outlawing discrimination against members of social groups who in one way or another do not conform or fit into the categories favored by the government.

The clash between an administrative preference for standardization and the constitutional one for diversity generates substantial litigation. Case 7.1 *Goldman v. Weinberger* (1986), illustrates how the Air Force's demand for standardized uniforms impedes religious diversity. Case 7.2, *Church of Lukumi Babalu Aye, Inc. v. City of Hialeah* (1993), provides an outstanding example of how the Constitution protects religious diversity from direct governmental regulation.

Equity

The Constitution also values equity, or the judiciary's power "…to dispense with the harsh rigor of general laws in particular cases."[19] As Gary McDowell explains, "Equity was necessary, in many cases, to fulfill the law. The law, being by its nature general in scope and application, always admits of exceptions."[20]

Equity is in tension with traditional administrative theory and practice, which look on exceptions to standardization as inefficient, improper, or corrupt. It sometimes requires that principled exceptions be made in order to prevent the misapplication of general rules. The NPM is very much in keeping with the constitutional view in this regard.

Case 8.2, *Sherbert v. Verner* (1963), presents an excellent example. The Supreme Court held that it was unconstitutional to deny a Sabbath observer unemployment compensation benefits on the basis that she voluntarily took herself out of the workforce by not working on Saturdays. From a traditional administrative perspective, an exception made for a Seventh Day Adventist would also have to be made for a Muslim who refused to work on Fridays, as well as for anyone else who claimed a religious basis for not working on a weekday. An exception for one individual could lead to exceptions for many, which would put the administrative scheme in disarray. But constitutionally speaking, the failure to make a principled exception for sincere religious belief constituted undue governmental interference with the individual's free exercise of religion. The different outcomes in *Goldman* and *Sherbert* are less indicative of inconsistent legal reasoning than an illustration of the constitutional flexibility to embrace principled exceptions, when circumstances are sufficiently compelling, without becoming locked into a standardized, "one-size-fits-all" approach.

Like constitutional law, the NPM weighs carefully the arguments for deviating from general rules to solve customers' problems. Presumably an empowered employee would consider whether an exception for one, when circumstances warranted it, would require exceptions for many more. Traditional administrative thinking fails to recognize that whether an exception for one person will lead others also to demand special treatment is an empirical question. If the Air Force had allowed Goldman to wear his religious skullcap, how many more personnel would have requested a religion-based exemption from its dress code?

Individuation

Constitutional values as reflected in contemporary constitutional law often favor individuation—that is, treatment of an individual as a distinct entity rather than as a member of a group or category of persons. The Supreme Court often evidences doubt about applying broad social scientific or biological generalizations to specific individuals. Cases 4.3 and 6.2, *Craig v. Boren* (1976) and *Cleveland Board of Education v. LaFleur* (1974), are examples.[21] Case 8.1, *Wyatt v. Stickney* (1971), combated administrative standardization in Alabama's public mental health facilities by requiring an individualized treatment plan for each patient. Procedural due process, as explained in Case 6.1, *Cleveland Board of Education v. Loudermill* (1985), specifically weighs individuals' interests. Balancing tests, as in Case 6.3, *Rankin v. McPherson* (1987), often assess individualized factors as well.

Equal Protection

Standardization can also violate equal protection. Case 7.3, *United States v. Virginia* (1996), discussed further on in this chapter, is a clear example. The current controversy over the use of profiles for traffic stops, particularly the issue of "driving while black,"[22] also illustrates the broad tension between standardization and equal protection.

Law enforcement profiles have two purposes. They are designed as standardized tools to increase efficiency and effectiveness in the use of police resources. They also provide objective criteria to guide police officers' decisions about whom to stop. (Recall Case 4.1, *Delaware v. Prouse,* 1979.) But what if race, ethnicity, or gender is part of the profile? The concern with "driving while black" arises from statistics indicating that black men are subject to traffic stops far out of proportion to their numbers on the roads.[23] This not only may reflect rampant discrimination, but may also exacerbate targeting: "racial stereotypes influence police to arrest minorities more frequently than nonminorities, thereby generating statistically disparate arrest patterns that in turn form the basis for future selectivity."[24]

The concern with profiles increased in 1996, when the Supreme Court handed down its decision in *Whren v. United States.*[25] The Court held that if a police officer has probable cause to stop a vehicle for any traffic violation, then the stop is justified under the Fourth Amendment. The Court flatly refused to make the constitutionality of the stop depend on what a reasonable officer might have done when confronted with a very minor violation, such as rolling through a stop sign or remaining stopped at one for too long: "Subjective intentions play no role in ordinary, probable-cause Fourth Amendment analysis."[26] In practice, *Whren* means that the police can use an infraction as a pretext for stopping a vehicle in order to check out the driver for illegal drug or other activity.

The Court has ruled that under the Fourth Amendment it is unreasonable for the U.S. Border Patrol to stop drivers on the basis that they "look Mexican," but it has not explicitly dealt with the use of race or ethnicity in a profile.[27] Is a profile a standardized, impersonal, objective, justifiable guide to decision making, or does it deny individualized consideration that is essential to constitutional values? When should a profile violate equal protection?

Standardization and Constitutional Competence

The cases in this chapter promote constitutional competence by explaining how to analyze the various tensions between administrative standardization and constitutional values. They are challenging—none was decided by a unanimous opinion. But they indicate the types of questions that must be asked and why.

Goldman offers a classic administrative rationale for standardization and clearly shows its impact on diversity. From one perspective it highlights a tension between military needs and the traditions of constitutional government.[28] From another it reflects a broad problem of reconciling religious freedom with governmental interests, which was intensely litigated during the 1990s.

In *Employment Division, Department of Human Resources of Oregon v. Smith* (1990),[29] the Supreme Court held that a generally applicable criminal law is enforceable irrespective of the burden it may impose on specific individuals' religious beliefs. The Court said that Native Americans are not entitled to an exemption from a law criminalizing the possession of peyote, a drug that some use as a central part of their religious ceremonies. The Court further held that the state was not required to balance its interests against the burden on religious beliefs.

Five justices rejected the argument that strict scrutiny should apply. If government has a rational basis for a general policy that interferes with particular religious practices, it will prevail. No compelling or paramount reason is necessary. The dissenters argued for strict scrutiny review.

The Court's decision in *Employment Division* created apprehension that religious freedom could be seriously compromised. Can using wine in rituals involving minors be prosecuted as a form of child abuse or endangerment? Could a general law against child abuse or mutilation be construed to prohibit male circumcision? Congress responded to the potential threat to diverse religious practices with the Religious Freedom Restoration Act of 1993. The act sought to reestablish the pre-*Employment Division* approach, which required the government to show a compelling interest in enforcing a general law in circumstances that abridged religious freedom.[30] However, in *City of Boerne v. Flores* (1997),[31] the Supreme Court held that the act unconstitutionally exceeded Congress's powers under the Fourteenth Amendment's enforcement clause. It reasoned that while Congress may pass laws to enforce the amendment, it cannot define the substance of constitutional rights, which is the perview of the judiciary and constitutional amendments.

In response to the controversy over government and religion, on August 14, 1997, President Bill Clinton issued a *Memorandum on Religious Exercise and Religious Expression in the Federal Workplace*.[32] It established three principles for federal personnel management with regard to religious practices. First, agencies should permit employees to engage in personal religious expression in the workplace to the greatest extent possible, consistent with efficiency and requirements of law. Second, the federal government may not discriminate in any aspect of employment on the basis of religion. This means that agencies are obligated to prevent supervisors or employees from engaging in harassment based on religion or creating a hostile environment through insult or ridicule of religious beliefs or practices.

> Third, agencies must reasonably accommodate employees' religious practices. The need for accommodation arises in many circumstances—for example, when work schedules interfere with Sabbath or other religious holiday observances or when work rules prevent an employee from wearing religiously compelled dress. Once again, governmental interests in workplace efficiency may be at stake in such cases. But an agency…must always accommodate an employee's religious practice in the absence of nonspeculative costs and may need to accommodate such practice even when doing so will impose some hardship on the agency's operations.[33]

Although the *Memorandum* does not apply to military personnel, it stands in stark contrast to the Air Force's effort to standardize Goldman's religious practice in Case 7.1.

Case 7.2, *Lukumi,* strongly asserts that strict scrutiny applies to government efforts to regulate religious practices per se. The Supreme Court found that under the guise of protecting animals and public health, the City of Hialeah had deliberately banned animal sacrifices by adherents to the Santeria religion.

From the perspective of standardization, the difference between *Goldman* and *Lukumi* lies in the principle of incidental burdensome effect. If an otherwise valid governmental action has the unintended effect of burdening religion, it probably will be upheld. However, an action that intentionally burdens a particular religion or all religion ordinarily will be struck down unless it satisfies a compelling governmental interest and withstands either the least restrictive alternative or narrow tailoring tests.

Case 7.3, *United States v. Virginia,* vividly shows how administrative standardization can clash with equal protection. Virginia Military Institute (VMI), a state school, had a males-only policy since its founding in the 1830s. Virginia defended the exclusion of females on the grounds that VMI's "adversative" approach to education was uniquely suitable for males and that the admission of females would destroy the school's culture. Among other practices were an almost complete absence of personal privacy and institutionalized abuse of new students by more senior ones. The Supreme Court held that VMI's policy violated the Equal Protection Clause by denying an equal educational opportunity to females. It also found Virginia's belated effort to provide leadership-oriented education for females in a single-sex institution constitutionally inadequate. The Court employed middle-level review, but emphasized that classifications based on gender require an "exceedingly persuasive justification."[34]

Case 7.4, *Zobel v. Williams* (1982), demonstrates how standardization can violate equal protection in another context. Alaska used years of residency in the state as a basis for giving its citizens a portion of the revenue derived annually from its mineral wealth. The longer one had lived there since statehood, the greater the yearly dividend he or she would receive. One of Alaska's objectives was to reward individuals for the tangible and intangible contributions they might have made to the state. Since assessing these on an individual basis would be very difficult and costly, if not impossible, Alaska relied on standardization in assuming that everyone made an equal contribution each year. The Supreme Court's decision is instructive with regard to constitutional competence because it explains two ways in which a nonsuspect classification, such as residency, can unconstitutionally abridge equal protection. The classification will be unconstitutional if it is not rationally related to a legitimate governmental purpose or if the government's objective is illegitimate.

Conclusion

Administrative standardization often advances important administrative concerns, including efficiency and procedural regularity. However, as this chapter illustrates, using it properly can require considerable constitutional competence. In some instances, standardization will run counter to the core constitutional interest in promoting and protecting diversity. Deviation from standardization may be necessary to protect individual rights. Subtlety is needed. It is not feasible to cling rigidly to standardization, as orthodox public administration sometimes advocates. Each use of standardization involving individual rights or interests has to be evaluated on its own merits in order to protect constitutional values. If the NPM is correct, a flexible response to particular circumstances will frequently be better public administration as well.

Notes

1. Alison Mitchell, "Posing as Welfare Recipient, Agency Head Finds Indignity," *New York Times,* February 5, 1993, pp. A1, B2.

2. Max Weber, *From Max Weber: Essays in Sociology,* trans. and ed. by H.H. Gerth and C. W. Mills (New York: Oxford University Press, 1958), p. 216.

3. Ibid.

4. Ibid., p. 228.

5. Ibid., p. 214.

6. Peter Blau and Marshall Meyer, *Bureaucracy in Modern Society,* 2nd ed. (New York: Random House, 1971), p. 9.

7. Jay Shafritz, Norma Riccucci, David Rosenbloom, and Albert Hyde, *Personnel Management in Government,* 4th ed. (New York: Marcel Dekker, 1992), p. 137.

8. Ralph Hummel, *The Bureaucratic Experience* (New York: St. Martin's Press, 1977), p. 56.

9. See David Rosenbloom and Rosemary O'Leary, *Public Administration and Law,* 2nd ed. (New York: Marcel Dekker, 1997), Chapter 7.

10. Erving Goffman, *Asylums* (Garden City, NY: Anchor, 1961), pp. 78–79.

11. Victor Thompson, *Without Sympathy or Enthusiasm* (University, AL: University of Alabama Press, 1975), p. 41.

12. For example, the federal merit system initially facilitated the employment of African Americans—so much so that, during Woodrow Wilson's presidency, photographs were required to make it easier to discriminate in hiring. See David Rosenbloom, *Federal Equal Employment Opportunity: Politics and Public Personnel Administration* (New York: Praeger, 1977), pp. 52–54.

13. Thompson, *Without Sympathy or Enthusiasm,* p. 18.

14. Al Gore, *Common Sense Government Works Better & Costs Less* (Washington, DC: U.S. Government Printing Office, 1995), pp. 18–19.

15. *The Federalist Papers,* ed. by Clinton Rossiter (New York: New American Library, 1961), p. 78.

16. Ibid.

17. Ibid.

18. See the various opinions in *Griswold v. Connecticut,* 381 U.S. 479 (1965).

19. Gary McDowell, *Equity and the Constitution* (Chicago: University of Chicago Press, 1982), p. 5.

20. Ibid.

21. See also *McClesky v. Kemp,* 481 U.S. 279 (1987), for a dramatic refusal to apply a social scientific generalization to an individual's case.

22. See Jennifer A. Larrabee, "'DWB (Driving While Black)' and Equal Protection: The Realities of an Unconstitutional Police Practice," *Journal of Law and Policy,* vol. 6 (1997): 291; Angela Davis, "Race, Cops, and Traffic Stops," *University of Miami Law Review,* vol. 51 (1997): 425; David Harris, "'Driving While Black' and All Other Traffic Offenses: The Supreme Court and Pretextual Traffic Stops," *Journal of Law and Criminology,* vol. 87 (1997): 544; Kathleen O'Day, "Pretextual Traffic Stops: Protecting Our Streets or Racist Police Tactics?" *University of Dayton Law Review,* vol. 23 (1998): 313.

23. See S. B. Duke and A.C. Gross, "Casualties of War," *Reason,* vol. 25 (February 1994): 20–27.

24. "Race and the Criminal Process, Racial Discrimination on the Beat: Extending the Racial Critique to Police Conduct," *Harvard Law Review,* vol. 101 (1988): 1494, at page 1508. See also Robin Magee, "The Myth of the Good Cop and the Inadequacy of Fourth Amendment Remedies for Black Men," *Capital University Law Review,* vol. 23 (1994): 151.

25. *Whren v. United States,* 135 L. Ed. 2d 89 (1996).

26. Ibid., p. 98.

27. See *United States v. Brignoni-Ponce,* 422 U.S. 873 (1975).

28. See Thomas Dienes, "When the First Amendment Is Not Preferred: The Military and Other Special Contexts," *University of Cincinnati Law Review,* vol. 56 (1987): 779; and John Carr, "Free Speech in the Military Community: Striking a Balance Between Personal Rights and Military Necessity," *The Air Force Law Review,* vol. 45 (1998): 303.

29. *Employment Division, Department of Human Resources of Oregon v. Smith,* 494 U.S. 872 (1990).

30. See *Wisconsin v. Yoder,* 406 U.S. 205 (1972), and the various opinions in *City of Boerne v. Flores,* 117 S.Ct. 2157 (1997).

31. *City of Boerne v. Flores,* 117 S.Ct. 2157 (1997).

32. *Weekly Compilation of Presidential Documents,* vol. 33 (August 14, 1997): 1246–1248.

33. Ibid., p. 1247.

34. *United States v. Virginia,* 518 U.S. 515, 531 (1996). See also *Miller v. Albright,* 118 S.Ct. 1428 (1998), which applies "skeptical scrutiny" to a gender classification.

Additional Reading

Barzelay, Michael. *Breaking Through Bureaucracy.* Berkeley: University of California Press, 1992.

Gore, Al. *Common Sense Government Works Better & Costs Less.* Washington, DC: U.S. Government Printing Office, 1992.

Hummel, Ralph. *The Bureaucratic Experience: A Critique of Life in the Modern Organization.* 4th ed. New York: St. Martin's Press, 1994.

Case 7.1
Conformity Versus Pluralism

GOLDMAN v. WEINBERGER, SECRETARY OF DEFENSE, et al.
Argued January 14, 1986
Decided March 25, 1986
475 US 503

JUSTICE REHNQUIST delivered the opinion of the Court.

Petitioner S. Simcha Goldman contends that the Free Exercise Clause of the First Amendment to the United States Constitution permits him to wear a yarmulke while in uniform, notwithstanding an Air Force regulation mandating uniform dress for Air Force personnel. The District Court for the District of Columbia permanently enjoined the Air Force from enforcing its regulation against petitioner and from penalizing him for wearing his yarmulke. The Court of Appeals for the District of Columbia Circuit reversed on the ground that the Air Force's strong interest in discipline justified the strict enforcement of its uniform dress requirements. We granted certiorari because of the importance of the question....

Petitioner Goldman is an Orthodox Jew and ordained rabbi. In 1973, he was accepted into the Armed Forces Health Professions Scholarship Program and placed on inactive reserve status in the Air Force while he studied clinical psychology at Loyola University of Chicago. During his three years in the scholarship program, he received a monthly stipend and an allowance for tuition, books, and fees. After completing his Ph.D. in psychology, petitioner entered active service in the United States Air Force as a commissioned officer, in accordance with a requirement that participants in the scholarship program serve one year of active duty for each year of subsidized education. Petitioner was stationed at March Air Force Base in Riverside, California, and served as a clinical psychologist at the mental health clinic on the base.

Until 1981, petitioner was not prevented from wearing his yarmulke on the base. He avoided controversy by remaining close to his duty station in the health clinic and by wearing his service cap over the yarmulke when out of doors. But in April 1981, after he testified as a defense witness at a court-martial wearing his yarmulke but not his service cap, opposing counsel lodged a complaint with Colonel Joseph Gregory, the Hospital Commander, arguing that petitioner's practice of wearing his yarmulke was a violation of Air Force Regulation (AFR) 35-10. This regulation states in pertinent part that "[h]eadgear will not be worn...[w]hile indoors except by armed security police in the performance of their duties." AFR 35-10 ¶ 1-6.h(2)(f) (1980).

Colonel Gregory informed petitioner that wearing a yarmulke while on duty does indeed violate AFR 35-10, and ordered him not to violate this regulation outside the hospital. Although virtually all of petitioner's time on the base was spent in the hospital, he refused. Later, after petitioner's attorney protested to the Air Force General Counsel, Colonel Gregory revised his order to prohibit petitioner from wearing the yarmulke even in the hospital. Petitioner's request to report for duty in civilian clothing pending legal resolution of the issue was denied. The next day he received a formal letter of reprimand, and was warned that failure to obey AFR 35-10 could subject him to a court-martial. Colonel Gregory also withdrew a recommendation that petitioner's application to extend the term of his active service be approved, and substituted a negative recommendation.

Petitioner then sued respondent Secretary of Defense and others, claiming that the application of AFR 35-10 to prevent him from wearing his yarmulke infringed upon his First Amendment freedom to exercise his religious beliefs.

• • •

Our review of military regulations challenged on First Amendment grounds is far more deferential than constitutional review of similar laws or regulations designed for civilian society. The military need not encourage debate or tolerate protest to the extent that such tolerance is required of the civilian state by the First Amendment; to accomplish its mission the military must foster instinctive obedience, unity, commitment, and espirit de corps....The essence of military service "is the subordination of the desires and interests of the individual to the needs of the service."

These aspects of military life do not, of course, render entirely nugatory in the military context the guarantees of the First Amendment....But "within the military community there is simply not the same [individual] autonomy as there is in the larger civilian community."...In the context of the present case, when evaluating whether military needs justify a particular restriction on religiously motivated conduct, courts must give great deference to the professional judgment of military authorities concerning the relative importance of a particular military interest....Not only are courts "'ill-equipped to determine the impact upon discipline that any particular intrusion upon military authority might have,'"...but the military authorities have been charged by the Executive and Legislative Branches with carrying out our Nation's military policy. "[J]udicial deference...is at its apogee when legislative action under the congressional authority to raise and support armies and make rules and regulations for their governance is challenged."...

The considered professional judgment of the Air Force is that the traditional outfitting of personnel in standardized uniforms encourages the subordination of personal preferences and identities in favor of the overall group mission. Uniforms encourage a sense of hierarchical unity by tending to eliminate outward individual distinctions except for those of rank. The Air Force considers them as vital during peacetime as during war because its personnel must be ready to provide an effective defense on a moment's notice; the necessary habits of discipline and unity must be developed in advance of trouble. We have acknowledged that "[t]he inescapable demands of military discipline and obedience to orders cannot be taught on battlefields; the habit of immediate compliance with military procedures and orders must be virtually reflex with no time for debate or reflection."...

To this end, the Air Force promulgated AFR 35-10, a 190-page document, which states that "Air Force members will wear the Air Force uniform while performing their military duties, except when authorized to wear civilian clothes on duty." AFR § 35-10, ¶ 1-6 (1980). The rest of the document describes in minute detail all of the various items of apparel that must be worn as part of the Air Force uniform. It authorizes a few individualized options with respect to certain pieces of jewelry and hair style, but even these are subject to severe limitations. See AFR 35-10, Table 1-1, and ¶ 1-12.b(1)(b) (1980). In general, authorized headgear may be worn only out of doors. See AFR § 35-10, ¶ 1-6.h (1980). Indoors, "[h]eadgear [may] not be worn...except by armed security police in the performance of their duties." AFR 35-10, ¶ 1-6.h(2)(f) (1980). A narrow exception to this rule exists for headgear worn during indoor religious ceremonies. See AFR 35-10, ¶ 1-6.h(2)(d) (1980). In addition, military commanders may in their discretion permit visible religious headgear and other such apparel in designated living quarters and nonvisible items generally. See Department of Defense Directive 1300.17 (June 18, 1985).

Petitioner Goldman contends that the Free Exercise Clause of the First Amendment requires the Air Force to make an exception to its uniform dress requirements for religious apparel unless the accouterments create a "clear danger" of undermining discipline and esprit de corps. He asserts that in general, visible but "unobtrusive" apparel will not create such a danger and must therefore be accommodated. He argues that the Air Force failed to prove that a specific exception for his practice of wearing an unobtrusive yarmulke would threaten discipline. He contends that the Air Force's assertion to the contrary is mere ipse dixit, with no support from actual experience or a scientific study in the record, and is contradicted by expert testimony that religious exceptions to AFR 35-10 are in fact desirable and will increase morale by making the Air Force a more humane place....

...The Air Force has drawn the line essentially between religious apparel that is visible and that which is not, and we hold that those portions of the regulations challenged here reasonably and evenhandedly regulate dress in the interest of the military's perceived need for uniformity. The First Amendment therefore does not prohibit them from being applied to petitioner even though their effect is to restrict the wearing of the headgear required by his religious beliefs.

Separate Opinions

Justice **Stevens**, with whom Justice **White** and Justice **Powell** join, concurring.

• • •

The interest in uniformity, however, has a dimension that is of still greater importance for me. It is the interest in uniform treatment for the members of all religious faiths. The very strength of Captain Goldman's claim creates the danger that a similar claim on behalf of a Sikh or a Rastafarian might readily be dismissed as "so extreme, so unusual, or so faddish an image that public confidence in his ability to perform his duties will be destroyed." …If exceptions from dress code regulations are to be granted on the basis of a multifactored test…, such as that proposed by Justice Brennan, inevitably the decisionmaker's evaluation of the character and the sincerity of the requester's faith—as well as the probable reaction of the majority to the favored treatment of a member of that faith—will play a critical part in the decision. For the difference between a turban or a dreadlock on the one hand, and a yarmulke on the other, is not merely a difference in "appearance"—it is also the difference between a Sikh or a Rastafarian, on the one hand, and an Orthodox Jew on the other. The Air Force has no business drawing distinctions between such persons when it is enforcing commands of universal application.

• • •

Justice **Brennan**, with whom Justice **Marshall** joins, dissenting.

• • •

The Government maintains in its brief that discipline is jeopardized whenever exceptions to military regulations are granted. Service personnel must be trained to obey even the most arbitrary command reflexively. Non-Jewish personnel will perceive the wearing of a yarmulke by an Orthodox Jew as an unautho-

rized departure from the rules and will begin to question the principle of unswerving obedience. Thus shall our fighting forces slip down the treacherous slope toward unkempt appearance, anarchy, and, ultimately, defeat at the hands of our enemies.

The contention that the discipline of the Armed Forces will be subverted if Orthodox Jews are allowed to wear yarmulkes with their uniforms surpasses belief. It lacks support in the record of this case, and the Air Force offers no basis for it as a general proposition. While the perilous slope permits the services arbitrarily to refuse exceptions requested to satisfy mere personal preferences, before the Air Force may burden free exercise rights it must advance, at the *very least,* a rational reason for doing so.

• • •

The Government also argues that the services have an important interest in uniform dress, because such dress establishes the pre-eminence of group identity, thus fostering esprit de corps and loyalty to the service that transcends individual bonds. In its brief, the Government characterizes the yarmulke as an assertion of individuality and as a badge of religious and ethnic identity, strongly suggesting that, as such, it could drive a wedge of divisiveness between members of the services.

First, the purported interests of the Air Force in complete uniformity of dress and in elimination of individuality or visible identification with any group other than itself are belied by the service's own regulations. The dress code expressly abjures the need for total uniformity:

"(1) The American public and its elected representatives draw certain conclusions on military effectiveness based on what they see; that is, the image the Air Force presents. The image must instill public confidence and leave no doubt that the service member lives by a common standard and responds to military order and discipline.

"(2) Appearance in uniform is an important part of this image.…Neither the Air Force nor the public expects absolute uniformity of appearance. Each member has the right, within limits, to express individuality through his or her appearance. However, the image of a disciplined service member who can be relied on to do his or her job excludes the extreme, the unusual, and the fad." AFR 35-10, ¶¶1-12a(1) and (2) (1978).

It cannot be seriously contended that a serviceman in a yarmulke presents so extreme, so unusual, or so faddish an image that public confidence in his ability to perform his duties will be destroyed. Under the Air Force's own standards, then, Dr. Goldman should have and could have been granted an exception to wear his yarmulke.

• • •

Implicit in Justice Stevens' concurrence, and in the Government's arguments, is what might be characterized as a fairness concern. It would be unfair to allow Orthodox Jews to wear yarmulkes, while prohibiting members of other minority faiths with visible dress and grooming requirements from wearing their saffron robes, dreadlocks, turbans, and so forth. While I appreciate and share this concern for the feelings and the free exercise rights of members of these other faiths, I am baffled by this formulation of the problem. What puzzles me is the implication that a neutral standard that could result in the disparate treatment of Orthodox Jews and, for example, Sikhs is *more* troublesome or unfair than the existing neutral standard that does result in the different treatment of Christians, on the one hand, and Orthodox Jews and Sikhs on the other. *Both* standards are constitutionally suspect; before either can be sustained, it must be shown to be a narrowly tailored means of promoting important military interests.

• • •

As I have shown, that uniformity is illusory, unless uniformity means uniformly accommodating majority religious practices and uniformly rejecting distinctive minority practices.

• • •

Justice **Blackmun**, dissenting.

• • •

The Air Force argues that it has no way of distinguishing fairly between Goldman's request for an exemption and the potential requests of others whose religious practices may conflict with the appearance code, perhaps in more conspicuous ways. In theory, this argument makes some sense. Like any rules prescribing a uniform, the Air Force dress code is by nature arbitrary; few of its requirements could be de-

fended on purely functional grounds. Particularly for personnel such as Goldman who serve in noncombat roles, variations from the prescribed attire frequently will interfere with no military goals other than those served by uniformity itself. There thus may be no basis on which to distinguish some variations from others, aside from the degree to which they detract from the overall image of the service, a criterion that raises special constitutional problems when applied to religious practices. To allow noncombat personnel to wear yarmulkes but not turbans or dreadlocks because the latter seem more obtrusive—or, as Justice Brennan suggests, less "polished" and "professional,"—would be to discriminate in favor of this country's more established, mainstream religions, the practices of which are more familiar to the average observer. Not only would conventional faiths receive special treatment under such an approach; they would receive special treatment precisely *because* they are conventional. In general, I see no constitutional difficulty in distinguishing between religious practices based on how difficult it would be to accommodate them, but favoritism based on how unobtrusive a practice appears to the majority could create serious problems of equal protection and religious establishment, problems the Air Force clearly has a strong interest in avoiding by drawing an objective line at visibility.

The problem with this argument, it seems to me, is not doctrinal but empirical. The Air Force simply has not shown any reason to fear that a significant number of enlisted personnel and officers would request religious exemptions that could not be denied on neutral grounds such as safety, let alone that granting these requests would noticeably impair the overall image of the service.

In these circumstances, deference seems unwarranted. Reasoned military judgments, of course, are entitled to respect, but the military has failed to show that this particular judgment with respect to Captain Goldman is a reasoned one. If, in the future, the Air Force is besieged with requests for religious exemptions from the dress code, and those requests cannot be distinguished on functional grounds from Goldman's, the service may be able to argue credibly that circumstances warrant a flat rule against any visible religious apparel. That, however, would be a case different from the one at hand.

Discussion Questions

1. What are the main rationales for administrative standardization discussed by the majority opinion, Justice Stevens's concurring opinion, and by Justice Blackmun's dissent? Are these rationales fully compatible with one another? Which, if any, are most convincing to you? What are the countervailing constitutional values raised by Justices Brennan and Blackmun? Do you think the outcome of the case was correct with regard to standardization versus free exercise of religion, or do you think the majority's opinion is better explained by its deference to the Air Force?

2. *Yarmulke* is a Yiddish word; many people prefer the Hebrew term *kipah* (pronounced key-*pah*) for the religious skullcap. An ordinary *kipah* measures about five inches in diameter, though some are as large as approximately eight inches. Although they come in a variety of designs and colors, unobtrusive black, brown, and grey ones that lie flat on the head are easily obtained. A *kipah* is not out of keeping with such public ideals as a nation "under God" or one in which "In God We Trust." Does the chain of causality by which the wearing of such an item could compromise the Air Force's effectiveness and compromise the nation's defense seem too attenuated to be believable, as Justice Brennan claims in his dissent? There is no barrier either to wearing or not wearing a *kipah* in the Israeli Air Force (and military generally). Does this fact have any bearing on your thinking about the standardization imposed in the U.S.? Why or why not?

3. Justice Brennan's dissent included a paragraph, not reprinted, to the effect that "Guardianship of this precious liberty [of free exercise of religion] is not the exclusive domain of the federal courts. It is the responsibility as well of the States and other branches of the Federal Government." He also claimed that "Our constitutional commitment to religious freedom is one of our greatest achievements...." If you were an Air Force official responsible for dealing with an issue like the one Goldman raised, what would you do? Is this the type of case in which the regulations should be read to require exceptions at various times?

4. Do you agree with Justice Blackmun that it is too facile to justify standardization on the claim that "if we make an exception for you, we'll have to make an exception for everyone"? Should the Air Force be required to wait and see how many claims like Goldman's arise and how difficult they are to resolve in a principled manner? Is there a conflict between administrative management and adjudication at work here?

Case 7.2
Regulating Religious Practices

CHURCH OF LUKUMI BABALU AYE, INC. v. CITY OF HIALEAH
Argued Nov. 4, 1992
Decided June 11, 1993
508 US 520

JUSTICE KENNEDY delivered the opinion of the Court, except as to Part II-A-2.

The principle that government may not enact laws that suppress religious belief or practice is so well understood that few violations are recorded in our opinions....Concerned that this fundamental nonpersecution principle of the First Amendment was implicated here, however, we granted certiorari....

Our review confirms that the laws in question were enacted by officials who did not understand, failed to perceive, or chose to ignore the fact that their official actions violated the Nation's essential commitment to religious freedom. The challenged laws had an impermissible object; and in all events, the principle of general applicability was violated because the secular ends asserted in defense of the laws were pursued only with respect to conduct motivated by religious beliefs. We invalidate the challenged enactments, and reverse the judgment of the Court of Appeals.

I

A

This case involves practices of the Santeria religion, which originated in the nineteenth century. When hundreds of thousands of members of the Yoruba people were brought as slaves from eastern Africa to Cuba, their traditional African religion absorbed significant elements of Roman Catholicism. The resulting syncretion, or fusion, is Santeria, "the way of the saints." The Cuban Yoruba express their devotion to spirits, called orishas, through the iconography of Catholic saints, Catholic symbols are often present at Santeria rites, and Santeria devotees attend the Catholic sacraments....

The Santeria faith teaches that every individual has a destiny from God, a destiny fulfilled with the aid and energy of the orishas. The basis of the Santeria religion is the nurture of a personal relation with the orishas, and one of the principal forms of devotion is an animal sacrifice....

According to Santeria teaching, the orishas are powerful, but not immortal. They depend for survival on the sacrifice. Sacrifices are performed at birth, marriage, and death rites, for the cure of the sick, for the initiation of new members and priests, and during an annual celebration. Animals sacrificed in Santeria rituals include chickens, pigeons, doves, ducks, guinea pigs, goats, sheep, and turtles. The animals are killed by the cutting of the carotid arteries in the neck. The sacrificed animal is cooked and eaten, except after healing and death rituals....

• • •

B

Petitioner Church of the Lukumi Babalu Aye, Inc. (Church), is a not-for-profit corporation organized under Florida law in 1973. The

Church and its congregants practice the Santeria religion. The president of the Church is petitioner Ernesto Pichardo, who is also the Church's priest and holds the religious title of Italero, the second highest in the Santeria faith. In April, 1987, the Church leased land in the city of Hialeah, Florida, and announced plans to establish a house of worship as well as a school, cultural center, and museum. Pichardo indicated that the Church's goal was to bring the practice of the Santeria faith, including its ritual of animal sacrifice, into the open. The Church began the process of obtaining utility service and receiving the necessary licensing, inspection, and zoning approvals. Although the Church's efforts at obtaining the necessary licenses and permits were far from smooth,...it appears that it received all needed approvals by early August, 1987.

The prospect of a Santeria church in their midst was distressing to many members of the Hialeah community, and the announcement of the plans to open a Santeria church in Hialeah prompted the city council to hold an emergency public session on June 9, 1987....

First, the city council adopted Resolution 87-66, which noted the "concern" expressed by residents of the city "that certain religions may propose to engage in practices which are inconsistent with public morals, peace or safety," and declared that

> [t]he City reiterates its commitment to a prohibition against any and all acts of any and all religious groups which are inconsistent with public morals, peace or safety.

Next, the council approved an emergency ordinance, Ordinance 87-40 that incorporated in full, except as to penalty, Florida's animal cruelty laws....Among other things, the incorporated state law subjected to criminal punishment "[w]hoever...unnecessarily or cruelly...kills any animal." § 828.12.

The city council desired to undertake further legislative action, but Florida law prohibited a municipality from enacting legislation relating to animal cruelty that conflicted with state law....To obtain clarification, Hialeah's city attorney requested an opinion from the attorney general of Florida as to whether § 828.12 prohibited "a religious group from sacrificing an animal in a religious ritual or practice," and whether the city could enact ordinances "making religious animal sacrifice unlawful." The attorney general responded in mid-July. He concluded that the "ritual sacrifice of animals for purposes other than food consumption" was not a "necessary" killing, and so was prohibited by § 828.12.... The attorney general appeared to define "unnecessary" as

> done without any useful motive, in a spirit of wanton cruelty or for the mere pleasure of destruction without being in any sense beneficial or useful to the person killing the animal.

...He advised that religious animal sacrifice was against state law, so that a city ordinance prohibiting it would not be in conflict....

The city council responded at first with a hortatory enactment, Resolution 87-90, that noted its residents'"great concern regarding the possibility of public ritualistic animal sacrifices" and the state law prohibition. The resolution declared the city policy "to oppose the ritual sacrifices of animals" within Hialeah, and announced that any person or organization practicing animal sacrifice "will be prosecuted."

In September, 1987, the city council adopted three substantive ordinances addressing the issue of religious animal sacrifice. Ordinance 87-52 defined "sacrifice" as

> to unnecessarily kill, torment, torture, or mutilate an animal in a public or private ritual or ceremony not for the primary purpose of food consumption,

and prohibited owning or possessing an animal "intending to use such animal for food purposes." It restricted application of this prohibition, however, to any individual or group that

> kills, slaughters or sacrifices animals for any type of ritual, regardless of whether or not the flesh or blood of the animal is to be consumed.

The ordinance contained an exemption for slaughtering by "licensed establishment[s]" of animals "specifically raised for food purposes." Declaring, moreover, that the city council

> has determined that the sacrificing of animals within the city limits is contrary to the public health, safety, welfare and morals of the community,

the city council adopted Ordinance 87-71. That ordinance defined sacrifice as had Ordinance 87-52, and then provided that

> [i]t shall be unlawful for any person, persons, corporations or associations to sacrifice any animal within the corporate limits of the City of Hialeah, Florida.

The final Ordinance, 87-72, defined "slaughter" as "the killing of animals for food," and prohibited slaughter outside of areas zoned for slaughterhouse use. The ordinance provided an exemption, however, for the slaughter or processing for sale of "small numbers of hogs and/or cattle per week in accordance with an exemption provided by state law." All ordinances and resolutions passed the city council by unanimous vote. Violations of each of the four ordinances were punishable by fines not exceeding $500 or imprisonment not exceeding 60 days, or both.

Following enactment of these ordinances, the Church and Pichardo filed this action pursuant to 42 U.S.C. § 1983 in the United States District Court for the Southern District of Florida. Named as defendants were the city of Hialeah and its mayor and members of its city council in their individual capacities. Alleging violations of petitioners' rights under, *inter alia,* the Free Exercise Clause, the complaint sought a declaratory judgment and injunctive and monetary relief. The District Court granted summary judgment to the individual defendants, finding that they had absolute immunity for their legislative acts and that the ordinances and resolutions adopted by the council did not constitute an official policy of harassment, as alleged by petitioners....

After a 9-day bench trial on the remaining claims, the District Court ruled for the city, finding no violation of petitioners' rights under the Free Exercise Clause.

• • •

II

• • •

In addressing the constitutional protection for free exercise of religion, our cases establish the general proposition that a law that is neutral and of general applicability need not be justified by a compelling governmental interest even if the law has the incidental effect of burdening a particular religious practice. *Employment Div., Dept. of Human Resources of Oregon v. Smith* [1990]. Neutrality and general applicability are interrelated, and, as becomes apparent in this case, failure to satisfy one requirement is a likely indication that the other has not been satisfied. A law failing to satisfy these requirements must be justified by a compelling governmental interest, and must be narrowly tailored to advance that interest. These ordinances fail to satisfy the *Smith* requirements. We begin by discussing neutrality.

A

• • •

At a minimum, the protections of the Free Exercise Clause pertain if the law at issue discriminates against some or all religious beliefs or regulates or prohibits conduct because it is undertaken for religious reasons....

1

Although a law targeting religious beliefs as such is never permissible,...if the object of a law is to infringe upon or restrict practices because of their religious motivation, the law is not neutral,...and it is invalid unless it is justified by a compelling interest and is narrowly tailored to advance that interest. There are, of course, many ways of demonstrating that the object or purpose of a law is the suppression of religion or religious conduct. To determine the object of a law, we must begin with its text, for the minimum requirement of neutrality is that a law not discriminate on its face. A law lacks facial neutrality if it refers to a religious practice without a secular meaning discernable from the language or context. Petitioners contend that three of the ordinances fail this test of facial neutrality because they use the words "sacrifice" and "ritual," words with strong religious connotations.... We agree that these words are consistent with the claim of facial discrimination, but the argument is not conclusive. The words "sacrifice" and "ritual" have a religious origin, but current use admits also of secular meanings.... The ordinances, furthermore, define "sacrifice" in secular terms, without referring to religious practices.

We reject the contention advanced by the city...that our inquiry must end with the text of the laws at issue. Facial neutrality is not determinative. The Free Exercise Clause, like the Establishment Clause, extends beyond facial discrimination. The Clause "forbids subtle departures from neutrality,"...and "covert suppression of particular religious beliefs."...Official action that targets religious conduct for distinctive treatment cannot be shielded by mere compliance with the requirement of facial neutrality. The Free Exercise Clause protects against governmental hostility which is masked, as well as overt....

• • •

3

In sum, the neutrality inquiry leads to one conclusion: the ordinances had as their object the suppression of religion. The pattern we have recited discloses animosity to Santeria adherents and their religious practices; the ordinances, by their own terms, target this religious exercise; the texts of the ordinances were gerrymandered with care to proscribe religious killings of animals but to exclude almost all secular killings; and the ordinances suppress much more religious conduct than is necessary in order to achieve the legitimate ends asserted in their defense. These ordinances are not neutral, and the court below committed clear error in failing to reach this conclusion.

B

We turn next to a second requirement of the Free Exercise Clause, the rule that laws burdening religious practice must be of general applicability.... All laws are selective to some extent, but categories of selection are of paramount concern when a law has the incidental effect of burdening religious practice. The Free Exercise Clause "protect[s] religious observers against unequal treatment,"...and inequality results when a legislature decides that the governmental interests it seeks to advance are worthy of being pursued only against conduct with a religious motivation.

The principle that government, in pursuit of legitimate interests, cannot in a selective manner impose burdens only on conduct motivated by religious belief is essential to the protection of the rights guaranteed by the Free Exercise Clause....In this case, we need not define with precision the standard used to evaluate whether a prohibition is of general application, for these ordinances fall well below the minimum standard necessary to protect First Amendment rights.

Respondent claims that Ordinances 87-40, 87-52, and 87-71 advance two interests: protecting the public health and preventing cruelty to animals. The ordinances are underinclusive for those ends. They fail to prohibit nonreligious conduct that endangers these interests in a similar or greater degree than Santeria sacrifice does. The underinclusion is substantial, not inconsequential. Despite the city's proffered interest in preventing cruelty to animals, the ordinances are drafted with care to forbid few killings but those occasioned by religious sacrifice. Many types of animal deaths or kills for nonreligious reasons are either not prohibited or approved by express provision. For example, fishing—which occurs in Hialeah...is legal. Extermination of mice and rats within a home is also permitted. Florida law incorporated by Ordinance 87-40 sanctions euthanasia of "stray, neglected, abandoned, or unwanted animals,"...destruction of animals judicially removed from their owners "for humanitarian reasons" or when the animal "is of no commercial value,"...the infliction of pain or suffering "in the interest of medical science,"...the placing of poison in one's yard or enclosure,...and the use of a live animal "to pursue or take wildlife or to participate in any hunting,"...and "to hunt wild hogs."...

The city concedes that "neither the State of Florida nor the City has enacted a generally applicable ban on the killing of animals."...It asserts, however, that animal sacrifice is "different" from the animal killings that are permitted by law....According to the city, it is "self-evident" that killing animals for food is "important"; the eradication of insects and pests is "obviously justified'; and the euthanasia of excess animals "makes sense."...These *ipse dixits* do not explain why religion alone must bear the burden of the ordinances, when many of these secular killings fall within the city's interest in preventing the cruel treatment of animals.

The ordinances are also underinclusive with regard to the city's interest in public health, which is threatened by the disposal of animal carcasses in open public places and the consumption of uninspected meat....Neither interest is pursued by respondent with regard to conduct that is not motivated by religious conviction. The health risks posed by the improper disposal of animal carcasses are the same whether Santeria sacrifice or some nonreligious killing preceded it. The city does not, however, prohibit hunters from bringing their kill to their houses, nor does it regulate disposal after their activity. Despite substantial testimony at trial that the same public health hazards result from improper disposal of garbage by restaurants,...restaurants are outside the scope of the ordinances. Improper disposal is a general problem that causes substantial health risks,...but which respondent addresses only when it results from religious exercise.

The ordinances are underinclusive as well with regard to the health risk posed by consumption of uninspected meat. Under the city's ordinances, hunters may eat their kill and fishermen may eat their catch without undergoing governmental inspection. Likewise, state law requires inspection of meat that is sold, but exempts meat from animals raised for the use of the owner and "members of his household and nonpaying guests and employees."...The asserted interest in inspected meat is not pursued in contexts similar to that of religious animal sacrifice.

Ordinance 87-72, which prohibits the slaughter of animals outside of areas zoned for slaughterhouses, is underinclusive on its face. The ordinance includes an exemption for "any person, group, or organization" that "slaughters or processes for sale, small numbers of hogs and/or cattle per week in accordance with an exemption provided by state law."...Respondent has not explained why commercial operations that slaughter "small numbers" of hogs and cattle do not implicate its professed desire to prevent cruelty to animals and preserve the public health. Although the city has classified Santeria sacrifice as slaughter, subjecting it to this ordinance, it does not regulate other killings for food in like manner.

We conclude, in sum, that each of Hialeah's ordinances pursues the city's governmental interests only against conduct motivated by religious belief....This precise evil is what the requirement of general applicability is designed to prevent.

III

A law burdening religious practice that is not neutral or not of general application must undergo the most rigorous of scrutiny. To satisfy the commands of the First Amendment, a law restrictive of religious practice must advance "'interests of the highest order,'" and must be narrowly tailored in pursuit of those interests....A law that targets religious conduct for distinctive treatment or advances legitimate governmental interests only against conduct with a religious motivation will survive strict scrutiny only in rare cases. It follows from what we have already said that these ordinances cannot withstand this scrutiny.

First, even were the governmental interests compelling, the ordinances are not drawn in narrow terms to accomplish those interests. As we have discussed,... all four ordinances are overbroad or underinclusive in substantial respects. The proffered objectives are not pursued with respect to analogous nonreligious conduct, and those interests could be achieved by narrower ordinances that burdened religion to a far lesser degree. The absence of narrow tailoring suffices to establish the invalidity of the ordinances....

Respondent has not demonstrated, moreover, that, in the context of these ordinances, its governmental interests are compelling. Where government restricts only conduct protected by the First Amendment and fails to enact feasible measures to restrict other conduct producing substantial harm or alleged harm of the same sort, the interest given in justification of the restriction is not compelling. It is established in our strict scrutiny jurisprudence that

> a law cannot be regarded as protecting an interest "of the highest order"...when it leaves appreciable damage to that supposedly vital interest unprohibited....

IV

The Free Exercise Clause commits government itself to religious tolerance, and upon even slight suspicion that proposals for state intervention stem from animosity to religion or distrust of its practices, all officials must pause to remember their own high duty to the Constitution and to the rights it secures. Those in office must be resolute in resisting importunate demands and must ensure that the sole reasons for imposing the burdens of law and regulation are secular. Legislators may not devise mechanisms, overt or disguised, designed to persecute or oppress a religion or its practices. The laws here in question were enacted contrary to these constitutional principles, and they are void.

Discussion Questions

1. Can the Court's decision in *Lukumi* be squared with its decision in *Goldman v. Weinberger?* How?
2. Some practices that are partly inspired by religious beliefs can be construed as child abuse, such as circumcision of males or females, and the use of wine for ceremonial purposes. Could a local government outlaw such practices? How? What constitutional tests would it have to pass?

Case 7.3
Standardization by Gender

UNITED STATES v. VIRGINIA
Argued January 17, 1996
Decided June 26, 1996
518 US 515

JUSTICE GINSBURG delivered the opinion of the Court.

Virginia's public institutions of higher learning include an incomparable military college, Virginia Military Institute (VMI). The United States maintains that the Constitution's equal protection guarantee precludes Virginia from reserving exclusively to men the unique educational opportunities VMI affords. We agree.

I

Founded in 1839, VMI is today the sole single-sex school among Virginia's 15 public institutions of higher learning. VMI's distinctive mission is to produce "citizen soldiers," men prepared for leadership in civilian life and in military service. VMI pursues this mission through pervasive training of a kind not available anywhere else in Virginia. Assigning prime place to character development, VMI uses an "adversative method" modeled on English public schools and once characteristic of military instruction. VMI constantly endeavors to instill physical and mental discipline in its cadets and impart to them a strong moral code. The school's graduates leave VMI with heightened comprehension of their capacity to deal with duress and stress, and a large sense of accomplishment for completing the hazardous course.

VMI has notably succeeded in its mission to produce leaders; among its alumni are military generals, Members of Congress, and business executives. The school's alumni overwhelmingly perceive that their VMI training helped them to realize their personal goals. VMI's endowment reflects the loyalty of its graduates; VMI has the largest per-student endowment of all undergraduate institutions in the Nation.

Neither the goal of producing citizen soldiers nor VMI's implementing methodology is inherently unsuitable to women. And the school's impressive record in producing leaders has made admission desirable to some women. Nevertheless, Virginia has elected to preserve exclusively for men the advantages and opportunities a VMI education affords.

• • •

IV

• • •

In 1971, for the first time in our Nation's history, this Court ruled in favor of a woman who complained that her State had denied her the equal protection of its laws. *Reed v. Reed,...* (holding unconstitutional Idaho Code prescription that, among "'several persons claiming and equally entitled to administer [a decedent's estate], males must be preferred to females'"). Since *Reed,* the Court has repeat-

edly recognized that neither federal nor state government acts compatibly with the equal protection principle when a law or official policy denies to women, simply because they are women, full citizenship stature—equal opportunity to aspire, achieve, participate in and contribute to society based on their individual talents and capacities....

Without equating gender classifications, for all purposes, to classifications based on race or national origin, the Court, in post-*Reed* decisions, has carefully inspected official action that closes a door or denies opportunity to women (or to men).... To summarize the Court's current directions for cases of official classification based on gender: focusing on the differential treatment or denial of opportunity for which relief is sought, the reviewing court must determine whether the proffered justification is "exceedingly persuasive." The burden of justification is demanding and it rests entirely on the State...[to show that the classification is substantially related to the achievement of important governmental objectives].

• • •

V

• • •

B

Virginia...argues that VMI's adversative method of training provides educational benefits that cannot be made available, unmodified, to women. Alterations to accommodate women would necessarily be "radical," so "drastic," Virginia asserts, as to transform, indeed "destroy," VMI's program.... Neither sex would be favored by the transformation, Virginia maintains: men would be deprived of the unique opportunity currently available to them; women would not gain that opportunity, because their participation would "eliminat[e] the very aspects of [the] program that distinguish [VMI] from...other institutions of higher education in Virginia."...

The District Court forecast from expert witness testimony, and the Court of Appeals accepted, that coeducation would materially affect "at least these three aspects of VMI's program—physical training, the absence of privacy, and the adversative approach."...And it is uncontested that women's admission would require accommodations, primarily in arranging housing assignments and physical training programs for female cadets....

• • •

The notion that admission of women would downgrade VMI's stature, destroy the adversative system and, with it, even the school, is a judgment hardly proved, a prediction hardly different from other "self-fulfilling prophec[ies]."

• • •

Women's successful entry into the federal military academies, and their participation in the Nation's military forces, indicate that Virginia's fears for the future of VMI may not be solidly grounded. The State's justification for excluding all women from "citizen soldier" training for which some are qualified, in any event, cannot rank as "exceedingly persuasive," as we have explained and applied that standard.

• • •

VI

In the second phase of litigation, Virginia presented its remedial plan—maintain VMI as a male-only college and create VWIL [Virginia Women's Institute for Leadership at Mary Baldwin College] as a separate program for women.

• • •

B

In myriad respects other than military training, VWIL does not qualify as VMI's equal. VWIL's student body, faculty, course offerings, and facilities hardly match VMI's. Nor can the VWIL graduate anticipate the benefits associated with VMI's 157-year history, the school's prestige, and its influential alumni network.

• • •

Virginia, in sum, while maintaining VMI for men only, has failed to provide any "comparable single-gender women's institution."... Instead, the Commonwealth has created a VWIL program fairly appraised as a "pale shadow" of VMI in terms of the range of curricular choices and faculty stature, funding, prestige, alumni support and influence....

• • •

Valuable as VWIL may prove for students who seek the program offered, Virginia's remedy affords no cure at all for the opportunities and advantages withheld from women who want a VMI education and can make the grade.... In sum, Virginia's remedy does not match the constitutional violation; the State has shown no "exceedingly persuasive justification" for withholding from women qualified for the experience premier training of the kind VMI affords.

VII

• • •

Women seeking and fit for a VMI-quality education cannot be offered anything less, under the State's obligation to afford them genuinely equal protection.

Discussion Questions

1. Suppose a city concluded that it would be sound educational policy to offer single-sex public school education for girls in kindergarten through eighth grade. How might it constitutionally justify such an all-girl's school?

2. Could a city or state assign only same-sex prison guards to work in male and female prisons? Public mental health wards? Could men be excluded from working in public sector rape crisis centers for women? Shelters for women? Could male police be barred from interviewing female rape victims? What are the principles that guide your answers? Do they comport with the Court's standards for gender classification in the VMI case?

Case 7.4
Standardization, Individuation, and Equal Protection

ZOBEL et ux v. WILLIAMS, COMMISSIONER OF REVENUE OF ALASKA, et al.
Argued October 7, 1981
Decided June 14, 1982
457 US 55

CHIEF JUSTICE BURGER delivered the opinion of the Court.

The question presented on this appeal is whether a statutory scheme by which a State distributes income derived from its natural resources to the adult citizens of the State in varying amounts, based on the length of each citizen's residence, violates the equal protection rights of newer state citizens....

• • •

I

The 1967 discovery of large oil reserves on state-owned land in the Prudhoe Bay area of Alaska resulted in a windfall to the State. The State, which had a total budget of $124 million in 1969, before the oil revenues began to flow into the state coffers, received $3.7 billion in petroleum revenues during the 1981 fiscal year. This income will continue, and most likely grow for some years in the future. Recognizing that its mineral reserves, although large, are finite and that the resulting income will not continue in perpetuity, the State took steps to assure that its current good fortune will bring long-range benefits. To accomplish this, Alaska in 1976 adopted a constitutional amendment establishing the Permanent Fund into which the State must deposit at least 25% of its mineral income each year. Alaska Const., Art. IX, § 15. The amendment prohibits the legislature from appropriating any of the principal of the Fund but permits use of the Fund's earnings for general governmental purposes.

In 1980, the legislature enacted a dividend program to distribute annually a portion of the Fund's earnings directly to the State's adult residents. Under the plan, each citizen 18 years of age or older receives one dividend unit for each year of residency subsequent to 1959, the first year of statehood. The statute fixed the value of each dividend unit at $50 for the 1979 fiscal

year; a one-year resident thus would receive one unit, or $50, while a resident of Alaska since it became a State in 1959 would receive 21 units, or $1,050. The value of a dividend unit will vary each year depending on the income of the Permanent Fund and the amount of that income the State allocates for other purposes. The State now estimates that the 1985 fiscal year dividend will be nearly four times as large as that for 1979.

Appellants, residents of Alaska since 1978, brought this suit in 1980 challenging the dividend distribution plan as violative of their right to equal protection guarantees and their constitutional right to migrate to Alaska, to establish residency there and thereafter to enjoy the full rights of Alaska citizenship on the same terms as all other citizens of the State. The Superior Court for Alaska's Third Judicial District granted summary judgment in appellants' favor, holding that the plan violated the rights of interstate travel and equal protection. A divided Alaska Supreme Court reversed and upheld the statute.

[II]

A

The State advanced and the Alaska Supreme Court accepted three purposes justifying the distinctions made by the dividend program: (a) creation of a financial incentive for individuals to establish and maintain residence in Alaska; (b) encouragement of prudent management of the Permanent Fund; and (c) apportionment of benefits in recognition of undefined "contributions of various kinds, both tangible and intangible, which residents have made during their years of residency."...

As the Alaska Supreme Court apparently realized, the first two state objectives—creating a financial incentive for individuals to establish and maintain Alaska residence, and assuring prudent management of the Permanent Fund and the State's natural and mineral resources—are not rationally related to the distinctions Alaska seeks to make between newer residents and those who have been in the State since 1959.

Assuming, *arguendo,* that granting increased dividend benefits for each year of continued Alaska residence might give some residents an incentive to stay in the State in order to reap increased dividend benefits in the future, the State's interest is not in any way served by granting greater dividends to persons for their residency during the 21 years prior to the enactment.

Nor does the State's purpose of furthering the prudent management of the Permanent Fund and the State's resources support retrospective application of its plan to the date of statehood.

• • •

The last of the State's objectives—to reward citizens for past contributions—alone was relied upon by the Alaska Supreme Court to support the retrospective application of the law to 1959. However, that objective is not a legitimate state purpose.

• • •

If the states can make the amount of a cash dividend depend on length of residence, what would preclude varying university tuition on a sliding scale based on years of residence—or even limiting access to finite public facilities, eligibility for student loans, for civil service jobs, or for government contracts by length of domicile? Could states impose different taxes based on length of residence? Alaska's reasoning could open the door to state apportionment of other rights, benefits, and services according to length of residency. It would permit the states to divide citizens into expanding numbers of permanent classes. Such a result would be clearly impermissible.

III

The only apparent justification for the retrospective aspect of the program, "favoring established residents over new residents," is constitutionally unacceptable.…In our view Alaska has shown no valid state interests which

are rationally served by the distinction it makes between citizens who established residence before 1959 and who have become residents since then.

We hold that the Alaska dividend distribution plan violates the guarantees of the Equal Protection Clause of the Fourteenth Amendment.

• • •

Justice Brennan, with whom Justice Marshall, Justice Blackmun, and Justice Powell join concurring.

I join the opinion of the Court, and agree with its conclusion that the retrospective aspects of Alaska's dividend-distribution law are not rationally related to a legitimate state purpose. I write separately only to emphasize that the pervasive discrimination embodied in the Alaska distribution scheme gives rise to constitutional concerns of somewhat larger proportions than may be evident on a cursory reading of the Court's opinion.

• • •

It is, of course, elementary that the Constitution does not bar the States from making reasoned distinctions between citizens: Insofar as those distinctions are rationally related to the legitimate ends of the State they present no constitutional difficulty, as our equal protection jurisprudence attests. But we have never suggested that duration of residence *vel non* provides a valid justification for discrimination.

• • •

Permissible discriminations between persons must bear a rational relationship to their *relevant* characteristics. While some imprecision is unavoidable in the process of legislative classification, the ideal of equal protection requires attention to individual merit, to individual need. In almost all instances, the business of the State is not with the past, but with the present: to remedy continuing injustices, to fill current needs, to build on the present in order to better the future. The past actions of individuals may be relevant in assessing their present needs; past actions may also be relevant in predicting current ability and future performance. In addition, to a limited extent, recognition and reward of past public service have independent utility for the State, for such recognition may encourage other people to engage in comparably meritorious service. But even the idea of rewarding past public service offers scarce support for the "past contribution" justification for durational-residence classifications since length of residence has only the most tenuous relation to the *actual* service of individuals to the State.

Thus, the past-contribution rationale proves much too little to provide a rational predicate for discrimination on the basis of length of residence. But it also proves far too much, for "it would permit the State to apportion all benefits and services according to the past...contributions of its citizens."...In effect, then, the past-contribution rationale is so far-reaching in its potential application, and the relationship between residence and contribution to the State so vague and insupportable, that it amounts to little more than a restatement of the criterion for discrimination that it purports to justify. But while duration of residence has minimal utility as a measure of things that are, in fact, constitutionally relevant, resort to duration of residence as the basis for a distribution of state largesse does closely track the constitutionally untenable position that the longer one's residence, the worthier one is of the State's favor. In my view, it is difficult to escape from the recognition that underlying any scheme of classification on the basis of duration of residence, we shall almost invariably find the unstated premise that "some citizens are more equal than others." We rejected that premise and, I believe, implicitly rejected most forms of discrimination based upon length of residence, when we adopted the Equal Protection Clause.

Discussion Questions

1. Seeking to reward individuals for "contributions of various kinds, both tangible and intangible, which residents have made during their years of residency" by treating all individuals with equal length of residency identically is obviously irrational. For instance, someone who had spent twenty years in jail for a horrible crime could receive the same benefits as a public school teacher with twenty years seniority. Why do you suppose the State wanted to use years of residence as a surrogate measure for actual contributions to Alaska? Is the individuation that Justice Brennan calls for in his concurring opinion administratively practicable? How could actual contributions be evaluated? If the state had sought to make past tax payments by individuals or families the basis for assessing contributions, what problems might have developed?

2. In *Zobel*, how is the Equal Protection Clause used to protect *pluralism* against governmental efforts to favor some groups? Consider how equal protection serves to promote both standardized treatment (procedural regularity and equality) and diversity (pluralism). Does the constitutional commitment to both procedural equality and pluralism draw acute attention to the way public policy and administration classifies individuals? For instance, what would be the problem if Alaska had made the benefit available to women only? What if only military veterans were eligible? What if everyone who had reached the age of majority were given an equal benefit, but minors received none? What if only indigenous peoples, such as Eskimos and Aleuts, were eligible or ineligible for benefits? What are some of the differences in these classifications?

EIGHT

Economy

Economy is another core public administrative value that often triggers a need for constitutional competence. The cost of government is almost always of interest to the public, politicians, and the media. For instance, an official investigation concluded that poor federal administration has "burdened the country with debt and taxes, and assisted to prostrate the trade and industry of the nation."[1] That was back in 1877! But the complaint has a contemporary ring. Today, on average, the federal government spends more than $40,000 per second every second of the year. The public sector accounts for about 32 percent of the nation's gross domestic product.[2] Perhaps as a result of news stories about incredibly exorbitant government spending on everything from ashtrays to bombers, Americans reportedly believe that the federal government wastes 48 cents of every tax dollar it collects![3]

No wonder public managers are under substantial pressure to reduce and control spending. In fact, a great deal of public administration is aimed precisely at achieving these goals. However, constitutional competence requires that economy not be attained at the expense of individuals' protected rights.

Economy, Budgets, and Accountability

Orthodox public administration views budgeting very largely as a tool for controlling costs and reducing waste. In the early part of the century, administrative reformers promoted the line-item veto to track expenditures very closely. For the past 50 years, the federal government has experimented with a number of formats—performance budgeting, program budgeting, zero-based budgeting, and deficit reduction budgeting.[4] In one way or another, all these approaches are intended to achieve economy by eliminating waste and making government operate more cost-effectively.

The various budget strategies have been accompanied by a number of accountability measures to further guard against waste, corruption, or other mismanagement of funds. Budgets may "earmark" funds for spending on specific projects or objects. They may also contain detailed limits on how much can be spent for staff, supplies, programs, or any object of expenditure. Auditing agencies, inspectors general, legislative committees, and financial officers monitor compliance with such budgetary requirements and recommend economizing measures.

The New Public Management (NPM) argues that much of the orthodox approach is counterproductive. Ideally, the NPM would rely on lump-sum or envelope budgeting, in which public managers are given clear missions and the funds to achieve them with few strings attached. Public managers would be held strictly responsible for results rather than for complying with myriad procedural requirements and detailed restrictions on spending.

The federal National Performance Review (NPR) incorporates several components of NPM budgeting. It advocates the following:

- [S]treamline the budget process, to remove the manifold restrictions that consume managers' time and literally force them to waste money.
- [S]treamline procurement, to reduce the enormous waste built into the process we use to buy $200 billion a year in goods and services.
- [R]eorient the inspectors general, to shift their focus from punishing those who violate rules and regulations to helping agencies learn to perform better.
- Institute biennial budgets and appropriations.
- [M]inimize budget restrictions such as apportionments and allotments.
- Allow agencies to roll over 50 percent of what they do not spend on internal operations during a fiscal year.[5]

Although the NPR's strategy for achieving economy is diametrically opposed to the orthodox approach, the goal is essentially the same. The NPR, the NPM more generally, and the orthodoxy all want government to work better and cost less.

Few will argue against administrative economy and financial accountability in the abstract. However, the pressure on agencies, programs, and public managers to economize sometimes leads to serious interference with protected constitutional rights. Indeed, the pursuit of economy can result in outright victimization. Prisoners have probably borne the brunt of this problem, but it extends to the mentally ill and, in some respects, to the poor as well.[6]

Holt v. Sarver (1970), a landmark prison reform case, well illustrates the tension between economy and constitutional rights.[7] The Arkansas penal system emphasized cost-effectiveness. The objective was to make the system self-supporting, if not profit making. Convicts spent long hours working the system's farms. Costs were cut to the point that a federal district court broke new legal ground in holding that confinement in the system violated the Eighth Amendment's ban on cruel and unusual punishment. At one facility, 35 paid personnel were responsible for 1,000 prisoners; at night, only two paid guards were on duty. The average prisoner was between 40 and 60 pounds underweight, and sanitation was very poor. Prisoner-on-prisoner violence and predation were rife. The court found the results of this economizing to be shocking: "It is one thing for the State not to pay a convict for his labor; it is something else to subject him to a situation in which he has to sell his blood to obtain money to pay for his own safety, or for adequate food, or for access to needed medical attention."[8]

Case 8.1, *Wyatt v. Stickney* (1971), is another ground-breaking proceeding. It deals with the conflict between administrative economy and humane treatment in the context of public mental health. The Alabama public mental health system was very seriously underfunded. Patients were essentially warehoused in harsh conditions. Inadequate staffing contributed to the death of four residents, a general lack of individualized treatment plans, and unsafe and unsanitary conditions. Some patients were brutalized.[9]

The federal district court responded to the patients' suit by declaring that the Fourteenth Amendment's protection of liberty provides those who are involuntarily confined in public mental health facilities with a right to treatment. Eventually, this new right required a humane psychological and physical environment, qualified staff in sufficient numbers, and an individualized treatment plan for each patient.

The following administrative conditions were judicially imposed on the system:

1. Protection of patients' right to wear their own clothes, have physical exercise, and freedom of religious worship.
2. No more than six patients per room.
3. No single room with less than 100 square feet.
4. At least one toilet for each eight patients.
5. At least one shower or tub for each 15 patients.
6. Not less than 50 square feet per person in the dayroom.
7. Not less than ten square feet per person in the dining room.
8. A temperature range of between 68 and 83 degrees Fahrenheit.
9. Various per-patient staffing ratios for professionals, clerical workers, and other personnel.

Technically, a violation of any of these conditions would be an infringement on the constitutional right to treatment as defined in the *Wyatt* litigation. If the administrators could not meet these conditions, they had the option of releasing the patients.[10]

Initially, at least, Alabama's commissioner of mental health, Dr. Stonewall B. Stickney, welcomed the court's ability to pry funding from the legislature. "Actually," he said, "it's kind of exhilarating to see that the courts may get the Legislature going. It's been our experience that they'd rather spend money for highways than mental health."[11]

Wyatt is one of the most famous of what are known as "remedial law" or "public law litigation" cases.[12] It became a significant precedent in efforts throughout the nation to use litigation to ensure that public institutions, including public mental hospitals, jails, and juvenile homes, do not economize to the point of depriving individuals of their constitutional rights. In many of these cases, a judge "took over" the institution by exercising the equity powers of federal courts to impose remedies for constitutional and statutory wrongs. Special masters were often used to help develop remedies and oversee their implementation.[13]

Remedial lawsuits such as *Wyatt* have generated considerable controversy. Both the appropriateness and effectiveness of judicial control of administrative institutions and systems have been broadly disputed.[14] So has the impact of the courts on public budgets.[15] However, as a legal principle it is now incontestable that economizing in public institutions must be subordinated to the protection of constitutional rights. Accountability is now for constitutional concerns as well as for funds. In fact, "there is an emerging new specialty in the corrections field, which according to some proponents of the idea, trains and designates officials to perform 'constitutional audits' of facilities and procedures in order to reduce legal liabilities."[16]

Economy in Safety-Net Programs

Economy plays a peculiar role in the administration of safety-net programs. In comparison with Great Britain and Western European nations, the welfare state developed relatively late in the United States. Social Security, which included Aid to Families with Dependent Children (AFDC) and other income-support programs, was introduced in 1935 as part of the New Deal. These initiatives were contested then and various safety-net programs have been intermittently controversial ever since. Tepid political support for some programs and the sheer expense of others—including Social Security, Medicaid, and Medicare—often translate into intense pressure on their administrators to keep payouts at the lowest level consistent with law. However, as in the case of prisons and public mental health systems, economy can conflict with constitutional rights.

In some respects, the constitutional scheme is skeptical of redistribution of wealth. As discussed in the previous chapter, James Madison argues in *Federalist No. 10* that the protection of different amounts and kinds of property is vital to the operation of the republican form of government established by the Constitution.[17] Different and unequal interests and abilities in acquiring property ensure a division of society into diverse and often competing parties and concerns. This prevents a majority faction from developing. It promotes vitality in federalism by increasing the likelihood that the individual states will be dominated by different interests. It also strengthens checks and balances within the separation of powers by enhancing the prospect that members of the House of Representatives will be responsive to different local majorities, Senators to interests aggregated at the state level, and the president to an even broader constituency. From this perspective, governmentally directed leveling of wealth through income redistribution programs is undesirable and counterproductive at the point that it reduces the nation's diversity of political outlooks and interests.

As Madison explains it, economic inequality is necessary for the proper operation of the constitutional design. Government will work best when each person has a basic liberty to pursue his or her economic self-interest in the marketplace consistent with the well-being of others. But public policy, the ideal of legal equality, and moral compassion impel government to ensure a reasonable standard of living to those who are unable to compete economically because of physical or mental disabilities, age, or other factors. The problem is that, as the public sector draws more of the society's wealth to provide a safety net, it reduces the resources available to the private sector. This can limit the economic opportunity available to some people.

Madisonian and economic perspectives indicate that there are constitutional reasons for economizing in safety-net programs. But the Constitution also places some basic constraints on how economy can be achieved.

Procedural due process is a constitutional requirement that is almost inherently in tension with administrative economy. The model explained earlier in Case 6.1,

Cleveland Board of Education v. Loudermill (1985), applies to the termination of welfare and disability benefits. As a general rule, individuals will have a constitutional right to notice of the government's reasons for terminating benefits, during the term for which they were offered, and an opportunity to respond either prior to or shortly after the cutoff. Depending on the circumstances, the response may take the form of an elaborate hearing. Procedural due process is not required when a fixed expiration date for benefits is reached.

Case 8.2, *Sherbert v. Verner* (1963), illustrates how the effort to economize in safety-net programs can interfere with the exercise of substantive rights. South Carolina's Employment Security Commission withheld unemployment benefits from Sherbert because, in its view, she took herself out of the labor market by refusing to work on Saturdays. But she did so in order to practice her religion, Seventh Day Adventism, and the Supreme Court likened the Commission's policy to imposing a fine on her Saturday worship. The Court was wholly unimpressed with the Commission's contention that its action was necessary to prevent fraudulent claims that could dilute the unemployment compensation fund. It reasoned that even if spurious claims were a threat, the Commission would have to show they could not be managed without abridging religious freedom. *Sherbert* was reinforced in several subsequent cases.[18]

The Supreme Court's decision in *Sherbert* is also noteworthy for its rejection of the doctrine of privilege and its application of the unconstitutional conditions doctrine to social welfare benefits (see the discussion in Chapter 2). Between 1963, when *Sherbert* was handed down, and 1990, the Court decided 23 cases involving constitutional challenges to conditions placed on public assistance benefits. It has been about as likely to uphold as reject their constitutionality and has not developed a clear theory to explain its decisions. However, there is a structure to its holdings:

> In cases in which the Court concluded that the challenged condition was impermissible, it typically found (1) that the condition operated as a "fine," "penalty," "burden," or "impingement" on the exercise of a constitutional right other than equal protection, and (2) that the government's interest in the condition was insufficiently "compelling" to justify the burden on the right. In contrast, in cases in which the Court concluded that the condition was permissible, it uniformly found (1) that the condition did not burden or impinge upon any constitutional right, and (2) there was, in any case, a "rational basis" for the condition.
>
> In reaching its result in each case, the Court's first determination—whether the condition impinges on or burdens a constitutional right—is virtually dispositive. Whether the challenge is brought under the equal protection clause or under another constitutional provision, the Court has explicitly applied a two-step test in which it inquires (1) whether the condition at issue impinges on, burdens, or penalizes the exercise of a constitutional right, and (2) whether the condition is justified by a "compelling state interest" (when the answer to (1) is "yes") or a "rational basis" (when the answer to (1) is "no"). In applying the test, the Court has *never* found the state's interest sufficiently compelling to justify a condition that burdens a constitutional right. The court has *always* been able to find a rational basis for conditions that impose no such burden.[19]

Case 8.3, *Shapiro v. Thompson* (1969), provides an illustration of how this decisional process operates. The Court struck down laws in Connecticut, the District of Columbia, and Pennsylvania that denied welfare benefits to individuals who had not resided in their jurisdictions for at least a year. In part, the regulations were intended to deter indigents and those seeking higher welfare benefits from moving into the jurisdictions. The classification, residential duration, is nonsuspect, but the Court held that the restrictions burdened the constitutional right of travel interstate. Such a right is derived from the structure of the federal union and the Constitution's protection of individual liberty. Consequently, the Court applied strict scrutiny and required the governments involved to meet the compelling interest and least restrictive alternative tests, which they were unable to do. Of particular interest to the administration of safety-net programs, the Court noted that although preventing fraud is a legitimate governmental purpose, it is not a compelling state interest. Moreover, in this instance, less restrictive means were available.

The constitutionally competent public manager should follow the law on residency requirements with some care. In 1974, the Court adhered to *Shapiro* in declaring unconstitutional a one-year residency requirement for indigent persons seeking nonemergency medical care in a public hospital.[20] Other litigation established that states may impose residency requirements for reduced in-state tuition at public colleges and universities as long as they afford individuals moving to the state an opportunity to become bona fide residents after a reasonable period of time.[21]

Questions about the constitutionality of residency requirements for welfare reemerged in the late 1990s. The welfare reform created by the Personal Responsibility and Work Opportunity Reconciliation Act of 1996 (PRWO) authorized the states to treat newcomers differently from those who have resided within their borders for a year or more. They could apply the rules of the state from which the indigent came for twelve months.[22] If the original state paid less, the new state could pay that amount. In one of the first legal challenges to this provision, a New York State court found the residency requirements unconstitutional.[23] The U.S. Supreme Court followed suit in *Saenz v. Roe* (1999).[24]

In summing up the Constitution's role in safety-net administration it can be said that while constitutional theory emphasizes economy, current constitutional law seeks to protect individuals' procedural due process, substantive, and equal protection rights from some forms of economizing. The vagaries of taxpayer penury and compassion reinforce the constitutional duality. The fundamental tension pervades welfare programs in which the general objective is to assist the deserving—though not too generously—and to screen out others—though not unfairly.

"Takings"

The Fifth Amendment prohibits the federal government from taking private property except for public use and with just compensation. The same restrictions apply to state and local governments through the Due Process Clause of the Fourteenth Amendment (see Chapter 1). Governments have broad zoning powers to eliminate nuisances and to make sure that one person's use of property is compatible with that of others. However, zoning that substantially takes away the right to use the property may require compensation.[25] In recent years, the Supreme Court extended greater constitutional protection to real property by ruling that conditions attached to building permits can violate the Takings Clause. This extension of the unconstitutional conditions doctrine is of considerable importance to local governmental efforts to economize by forcing real property owners to modify the use of their land for public purposes.

The issues involved are well illustrated by Case 8.4, *Dolan v. City of Tigard* (1994). Dolan wanted to expand her plumbing and electrical supply store. The city was concerned about increased traffic and surface water run-off into a river that periodically flooded. As a condition of receiving a building permit for the new use of her property, the city required that Dolan dedicate about 10 percent of her land to a greenway and pedestrian/bicycle path. The Supreme Court expanded on an earlier ruling, *Nollan v. California Coastal Commission* (1987),[26] in strengthening property rights.

Dolan holds that, first, the means government chooses to reach a legitimate specified end must substantially advance the achievement of that objective. Government cannot take property simply because taking it is a convenient means to an end. There must be a very close fit or "essential nexus" between the taking and the objective. Second, in the case of a building or other permit, there must be "rough proportionality" between the burden a new use of land will impose, such as greater traffic congestion, and what the landowner is required to surrender (control over a strip of land in *Dolan*). Government cannot take significantly more than is necessary to achieve its public purpose, such as facilitating the flow of traffic. Third, the government bears the burden of persuasion in demonstrating the essential nexus and rough proportionality. This has to be done on an individualized basis. The requirement strengthens the property owner's position in bargaining, settling, and litigating. As Justice John Paul Stevens said in dissent, "property owners have surely found a new friend today."[27]

The full ramifications of *Dolan* are still uncertain. Presumably the Court's decision will put a damper on some forms of NPM entrepreneurship, especially at the local level. In *Dolan,* the city wanted to obtain its pedestrian/bicycle path without paying for all the land. Elsewhere, any number of conditions, such as providing space for public libraries and fire departments, have been attached to permission to build shopping malls. For developers, these were the price of doing business. Now landowners have constitutional protection and can demand to be compensated when an essential nexus or rough proportionality is missing. And, of great practical importance, the legal structure of protection against takings favors the property owner.

Conclusion

This chapter completes our analysis of the requirements for constitutional competence. Public managers must integrate core constitutional requirements into their practice while attempting to maximize conflicting key administrative values. There is no general formula. Constitutional competence is a prerequisite, but not a blueprint. Taking "constitutional audits," as described earlier, is a good way of guarding against unconstitutional action.

The next chapter addresses the limits of the judiciary's effort to constitutionalize public administration. If the United States is to fulfill Woodrow Wilson's initial call for public management based on "principles which have democratic policy very much at heart,"[28] much of the progress will occur through the daily work of constitutionally competent public managers.

Notes

1. U.S. Congress, House, Executive Document No. 8, 45th Congress, 1st Session, p. 15 (October 25, 1877).

2. See U.S. Office of Management and Budget, *A Citizen's Guide to the Federal Budget, Fiscal Year 1997* (Washington, DC: U.S. Government Printing Office, 1996), p. 2.

3. Al Gore, *From Red Tape to Results: Creating a Government that Works Better & Costs Less* (Washington, DC: U.S. Government Printing Office, 1993), p.1.

4. See David Rosenbloom, *Public Administration: Understanding Management, Politics, and Law in the Public Sector,* 4th ed. (New York: McGraw-Hill, 1998), Chapter 6.

5. Gore, *From Red Tape to Results,* pp. 13–20.

6. See David Rosenbloom and Rosemary O'Leary, *Public Administration and Law,* 2nd ed. (New York: Marcel Dekker, 1997), Chapter 7; John La Fond and Mary Durham, *Back to the Asylum* (New York: Oxford University Press, 1992); and John DiIulio, ed., *The Courts, Corrections, and the Constitution* (New York: Oxford University Press, 1990).

7. *Holt v. Sarver,* 309 F. Supp. 362 (1970); see also Rosenbloom and O'Leary, *Public Administration and Law,* Chapter 7.

8. *Holt v. Sarver,* 309 F. Supp. 362, 381 (1970).

9. *Wyatt v. Stickney,* 325 F. Supp. 781; 334 F. Supp. 1314 (1971); 344 F. Supp. 373; 344 F. Supp. 387; 503 F.2d 1305 (1972); Rosenbloom and O'Leary, *Public Administration and Law,* Chapter 7.

10. "The *Wyatt* Case: Implementation of a Judicial Decree Ordering Institutional Change," *Yale Law Journal,* vol. 84 (1975): 1338–1379. See also Rosenbloom and O'Leary, *Public Administration and Law,* pp. 246–249.

11. Tinsley Yarbrough, "The Judge as Manager," *Journal of Policy Analysis and Management,* vol. 1 (1982): 397.

12. Robert Wood, *Remedial Law: When Courts Become Administrators* (Amherst, MA: University of Massachusetts Press, 1990); Abram Chayes, "The Role of the Judge in Public Law Litigation," *Harvard University Law Review,* vol. 89 (1976): 1281–1316.

13. David Levine, "The Authority for the Appointment of Remedial Special Masters in Federal Institutional Reform Litigation," *University of California at Davis Law Review,* vol. 17 (1984): 753; Wood, *Remedial Law;* David Schoenbrod, Angus MacBeth, David Levine, and David Jung, *Remedies: Public and Private* (Belmont, CA: West/Wadsworth, 1996).

14. See Rosenbloom and O'Leary, *Public Administration and Law,* Chapter 9, for a summary of the literature. See also David Schultz and Stephen E. Gottlieb, "Legal Functionalism and Social Change," *Journal of Law and Politics,* vol. 12 (1996): 63.

15. Rosenbloom and O'Leary, *Public Administration and Law,* pp. 317–318.

16. Malcom Feeley and Roger Hanson, "The Impact of Judicial Intervention on Prisons and Jails: A Framework for Analysis and a Review of the Literature," in DiIulio, ed., *The Courts, Corrections, and the Constitution,* p. 26.

17. *The Federalist Papers,* ed. by Clinton Rossiter (New York: The New American Library, 1961), p. 80.

18. *Thomas v. Review Board,* 450 U.S. 707 (1981); *Hobbie v. Unemployment Appeals Commission,* 480 U.S. 136 (1987); *Frazee v. Illinois Employment Security Department,* 489 U.S. 829 (1989).

19. Lynn Baker, "The Prices of Rights," *Cornell University Law Review,* vol. 75 (1990): 1202–1203.

20. *Memorial Hospital v. Maricopa County,* 415 U.S. 250 (1974).

21. *Starns v. Malkerson,* 326 F. Supp. 234 (1970), affirmed 401 U.S. 985 (1971); *Vlandis v. Kline,* 412 U.S. 441 (1973). For a recent example of litigation on the issue of tuition payments, see *Buchwald v. University of New Mexico School of Medicine,* 1998 U.S. App. Lexis 26598.

22. Brenna Binns, "Fencing Out the Poor: The Constitutionality of Residency Requirements in Welfare Reform," *Wisconsin Law Review,* vol. 1996 (1996): 1255; Todd Zubler, "The Right to Migrate and Welfare Reform: Time for *Shapiro v. Thompson* to Take a Hike," *Valparaiso University Law Review,* vol. 31 (1977): 893.

23. *Brown v. Wing,* New York Supreme Court, No. 96-09067 (December 1996).

24. *Saenz v. Roe,* No. 98-97 (1999).

25. See Richard Epstein, *Taking Private Property and the Power of Eminent Domain* (Cambridge, MA: Harvard University Press, 1985); *Lucas v. South Carolina Coastal Council,* 502 U.S. 966 (1991).

26. *Nollan v. California Coastal Commission,* 483 U.S. 825 (1987).

27. *Dolan v. City of Tigard,* 512 U.S. 374, 405 (1994).

28. Woodrow Wilson, "The Study of Administration," J. Shafritz and A. Hyde, eds., *Classics of Public Administration,* 2nd ed. (Chicago: Dorsey Press, 1987), p. 24. (Originally published in 1887.)

Additional Reading

Okun, Arthur. *Equality and Efficiency: The Big Tradeoff.* Washington, DC: Brookings Institution, 1975.

Case 8.1
Constitutional Rights and Budget Constraints

WYATT v. STICKNEY, AS COMMISSIONER OF MENTAL HEALTH AND THE
STATE OF ALABAMA MENTAL HEALTH OFFICER, et al.
United States District Court, M.D.
Alabama, N.D. March 12, 1971
325 F. Supp. 781

JOHNSON, Chief Judge.

This is a class action that was initiated by guardians of patients confined at Bryce Hospital, Tuscaloosa, Alabama, and by certain employees of the Alabama Mental Health Board who are assigned to Bryce Hospital. The plaintiffs sue on behalf of themselves and on behalf of other members of their respective classes.

The defendants are the commissioner and the deputy commissioner of the Department of Mental Health of the State of Alabama, the members of the Alabama Mental Health Board, the Governor of the State of Alabama, and the probate judge of Montgomery County, Alabama, as representative of the other judges of probate in the State of Alabama.

• • •

The Alabama Mental Health Board is a public corporation created by the State of Alabama.... This board is responsible for the administration of all State mental health facilities and treatment centers, including Bryce Hospital, Tuscaloosa, Alabama. When not in session, the Alabama Mental Health Board acts through its chief administrative officer whose title is State Mental Health Officer. This position is presently held by Dr. Stonewall B. Stickney.

Bryce Hospital is located in Tuscaloosa, Alabama, and is a part of the mental health service delivery system for the State of Alabama. Bryce Hospital has approximately 5,000 patients, the majority of whom are involuntarily committed through civil proceedings by the various probate judges in Alabama. Approximately 1,600 employees were assigned to various duties at the Bryce Hospital facility when this case was heard on plaintiff's motion for a preliminary injunction.

During October 1970, the Alabama Mental Health Board and the administration of the Department of Mental Health terminated 99 of these employees. These terminations were made

due to budgetary considerations and, according to the evidence, were necessary to bring the expenditures at Bryce Hospital within the framework of available resources. This budget cut at Bryce Hospital was allegedly necessary because of a reduction in the tax revenues available to the Department of Mental Health of the State of Alabama, and also because an adjustment in the pay periods for personnel which had been directed by the Alabama legislature would require additional expenditures. The employees who were terminated included 41 persons who were assigned to duties such as food service, maintenance, typing, and other functional duties not involving direct patient care in the hospital therapeutic programs. Twenty-six persons were discharged who were involved in patient activity and recreational programs. These workers were involved in planning social and other types of recreational programs for the patient population. The remaining 32 employees who were discharged included 9 in the department of psychology, 11 in the social service department, with varying degrees of educational background and experience, three registered nurses, two physicians, one dentist, and six dental aides. After the termination of these employees, there remained at Bryce Hospital 17 physicians, approximately 850 psychiatric aides, 21 registered nurses, 12 patient activity workers, and 12 psychologists with varying academic qualifications and experience, together with 13 social service workers. Of the employees remaining whose duties involved direct patient care in the hospital therapeutic programs, there are only one Ph.D. clinical psychologist, three medical doctors with some psychiatric training (including one board eligible but no board-certified psychiatrist) and two M.S.W. social workers.

• • •

Included in the Bryce Hospital patient population are between 1,500 and 1,600 geriatric patients who are provided custodial care but no treatment. The evidence is without dispute that these patients are not properly confined at Bryce Hospital since these geriatric patients cannot benefit from any psychiatric treatment or are not mentally ill. Also included in the Bryce patient population are approximately 1,000 mental retardates, most of whom receive only custodial care without any psychiatric treatment. Thus, the evidence reflects that there is considerable confusion regarding the primary mission and function of Bryce Hospital since certain nonpsychotic geriatric patients and the mental retardates, and perhaps other non–mentally ill persons, have been and remain committed there for a variety of reasons.

The evidence further reflects that Alabama ranks fiftieth among all the states in the Union in per-patient expenditures per day. This Court must, and does, find from the evidence that the programs of treatment in use at Bryce Hospital…were scientifically and medically inadequate. These programs of treatment failed to conform to any known minimums established for providing treatment for the mentally ill.

The patients at Bryce Hospital, for the most part, were involuntarily committed through noncriminal procedures and without the constitutional protections that are afforded defendants in criminal proceedings. When patients are so committed for treatment purposes they unquestionably have a constitutional right to receive such individual treatment as will give each of them a realistic opportunity to be cured or to improve his or her mental condition…. Adequate and effective treatment is constitutionally required because, absent treatment, the hospital is transformed "into a penitentiary where one could be held indefinitely for no convicted offense."… The purpose of involuntary hospitalization for treatment purposes is *treatment* and not mere custodial care or punishment. This is the only justification, from a constitutional standpoint, that allows civil commitments to mental institutions such as Bryce. According to the evidence in this case, the failure of Bryce Hospital to supply adequate treatment is due to a lack of operating funds. The failure to provide suitable and adequate treatment to the mentally ill cannot be justified by lack of staff or facilities….

There can be no legal (or moral) justification for the State of Alabama's failing to afford treatment—and adequate treatment from a medical standpoint—to the several thousand patients who have been civilly committed to Bryce's for treatment purposes. To deprive any citizen of his or her liberty upon the altruistic theory that the confinement is for humane therapeutic reasons and then fail to provide adequate treatment violates the very fundamentals of due process.

• • •

… The evidence reflects that the defendant Dr. Stonewall B. Stickney is, if he is afforded adequate funds for staffing and facilities, qualified to study, to evaluate, to institute, and to implement fully appropriate mental health treatment programs. A failure on the part of the defendants to implement fully, within six months from the date of this order, a treatment program so as to give each of the treatable patients committed to Bryce facility a realistic opportunity to be cured or to improve his or her mental condition, will necessitate this Court's appointing a panel of experts in the area of mental health to determine what objective and subjective hospital standards will be required to furnish adequate treatment to the treatable mentally ill in the Bryce facility. This will include an order requiring a full inspection of the existing facilities, a study of the operational and treatment practices and programs, and recommendations that will enable this Court to determine what will be necessary in order to render the Bryce facilities a mental health unit providing adequate and effective treatment, in a constitutional sense, for the patients who have been involuntarily committed and are confined there.*

---

*Editor's note: Subsequently, the court held

"…that defendants had failed to promulgate and implement a treatment program satisfying minimum medical and constitutional requisites. Generally, the Court found that defendants' treatment program was deficient in three fundamental areas. It failed to provide: (1) a humane psychological and physical environment, (2) qualified staff in numbers sufficient to administer adequate treatment and (3) individualized treatment plans."

As a result, in *Wyatt v. Stickney*, 344 F. Supp. 373 (1972), the court mandated massive reforms that would achieve these three conditions. Among the reforms were specific treatment rules, such as a right to be free of unnecessary or excessive medication; staffing ratios; and physical improvements, including a temperature range of between 68 and 83 degrees F and one tub or shower for each fifteen patients.

Discussion Questions

1. In *Wyatt,* the court held that "the failure to provide suitable and adequate treatment to the mentally ill cannot be justified by the lack of staff or facilities." Consider the relationship between constitutional rights and budgetary costs. There are rights, as in *Wyatt* and under the Eighth Amendment's ban on cruel and unusual punishment, that can entail substantial administrative costs. Compare how judges and legislators think about such rights and budgetary costs generally. For instance, does the judge in *Wyatt* appear to be concerned with the source of the revenues necessary to accomplish the reforms he finds constitutionally required? Identify some plausible sources from which such revenues might be drawn. What might be the legislative reaction to drawing on each of these? How do the "constituencies" of courts and legislatures differ? Should the principles of U.S. constitutional democracy support majority sentiment as reflected by legislatures even when it is mean-spirited, though not in violation of *specific* constitutional rights, such as freedom of speech?

2. If you were in Dr. Stonewall B. Stickney's place, how would you respond to the Court's ruling? How can public administratiors respond effectively when they are caught in the crossfire between state legislatures' cost-cutting and federal courts' "rights-funding"?

3. Technically speaking, after the court's ruling in *Wyatt,* 344 F. Supp. 373 (1972), patients at Bryce Hospital had a *constitutional* right to a temperature range of between 68 and 83 degrees F, as well as to certain amounts of square footage in the various rooms. Restate and explore the logic through which these rights were established. What might be some of the administrative ramifications of such detailed judicial involvement in the management of public institutions? For instance, what might be some of the consequences of making state health administrators "subordinates" of federal judges?

Case 8.2
Cost Reduction Versus Free Exercise of Religion

SHERBERT v. VERNER et al., MEMBERS OF SOUTH CAROLINA
EMPLOYMENT SECURITY COMMISSION et al.
Argued April 24, 1963
Decided June 17, 1963
374 US 398

MR. JUSTICE BRENNAN delivered the opinion of the Court.

Appellant, a member of the Seventh-Day Adventist Church, was discharged by her South Carolina employer because she would not work on Saturday, the Sabbath Day of her faith. When she was unable to obtain other employment because from conscientious scruples she would not take Saturday work, she filed a claim for unemployment compensation benefits under the South Carolina Unemployment Compensation Act. That law provides that, to be eligible for benefits, a claimant must be "able to work and...available for work"; and, further, that a

claimant is ineligible for benefits "[i]f...he has failed, without good cause...to accept available suitable work when offered him by the employment office or the employer...." The appellee Employment Security Commission, in administrative proceedings under the statute, found that appellant's restriction upon her availability for Saturday work brought her within the provision disqualifying for benefits insured workers who fail, without good cause, to accept "suitable work when offered...by the employment office or the employer...." The Commission's finding was sustained by the Court of Common Pleas for Spartanburg

County. That court's judgment was in turn affirmed by the South Carolina Supreme Court, which rejected appellant's contention that, as applied to her, the disqualifying provisions of the South Carolina statute abridged her right to the free exercise of her religion secured under the Free Exercise Clause of the First Amendment through the Fourteenth Amendment. The State Supreme Court held specifically that appellant's ineligibility infringed no constitutional liberties because such a construction of the statute "places no restriction upon the appellant's freedom of religion nor does it in any way prevent her in the exercise of her right and freedom to observe her religious beliefs in accordance with the dictates of her conscience."

...We reverse the judgment of the South Carolina Supreme Court and remand for further proceedings not inconsistent with this opinion.

I

The door of the Free Exercise Clause stands tightly closed against any governmental regulation of religious *beliefs* as such....Government may neither compel affirmation of a repugnant belief...nor penalize or discriminate against individuals or groups because they hold religious views abhorrent to the authorities...nor employ the taxing power to inhibit the dissemination of particular religious views.... On the other hand, the Court has rejected challenges under the Free Exercise Clause to governmental regulation of certain overt acts prompted by religious beliefs or principles, for "even when the action is in accord with one's religious convictions, [it] is not totally free from legislative restrictions."... The conduct or actions so regulated have invariably posed some substantial threat to public safety, peace or order.

Plainly enough, appellant's conscientious objection to Saturday work constitutes no conduct prompted by religious principles of a kind within the reach of state legislation. If, therefore, the decision of the South Carolina Supreme Court is to withstand appellant's constitutional challenge, it must be either because her disqualification as a beneficiary represents no infringement by the State of her constitutional rights of free exercise, or because any incidental burden on the free exercise of appellant's religion may be justified by a "compelling state interest in the regulation of a subject within the State's constitutional power to regulate...."

II

We turn first to the question whether the disqualification for benefits imposes any burden on the free exercise of appellant's religion. We think it is clear that it does. In a sense the consequences of such a disqualification to religious principles and practices may be only an indirect result of welfare legislation within the State's general competence to enact: it is true that no criminal sanctions directly compel appellant to work a six-day week. But this is only the beginning, not the end, of our inquiry. For "[i]f the purpose or effect of a law is to impede the observance of one or all religions or is to discriminate invidiously between religions, that law is constitutionally invalid even though the burden may be characterized as being only indirect."... Here not only is it apparent that appellant's declared ineligibility for benefits derives solely from the practice of her religion, but the pressure upon her to forego that practice is unmistakable. The ruling forces her to choose between following the precepts of her religion and forfeiting benefits, on the one hand, and abandoning one of the precepts of her religion in order to accept work, on the other hand. Governmental imposition of such a choice puts the same kind of burden upon the free exercise of religion as would a fine imposed against appellant for her Saturday worship.

Nor may the South Carolina court's construction of the statute be saved from constitutional infirmity on the ground that unemployment compensation benefits are not appellant's "right" but merely a "privilege." It is too late in the day to doubt that the liberties of religion and expression may be infringed by the denial of or placing of conditions upon a benefit or privilege.... [T]he Court recognized with respect to Federal Social Security benefits that "[t]he interest of a covered employee under the Act is of sufficient substance to fall within the protection from arbitrary governmental action afforded by the Due Process Clause." In Speiser v Randall [1958]...we emphasized that conditions upon public benefits cannot be sustained if they so operate, whatever their purpose, as to inhibit or deter the exercise of First Amendment freedoms. We there struck down a condition which limited the availability of a tax exemption to those members of the exempted class who affirmed their loyalty to the state government granting the exemption. While the State was surely under no obligation to afford such an exemption, we held that the imposition of such a condition upon even a gratuitous benefit inevitably deterred or discouraged the exercise of First Amendment rights of expression and thereby threatened to "produce a result which the State could not command directly."... "To deny an exemption to claimants who engage in certain forms of speech is in effect to penalize them for such speech."... Likewise, to condition the availability of benefits upon this appellant's willingness to violate a cardinal principle of her religious faith effectively penalizes the free exercise of her constitutional liberties.

Significantly South Carolina expressly saves the Sunday worshipper from having to make the kind of choice which we here hold infringes the Sabbatarian's religious liberty. When in times of "national emergency" the textile plants are authorized by the State Commissioner of Labor to operate on Sunday, "no employee shall be required to work on Sunday...who is conscientiously opposed to Sunday work; and if any employee should refuse to work on Sunday on account of conscientious...objections he or she shall not jeopardize his or her seniority by such refusal or be discriminated against in any other manner."... No question of the disqualification of a Sunday worshipper for benefits is likely to arise, since we cannot suppose that an employer will discharge him in violation of this statute. The unconstitutionality of the disqualification of the Sabbatarian is thus compounded by the religious discrimination which South Carolina's general statutory scheme necessarily effects.

III

We must next consider whether some compelling state interest enforced in the eligibility provisions of the South Carolina statute justifies the substantial infringement of appellant's First Amendment right. It is basic that no showing merely of a rational relationship to some colorable state interest would suffice; in this highly sensitive constitutional area, "[o]nly the

gravest abuses, endangering paramount interests, give occasion for permissible limitation."... No such abuse or danger has been advanced in the present case. The appellees suggest no more than a possibility that the filing of fraudulent claims by unscrupulous claimants feigning religious objections to Saturday work might not only dilute the unemployment compensation fund but also hinder the scheduling by employers of necessary Saturday work. But that possibility is not apposite here because no such objection appears to have been made before the South Carolina Supreme Court, and we are unwilling to assess the importance of an asserted state interest without the views of the state court. Nor, if the contention had been made below, would the record appear to sustain it; there is no proof whatever to warrant such fears of malingering or deceit as those which the respondents now advance. Even if consideration of such evidence is not foreclosed by the prohibition against judicial inquiry into the truth or falsity of religious beliefs,...—a question as to which we intimate no view since it is not before us—it is highly doubtful whether such evidence would be sufficient to warrant a substantial infringement of religious liberties. For even if the possibility of spurious claims did threaten to dilute the fund and disrupt the scheduling of work, it would plainly be incumbent upon the appellees to demonstrate that no alternative forms of regulation would combat such abuses without infringing First Amendment rights....

•   •   •

IV

In holding as we do, plainly we are not fostering the "establishment" of the Seventh-Day Adventist religion in South Carolina, for the extension of unemployment benefits to Sabbatarians in common with Sunday worshippers reflects nothing more than the governmental obligation of neutrality in the face of religious differences, and does not represent that involvement of religious with secular institutions which it is the object of the Establishment Clause to forestall.... Nor does the recognition of the appellant's right to unemployment benefits under the state statute serve to abridge any other person's religious liberties. Nor do we, by our decision today, declare the existence of a constitutional right to unemployment benefits on the part of all persons whose religious convictions are the cause of their unemployment. This is not a case in which an employee's religious convictions serve to make him a nonproductive member of society.... Finally, nothing we say today constrains the States to adopt any particular form or scheme of unemployment compensation. Our holding today is only that South Carolina may not constitutionally apply the eligibility provisions so as to constrain a worker to abandon his religious convictions respecting the day of rest....

Discussion Questions

1. *Sherbert* was one of the first Supreme Court decisions to reject the historic "doctrine of privilege." Under that doctrine, governments were permitted to place conditions on individuals' receipt of benefits, such as public employment and welfare, that interfered with the exercise of their ordinary constitutional rights. The doctrine did not require governments to demonstrate a compelling state interest for such conditions or that they were the least restrictive alternatives. For instance, as the South Carolina State Supreme Court reasoned, under this doctrine the government did not abridge Sherbert's constitutional right to free exercise of religion because it left her free to observe the Sabbath as she saw fit; the government merely denied her a benefit to which she had no right (and which, therefore, was considered a "privilege"). The demise of the doctrine of privilege during the 1960s and early 1970s dramatically changed the relationship between the Constitution and public administration; but in *Sherbert,* the U.S. Supreme Court took only a few terse sentences to reject it.

   Think back over the cases presented earlier in this book. Identify those that implicitly or explicitly reject the logic of the doctrine of privilege and consider how public management has been changed by its demise.

2. In dissent, Justice Harlan, joined by Justice White, argued that under the majority's decision, "The State...must *single out* for financial assistance those whose behavior is religiously motivated, even though it denies such assistance to others whose identical behavior...is not religiously motivated." Thus, Sherbert can receive assistance if her reason for not working on Saturdays is based on her religion, but not if it is because she likes to watch Saturday morning TV. To what extent does there appear to be a tension between the two prongs of the Constitution's guarantee of freedom of religion in this case; that is, between the rights of individuals to free exercise of religion and the prohibition on governmental establishment of religion? What criteria would you use to determine the extent to which government should be required to accommodate individuals' religious practices? Suppose, for example, Sherbert's religion required so many hours of daily prayer that she could be available for work only for six hours, rather than eight. Under the Court's ruling, would she be eligible for unemployment compensation benefits?

3. Consider the extent to which *Goldman v. Weinberger* (Case 7.1) is consistent with *Sherbert.*

Case 8.3
Administrative Costs Versus Equal Protection and the Right to Travel

---

SHAPIRO, COMMISSIONER OF WELFARE OF CONNECTICUT v. THOMPSON
Argued May 1, 1968
Reargued October 23–24, 1968
Decided April 21, 1969
394 US 618

MR. JUSTICE BRENNAN delivered the opinion of the Court.

These three appeals were restored to the calendar for reargument.... Each is an appeal from a decision of a three-judge District Court holding unconstitutional a State or District of Columbia statutory provision which denies welfare assistance to residents of the State or District who have not resided within their jurisdictions for at least one year immediately preceding their applications for such assistance. We affirm the judgments of the District Courts in the three cases.

I

In No. 9, the Connecticut Welfare Department invoked § 17-2d of the Connecticut General Statutes to deny the application of appellee Vivian Marie Thompson for assistance under the program for Aid to Families with Dependent Children (AFDC). She was a 19-year-old unwed mother of one child and pregnant with her second child when she changed her residence in June 1966 from Dorchester, Massachusetts, to Hartford, Connecticut, to live with her mother, a Hartford resident. She moved to her own apartment in Hartford in August 1966, when her mother was no longer able to support her and her infant son. Because of her pregnancy, she was unable to work or enter a work training program. Her application for AFDC assistance, filed in August, was denied in November solely on the ground that, as required by § 17-2d, she had not lived in the State for a year before her application was filed. She brought this action in the District Court for the District of Connecticut where a three-judge court, one judge dissenting, declared § 17-2d unconstitutional.... The majority held that the waiting-period requirement is unconstitutional because it "has a chilling effect on the right to travel."... The majority also held that the provision was a violation of the Equal

Protection Clause of the Fourteenth Amendment because the denial of relief to those resident in the State for less than a year is not based on any permissible purpose but is solely designed, as "Connecticut states quite frankly," "to protect its fisc by discouraging entry of those who come needing relief."...

In No. 33, there are four appellees. Three of them—appellees Harrell, Brown, and Legrant—applied for and were denied AFDC aid. The fourth, appellee Barley, applied for and was denied benefits under the program for Aid to the Permanently and Totally Disabled. The denial in each case was on the ground that the applicant had not resided in the District of Columbia for one year immediately preceding the filing of her application, as required by § 3-203 of the District of Columbia Code.

Appellee Minnie Harrell, now deceased, had moved with her three children from New York to Washington in September 1966. She suffered from cancer and moved to be near members of her family who lived in Washington.

Appellee Barley, a former resident of the District of Columbia, returned to the District in March 1941 and was committed a month later to St. Elizabeth's Hospital as mentally ill. She has remained in that hospital ever since. She was deemed eligible for release in 1965, and a plan was made to transfer her from the hospital to a foster home. The plan depended, however, upon Mrs. Barley's obtaining welfare assistance for her support. Her application for assistance under the program for Aid to the Permanently and Totally Disabled was denied because her time spent in the hospital did not count in determining compliance with the one-year requirement.

Appellee Brown lived with her mother and two of her three children in Fort Smith, Arkansas. Her third child was living with appellee Brown's father in the District of Columbia. When her mother moved from Fort Smith to Oklahoma, appellee Brown, in February 1966, returned to the District of Columbia where she had lived as a child. Her application for AFDC assistance was approved insofar as it sought assistance for the child who had lived in the District with her father but was denied to the extent it sought assistance for the two other children.

Appellee Legrant moved with her two children from South Carolina to the District of Columbia in March 1967 after the death of her mother. She planned to live with a sister and brother in Washington. She was pregnant and in ill health when she applied for and was denied AFDC assistance in July 1967.

The several cases were consolidated for trial, and a three-judge District Court was convened. The court, one judge dissenting, held § 3-203 unconstitutional.... The majority rested its decision on the ground that the one-year requirement was unconstitutional as a denial of the right to equal protection secured by the Due Process Clause of the Fifth Amendment. We noted probable jurisdiction....

In No. 34, there are two appellees, Smith and Foster, who were denied AFDC aid on the sole ground that they had not been residents of Pennsylvania for a year prior to their applications as required by § 432(6) of the Pennsylvania Welfare Code. Appellee Smith and her five minor children moved in December 1966 from Delaware to Philadelphia, Pennsylvania, where her father lived. Her father supported her and her children for several months until he lost his job. Appellee then applied for AFDC assistance and had received two checks when the aid was terminated. Appellee Foster, after living in Pennsylvania from 1953 to 1965, had moved with her four children to South Carolina to care for her grandfather and invalid grandmother and had returned to Pennsylvania in 1967. A three-judge District Court for the Eastern District of Pennsylvania, one judge dissenting, declared § 432(6) unconstitutional.... The majority held that the classification established by the waiting-period requirement is "without rational basis and without legitimate purpose or function" and therefore a violation of the Equal Protection Clause.... The majority noted further that if the purpose of the statute was "to erect a barrier against the movement of indigent persons into the State or to

effect their prompt departure after they have gotten there," it would be "patently improper and its implementation plainly impermissible."... We noted probably jurisdiction....

II

There is no dispute that the effect of the waiting-period requirement in each case is to create two classes of needy resident families indistinguishable from each other except that one is composed of residents who have resided a year or more, and the second of residents who have resided less than a year, in the jurisdiction. On the basis of this sole difference the first class is granted and the second class is denied welfare aid upon which may depend the ability of the families to obtain the very means to subsist— food, shelter, and other necessities of life. In each case, the District Court found that appellees met the test for residence in their jurisdictions, as well as all other eligibility requirements except the requirement of residence for a full year prior to their applications. On reargument, appellees' central contention is that the statutory prohibition of benefits to residents of less than a year creates a classification which constitutes an invidious discrimination denying them equal protection of the laws. We agree. The interests which appellants assert are promoted by the classification either may not constitutionally be promoted by government or are not compelling governmental interests.

III

Primarily, appellants justify the waiting-period requirement as a protective device to preserve the fiscal integrity of state public assistance programs. It is asserted that people who require welfare assistance during their first year of residence in a State are likely to become continuing burdens on state welfare programs. Therefore, the argument runs, if such people can be deterred from entering the jurisdiction by denying them welfare benefits during the first year, state programs to assist long-time residents will not be impaired by a substantial influx of indigent newcomers.

There is weighty evidence that exclusion from the jurisdiction of the poor who need or may need relief was the specific objective of these provisions. In the Congress, sponsors of federal legislation to eliminate all residence requirements have been consistently opposed by representatives of state and local welfare agencies who have stressed the fears of the States that elimination of the requirements would result in a heavy influx of individuals into States providing the most generous benefits....

We do not doubt that the one-year waiting-period device is well suited to discourage the influx of poor families in need of assistance. An indigent who desires to migrate, resettle, find a new job, and start a new life will doubtless hesitate if he knows that he must risk making the move without the possibility of falling back on state welfare assistance during his first year of residence when his need may be most acute. But the purpose of inhibiting migration by needy persons into the State is constitutionally impermissible.

This Court long ago recognized that the nature of our Federal Union and our constitutional concepts of personal liberty unite to require that all citizens be free to travel throughout the length and breadth of our land uninhibited by statutes, rules, or regulations which unreasonably burden or restrict this movement. That proposition was early stated by Chief Justice Taney in the Passenger Cases...(1849):

> "For all the great purposes for which the Federal government was formed, we are one people, with one common country. We are all citizens of the United States; and, as members of the same community, must have the right to pass and repass through every part of it without interruption, as freely as in our own States."

We have no occasion to ascribe the source of this right to travel interstate to a particular constitutional provision. It suffices that, as Mr. Justice Stewart said for the Court in United States v Guest...(1966):

> "The constitutional right to travel from one State to another...occupies a position fundamental to the concept of our Federal Union. It is a right that has been firmly established and repeatedly recognized.
>
> "...[The] right finds no explicit mention in the Constitution. The reason, it has been suggested, is that a right so elementary was conceived from the beginning to be a necessary concomitant of the stronger Union the Constitution created. In any event, freedom to travel throughout the United States has long been recognized as a basic right under the Constitution."

Thus, the purpose of deterring the in-migration of indigents cannot serve as justification for the classification created by the one-year waiting period, since that purpose is constitutionally impermissible. If a law has "no other purpose...than to chill the assertion of constitutional rights by penalizing those who choose to exercise them, then it [is] patently unconstitutional."... Alternatively, appellants argue that even if it is impermissible for a State to attempt to deter the entry of all indigents, the challenged classification may be justified as a permissible state attempt to discourage those indigents who would enter the State solely to obtain larger benefits. We observe first that none of the statutes before us is tailored to serve that objective. Rather, the class of barred newcomers is all-inclusive, lumping the great majority who come to the State for other purposes with those who come for the sole purpose of collecting higher benefits. In actual operation, therefore, the three statutes enact what in effect are nonrebuttable presumptions that every applicant for assistance in his first year of residence came to the jurisdiction solely to obtain higher benefits. Nothing whatever in any of these records supplies any basis in fact for such a presumption.

More fundamentally, a State may no more try to fence out those indigents who seek higher welfare benefits than it may try to fence out indigents generally. Implicit in any such distinction is the notion that indigents who enter a State with the hope of securing higher welfare benefits are somehow less deserving than indigents who do not take this consideration into account. But we do not perceive why a mother who is seeking to make a new life for herself and her children should be regarded as less deserving because she considers, among other factors, the level of a State's public assistance. Surely such a mother is no less deserving than a mother who moves into a particular State in order to take advantage of its better educational facilities.

Appellants argue further that the challenged classification may be sustained as an attempt to distinguish between new and old residents on the basis of the contribution they have made to the community through the payment of taxes.... Appellants' reasoning would logically permit the State to bar new residents from schools, parks, and libraries or deprive them of police and fire protection. Indeed it would permit the State to apportion all benefits and services according to the past tax contributions of its citizens. The Equal Protection Clause prohibits such an apportionment of state services.

We recognize that a State has a valid interest in preserving the fiscal integrity of its programs. It may legitimately attempt to limit its expenditures, whether for public assistance, public education, or any other program. But a State may not accomplish such a purpose by invidious distinctions between classes of its citizens. It could not, for example, reduce expenditures for education by barring indigent children from its schools. Similarly, in the cases before us, appellants must do more than show that denying welfare benefits to new residents saves money. The saving of welfare costs cannot justify an otherwise invidious classification.

In sum, neither deterrence of indigents from migrating to the State nor limitation of welfare benefits to those regarded as contributing to the State is a constitutionally permissible state objective.

IV

Appellants next advance as justification certain administrative and related governmental objectives allegedly served by the waiting-period requirement. They argue that the requirement (1) facilitates the planning of the welfare budget; (2) provides an objective test of residency; (3) minimizes the opportunity for recipients fraudulently to receive payments from more than one jurisdiction; and (4) encourages early entry of new residents into the labor force.

At the outset, we reject appellants' argument that a mere showing of a rational relationship between the waiting period and these four admittedly permissible state objectives will suffice to justify the classification.... The waiting-period provision denies welfare benefits to otherwise eligible applicants solely because they have recently moved into the jurisdiction. But in moving from State to State or to the District of Columbia appellees were exercising a constitutional right, and any classification which serves to penalize the exercise of that right, unless shown to be necessary to promote a *compelling* governmental interest, is unconstitutional....

The argument that the waiting-period requirement facilitates budget predictability is wholly unfounded. The records in all three cases are utterly devoid of evidence that either State or the District of Columbia in fact uses the one-year requirement as a means to predict the number of people who will require assistance in the budget year....

The argument that the waiting period serves as an administratively efficient rule of thumb for determining residency similarly will not withstand scrutiny. The residence requirement and the one-year waiting-period requirement are distinct and independent prerequisites for assistance under these three statutes, and the facts relevant to the determination of each are directly examined by the welfare authorities. Before granting an application, the welfare authorities investigate the applicant's employment, housing, and family situation and in the course of the inquiry necessarily learn the facts upon which to determine whether the applicant is a resident.

Similarly, there is no need for a State to use the one-year waiting period as a safeguard against fraudulent receipt of benefits; for less drastic means are available, and are employed, to minimize that hazard. Of course, a State has a valid interest in preventing fraud by any applicant, whether a newcomer or a long-time resident. It is not denied, however, that the investigations now conducted entail inquiries into facts relevant to that subject. In addition, cooperation among state welfare departments is common.... Since double payments can be prevented by a letter or a telephone call, it is unreasonable to accomplish this objective by the blunderbuss method of denying assistance to all indigent newcomers for an entire year.

Pennsylvania suggests that the one-year waiting period is justified as a means of encouraging new residents to join the labor force promptly. But this logic would also require a similar waiting period for long-term residents of the State. A state purpose to encourage employment provides no rational basis for imposing a one-year waiting period restriction on new residents only.

We conclude therefore that appellants in these cases do not use and have no need to use the one-year requirement for the governmental purposes suggested. Thus, even under traditional equal protection tests a classification of welfare applicants according to whether they have lived in the State for one year would seem irrational and unconstitutional. But, of course, the traditional criteria do not apply in these cases. Since the classification here touches on the fundamental right of interstate movement, its constitutionality must be judged by the stricter standard of whether it promotes a *compelling* state interest. Under this standard, the waiting-period requirement clearly violates the Equal Protection Clause.

Discussion Questions

1. Under what circumstances, if any, do you believe that residency requirements might be justified to preserve the fiscal integrity of state programs? Would you draw a distinction between the circumstances in *Shapiro* and those presented by state universities that charge less tuition for "in-staters" than for "out-of-staters"? Why or why not?

2. What might the ramifications of the Court's decision be on state or local governmental budgeting? Suppose the number of claimants exceeded the government's ability to provide an adequate level of benefits, would that affect the Court's conclusion according to its opinion in *Shapiro?*

3. How do residency requirements interfere with the right to travel?

Case 8.4
Taking Private Property

DOLAN v. CITY OF TIGARD
Argued March 23, 1994
Decided June 24, 1994
512 US 374

CHIEF JUSTICE REHNQUIST delivered the opinion of the Court.

Petitioner challenges the decision of the Oregon Supreme Court which held that the city of Tigard could condition the approval of her building permit on the dedication of a portion of her property for flood control and traffic improvements.... We granted certiorari to resolve a question left open by our decision in *Nollan v. California Coastal Comm'n...*(1987), of what is the required degree of connection between the exactions imposed by the city and the projected impacts of the proposed development.

I

The State of Oregon enacted a comprehensive land use management program in 1973.... The program required all Oregon cities and counties to adopt new comprehensive land use plans that were consistent with the statewide planning goals.... The plans are implemented by land use regulations which are part of an integrated hierarchy of legally binding goals, plans, and regulations... Pursuant to the State's requirements, the city of Tigard, a community of some 30,000 residents on the southwest edge of Portland, developed a comprehensive plan and codified it in its Community Development Code (CDC). The CDC requires property owners in the area zoned Central Business District to comply with a 15% open space and landscaping requirement, which limits total site coverage, including all structures and paved parking, to 85% of the parcel.... After the completion of a transportation study that identified congestion in the Central

Business District as a particular problem, the city adopted a plan for a pedestrian/bicycle pathway intended to encourage alternatives to automobile transportation for short trips. The CDC requires that new development facilitate this plan by dedicating land for pedestrian pathways where provided for in the pedestrian/bicycle pathway plan.

The city also adopted a Master Drainage Plan (Drainage Plan). The Drainage Plan noted that flooding occurred in several areas along Fanno Creek, including areas near petitioner's property.... The Drainage Plan also established that the increase in impervious surfaces associated with continued urbanization would exacerbate these flooding problems. To combat these risks, the Drainage Plan suggested a series of improvements to the Fanno Creek Basin, including channel excavation in the area next to petitioner's property.... Other recommendations included ensuring that the floodplain remains free of structures and that it be preserved as greenways to minimize flood damage to structures.... The Drainage Plan concluded that the cost of these improvements should be shared based on both direct and indirect benefits, with property owners along the waterways paying more due to the direct benefit that they would receive....

Petitioner Florence Dolan owns a plumbing and electric supply store located on Main Street in the Central Business District of the city. The store covers approximately 9,700 square feet on the eastern side of a 1.67-acre parcel, which includes a gravel parking lot. Fanno Creek flows through the southwestern corner of the lot and along its western boundary. The year-round flow of the creek renders the area within the creek's 100-year floodplain virtually unusable for commercial development. The city's comprehensive plan includes the Fanno Creek floodplain as part of the city's greenway system.

Petitioner applied to the city for a permit to redevelop the site. Her proposed plans called for nearly doubling the size of the store to 17,600 square feet, and paving a 39-space parking lot. The existing store, located on the opposite side of the parcel, would be razed in sections as construction progressed on the new building. In the second phase of the project, petitioner proposed to build an additional struc-

ture on the northeast side of the site for complementary businesses, and to provide more parking. The proposed expansion and intensified use are consistent with the city's zoning scheme in the Central Business District....

[T]he Commission required that petitioner dedicate the portion of her property lying within the 100-year floodplain for improvement of a storm drainage system along Fanno Creek, and that she dedicate an additional 15-foot strip of land adjacent to the floodplain as a pedestrian/bicycle pathway. The dedication required by that condition encompasses approximately 7,000 square feet, or roughly 10% of the property. In accordance with city practice, petitioner could rely on the dedicated property to meet the 15% open space and landscaping requirement mandated by the city's zoning scheme.... The city would bear the cost of maintaining a landscaped buffer between the dedicated area and the new store....

Petitioner requested variances from the CDC standards.... [P]etitioner simply argued that her proposed development would not conflict with the policies of the comprehensive plan.... The [City Planning] Commission denied the request....

• • •

II

The Takings Clause of the Fifth Amendment of the United States Constitution, made applicable to the States through the Fourteenth Amendment..., provides: "[N]or shall private property be taken for public use, without just compensation." One of the principal purposes of the Takings Clause is

> to bar government from forcing some people alone to bear public burdens which, in all fairness and justice, should be borne by the public as a whole....

Without question, had the city simply required petitioner to dedicate a strip of land along Fanno Creek for public use, rather than conditioning the grant of her permit to redevelop her property on such a dedication, a taking would have occurred.... Such public access would deprive petitioner of the right to exclude others, "one of the most essential sticks in the bundle of rights that are commonly characterized as property."...

On the other side of the ledger, the authority of state and local governments to engage in land use planning has been sustained against constitutional challenge as long ago as our decision in *Euclid v. Ambler Realty Co.*...(1926).

> Government hardly could go on if to some extent values incident to property could not be diminished without paying for every such change in the general law....

A land use regulation does not effect a taking if it "substantially advance[s] legitimate state interests" and does not "den[y] an owner economically viable use of his land."...

The sort of land use regulations discussed in the cases just cited, however, differ in two relevant particulars from the present case. First, they involved essentially legislative determinations classifying entire areas of the city, whereas here, the city made an adjudicative decision to condition petitioner's application for a building permit on an individual parcel. Second, the conditions imposed were not simply a limitation on the use petitioner might make of her own parcel, but a requirement that she deed portions of the property to the city. In *Nollan*..., we held that governmental authority to exact such a condition was circumscribed by the Fifth and Fourteenth Amendments. Under the well settled doctrine of "unconstitutional conditions," the government may not require a person to give up a constitutional right—here the right to receive just compensation when property is taken for a public use—in exchange for a discretionary benefit conferred by the government where the property sought has little or no relationship to the benefit....

Petitioner contends that the city has forced her to choose between the building permit and her right under the Fifth Amendment to just compensation for the public easements. Petitioner does not quarrel with the city's authority to exact some forms of dedication as a condition for the grant of a building permit, but challenges the showing made by the city to justify these exactions. She argues that the city has identified "no special benefits" conferred on her, and has not identified any "special quantifiable burdens" created by her new store that would justify the particular dedications required from her which are not required from the public at large.

III

In evaluating petitioner's claim, we must first determine whether the "essential nexus" exists between the "legitimate state interest" and the permit condition exacted by the city.... If we find that a nexus exists, we must then decide the required degree of connection between the exactions and the projected impact of the proposed development. We were not required to reach this question in *Nollan,* because we concluded that the connection did not meet even the loosest standard.... Here, however, we must decide this question.

A

We addressed the essential nexus question in *Nollan.* The California Coastal Commission demanded a lateral public easement across the Nollan's beachfront lot in exchange for a permit to demolish an existing bungalow and replace it with a three-bedroom house.... The public easement was designed to connect two public beaches that were separated by the Nollan's property. The Coastal Commission had asserted that the public easement condition was imposed to promote the legitimate state interest of diminishing the "blockage of the view of the ocean" caused by construction of the larger house.

We agreed that the Coastal Commission's concern with protecting visual access to the ocean constituted a legitimate public interest.... We also agreed that the permit condition would have been constitutional

> even if it consisted of the requirement that the Nollans provide a viewing spot on their property for passersby with whose sighting of the ocean their new house would interfere....

We resolved, however, that the Coastal Commission's regulatory authority was set completely adrift from its constitutional moorings when it claimed that a nexus existed between visual access to the ocean and a permit condition requiring lateral public access along the Nollan's beachfront lot.... How enhancing the public's ability to "traverse to and along the shorefront" served the same governmental purpose of "visual access to the ocean" from the roadway was beyond our ability to countenance. The absence of a nexus left the Coastal Commission in the position of simply trying to obtain an easement through gimmickry, which converted a valid regulation of land use into "an out-and-out plan of extortion."...

No such gimmicks are associated with the permit conditions imposed by the city in this case. Undoubtedly, the prevention of flooding along Fanno Creek and the reduction of traffic congestion in the Central Business District qualify as the type of legitimate public purposes we have upheld.... It seems equally obvious that a nexus exists between preventing flooding along Fanno Creek and limiting development within the creek's 100-year floodplain. Petitioner proposes to double the size of her retail store and to pave her now-gravel parking lot, thereby expanding the impervious surface on the property and increasing the amount of stormwater run-off into Fanno Creek.

The same may be said for the city's attempt to reduce traffic congestion by providing for alternative means of transportation. In theory, a pedestrian/bicycle pathway provides a useful alternative means of transportation for workers and shoppers....

B

The second part of our analysis requires us to determine whether the degree of the exactions demanded by the city's permit conditions bear the required relationship to the projected impact of petitioner's proposed development....

• • •

Some form of the reasonable relationship test has been adopted in many other jurisdictions.... Despite any semantic differences, general agreement exists among the courts "that the dedication should have some reasonable relationship to the needs created by the [development]."...

We think the "reasonable relationship" test adopted by a majority of the state courts is closer to the federal constitutional norm than either of those previously discussed. But we do not adopt it as such, partly because the term "reasonable relationship" seems confusingly similar to the term "rational basis" which describes the minimal level of scrutiny under the Equal Protection Clause of the Fourteenth Amendment. We think a term such as "rough proportionality" best encapsulates what we hold to be the requirement of the Fifth Amendment. No pre-

cise mathematical calculation is required, but the city must make some sort of individualized determination that the required dedication is related both in nature and extent to the impact of the proposed development.

... We see no reason why the Takings Clause of the Fifth Amendment, as much a part of the Bill of Rights as the First Amendment or Fourth Amendment, should be relegated to the status of a poor relation in these comparable circumstances. We turn now to analysis of whether the findings relied upon by the city here, first with respect to the floodplain easement, and second with respect to the pedestrian/bicycle path, satisfied these requirements.

It is axiomatic that increasing the amount of impervious surface will increase the quantity and rate of stormwater flow from petitioner's property.... Therefore, keeping the floodplain open and free from development would likely confine the pressures on Fanno Creek created by petitioner's development. In fact, because petitioner's property lies within the Central Business District, the Community Development Code already required that petitioner leave 15% of it as open space and the undeveloped floodplain would have nearly satisfied that requirement.... But the city demanded more—it not only wanted petitioner not to build in the floodplain, but it also wanted petitioner's property along Fanno Creek for its Greenway system. The city has never said why a public greenway, as opposed to a private one, was required in the interest of flood control.

The difference to petitioner, of course, is the loss of her ability to exclude others. As we have noted, this right to exclude others is "one of the most essential sticks in the bundle of rights that are commonly characterized as property."... It is difficult to see why recreational visitors trampling along petitioner's floodplain easement are sufficiently related to the city's legitimate interest in reducing flooding problems along Fanno Creek, and the city has not attempted to make any individualized determination to support this part of its request.

The city contends that recreational easement along the Greenway is only ancillary to the city's chief purpose in controlling flood hazards. It further asserts that, unlike the residential property at issue in *Nollan*, petitioner's property is commercial in character....

Admittedly, petitioner wants to build a bigger store to attract members of the public to her property. She also wants, however, to be able to control the time and manner in which they enter.… By contrast, the city wants to impose a permanent recreational easement upon petitioner's property that borders Fanno Creek. Petitioner would lose all rights to regulate the time in which the public entered onto the Greenway, regardless of any interference it might pose with her retail store. Her right to exclude would not be regulated, it would be eviscerated.

If petitioner's proposed development had somehow encroached on existing greenway space in the city, it would have been reasonable to require petitioner to provide some alternative greenway space for the public either on her property or elsewhere.… But that is not the case here. We conclude that the findings upon which the city relies do not show the required reasonable relationship between the floodplain easement and the petitioner's proposed new building.

With respect to the pedestrian/bicycle pathway, we have no doubt that the city was correct in finding that the larger retail sales facility proposed by petitioner will increase traffic on the streets of the Central Business District. The city estimates that the proposed development would generate roughly 435 additional trips per day. Dedications for streets, sidewalks, and other public ways are generally reasonable exactions to avoid excessive congestion from a proposed property use. But, on the record before us, the city has not met its burden of demonstrating that the additional number of vehicle and bicycle trips generated by the petitioner's development reasonably relate to the city's requirement for a dedication of the pedestrian/bicycle pathway easement. The city simply found that the creation of the pathway "could offset some of the traffic demand…and lessen the increase in traffic congestion."

…No precise mathematical calculation is required, but the city must make some effort to quantify its findings in support of the dedication for the pedestrian/bicycle pathway beyond the conclusory statement that it could offset some of the traffic demand generated.

IV

Cities have long engaged in the commendable task of land use planning, made necessary by increasing urbanization particularly in metropolitan areas such as Portland. The city's goals of reducing flooding hazards and traffic congestion, and providing for public greenways, are laudable, but there are outer limits to how this may be done.

A strong public desire to improve the public condition [will not] warrant achieving the desire by a shorter cut than the constitutional way of paying for the change.…

• • •

Discussion Questions

1. *Dolan* places the burden of persuasion on the government. What are the implications for public administration involving building permits and zoning regulations?
2. Is there any reason why property rights should be weaker than civil liberties such as free exercise of religion? Why don't we compensate people such as Goldman, in Case 7.1, when we require them to sacrifice liberty for a public good?

NINE

The Promise of Constitutional Competence

"Single-minded inspector Javert is a monster, even though he focused only on his duty."[1] These are not very judicious words. In 1993, a judge used them in response to a prison warden's search policy that literally compelled male guards to sexually abuse female prisoners. The judge elaborated:

> A bland American civil servant can be as much of a beast as a ferocious concentration camp guard if he does not think about what his actions are doing.... Half the cruelties of human history have been inflicted by conscientious servants of the state. The mildest of bureaucrats can be a brute if he does not raise his eyes from his task and consider the human beings on whom he is having an impact....
>
> How did a civilized country and a civilized state like Washington get into this fix where it takes federal judges to tell a responsible state official to stop his approval of indecency because he is violating the Constitution?[2]

How indeed?

The public administrators and policymakers involved in the cases in this book were not monsters. Most were trying to promote important public or organizational interests. Some were impelled by cultural norms whose day has past. Others were hampered by inadequate funding. But most would have benefited from a higher level of constitutional competence.

As the judge in "Javert's" case suggests, it is inappropriate to expect the judiciary alone to make public management operate firmly within constitutional boundaries. There are limits to what the courts can achieve. Litigation is expensive. And it is usually after the fact. A better approach is for every public administrator to have constitutional competence and to integrate it into the day-to-day performance of his or her job.

Public Administration and Constitutional Governance

The stakes are high, and not just because one may be sued and held liable. Public administration goes hand-in-hand with civilization.[3] Public managers manage complexity, which increases at an accelerating rate. Governments may or may not do as much "rowing" in the future, but they will continue to do a great deal of steering. The values that public administration incorporates will have a major impact on the quality of life and human rights. Infusing American public administration with constitutional values while enhancing its operational performance can be challenging.

But what would be better? Recall Chief Justice Warren Burger's point in *Chadha* (Case 1.1): constitutional arrangements "impose burdens on governmental processes that often seem clumsy, inefficient, even unworkable" but "we have not yet found a better way to preserve freedom than by making the exercise of power subject to the carefully crafted restraints spelled out in the Constitution."[4]

Our traditional public administrative doctrine developed with scant attention to constitutional questions. The orthodoxy viewed public administration as a managerial—not governmental—endeavor. It held that "good" public administration is simply effective, efficient, and economical; that it can be achieved through the proper organization and funding of a civil service based solely on technical competence and political neutrality. This approach is no longer viable.[5] As even the few cases in this volume indicate, the federal judiciary will not accept indifference to constitutional rights and values.

The New Public Management (NPM) views the orthodoxy as *the problem* and seeks to replace it. The orthodoxy had a tendency to think it knew what was best for the average person.[6] The NPM wants public administration to be customer driven. It explicitly values people. But it speaks the language of customer service, not human rights. Moreover, the American incarnation, like Woodrow Wilson's foundational essay more than a century ago, is apt to borrow from parliamentary systems and unitary states as though the separation of powers and federalism are irrelevant to public administration.[7] Even if the NPM succeeds in the United States, it will not solve the basic problem of making public administrative practice and theory comport better with the Constitution.

"Retrofitting" the Administrative State into the Constitutional Regime

Over the past half-century, the federal courts have been calling upon public administrators and policymakers to "retrofit" the administrative state into the constitutional regime. Retrofitting cannot be done by the judiciary alone. It is a job for everyone—public managers, political executives, legislators, rank-and-file civil servants, third-party service providers, and citizens. At the broadest level, it requires a change in administrative culture. What can public managers do to make sure their programs and daily operations embrace constitutional values and respect constitutional constraints?

 1. Gain constitutional competence. Understanding the basic structure of constitutional rights, the separation of powers, and federalism is a strong start. So is the ability to follow judicial reasoning. But there is more. A leading constitutional scholar once remarked that "The Constitution is largely a document of the imagination, but always treated as if it were real."[8] Constitutional competence requires serious reflection on the substantive and procedural values embodied in the Constitution and its interpretation by the courts. Constitutional values have to be internalized in administrative practice, not viewed as external constraints on it.

2. Maintain constitutional competence. Follow the constitutional law. A variety of professional magazines, journals, and newsletters report on new legal developments.[9] Ask agency attorneys to circulate information about court decisions that bear on the way business is done. E-mail makes it easy for those who believe a case has implications for daily practice to alert everyone involved. Building law into agency information networks should be a high priority. Beyond that, there are many excellent books on the Constitution that are written for an intelligent general audience.[10]

3. Talk constitutional talk. As noted in the first chapter, Constance Horner, former Director of the U.S. Office of Personnel Management, viewed constitutional discourse as the "common language of the Federal executive."[11] In a government chartered by the Constitution, public administrators should think about questions from constitutional perspectives and discuss them with coworkers. Constitutional talk improves constitutional reasoning and knowledge. The Constitution is not an exclusive domain for judges and lawyers. It begins with "We the People." There are gaps, paradoxes, and silences in the text that sometimes require discussion.[12] Enough constitutional talk will have a significant impact on the administrative culture of agencies and, ultimately, the nation.

4. Conduct constitutional audits. Are programs and systems well within constitutional limits? Do they promote constitutional values as fully as practicable? Reengineer work from a constitutional standpoint. Think in terms of *constitutional* best practices and exchange information about them. Change can come from the top, bottom, or in between. Large-scale changes are sometimes the aggregate of myriad small individual decisions.

These are important steps in integrating public administration into the constitutional regime. But there is no blueprint or map. The art of administration requires balancing values and meeting legal requirements in a broad variety of circumstances. In the 1970s, when the contemporary scale of judicial involvement in public administration was relatively new, some considered the emerging constitutional law to be an obstacle. Today, after courts and administrators have had more time to adjust to one another, it may be easier to view constitutional interpretation as a guide to a better government and society. Who would disagree with the proposition that there is no place for "Javerts," or at least Javert-like actions in American government?

Conclusion: No One Else Can Do the Whole Job

Retrofitting cannot be accomplished unless public managers actively promote it. Legislatures have not mandated it—and may actually undercut it with underfunding and inconsistent oversight. Elected and politically appointed executives generally have other priorities and, often, short tenure. The Supreme Court has served notice that there are real limits to how far constitutional law may reach into public administration.

Case 9.1, *DeShaney v. Winnebago County Department of Social Services* (1989), illustrates two of the Constitution's limits. First, it generally does not apply to private action.[13] Second, its fundamental protections of individual rights restrict governmental action but do not require it. For example, the people have a Fourth Amendment right to be secure against unreasonable searches and seizures in their houses, but no one has a federal constitutional right to shelter. We are protected against governmental "takings" of property, but can invoke no constitutional claim on the government to receive property.

DeShaney also makes two points about why public administration is so important to the constitutional regime. Administrative action comes to replace social action. When administrators fail, the people involved may have nowhere else to turn for protection. By contrast, when the Constitution fails to protect human rights, administrators may nevertheless be able to do so.

Case 9.2, *Missouri v. Jenkins* (1995), demonstrates that even massive judicial involvement in a public administrative system may be insufficient to cure a basic ill. Even with the equity powers available to them, the courts cannot always go it alone. Moreover, the Supreme Court indicates deep skepticism about judicially imposed remedies that deepen the courts' role in managing public institutions. A better approach could be what Judge David Bazelon referred to as a "partnership" between judges and administrators.[14] Constitutional competence enhances the ability of public managers to uphold their end of the partnership, the one they agreed to when they became "bound by Oath of Affirmation, to support this Constitution."[15]

Notes

1. *Jordan v. Gardner*, 986 F. 2d 1521, 1544 (1993).

2. Ibid., p. 1523. As the court described the procedure: "the male guard stands next to the female inmate and thoroughly runs his hands over her clothed body starting with their neck and working down to her feet. According to the prison training material, a guard is to '[u]se a flat hand and pushing motion across the [inmate's] crotch area.'… The guard must 'push inward and upward when searching the crotch and upper thighs of the inmate.'…All seams in the leg and crotch area are to be 'squeez[ed] and knead[ed].'…Using the back of the hand, the guard also is to search the breast area in a sweeping motion, so that the breasts will be 'flattened.'"

3. See Dwight Waldo, *The Enterprise of Public Administration* (Novato CA: Chandler and Sharp, 1980).

4. *Immigration and Naturalization Service v. Chadha*, 462 U.S. 919, 959 (1983).

5. The orthodoxy lost a great deal of credibility as a result of the writings of Herbert Simon, *Administrative Behavior* (New York: Free Press, 1947); Dwight Waldo, *The Administrative State* (New York: Ronald Press, 1948); and Paul Appleby, *Policy and Administration* (University, AL: University of Alabama Press, 1949).

6. See Luther Gulick, "Notes on the Theory of Organization," in Luther Gulick and L. Urwick, eds., *Papers on the Science of Administration* (New York:

Institute of Public Administration, 1937), pp. 3–13. Gulick says democracy is a system in which the people are the final judge of what is good for them and then, in the next paragraph, says efficiency is one of the things that is good for them! The larger problem with the orthodoxy was that part of its mission was to reduce the impact of the electorate on government. See David Rosenbloom, *Federal Service and the Constitution* (Ithaca, NY: Cornell University Press, 1971), Chapter 3; David H. Rosenbloom and Rosemary O'Leary, *Public Administration and Law,* 2nd ed. (New York: Marcel Dekker, 1997), Chapter 1.

7. There is a good deal of recitation of experiences in New Zealand and Australia. See David Rosenbloom, "Constitutional Problems for the New Public Management," in Khi Thai and Rosalyn Carter, eds., *Current Public Policy Issues: The 1998 Annals* (Boca Raton, FL: PrAcademics Press, 1999). See also Fred Riggs, "Bureaucracy and the Constitution," *Public Administration Review,* vol. 54 (January/February 1994): 65.

8. Philip Kurland, "Some Reflections on Privacy and the Constitution," *University of Chicago Magazine,* vol. 69 (1976): 7.

9. *Public Administration Review, American Review of Public Administration, Review of Public Personnel Administration,* and *National Law Journal,* as well as publications by the International City/County Management Association and various police newsletters.

10. Michael Kammen, *A Machine That Would Go of Itself: The Constitution in American Culture* (New York: Knopf, 1987); Melvin Urofsky, *A March of Liberty* (New York: Knopf, 1988); Catherine Bowen, *Miracle at Philadelphia* (Boston: Little, Brown, 1986).

11. Constance Horner, "Remarks on FEI's [Federal Executive Institute's] 20th Anniversary Dinner," Charlottesville, Virginia, October 14, 1988, p. 14.

12. Daniel Hoffman, *Our Elusive Constitution: Silences, Paradoxes, Priorities* (Albany, NY: State University of New York Press, 1997).

13. See Larry Alexander and Paul Horton, *Whom Does the Constitution Command?* (Westport, CT: Green-wood Press, 1988); John Garvey and T. Alexander Aleinikoff, eds., *Modern Constitutional Theory* (St. Paul, MN: West Publishing, 1994); Akhil Reed Amar and Daniel Widawsky, "Child Abuse as Slavery: A Thirteenth Amendment Response to *DeShaney*," *Harvard Law Review*, vol. 105 (1992): 105.

14. David Bazelon, "The Impact of the Courts on Public Administration," *Indiana Law Journal*, vol. 52 (1976): 101.

15. Article VI. See also John A. Rohr, *Ethics for Bureaucrats*, 2nd ed. (New York: Marcel Dekker, 1989).

Additional Reading

Bowen, Catherine. *Miracle at Philadelphia*. Boston: Little, Brown, 1986.

Kammen, Michael. *A Machine That Would Go of Itself: The Constitution in American Culture*. New York: Knopf, 1987.

Urofsky, Melvin. *A March of Liberty*. New York: Knopf, 1988.

Case 9.1
Public Versus Private Harm

DeSHANEY v. WINNEBAGO COUNTY DEPARTMENT OF SOCIAL SERVICES
Argued November 2, 1988
Decided February 22, 1989
489 US 189

CHIEF JUSTICE REHNQUIST delivered the opinion of the Court.

Petitioner is a boy who was beaten and permanently injured by his father, with whom he lived. Respondents are social workers and other local officials who received complaints that petitioner was being abused by his father and had reason to believe that this was the case, but nonetheless did not act to remove petitioner from his father's custody. Petitioner sued respondents claiming that their failure to act deprived him of his liberty in violation of the Due Process Clause of the Fourteenth Amendment to the United States Constitution. We hold that it did not.

I

The facts of this case are undeniably tragic. Petitioner Joshua DeShaney was born in 1979. In 1980, a Wyoming court granted his parents a divorce and awarded custody of Joshua to his father, Randy DeShaney. The father shortly thereafter moved to Neenah, a city located in Winnebago County, Wisconsin, taking the infant Joshua with him. There he entered into a second marriage, which also ended in divorce.

The Winnebago County authorities first learned that Joshua DeShaney might be a victim of child abuse in January, 1982, when his father's second wife complained to the police, at the time of their divorce, that he had previously "hit the boy, causing marks, and [was] a prime case for child abuse."... The Winnebago County Department of Social Services (DSS) interviewed the father, but he denied the accusations, and DSS did not pursue them further. In January, 1983, Joshua was admitted to a local hospital with multiple bruises and abrasions. The examining physician suspected child abuse and notified DSS, which immediately obtained an order from a Wisconsin juvenile court placing Joshua in the temporary custody of the hospital. Three days later, the county convened

an *ad hoc* "Child Protection Team"—consisting of a pediatrician, a psychologist, a police detective, the county's lawyer, several DSS caseworkers, and various hospital personnel—to consider Joshua's situation. At this meeting, the Team decided that there was insufficient evidence of child abuse to retain Joshua in the custody of the court. The Team did, however, decide to recommend several measures to protect Joshua, including enrolling him in a preschool program, providing his father with certain counselling services, and encouraging his father's girlfriend to move out of the home. Randy DeShaney entered into a voluntary agreement with DSS in which he promised to cooperate with them in accomplishing these goals.

Based on the recommendation of the Child Protection Team, the juvenile court dismissed the child protection case and returned Joshua to the custody of his father. A month later, emergency room personnel called the DSS caseworker handling Joshua's case to report that he had once again been treated for suspicious injuries. The caseworker concluded that there was no basis for action. For the next six months, the caseworker made monthly visits to the DeShaney home, during which she observed a number of suspicious injuries on Joshua's head; she also noticed that he had not been enrolled in school, and that the girlfriend had not moved out. The caseworker dutifully recorded these incidents in her files, along with her continuing suspicions that someone in the DeShaney household was physically abusing Joshua, but she did nothing more. In November, 1983, the emergency room notified DSS that Joshua had been treated once again for injuries that they believed to be caused by child abuse. On the caseworker's next two visits to the DeShaney home, she was told that Joshua was too ill to see her. Still DSS took no action.

In March, 1984, Randy DeShaney beat 4-year-old Joshua so severely that he fell into a life-threatening coma. Emergency brain surgery revealed a series of hemorrhages caused by traumatic injuries to the head inflicted over a long period of time. Joshua did not die, but he suffered brain damage so severe that he is expected to spend the rest of his life confined to an institution for the profoundly retarded. Randy DeShaney was subsequently tried and convicted of child abuse.

Joshua and his mother brought this action under 42 U.S.C. § 1983 in the United States District Court for the Eastern District of Wisconsin against respondents Winnebago County, DSS, and various individual employees of DSS. The complaint alleged that respondents had deprived Joshua of his liberty without due process of law, in violation of his rights under the Fourteenth Amendment, by failing to intervene to protect him against a risk of violence at his father's hands of which they knew or should have known....

• • •

Because of the inconsistent approaches taken by the lower courts in determining when, if ever, the failure of a state or local governmental entity or its agents to provide an individual with adequate protective services constitutes a violation of the individual's due process rights..., and the importance of the issue to the administration of state and local governments, we granted certiorari....

II

The Due Process Clause of the Fourteenth Amendment provides that "[n]o State shall... deprive any person of life, liberty, or property, without due process of law." Petitioners contend that the State deprived Joshua of his liberty interest in "free[dom] from...unjustified intrusions on personal security"... by failing to provide him with adequate protection against his father's violence. The claim is one invoking the substantive, rather than the procedural, component of the Due Process Clause; petitioners do not claim that the State denied Joshua protection without according him appropriate procedural safeguards..., but that it was categorically obligated to protect him in these circumstances....

But nothing in the language of the Due Process Clause itself requires the State to protect the life, liberty, and property of its citizens against invasion by private actors. The Clause is phrased as a limitation on the State's power to act, not as a guarantee of certain minimal levels of safety and security. It forbids the State itself to deprive individuals of life, liberty, or property without "due process of law," but its language cannot fairly be extended to impose an affirmative obligation on the State to ensure that those interests do not come to harm through other means. Nor does history support such an expansive reading of the constitutional text. Like its counterpart in the Fifth Amendment, the Due Process Clause of the Fourteenth Amendment was intended to prevent government "from abusing [its] power, or employing it as an instrument of oppression."... Its purpose was to protect the people from the State, not to ensure that the State protected them from each other. The Framers were content to leave the extent of governmental obligation in the latter area to the democratic political processes.

Consistent with these principles, our cases have recognized that the Due Process Clauses generally confer no affirmative right to governmental aid, even where such aid may be necessary to secure life, liberty, or property interests of which the government itself may not deprive the individual.... As we said in *Harris v. McRae* [1980]:

> Although the liberty protected by the Due Process Clause affords protection against unwarranted *government* interference,... it does not confer an entitlement to such [governmental aid] as may be necessary to realize all the advantages of that freedom....

If the Due Process Clause does not require the State to provide its citizens with particular protective services, it follows that the State cannot be held liable under the Clause for injuries that could have been averted had it chosen to provide them. As a general matter, then, we conclude that a State's failure to protect an individual against private violence simply does not constitute a violation of the Due Process Clause.

Petitioners contend, however, that even if the Due Process Clause imposes no affirmative obligation on the State to provide the general public with adequate protective services, such a duty may arise out of certain "special relationships" created or assumed by the State with respect to particular individuals.... Petitioners argue that such a "special relationship" existed here because the State knew that Joshua faced a special danger of abuse at his father's hands, and specifically proclaimed, by word and by deed, its intention to protect him against that danger.... Having actually undertaken to protect Joshua from this danger—which petitioners concede the State played no part in creating—the State acquired an affirmative "duty," enforceable through the Due Process Clause, to do so in a reasonably competent fashion....

We reject this argument. It is true that, in certain limited circumstances, the Constitution imposes upon the State affirmative duties of care and protection with respect to particular individuals [held in its custody]....

In *Youngberg v. Romeo*... (1982), we extended this analysis beyond the Eighth Amendment setting, holding that the substantive component of the Fourteenth Amendment's Due Process Clause requires the State to provide involuntarily committed mental patients with such services as are necessary to ensure their "reasonable safety" from themselves and others.... As we explained:

> If it is cruel and unusual punishment to hold convicted criminals in unsafe conditions, it must be unconstitutional [under the Due Process Clause] to confine the involuntarily committed—who may not be punished at all—in unsafe conditions....

But these cases afford petitioners no help. Taken together, they stand only for the proposition that, when the State takes a person into its custody and holds him there against his will, the Constitution imposes upon it a corresponding duty to assume some responsibility for his safety and general wellbeing.... The rationale for this principle is simple enough: when the State, by the affirmative exercise of its power, so restrains an individual's liberty that it renders him unable to care for himself, and at the same time fails to provide for his basic human needs—*e.g.,* food, clothing, shelter, medical care, and reasonable safety—it transgresses the substantive limits on state action set by the Eighth Amendment and the Due Process Clause.... The affirmative duty to protect arises not from the State's knowledge of the individual's predicament or from its expressions of intent to help him, but from the limitation

which it has imposed on his freedom to act on his own behalf.... In the substantive due process analysis, it is the State's affirmative act of restraining the individual's freedom to act on his own behalf—through incarceration, institutionalization, or other similar restraint of personal liberty—which is the "deprivation of liberty" triggering the protections of the Due Process Clause, not its failure to act to protect his liberty interests against harms inflicted by other means.

The [custodial] analysis simply has no applicability in the present case. Petitioners concede that the harms Joshua suffered did not occur while he was in the State's custody, but while he was in the custody of his natural father, who was in no sense a state actor. While the State may have been aware of the dangers that Joshua faced in the free world, it played no part in their creation, nor did it do anything to render him any more vulnerable to them. That the State once took temporary custody of Joshua does not alter the analysis, for, when it returned him to his father's custody, it placed him in no worse position than that in which he would have been had it not acted at all; the State does not become the permanent guarantor of an individual's safety by having once offered him shelter. Under these circumstances, the State had no constitutional duty to protect Joshua....

• • •

Judges and lawyers, like other humans, are moved by natural sympathy in a case like this to find a way for Joshua and his mother to receive adequate compensation for the grievous harm inflicted upon them. But before yielding to that impulse, it is well to remember once again that the harm was inflicted not by the State of Wisconsin, but by Joshua's father. The most that can be said of the state functionaries in this case is that they stood by and did nothing when suspicious circumstances dictated a more active role for them. In defense of them, it must also be said that, had they moved too soon to take custody of the son away from the father, they would likely have been met with charges of improperly intruding into the parent-child relationship, charges based on the same Due Process Clause that forms the basis for the present charge of failure to provide adequate protection.

The people of Wisconsin may well prefer a system of liability which would place upon the State and its officials the responsibility for failure to act in situations such as the present one. They may create such a system, if they do not have it already, by changing the tort law of the State in accordance with the regular lawmaking process. But they should not have it thrust upon them by this Court's expansion of the Due Process Clause of the Fourteenth Amendment.

Discussion Questions

1. If Joshua had been in state custody and were beaten, it most certainly would have violated his due process rights. Thinking back on the concept of state action, discussed in Chapter 3, would Joshua have been entitled to constitutional protection if the county had consigned him to: (a) a private foster home? (b) a private orphanage? (c) a state orphanage? Based on your answers, what conclusions about state action do you draw?

2. If you were Joshua's case worker, what would you have done?

3. Overall, how convincing do you find the Court's decision? Why?

Case 9.2
The Limits of Judicial Remedies

MISSOURI v. JENKINS
Argued January 11, 1995
Decided June 12, 1995
515 US 70

CHIEF JUSTICE REHNQUIST delivered the opinion of the Court.

As this school desegregation litigation enters its 18th year, we are called upon again to review the decisions of the lower courts. In this case, the State of Missouri has challenged the District Court's order of salary increases for virtually all instructional and noninstructional staff within the Kansas City, Missouri, School District (KCMSD) and the District Court's order requiring the State to continue to fund remedial "quality education" programs because student achievement levels were still "at or below national norms at many grade levels."

I

A general overview of this litigation is necessary for proper resolution of the issues upon which we granted certiorari. This case has been before the same United States District Judge since 1977.... In that year, the KCMSD, the school board, and the children of two school board members brought suit against the State and other defendants. Plaintiffs alleged that the State, the surrounding suburban school districts (SSD's), and various federal agencies had caused and perpetuated a system of racial segregation in the schools of the Kansas City metropolitan area. The District Court realigned the KCMSD as a nominal defendant and certified as a class, present and future KCMSD students. The KCMSD brought a cross-claim against the State for its failure to eliminate the vestiges of its prior dual school system.

After a trial that lasted 7½ months, the District Court dismissed the case against the federal defendants and the SSD's, but determined that the State and the KCMSD were liable for an intradistrict violation, *i.e.,* they had operated a segregated school system within the KCMSD.... The District Court determined that prior to 1954 "Missouri mandated segregated schools for black and white children."... Furthermore, the KCMSD and the State had failed in their affirmative obligations to eliminate the vestiges of the State's dual school system within the KCMSD....

In June, 1985, the District Court issued its first remedial order and established as its goal the "elimination of all vestiges of state imposed segregation."... The District Court determined that "[s]egregation ha[d] caused a system-wide *reduction* in student achievement in the schools of the KCMSD."... The District Court made no particularized findings regarding the extent that student achievement had been reduced or what portion of that reduction was attributable to segregation. The District Court also identified 25 schools within the KCMSD that had enrollments of 90% or more black students....

... Under the "effective schools" program, the State was required to fund programs at both the 25 racially identifiable schools as well as the 43 other schools within the KCMSD....

• • •

The District Court also set out to desegregate the KCMSD but believed that "[t]o accomplish desegregation within the boundary lines of a school district whose enrollment remains 68.3% black is a difficult task."... Because it had found no interdistrict violation, the District Court could not order mandatory interdistrict redistribution of students between the KCMSD and the surrounding SSD's....

In November, 1986, the District Court approved a comprehensive magnet school and capital improvements plan and held the State and the KCMSD jointly and severally liable for its funding....

... Since its inception, the magnet school program has operated at a cost, including magnet transportation, in excess of $448 million....

• • •

The District Court's desegregation plan has been described as the most ambitious and expensive remedial program in the history of school desegregation.... The annual cost per pupil at the KCMSD far exceeds that of the neighboring SSD's or of any school district in Missouri. Nevertheless, the KCMSD, which has pursued a "friendly adversary" relationship with the plaintiffs, has continued to propose ever more expensive programs. As a result, the desegregation costs have escalated and now are approaching an annual cost of $200 million. These massive expenditures have financed

high schools in which every classroom will have air conditioning, an alarm system, and 15 microcomputers; a 2,000-square-foot planetarium; green houses and vivariums; a 25-acre farm with an airconditioned meeting room for 104 people; a Model United Nations wired for language translation; broadcast capable radio and television studios with an editing and animation lab; a temperature controlled art gallery; movie editing and screening rooms; a 3,500-square-foot dust-free diesel mechanics room; 1,875-square-foot elementary school animal rooms for use in a zoo project; swimming pools; and numerous other facilities....

Not surprisingly, the cost of this remedial plan has "far exceeded KCMSD's budget, or for that matter, its authority to tax."... The State, through the operation of joint and several liability, has borne the brunt of these costs. The District Court candidly has acknowledged that it has "allowed the District planners to dream" and "provided the mechanism for th[ose] dreams to be realized."... In short, the District Court "has gone to great lengths to provide KCMSD with facilities and opportunities not available anywhere else in the country."...

II

With this background, we turn to the present controversy. First, the State has challenged the District Court's requirement that it fund salary increases for KCMSD instructional and noninstructional staff.... The State claimed that funding for salaries was beyond the scope of the District Court's remedial authority.... Second, the State has challenged the District Court's order requiring it to continue to fund the remedial quality education programs for the 1992–1993 school year.... The State contended that...it had achieved partial unitary status with respect to the quality education programs already in place. As a result, the State argued that the District Court should have relieved it of responsibility for funding those programs.

• • •

The District Court and Court of Appeals...have felt that because the KCMSD's enrollment remained 68.3% black, a purely *intra*district remedy would be insufficient.... But, ... we have rejected the suggestion

> that schools which have a majority of Negro students are not "desegregated" whatever the racial makeup of the school district's population and however neutrally the district lines have been drawn and administered....

("[T]he Court has consistently held that the Constitution is not violated by racial imbalance in the schools, without more")....

Instead of seeking to remove the racial identity of the various schools within the KCMSD, the District Court has set out on a program to create a school district that was equal to or superior to the surrounding SSD's. Its remedy has focused on "desegregative attractiveness," coupled with "suburban comparability."...

The purpose of desegregative attractiveness has been not only to remedy the system-wide reduction in student achievement, but also to attract nonminority students not presently enrolled in the KCMSD. This remedy has included an elaborate program of capital improvements, course enrichment, and extracurricular enhancement not simply in the formerly identifiable black schools, but in schools throughout the district. The District Court's remedial orders have converted every senior high school, every middle school, and one-half of the elementary schools in the KCMSD into "magnet" schools. The District Court's remedial order has all but made the KCMSD itself into a magnet district.

The District Court's remedial plan in this case, however, is not designed solely to redistribute the students within the KCMSD in order to eliminate racially identifiable schools within the KCMSD. Instead, its purpose is to attract nonminority students from outside the KCMSD schools. But this *inter*district goal is beyond the scope of the *intra*district violation identified by the District Court. In effect, the District Court has devised a remedy to accomplish indirectly what it admittedly lacks the remedial authority to mandate directly: the interdistrict transfer of students....

• • •

The District Court's pursuit of "desegregative attractiveness" cannot be reconciled with our cases placing limitations on a district court's remedial authority. It is certainly theoretically possible that the greater the expenditure per pupil within the KCMSD, the more likely it is that some unknowable number of nonminority students not presently attending schools in the KCMSD will choose to enroll in those schools. Under this reasoning, however, every increased expenditure, whether it be for teachers, noninstructional employees, books, or buildings, will make the KCMSD in some way more attractive, and thereby perhaps induce nonminority students to enroll in its schools. But this rationale is not susceptible to any objective limitation.... This case provides numerous examples demonstrating the limitless authority of the District Court operating under this rationale....[For example,] (The District Court has recognized that it has "provide[d] the KCMSD with facilities and opportunities not available anywhere else in the country");... ("The District has repeatedly requested that the [District Court] provide extravagant programs based on the hopes that they will succeed in the desegregation effort"). In short, desegregative attractiveness has been used "as the hook on which to hang numerous policy choices about improving the quality of education in general within the KCMSD."...

Nor are there limits to the duration of the District Court's involvement. The expenditures per pupil in the KCMSD currently far exceed those in the neighboring SSD's.... Sixteen years after this litigation began, the District Court recognized that the KCMSD has yet to offer a viable method of financing the "wonderful school system being built."... Each additional program ordered by the District Court—and financed by the State—to increase the "desegregative attractiveness" of the school district makes the KCMSD more and more dependent on additional funding from the State; in turn, the greater the KCMSD's dependence on state funding, the greater its reliance on continued supervision by the District Court. But our cases recognize that local autonomy of school districts is a vital national tradition..., and that a district court must strive to restore state and local authorities to the control of a school system operating in compliance with the Constitution....

The District Court's pursuit of the goal of "desegregative attractiveness" results in so many imponderables and is so far removed from the task of eliminating the racial identifiability of the schools within the KCMSD that we believe it is beyond the admittedly broad discretion of the District Court. In this posture, we conclude that the District Court's order of salary increases, which was "grounded in remedying the vestiges of segregation by improving the desegregative attractiveness of the KCMSD"..., is simply too far removed from an acceptable implementation of a permissible means to remedy previous legally mandated segregation....

Similar considerations lead us to conclude that the District Court's order requiring the State to continue to fund the quality education programs because student achievement levels were still "at or below national norms at many grade levels" cannot be sustained....

• • •

On remand, the District Court must bear in mind that its end purpose is not only "to remedy the violation" to the extent practicable, but also "to restore state and local authorities to the control of a school system that is operating in compliance with the Constitution."...

• • •

Discussion Questions

1. Think back on all the cases in this book:
    a. What are the primary value disagreements between public administration and constitutional law?
    b. How well would you say the courts understand public administration?
    c. Is there a general strategy for managing within the confines of ever-changing constitutional law?
    d. It is axiomatic that public management must be subordinate to constitutional law. Write a letter to the Chief Justice of the United States explaining how Supreme Court decisions could be improved from your perspective. Share the letter with your class.

2. Do you think *Missouri v. Jenkins* was properly decided by the Supreme Court? Why?

APPENDIX A

Table of Cases

APPENDIX B

Index of Cases
by Primary Legal Topic

Due Process

Equal Protection

Federalism

Fourth Amendment Privacy

Freedom of Religion

Freedom of Speech

Liability

Separation of Powers

State Action

"Takings"

APPENDIX C

The Bill of Rights

The first ten Amendments (Bill of Rights) were ratified effective December 15, 1791.

Amendment I.

Congress shall make no law respecting an establishment of religion, or prohibiting the free exercise thereof; or abridging the freedom of speech, or of the press, or the right of the people peaceably to assemble, and to petition the Government for a redress of grievances.

Amendment II.

A well regulated Militia, being necessary to the security of a free State, the right of the people to keep and bear Arms, shall not be infringed.

Amendment III.

No Soldier shall, in time of peace be quartered in any house, without the consent of the Owner, nor in time of war, but in a manner to be prescribed by law.

Amendment IV.

The right of the people to be secure in their persons, houses, papers, and effects, against unreasonable searches and seizures, shall not be violated, and no Warrants shall issue, but upon probable cause, supported by Oath or affirmation, and particularly describing the place to be searched, and the persons or things to be seized.

Amendment V.

No person shall be held to answer for a capital, or otherwise infamous crime, unless on a presentment or indictment of a Grand Jury, except in cases arising in the land or naval forces, or in the Militia, when in actual service in time of War or public danger; nor shall any person be subject for the same offence to be twice put in jeopardy of life or limb, nor shall be compelled in any criminal case to be a witness against himself, nor be deprived of life, liberty, or property, without due process of law; nor shall private property be taken for public use without just compensation.

Amendment VI.

In all criminal prosecutions, the accused shall enjoy the right to a speedy and public trial, by an impartial jury of the State and district wherein the crime shall have been committed; which district shall have been previously ascertained by law, and to be informed of the nature and cause of the accusation; to be confronted with the witnesses against him; to have compulsory process for obtaining witnesses in his favor, and to have the assistance of counsel for his defence.

Amendment VII.

In Suits at common law, where the value in controversy shall exceed twenty dollars, the right of trial by jury shall be preserved, and no fact tried by a jury shall be otherwise re-examined in any Court of the United States, than according to the rules of the common law.

Amendment VIII.

Excessive bail shall not be required, nor excessive fines imposed, nor cruel and unusual punishments inflicted.

Amendment IX.

The enumeration in the Constitution of certain rights shall not be construed to deny or disparage others retained by the people.

Amendment X.

The powers not delegated to the United States by the Constitution, nor prohibited by it to the States, are reserved to the States respectively, or to the people.

INDEX

New Deal, delegation of legislative authority to
  executive branch during, 106–107
New Jersey v. T.L.O. (1985), 85, 88
"New property," government benefits as, 44
New Public Management (NPM), 62–63, 64, 66
  administrative decisionmaking and, 81, 87
  administrative effectiveness and, 105
  administrative standardization and, 149
  budgeting and, 174
  efficiency and, 126–127
  meeting public administrative objectives and, 84
  public administration doctrine and, 197
  and standardization, 151–152
Ninth Amendment, 13
Nollan v. California Coastal Commission (1987), 179
Nonsuspect classifications, 12
NPM. *See* New Public Management
NPR. *See* National Performance Review

Objectives
  means for accomplishing, 84
  of public policy, 83–84
Occupational Safety and Health Act (1970),
  incrementalism and, 85, 86
O'Connor, Sandra Day, 6
Open public forum, 8
Outcomes, efficiency and, 126
Outputs, outcomes and, 126
Outsourcing
  and constraints on dealing with contractors, 66–67
  privatization and, 62–67
  state action doctrine and, 63–65
Overbreadth, 14

Papachristou v. City of Jacksonville (1972), 110–111
Paramount objective test, 7
Pembaur v. Cincinnati (1986), 48
Performance, achieving, 105
Performance-based organizations, 62
Performance budgeting, 173
Personal Responsibility and Work Opportunity
  Reconciliation Act (1996) (PRWO), 178
Police officers
  law enforcement profiles and, 154
  traffic stops by, 154
Political association, Fourteenth Amendment and, 66
Position classification, rank and, 150
Pound, Roscoe, 80
Powell, Lewis, 111
Precedent in case law, 5
President of the United States, absolute
  immunity and, 47
Press, freedom of, 8
Printz v. United States (1997), 5, 17
Prisoners, constitutional rights of, 45
Prisons
  budgetary considerations and reform of, 174
  cruel and unusual punishment in, 45
  desegregation of, 108
Pritchett, C. Herman, 107
Privacy rights, Fourth Amendment and, 9–10, 66
Private parties
  governmental authorization to violate constitutional
    rights and, 64

governmental subsidization of clientele and, 64
government regulation or subsidization and, 64
public functions of, 64
public-private partnerships and, 64
as state actors, 64
testing for engagement in state action, 64
Private property
  protection of, 13–14
  taking of, 178–179
Private state actors, liability for constitutional
  torts, 65–66
Privatization
  and constraints on dealing with
    contractors, 66–67
  outsourcing and, 62–67
  state action doctrine and, 63–65
  Supreme Court and, 45
"Privileges," government benefits as, 44
Problem solving, 83. *See also* Decisionmaking,
  rational-comprehensiveness model and
Procedural due process
  administrative economy and, 176–177
  application to routine public management, 129
  employee dismissals and, 129–130
  Fourteenth Amendment, 10
  fundamental fairness and, 130
Program budgeting, 173
Property, Takings Clause and, 178–179
Property interests, procedural due process and, 129
Property rights, 13–14, 45
  administrative economy and, 178–179
Protected rights
  chilling effect and, 14
  indirect interference with, 14–15
  overbreadth and, 14
  underinclusiveness, 15
  vagueness and, 14–15
Protected speech, 130–131. *See also*
  Freedom of speech
Public administration
  and constitutional governance, 196–197
  impact of constitutional limits on means, 109–111
Public administrators
  absolute immunity of, 46
  decisionmaking by, 80–88
  liability for violating individuals' constitutional
    rights, 43–49
Public assistance benefits, administrative
  economy and, 177–178
Public concern, freedom of speech and, 130–131
Public employees
  contractors' rights and, 45
  freedom of speech for, 130–131
  during "red scare," 108
  right to disobey unconstitutional orders, 48
Public employment, individuals' rights and, 44
Public forum, freedom of speech and, 8
Public functions, of private parties, 64
Public housing, individuals' rights and, 44
Public institutions
  desegregation of, 108
  economizing in, 174–176
Public law litigation, 46
  Wyatt case as, 175

CPSIA information can be obtained
at www.ICGtesting.com
Printed in the USA
FFOW01n1644080715
15018FF

9 780534 270780